D1286302

# CATHOLIC CONVERTS

## BRITISH AND AMERICAN
### INTELLECTUALS TURN TO ROME

## Patrick Allitt

CORNELL UNIVERSITY PRESS   *Ithaca and London*

This book has been published with the aid of a grant from Emory University.

First published 1997 by Cornell University Press

Printed in the United States of America

Cornell University Press strives to use environmentally responsible suppliers and materials to the fullest extent possible in the publishing of its books. Such materials include vegetable-based, low-VOC inks and acid-free papers that are recycled, totally chlorine-free, or partly composed of nonwood fibers.

Library of Congress Cataloging-in-Publication Data

Allitt, Patrick.
   Catholic Converts : British and American intellectuals turn to Rome / Patrick Allitt.
     p.  cm.
   Includes bibliographical references and index.
   ISBN 0-8014-2996-X (cloth : alk. paper)
   1. Catholic Converts—Great Britain—History. 2. Intellectuals—Religious life—Great Britain—History. 3. Catholic converts—United States—History. 4. Intellectuals—Religious life—United States—History. 5. Catholic Church—History—19th century. 6. Catholic Church—History—20th century. I. Title.
BX4668.A1A44   1997
248.2′42′0941—dc21
                                            96-29989

Cloth printing   10  9  8  7  6  5  4  3  2

*For Eric Allitt, my father*

# CONTENTS

Preface                                                          ix

I      Introduction: Intellectuals Becoming Catholics             1

II     New Pride and Old Prejudice                                17

III    Loss and Gain: The First English Converts                 43

IV     Tractarians and Transcendentalists in America             61

V      Infallibility and Its Discontents                         87

VI     America, Modernism, and Hell                              107

VII    The Lowliness of His Handmaidens:
       Women and Conversion                                      127

VIII   The British Apologists' Spiritual Aeneid                  159

IX     Revival and Departure                                     191

X      Fascists, Communists, Catholics, and Total War            219

XI     Transforming the Past: The Convert Historians             237

XII    Novels from *Hadrian* to *Brideshead*                     277

XIII   The Preconciliar Generation: 1935–1962                    309

       Index                                                     333

# PREFACE

Nearly all the major Catholic intellectuals writing in English between 1840 and 1960 were converts to Catholicism. Having been raised outside the Catholic faith, they enjoyed greater educational advantages than their born-Catholic contemporaries and developed a spirit of intellectual adventurousness. Even the disadvantages of being Catholic in traditionally anti-Catholic countries did not deter them from converting, and they continued to write imaginative and controversial work after conversion.

There was a close correspondence between Catholic developments in Britain and the United States, and the convert intellectuals in each nation were aware of and cooperated with those in the other. For much of the nineteenth and early twentieth centuries, U.S. intellectual life was subordinate to British, and the Catholic element of this story is no exception. In this period the more provincial Americans drew inspiration from their British counterparts, whose work they republished and read widely.

The convert intellectuals wanted to persuade other Protestants, Jews, atheists, and agnostics to follow their example and convert to Catholicism. They generally wrote with this audience in mind and not solely to their fellow Catholics, whereas most born-Catholic writers attended only to the needs of their own flock. As a result the converts' work was generally more likely than that of born Catholics to conform to intellectual standards prevailing outside their church. The converts tried at the same time to raise intellectual standards within the Catholic community. They pointed out to other Catholics that they had too few rigorously educated luminaries and that even in more highly populated fields such as philosophy and theology there was too much emphasis on an ahistorical scholasticism.

Throughout the later years of the nineteenth century converts were eager to show doubting outsiders that their church believed in intellectual freedom and would pursue truth fearlessly. But they soon encountered obstructions from their local bishops and from the hierarchy in Rome, which feared that these convert intellectuals were treading on dangerous or forbidden ground. Converts who tried to embrace evolutionary theory, historical-critical methods of biblical criticism, and comparative religion were especially likely to meet with censure. Some of them also accepted the "Teutonic" theory, which accorded racial primacy to the Anglo-Saxons, and this belief also provoked a Vatican challenge. The converts, therefore, had to keep an eye on the authorities to their "right" as well as the skeptical non-Catholic audience on their "left."

In the early twentieth century the Vatican made a series of definite prohibitions against modernism and resolutely turned its face away from modernity. Aspiring intellectual modernists would no longer be likely to convert, but the church attracted a generation of men and women who were disillusioned by elements of modernity, especially following the catastrophic First World War. Catholicism now seemed to them a haven against the icy storms of the modern world. Converts in this generation gladly accepted the disciplinary guidance of the church and maintained that its apparent restrictions cloaked a far greater intellectual freedom than that offered by the philosophical systems it opposed. Some members of this generation, such as Christopher Dawson in England and Carlton Hayes in America, made methodological innovations in the study of history and impressed their non-Catholic colleagues quite favorably, especially in the 1930s and 1940s when their criticisms of progress and nationalism seemed germane to the world crisis.

The decade of the 1950s saw a continued flow of convert intellectuals into British and American Catholicism, but by then distinguished intellectuals were growing up inside the church. In Britain they faced no educational discrimination and were free to compete for places at Oxford, Cambridge, and the other universities. In the United States a complex of Catholic universities, with converts prominent among their faculty members, provided a moderately high quality education. Converts were, therefore, less conspicuous among leading Catholic intellectuals by 1962, the eve of the Second Vatican Council (Vatican II). Moreover, some Catholic scholars were beginning to question the assumption that Catholicism was the only avenue to salvation; they encouraged the irenic spirit that blossomed in the era of Vatican II. The conversion of intellectuals has continued up to the present but has been a less distinctive feature of postconciliar Catholicism than it was in the hundred and twenty years before the council.

A book covering such a long period of time necessarily deals only superficially with many issues and personalities, and I pass hastily over the work of many convert intellectuals with regret. The poets Gerard Manley Hopkins, Coventry Patmore, Alice Meynell, Allen Tate, and Robert Lowell get particularly short shrift. I feel justified in taking this approach, however, in order to show that converts' dominance of English-language Catholic intellectual life was a sustained phenomenon of more than a century's duration. Several historians have mentioned it in passing but it has not yet been the central theme of any study. Most of the people whose work I consider here have already been the subjects of biographies. Indeed, John Henry Newman, G. K. Chesterton, Dorothy Day, and Thomas Merton are, between them, the subject of well over a hundred books. But the imperative of the genre often leads biographers to emphasize uniqueness rather than their subject's similarity to many other members of a group. Without scanting individual differences among this colorful and often brilliant group, I have been struck by common issues with which each of them in turn was forced to struggle.

Friends and family members have helped make the work a pleasure. I began the research at Princeton, as a fellow at the Center for the Study of American Religion in 1992–93. Working in the shadow of Princeton Chapel, America's finest Gothic revival building, is just right for a project like this. Robert Wuthnow was a kind, thoughtful, and rigorous critic of early chapters, but it was discouraging to see him publishing about three books during that year while I made a modest start on one. Among the students there I had the good fortune to meet Kate Joyce (now a professor at Duke), who has unerring judgment and gives me shrewd critical advice on everything I write. Other friends and colleagues, especially Philip Gleason, John McGreevy, Derek Wagg, and Tom Tanner, read various drafts and made criticisms I needed to hear. Jim Fisher was inspirational as always. His wedding was a welcome respite from writing footnotes. Catherine Bennett in London was a gracious host for a couple of weeks while I was working there. I did the research at Emory, Princeton, Notre Dame, Berkeley, the Paulist Archives in Washington, D.C., Rutgers, Campion Hall in Oxford, and the Catholic Central Library in London, and I am grateful for the help of the librarians at these institutions. Special thanks to Emory University, whose history department is a great place to work, to Jonathan Heller, an energetic research assistant, and to the Emory University Research Council for a research and travel grant. Peter Agree at Cornell University Press was friendly, helpful, calm, and patient, even when I asked him on thirty-seven consecutive days whether he had yet received readers' reports. Lovely, long-suffering Toni Allitt read the complete works of Dickens, Hardy, George Eliot, the Brontës, and Trollope while I was working on this project, and she provided the Victorian literary color. Coaching a girls' soccer team, the Under Eight Tornados, provided a lively diversion and taught our daughter Frances to kick hard. Special thanks to them both. The dedication is to my father, who has been a lifelong inspira-

PREFACE

tion to me, personally and intellectually. He used to think history was something we could safely leave behind, but although he is still a scientific positivist at heart, I think I have helped turn his mind a little more toward the past.

PATRICK ALLITT

*Atlanta, Georgia*

# CATHOLIC CONVERTS

# I

# INTRODUCTION

## *Intellectuals Becoming Catholics*

F ROM THE MID-NINETEENTH century to the mid-twentieth, a succession of English-speaking intellectuals converted to Catholicism. Since the Reformation almost no English-language writers of any influence had tried to advance the cause of the Catholic Church. When the church began to reassert itself in the nineteenth century, it used converts as its principal advocates. Outspoken, intellectually gifted, and impressed by their own example, Catholic converts said that they would show up the fallacies of Protestants and religious skeptics, end the long schism in Christendom, and place Catholics once more at the center of Western intellectual life.

Some of the names of these convert intellectuals are widely familiar, and among them John Henry Newman, G. K. Chesterton, Isaac Hecker, Orestes Brownson, Graham Greene, Evelyn Waugh, Thomas Merton, and Dorothy Day have all been the subject of more than one major biography. Around Newman, Day, and Merton, indeed, academic subfields have formed, and the existence of the *Chesterton Review* suggests that the memory of this prolific Londoner is also well tended. But no one has yet written a study of the general impact of converts on Catholic intellectual life in this era or the distinctive style of Catholicism they helped to create. Nor has anyone investigated the extensive transatlantic contacts among these English-speaking Catholic writers. Such is the purpose of this book.

Many of their contemporaries regarded the idea of a "Catholic intellectual" as a contradiction in terms, believing that the repressive Roman church prohibited freedom of thought. The converts were eager to prove otherwise; their work in history, science, literature, and philosophy was designed to substantiate their belief that Catholicism was intellectually

1

liberating rather than restrictive, despite the church's dogmatic style and hierarchical structure. They wrote partly for a Catholic audience, to be sure, but more for their Protestant and skeptical contemporaries, hoping to vindicate their own conversions by persuading others to follow them. To win more converts they knew that they would have to improve intellectual standards within Catholicism. History written in the form of pious hagiography and retrospective justification of every Catholic position, for example, would never convince Protestants and skeptics; it was annoying rather than persuasive to all but the most devout believer. Catholic history would henceforth have to be deeply researched, impartial in evaluating evidence, stylistically elegant, and vigorously argued. The same would have to be true in all other disciplines too. In urging such changes and in trying to set an example in their own work, however, convert intellectuals did not mean to abandon apologetics. Rather, they introduced a more circumspect apologetics, calculated to attract other intellectuals by appealing to them in their own idiom.

Sharing a common language and literary heritage, the British and American Catholic converts followed each other's progress closely. In both countries Catholics were a numerical minority, more or less resented by the Protestant majority and sometimes victimized by anti-Catholic uprisings, anti-Catholic political organizations such as the Know-Nothings, and a general cultural antipathy to all aspects of "popery." Because Catholicism was a minority religion in the English-speaking nations, its adherents tended to cleave to one another and to respect their clergy. Anticlericalism, a fact of life in Italy, France, and Mexico, was very rare in Britain and America, although English-speaking Catholics had good reason to think that the Catholic hierarchy in Rome did not understand the situation in their nations. They sometimes found it vexing to act upon Vatican directives that had no relevance to their situation. Convert intellectuals responded to their shared problems by encouraging and aiding one another. A regular traffic developed as they crossed and recrossed the Atlantic to confer, teach, and spread the word in each other's nations.

As they tried to make a place for themselves in the Catholic Church and a case for this church in the wider intellectual world, the first generation of converts found little Catholic literature in English on which to build. They had to start almost from scratch in trying to show what Catholic science or Catholic history as serious intellectual enterprises would be like. "We Catholics have no philosophy," wrote John Acton, an English "cradle" Catholic, in a letter of 1854 to the American convert writer Orestes Brownson. "You alone can prepare us for the great controversies by founding among us a school and arming it with the principles of a sound philosophy."[1] For Brownson and his fellow converts Catholicism was something quite new, but at the same time they were aware that it was far more ancient than its Christian rivals and that they had inherited a vast intellectual patrimony. They set to work, exploring and reinterpreting the Catholic past, trying to recover it from the obloquy of Protestant historiography as well as from the syrup of Catholic hagiography.

This paradoxical antiquity and novelty of Catholicism was complemented by another paradox: the converts' sense that Catholicism was both different from their former faiths and yet also very similar. They accepted their new faith as adults, having spent their youth and years of education outside the Catholic fold. In many cases a long intellectual preparation for conversion took place within other churches. The best-known British convert, John Henry Newman, for example, converted from Anglicanism at the age of forty-four after more than two decades of study and writing in Patristics. For many years he believed that the church Fathers were the precursors of Anglicanism, but at last in 1845, he admitted to himself that if they pointed in any direction, it was to Rome. Conversion changed his explicit allegiance and had immense consequences for the course of his life, but it did not overturn his pattern of thinking. The continuities in his thought before and after conversion are in many ways more striking than the discontinuities.[2] The same was true a generation later of G. K. Chesterton, who converted at the age of forty-six. His book *Orthodoxy* (1908), written while he was still an Anglican, became a favorite among his Catholic admirers, who in this way acknowledged the continuity.[3] Intellectually, then, conversion was often incremental, but institutionally (as well as perceptually, to outside observers), the jump was immense, from the establishment into the wilderness. The Catholic Church saw itself as embattled against the rest of the world and tried to recruit its converts as polemicists, but they, more often than not, retained heavy intellectual

1. Acton, quoted in Thomas P. Ryan, *Orestes A. Brownson: A Definitive Biography* (Huntington, Ind.: Our Sunday Visitor, 1976), 501.

2. The literature on Newman's life and work is very extensive. Here I have relied primarily on Ian Ker, *John Henry Newman: A Biography* (Oxford: Clarendon Press, 1988); Sheridan Gilley, *Newman and His Age* (Westminster, Md.: Christian Classics, 1990); David Newsome, *The Convert Cardinals: John Henry Newman and Henry Edward Manning* (London: John Murray, 1993). Indispensable to a fuller study of Newman is Stephen Dessain, ed., *Letters and Diaries of John Henry Newman*, 31 vols. (London: Thomas Nelson, 1961–84).

3. Here I have relied primarily on Chesterton's own works, including *Orthodoxy* (1908; Garden City, N.Y.: Doubleday, 1959); and on Maisie Ward, *Gilbert Keith Chesterton* (London: Sheed and Ward, 1944); Michael Ffinch, *G. K. Chesterton: A Biography* (London: Weidenfeld and Nicolson, 1986).

debts to their Protestant past and could not repudiate their personal and intellectual heritage. Paradoxically, then, Catholicism was both totally different from its rivals and yet, at the same time, remarkably continuous with them. It was a paradox that frequently caused friction between the new and old Catholics.

The outcome of the convert intellectuals' labors was not what they themselves had hoped. Although for three or four generations they were highly influential within the Catholic Church, playing a crucial role in transforming English-language Catholicism, they were powerless to halt or reverse the dominant intellectual trends of their era. The church was certainly unable to resume the central place in Western intellectual life which it had enjoyed prior to the Reformation. While the new Catholics challenged non-Catholic scholars on the vital issues of the era, the non-Catholics rarely deigned even to notice them in return and made little effort to incorporate their insights into their work. For example, William George Ward, a friend of Newman's and a fiery controversialist, converted in 1845 and later became editor of the *Dublin Review*, one of the leading British Catholic journals. His biographer (and son) describes at length Ward's fifteen-year correspondence with John Stuart Mill, giving the impression that Ward had a large effect on the utilitarian philosopher's outlook.[4] But no biographer of Mill has found evidence of this supposed influence, and it is likely that the Wards indulged in wishful thinking when they came to assess the importance of the correspondence to Mill's own life and work.

The flow of conversions in Britain and America between the mid-1840s and the late 1950s was sufficient to indicate the continuing allure of Catholicism, but it was hardly large enough to throw non-Catholic intellectuals into a panic. Although Newman was widely admired and stimulated other members of the Oxford Movement to follow his example, he was unable to lead his own brother into the Catholic fold, and most of his erstwhile followers, including the other movement leaders, Nathan Pusey and John Keble, remained staunch Anglicans.[5] As in Britain, so in the United States. Orestes Brownson, a member of the Transcendentalist circle, carried his family and a few friends into the embrace of Rome in 1844 but not his twin or his other siblings. Most of his New England cronies,

---

4. Wilfrid Ward, *William George Ward and the Catholic Revival* (New York: Macmillan, 1893), 17–30.

5. Marvin O'Connell, *The Oxford Conspirators: A History of the Oxford Movement, 1833–1845* (London: Macmillan, 1969), 420–21. On Francis Newman, see Geoffrey Faber, *Oxford Apostles: A Character Study of the Oxford Movement* (1933; London: Penguin, 1954), 146–48.

accustomed to Brownson's frequent changes of opinion, treated him as a mercurial spirit who had finally stepped off the edge of the world rather than as a role model.[6] Among them, only Isaac Hecker and the group who later founded the Paulist fathers went with Brownson to Rome.[7]

At times events in other churches could prompt a new spate of conversions. In the early 1890s, for example, a group of High Church Anglicans led by Lord Halifax raised the question of corporate reunion, the collective readmission of the Church of England into the Catholic Church. Hopes ran high among Anglo-Catholics for a time, but in 1896 Pope Leo XIII made a categorical declaration in the papal bull *Apostolicae Curae* that Anglican orders were invalid and that, in effect, there was nothing to discuss. In reaction a cluster of Anglican clergymen who had seen themselves as members of the worldwide Catholic communion and had been hoping for a different answer, resigned from their livings and converted to Catholicism.[8] A "push" came for American Episcopal priests in 1908 when their church decided to inaugurate an "open pulpits" policy, permitting all varieties of Protestant ministers to preach in Episcopal churches. American Episcopalians who saw themselves as Anglo-Catholics revolted at the prospect, and here too the result was a large handful of conversions.[9]

There were, however, plenty of good reasons for *not* converting. Quite apart from the religious wrench of conversion, becoming a Catholic in Britain or the United States often prompted accusations of disloyalty to the nation, its Protestant heritage, even its sense of common decency. When Thomas Arnold (Matthew Arnold's brother) converted, his wife wrote a furious letter to Newman, accusing him of persuading her husband "to ignore every social duty and become a pervert." She added, "From the bottom of my heart I curse you for it."[10] In 1848 the poet Christina Rossetti refused an offer of marriage from a young artist, James Collinson, because he had converted. She accepted him when he reverted to Anglicanism but canceled their wedding plans when he "went over to"

6. Arthur Schlesinger Jr., *Orestes A. Brownson: A Pilgrim's Progress* (Boston: Little, Brown, 1939), 186–87.

7. On Hecker's conversion, see David O'Brien, *Isaac Hecker, an American Catholic* (New York: Paulist Press, 1992), 49–65; Patrick Allitt, "The Meanings of Isaac Hecker's Conversion," *Journal of Paulist Studies* 3 (1994): 9–29.

8. H. R. McAdoo, "Anglican-Roman Catholic Relations, 1717–1980," in J. C. H. Aveling, D. M. Loades, and H. R. McAdoo, eds., *Rome and the Anglicans* (New York: Walter DeGruyter, 1982), esp. 189–94.

9. Raymond W. Albright, *A History of the Protestant Episcopal Church* (New York: Macmillan, 1964), 350–51; David L. Holmes, *A Brief History of the Episcopalian Church* (Valley Forge, Pa.: Trinity Press, 1993), 124–26.

10. Mrs. Arnold, quoted in Ker, *Newman*, 700–701.

Rome for a second time. Collinson's parents disowned him, and he was reduced to begging from his friends in the Pre-Raphaelite Brotherhood.[11]

Conversion usually entailed a jolting loss of social status. George Tyrrell, a young Anglican from a poor but genteel Irish family, was intellectually convinced by Catholic arguments, but his biographer notes, "he recoiled from 'the dirt and tinsel, and flashy gew gaws' in the Catholic chapels, from the 'essential commonness' of Romanism," and when he overcame his distaste and announced his conversion to his parents, "what pained his mother was 'that a son of mine should go to Mass with the cook.'"[12] Moreover, as David Newsome writes, the convert "became, as it were, an exile in his own land. . . . In addition to the humiliation of social ostracism, the pain of severed friendships and the torment of past memories, there was the inescapable problem of beginning life again within an alien community," while "recognizing that all one's past distinctions and achievements counted for nothing."[13] It is difficult to find any example of an intellectual who derived either social or monetary gain from conversion. For many, on the contrary, the material and prestige losses were considerable. The many Anglican and Episcopalian priests who converted were especially hard hit. Being, in many cases, married, they were ineligible to join the Catholic priesthood and so faced an economically precarious future. One such married clergyman, T. W. Allies, reported "extreme depression of spirits" due to "the utter destitution of my temporal fortunes." He longed "to produce some work for the glory of God" but was condemned "to the most anxious thoughts as to what I shall eat and what I shall drink, wherewithal I shall be clothed, I and mine, and to the drudgery of teaching dunces."[14] Such cases strongly suggest that the motive for conversion was genuine religious conviction. There are few plausible ulterior motives to explain it, though it may be true that certain

11. Georgina Battiscombe, *Christina Rossetti: A Divided Life* (New York: Holt, Rinehart, and Winston, 1981), 43–48. Rossetti was a staunch Anglican and a supporter of the Oxford Movement, but as Battiscombe says, "the adherents of the Oxford Movement, while stressing the Catholic nature of the Church of England, were especially horrified when any of their number went over to Rome. As well as being a denial of the Catholicity of the Church of England such a conversion gave substance to the charge that the 'Puseyites' were Papists in disguise" (56). Her own brother William wrote that "I have often thought that Christina's proper place was in the Roman Catholic Church" and that "her satisfaction in remaining a member of the English church may have been partly due to her deep affection for her mother" (33).

12. Nicholas Sagovsky, *On God's Side: A Life of George Tyrrell* (New York: Oxford University Press, 1990), 10.

13. David Newsome, *The Parting of Friends: The Wilberforces and Henry Manning* (1966; Grand Rapids, Mich.: Eerdman's, 1993), 403.

14. Ibid., 404.

character types were more receptive to the demands of Catholic life than others.[15]

The converts' position was doubly difficult because the Catholic Church received them with mixed feelings, an uneasy blend of gratitude and disdain. Catholic bishops were understandably glad that brilliant and influential men and women had decided that Rome represented the one true church, and delighted to learn that they were willing to put their skills at the service of Catholicism. But the bishops soon discovered that converts, intellectually adventurous and unused to clerical censorship, were likely to take speculative excursions that challenged orthodoxy rather than fortifying it. One part of the history of these converts is, accordingly, the story of conflicts with their bishops over what was or was not intellectually permissible. Newman, whose superiors often viewed him with suspicion for his ideas on the development of doctrine, the role of the laity, and the nature of religious certainty, once told Lord Acton that in the hierarchy's view "all converts are dangerous."[16] His fellow Oxford convert Richard Simpson, coeditor of the *Rambler*, the leading "liberal Catholic" journal of the mid-nineteenth century, had a long succession of conflicts with the hierarchy, which threatened to close the journal down as a hazard to the religion of the faithful.[17] Isaac Hecker, the American Transcendentalist and Brook Farm communard who converted in 1844, also ran into official disapproval when his book *Aspirations of Nature* (1857) appeared to maintain that by nature human beings were good, minimizing the power of original sin, and hence the need for grace, well beyond what his superiors found admissible.[18]

On the other hand, another group of converts, the Ultramontanes, became such fervent "Romanizers" that they dismayed the pragmatic "Old Catholics" of England. Henry Manning and William George Ward, for example, two Oxford converts, were among the leaders of the movement to declare the pope infallible on questions of faith and morals at the First Vatican Council (1869–1870) and some of the most passionate defenders of the pope's temporal power, which was threatened by the unifi-

---

15. In both countries Anglo-Catholicism, which is religiously the closest rival of Roman Catholicism, was an attractive option because it brought with it very *high* social status. It proved to be the sticking point for T. S. Eliot, C. S. Lewis, and Dorothy Sayers, and many other lesser literary figures whom the Roman Catholics hoped to convert in the mid-twentieth century.

16. Ker, *Newman*, 473.

17. In the event, Newman temporarily took over the editorship in 1859. See Josef L. Altholz, *The Liberal Catholic Movement in England: The "Rambler" and Its Contributors, 1848–1962* (London: Burns and Oates, 1962), esp. 63–82.

18. O'Brien, *Hecker*, 120.

cation of Italy.[19] These converts' views dismayed English Old Catholics who, over three centuries or more, had gradually adapted their faith to indigenous conditions. The converts were, then, anything but unanimous among themselves but tended toward radical or extreme positions in one direction or another, arousing resentment from their new coreligionists in either instance.

The later nineteenth and early twentieth centuries showed unmistakably that the Catholic Church had decided to climb out of the river of contemporary intellectual life rather than swim along in midstream, despite the hopes of Newman, Brownson, Hecker, and many other converts. The papal hammer fell frequently on efforts to "modernize" Catholic thinking, an enterprise in which converts were often closely involved. For example, Pope Pius IX (1846–1878) issued the *Syllabus of Errors* in 1864, condemning many of the principles upon which contemporary scientists, social scientists, and biblical critics outside the Catholic Church were then working. It concluded by condemning the proposition that "the Roman Pontiff can and ought to reconcile himself to, and come to terms with, progress, liberalism, and modern civilization."[20] The condemnation brought the work of several convert intellectuals under scrutiny, and it discouraged them from showing the consonance of their work with contemporary philosophy and science. Among the converts affected was the English evolutionary biologist St. George Mivart, who was ultimately excommunicated for his assertion that the Catholic doctrine of hell was untenable.[21] The seemingly antiintellectual animus of the syllabus also disillusioned some converts, among them Thomas Arnold, who reverted to Anglicanism when he learned of it.[22]

Six years later Pius IX organized the declaration of papal infallibility at the First Vatican Council (1870), declining to countenance historical evidence (provided by Newman, among others) which showed that papal supremacy itself, let alone papal infallibility, was based on several centuries of development out of an early church that had been constituted quite differently. Papal infallibility, whatever its other consequences, represented a disastrous reversal for Catholic historians, who had dedicated themselves to close analysis of the early church. The pontificate of Leo XIII (1878–1903) promised them some relief, but his encyclical letter *Aeterni Patris*

19. On Vatican I, see Robert Gray, *Cardinal Manning: A Biography* (New York: St. Martin's Press, 1985), 227–36.
20. Altholz, *Liberal Catholic Movement*, 231.
21. Jacob W. Gruber, *A Conscience in Conflict: The Life of St. George Jackson Mivart* (Philadelphia: Temple University Press, 1960), 197–212.
22. Ker, *Newman*, 576. He reconverted to Catholicism in 1877. See ibid., 700–701; and Gilley, *Newman*, 384.

(1879) aimed to revive scholasticism, keeping new philosophical and historical approaches at arm's length. Its successor, *Providentissimus Deus* (1893), set sharp limits on Catholic participation in historical-critical study of the Bible.[23]

A third abrupt check for adventurous Catholic intellectuals came in 1907 when Pope Pius X's decree *Lamentabili* (1907) and the encyclical *Pascendi* (1907) sweepingly condemned "modernism" in theology; in response, one English convert, George Tyrrell, S.J., courted excommunication.[24] In the following years seminaries and Catholic colleges in Britain and America were purged of all traces of "modernism." Outsiders regarded these episodes as further evidence that Catholic intellectuals were hamstrung by intrusive, censorious, and often ignorant authorities. This was the age in which Andrew Dickson White, first president of Cornell University, wrote his influential *History of the Warfare of Science with Theology in Christendom* (1896), casting the scientists as truth-loving heroes through the ages and the Catholic Church as an antiintellectual villain trying to squeeze the life out of them. White made enormous capital out of the famous Galileo case and treated it as typical of Catholicism at all times.[25] Converts who remained committed to contemporary intellectual principles found themselves walking a tightrope between the guardians of orthodoxy on their right and their former friends and colleagues to their left.

It should not be supposed that intellectual converts to Catholicism were reliably more "liberal" in their outlook than born Catholics. The convert who is more punctilious in his new faith than the lifelong communicant is a familiar figure in Catholic lore, and the nineteenth and twentieth centuries provided plentiful examples of such characters. The most notable was Henry Manning, the Anglican archdeacon of Chichester, who converted in 1851 and rose in the next fifteen years to leadership of England's Catholic community, becoming archbishop of Westminster in 1865 (cardinal from 1875). Manning supported papal infallibility, as did Newman's former Oxford colleagues William George Ward and Frederick Faber, and

23. Gerald Fogarty, S.J., *American Catholic Biblical Scholarship: A History from the Early Republic to Vatican II* (San Francisco: Harper and Row, 1989), 34, 37, 44–50. On *Aeterni Patris*, see also René Fulop Miller, *Leo XIII and Our Times* (New York: Longmans, Green, 1937), 70–73. On *Providentissimus Deus*, see James J. Megivern, *Bible Interpretation* (Wilmington, N.C.: Consortium, 1978), xxi–xxv, 193–220.

24. On the excommunication of Tyrrell, see Gabriel Daly, foreword to George Tyrrell, *Medievalism*, ed. Daly (Tunbridge Wells, Kent: Burns and Oates, 1994), 10–12; Sagovsky, *On God's Side*, 227–29; Thomas Bokenkotter, *A Concise History of the Catholic Church*, rev. ed. (Garden City, N.Y.: Doubleday, 1979), 356–67.

25. Andrew Dickson White, *A History of the Warfare of Science with Theology in Christendom* (1895; New York: D. Appleton, 1925), 130–70.

the American convert Augustine Hewit. Subsequent Catholic historians, most of them opposed to the Ultramontane position, have given Manning in particular a bad press and found Newman's antiinfallibilist views much more palatable.[26] But we should remember that to Manning Ultramontanism seemed to be the most liberating position. Like many of the converts, he hated the subordination of the Church of England to the civil state; indeed, he left it in protest over the Gorham case of 1851, in which the state overruled an Anglican bishop and installed as parish priest a man he considered a heretic.[27] Setting up the papacy as a powerful counterweight to the state seemed to Ultramontanists the surest way of assuring themselves of religious and intellectual freedom. Even Isaac Hecker, who had misgivings about infallibility during the Vatican Council, accepted it later as an assertion of the "external" dignity of the church, which could now be ideally complemented by a full development of its "internal" or intellectual life.[28]

Ultramontanists placed their faith in Thomism. In an effort to assure intellectual coherence between disciplines and a foundation for all studies in theology, the popes who reigned in the second half of the nineteenth century placed a renewed emphasis on the work of Thomas Aquinas and his scholastic successors. Scholasticism and natural law theory have many strengths, among them an orderly rationalism and a conceptual framework into which every discrete item of information can be fitted, showing its connection to the whole and to the divine will from which it springs. But scholastic philosophy and natural law encountered a succession of powerful challengers in the nineteenth and early twentieth centuries, including pragmatism, vitalism, existentialism, and logical positivism, each of which debunked scholasticism's claims to intellectual respectability. Similarly, in the physical sciences and in the study of history, the developing academic

26. The historiography of Manning has suffered under the shadow of Edmund Sheridan Purcell, whose *Life of Cardinal Manning, Archbishop of Westminster* (New York: Macmillan, 1895) painted the cardinal as worldly, ambitious, and unscrupulous. Lytton Strachey was even more cutting in *Eminent Victorians: Cardinal Manning, Florence Nightingale, Dr. Arnold, General Gordon* (1918; London: Chatto and Windus, 1948), 13–128. Subsequent biographers have been more sympathetic, notably Shane Leslie, *Henry Edward Manning: His Life and Labours* (1921; Westport, Conn.: Greenwood, 1970); Gray, *Cardinal Manning*; Newsome, *Convert Cardinals*. See also Peter Erb, ed., *The Manning-Gladstone Correspondence*, 3 vols. (forthcoming). The biographers of Newman still often treat Manning harshly. See, for example, Ker, *Newman*, 597–600.

27. George C. Gorham, an evangelical Church of England priest who denied the efficacy of baptismal regeneration, was assigned to a parish in the diocese of Bishop Henry Philpotts of Exeter. See Leslie, *Manning*, 88–98.

28. O'Brien, *Hecker*, 225–41.

orthodoxy in Britain and America, strongly empirical and increasingly based on evolutionary, probabilist, and materialist assumptions, was at variance with the scholastic framework, which, while granting science some autonomy, linked worldly phenomena to their supernatural origins.[29] The scholastic criticism of materialism and positivism was not so much refuted as blithely ignored by most of the scientists. Protestant conservatives were also polemicizing against the new secular sciences, but for religious and traditional reasons, Catholic and Protestant objectors to secular scholarship were unable to make common cause.[30] Meanwhile, the development of a "Catholic ghetto," especially in the United States, with its own set of self-segregating schools, colleges, and journals, made ignoring the Catholics easier than if they had been forcing their attention upon their antagonists from adjoining offices. Non-Catholics rarely investigated the work of intellectuals in the Catholic Church unless they were searching for polemical ammunition.

After Vatican I, and especially after *Pascendi*, English and American convert intellectuals tended to stay away from strictly theological questions altogether and work in the safer realms of literature, history, and the social sciences. Like their nineteenth-century predecessors, however, they too aimed to draw more converts into the faith that had won them. A succession of British converts, including Hugh Benson, Ronald Knox, G. K. Chesterton, and others, tried to dazzle their readers with wit, erudition, and ostentatious orthodoxy. Even so the experience of their earlier lives made their view of the outside world different from that of born Catholics and enabled them to make distinctions that sometimes escaped their born-Catholic fellows. These converts usually had relatives still outside the church; their own education outside Catholicism had formed their minds; and they found it difficult to demonize a non-Catholic society with which they were still intimately connected. Their chief line of attack was to criticize the premises of non-Catholic philosophy and science, to demonstrate its epistemological vulnerability, and to expose its links to a callow idealization of progress, sometimes with wry admissions that they too had once been deceived by its charms. They also brought their Catholic insight

29. On the scientific changes, see Robert V. Bruce, *The Launching of Modern American Science, 1846–1876* (Ithaca: Cornell University Press, 1987); Paul Jerome Croce, *Science and Religion in the Age of William James: The Eclipse of Certainty, 1820–1880* (Chapel Hill: University of North Carolina Press, 1995). On history, see Peter Novick, *That Noble Dream: The Objectivity Question and the American Historical Profession* (New York: Cambridge University Press, 1988).

30. Jan Roberts, *Darwinism and the Divine in America: Protestant Intellectuals and Organic Evolution, 1859–1900* (Madison: University of Wisconsin Press, 1988).

to bear on the political changes of their era, arguing that without the guidance of faith the world was out of control. The First World War gave their critique of progress a new plausibility.

The train of conversions continued during and after the war. Men and women disabused of their faith in progress as a force immanent in history found consolation in Catholicism. In the interwar years a distinguished group of British novelists converted to Catholicism, including Compton Mackenzie, Graham Greene, and Evelyn Waugh, and began to make lasting contributions to the canon of English literature. In the 1850s Newman had lamented that the great classics of English literature were Protestant to the core and that English was in effect a Protestant language.[31] Now for the first time since the Reformation, English literature enjoyed a significant Catholic leavening. Convert writers took turns touring the United States, teaching at Georgetown, Fordham, and Notre Dame and trying to encourage a Catholic literary revival across the sea. They were joined by another group of gifted and prolific controversialists, including Shane Leslie, Arnold Lunn, and Christopher Hollis, who took up the mantle of Chesterton and tried to carry on his message that Catholicism was synonymous with urbanity, erudition, and wit. Aptly enough, the first holder of the Stillman Chair in Catholic Studies at Harvard Divinity School was the English convert Christopher Dawson.

A new generation of converts in the United States joined the Catholic Church in the interwar years. The best known, Dorothy Day and Thomas Merton, each gradually won a wide and sympathetic audience in the non-Catholic world, eventually becoming spiritual celebrities. Less celebrated but equally important, a succession of converts from the ranks of academia—among them the historians Carlton Hayes, Ross Hoffman, and Elizabeth Kite, and the sociologist Eva Ross—brought a measure of intellectual respectability to Catholic education. This generation of converts was made up of white Anglo-Saxon Protestants. They had enjoyed an education in the leading American graduate schools—Hayes at Columbia and Hoffman at the University of Pennsylvania, for example—and they felt none of the immigrant insecurities and defensive belligerence still common among their ethnically assimilating Catholic contemporaries. They were as much a part of the American "establishment" as the convert sons of English Anglican bishops were part of the British establishment. They brought to Catholic academic life a new sense of ease and possession. Demonstrating a high level of technical skill in their disciplines, they began

31. John Henry Newman, *The Idea of a University*, ed. Charles Harrold (1853; New York: Longmans, Green, 1947), 271.

to win more sympathetic attention from non-Catholic academics. They also ran graduate programs, training young cradle Catholics to high standards, with the eventual effect of reducing the prominence of converts. Many non-Catholics found their critique of science and their philosophical antitotalitarianism germane to the total war of the 1940s and the Cold War of the 1950s. But whereas Brownson could rely only on himself and other converts, convert scholars a century later worked alongside born Catholics such as the Jesuit luminaries John Courtney Murray and Walter Ong.

By the 1950s some converts had persuaded themselves that their highbrow evangelizing effort was gaining ever more ground and that a demoralized secularist enemy was on the verge of capitulation, ready to throw itself into the arms of the pope. Not for the first time they were indulging in wishful thinking. Even as they made their hopeful prophecies, the long Catholic rear guard against modernity began to collapse from within. Catholic academics, priests and laity alike, began to question the adequacy of a scholastic and natural law approach to all issues. The church reformed itself at the Second Vatican Council (1962–1965), abandoning its intransigence toward the outside world and looking with a new sympathy both on the Catholic innovations of recent decades and on the non-Catholic branches of Christianity. It belatedly opened itself to scientific and philosophical systems that for a century it had repudiated, and at the same time it surrendered some of the characteristics that had made its outlook distinctive.[32] By the 1970s many of the special qualities of Catholic scholarship were disappearing, or else were confined to the angry handful of traditionalists who refused to forsake the ways of a lifetime. Ironically some of the intransigents were intellectuals who had converted to get away from modernism in its many guises, only to find that their church too was now negotiating with modernist teachings on all sides.[33] It only compounded the irony that converts had done much to pave the way for these changes. They had insisted on higher standards and more rigorous research, had declined to demonize the outside world, but had never meant to break down the fortress walls of what was to them the one, true Catholic faith.

In the first flush of success, Catholic intellectuals who had been pressing

32. Philip Gleason, "A Look Back at the Catholic Intellectualism Issue," in *U.S. Catholic Historian* 13 (Winter 1995): 19–37; Gleason, "Immigrant Assimilation and the Crisis of Americanization" and "Catholicism and Cultural Change in the 1960s," both in his *Keeping the Faith: American Catholicism Past and Present* (Notre Dame, Ind.: University of Notre Dame Press, 1987), 58–81, 82–96; Patrick Allitt, *Catholic Intellectuals and Conservative Politics in America, 1950–1985* (Ithaca: Cornell University Press, 1993), 41–48.
33. Allitt, *Catholic Intellectuals*, 147–59.

for reforms—an end to censorship and the exclusive reliance on scholasticism—celebrated victory over the bad old days.[34] Enough time has now passed since the Second Vatican Council that we can evaluate the rights and wrongs of this history in a new way, temper the exuberance of the modernizers, and pay at least a guarded tribute to the convert intellectuals and their work. In the late nineteenth and early twentieth centuries the Promethean self-confidence of the new sciences had seemed likely to sweep everything before it. Darwinism and the principle of evolutionary development had been applied widely to other phenomena and appeared irresistibly compelling to several generations of scientists, historians, philosophers, and social scientists. Evolutionists had scornfully dismissed the fixed principles and the unchanging universe of scholasticism and regarded it as easy to refute, if they bothered to look at it at all. Marxism, another developmental theory, which enjoyed its greatest vogue in the English-speaking countries between about 1890 and 1950, was no less scornful of Catholic thought, treating it either as an opiate for the oppressed or as the instrument of domination which a master class wielded against its subordinates.[35] By now, however, these rival orthodoxies have, in their turn, worn thin. Evolution is still a central theory in biology but hardly in economics, anthropology, political science, or psychology, where it once ruled imperiously. From evolution sprang eugenics, the science of population manipulation, whose horrific face Hitler displayed to the world. In the same way marxism, for complex political and intellectual reasons, lost its allure; its predictions were falsified, its scientific pretensions exposed as a sham, and it too became closely linked with a brutal tyrant, Stalin, whose career in "scientific" politics was almost enough to give political science itself a bad name. The failure of the alternatives does not, in itself, demonstrate the "correctness" of the Catholic faith, to be sure, but it lends credence to the Catholic opposition to marxism and eugenics. It seems now that dogmatic Catholics enjoyed an insulation against some of the utopian currents that swept the Western nations in the first half of this century. It would be rash today to say that Catholicism was wrong when its adversaries were right. Our age, more jaded and skeptical in the face of successive disappointments, can pay it at least backhanded compliments, acknowledge its strengths as well as its weaknesses, and recognize that it provided the standpoint from which to make a telling critique of its secular rivals.

34. See, for example, Michael Novak, *The Open Church: Vatican II, Act II* (New York: Macmillan, 1964).

35. Ironically, the only time a significant number of Catholic intellectuals took a sympathetic view of marxism was the 1960s and 1970s, when it formed the economic basis of "Liberation Theology."

A project of this kind, covering more than a century and two nations (with frequent glances at Ireland, Germany, France, Spain, Canada, and Italy), is obliged to move rapidly or become impossibly long. My approach is to single out the most influential figures from each generation and explain their work, rather than attempt to give a comprehensive account of all convert writers, though at times I have tried to rescue from obscurity characters who seem to me to deserve more fame than history has granted them, including Richard Simpson (Chapter 4), Elizabeth Kite (Chapter 7), and Bertram Windle (Chapter 8). "Influence" is, of course, an elusive phenomenon, not really amenable to accurate measurement. Such figures as Newman, Brownson, Hecker, Dawson, and Chesterton get comparatively thorough treatment not because they are typical of anything but because of their exceptional qualities; few of their fellow converts could rival them for insight or write so much and so well. In general I aim to demonstrate qualitative rather than quantitative changes throughout, arguing that the converts, who were never more than 2 or 3 percent of the Catholic population in either nation, were disproportionately represented in the ranks of Catholic writers, lecturers, editors, and professors, that their ideas often set the agenda for other Catholic intellectuals working within the tradition, and that non-Catholics looked to the more persuasive convert writers when they wanted to find "the Catholic position" on a controversial issue.

Another elusive yet important issue for a project of this kind is the question of the relationship between truth and intellectual respectability. The convert intellectuals were aware, in many cases, that what they believed to be true was not regarded by non-Catholics as plausible or reasonable or, indeed, respectable. On some points both groups could agree, of course, and the convert writers' intention was to make a closer fit between "Catholic truth" and "intellectual respectability." At any given moment in the era from about 1825 to 1962, Catholic intellectuals knew that a range of ideas was considered respectable in the two nations. They also knew that some Catholic ideas sat comfortably inside this area and others remained well beyond its boundaries. Their job, as they saw it, was to drag the recalcitrant Catholics into the realm of the respectable, while trying to shift the zone of respectable ideas in the society at large, in order that Catholic truth and respectable ideas might coincide more fully. They wanted to convince Protestant and atheist contemporaries that much of their work was in error or based on fallacious premises, encouraging them to become more Catholic *and* more intellectually respectable.

But the general trend bore the range of intellectually respectable ideas steadily away from religion in general and Catholicism in particular. This trend, often labeled "secularization," appeared for decades to be unstoppable, so that many convert intellectuals, far from reversing its momentum, found their own views gradually moving outside the realm of what other intellectuals considered plausible. The consequence was marginalization, and convert intellectuals in general *lost* influence with the passing decades, so that none in the twentieth century could have an effect on his or her non-Catholic contemporaries to match that of Newman and Brownson in the mid-nineteenth. Certain writers, such as Chesterton or Christopher Dawson, could still find admirers, but neither created a major school of thought, and non-Catholic admirers saw their religion as a colorful aberration rather than a central element in their work. In that sense this book is the history of a momentous and protracted failure.

# II
# NEW PRIDE
# AND OLD PREJUDICE

T HE CATHOLIC CHURCH in Britain and the United States was small and weak in 1825. The populations of both nations were emphatically Protestant, ill-disposed toward Catholicism after three centuries of antagonism and mistrust. Popular and educated opinion alike held Catholicism to be an odious mixture of atavism and tyranny. The handful of Catholic intellectuals writing in English knew they faced formidable obstacles in their search for a sympathetic hearing.

Catholic weakness and unpopularity in the English-speaking world are not hard to explain.[1] Ever since the Reformation, religious and political issues and events had combined to poison Protestant-Catholic relations. On the religious side, Protestants regarded themselves as reformers of a debased and idolatrous Christianity, who had turned their backs on Rome in order to get back to the simplicity of the early church by placing their full faith in the Bible. The English Reformation was triggered as much by Henry VIII's marital problems as by doctrinal or moral questions, but it soon tapped into an indigenous tradition of antipapal sentiment and gave rise to a body of convinced and influential Protestants. Under Edward VI (1547–1553), Henry's son and successor, the English church took further steps toward a doctrinal Protestantism and continued Henry's policy of dissolving the monasteries and redistributing their estates.

Queen Mary I (1553–1558), Edward's half sister, repudiated these reforms and tried to reestablish England on its old Catholic foundations. She married King Philip II of Spain, Europe's most powerful Catholic monarch, and persecuted Protestant ministers and bishops. In the five years of her reign she put to death almost three hundred prominent Protestants, burning many of them at the stake. These deaths held the place of

1. The following passage is based on A. G. Dickens, *The English Reformation*, 2d ed. (London: B. T. Batsford, 1989).

honor in John Foxe's twelve-volume *Acts and Monuments* (1563), better known as *Foxe's Book of Martyrs*, which became the central text of Protestant anti-Catholicism for the next three hundred years. Generations of British and American Protestants thrilled to Foxe's account of Archbishop Cranmer of Canterbury, who on his way to the stake stoutly declared: "As for the Pope I refuse him as Christ's enemy and Antichrist, with all his false doctrine." At the Last Judgment, he added, "the Papistical doctrine . . . shall be ashamed to show her face."[2] Charles Dickens's David Copperfield describes his boyhood fascination with the "dismal horrors" he discovered in Foxe's book.[3] As the historian E. R. Norman shows, Foxe gave Protestants their idea of what Catholicism was like: "Foxe represented it as inherently corrupt, authoritarian, foreign, and, above all, as implacably opposed to personal liberty. The association of English constitutional freedom, liberal institutions, and the rule of common law with national Protestantism has always involved, in contrast, a condemnation of 'popery' as the embodiment of 'medieval' subservience."[4]

As this quotation suggests, the political sources of anti-Catholicism were closely intertwined with the religious. Queen Elizabeth I and her ministers, establishing the Thirty-nine Articles as the basis of the Church of England in 1559, tried to be as inclusive as possible for the sake of civil peace, but they were adamant on the question of royal supremacy. The monarch, not the pope, was head of the church, and anyone who denied her supremacy was subject to persecution. Most Britons accepted the new arrangement, the transition being made easier by a long history of anti-papalism in England. A Catholic uprising in 1569 failed to gather broad support.[5] Nevertheless, Pope Pius V (1566–1572), unwilling to see England move permanently beyond his reach and hoping to foment further Catholic uprisings, issued the bull *Regnans in Excelsis* in 1570, deposing Queen Elizabeth. It forbade Catholics to swear oaths of loyalty to her. In consequence the English government took the view that every Catholic was actively or latently a traitor, and it persecuted all the Catholic priests it could find as presumptive conspirators. The British historian and Catholic convert E. I. Watkin observed:

The deposition was a blunder, worse than a blunder, a disaster, probably the most serious blow inflicted on English Catholicism between the Reforma-

---

2. G. A. Williamson, ed., *Foxe's Book of Martyrs* (Boston: Little, Brown, 1965), 355.

3. Charles Dickens, *David Copperfield* (1850; Oxford: Clarendon Press, 1981), 127–28.

4. Edward R. Norman, *Roman Catholicism in England: From the Elizabethan Settlement to the Second Vatican Council* (Oxford: Oxford Univerity Press, 1985), 4.

5. Dickens, *English Reformation*, 366.

tion and the present day [1957]. It identified Catholic allegiance to the papacy with a disloyalty to the sovereign which the vast majority of the English Catholics did not entertain. Protestants saw it, and have seen it ever since, as a declaration by the Holy See that a loyal Roman Catholic cannot also be a loyal Englishman.[6]

Protestant fears were not entirely groundless, in fact, and exposure of another Catholic conspiracy, the Ridolfi Plot of 1571, intensified them. Anti-Catholic persecution reached its height in the years of the execution of Mary Queen of Scots (1585) and the attack of the Spanish Armada (1588), when fear of encirclement by hostile Catholic powers lent urgency and harshness to English policy. Among the victims of the Elizabethan persecution was Edmund Campion, a distinguished Oxford scholar who had become a Jesuit priest and tried to keep the old faith alive in the face of intense adversity. Tortured and executed in 1581, he was to become an object of particular fascination to Catholic scholars in the nineteenth and twentieth centuries.[7] By 1600 the English Catholics were a small and dwindling minority of the population, strongest in the north where remoteness from royal power and the strength of local Catholic noblemen afforded them a degree of protection.[8]

The accession of James Stuart (James I) in 1603 did little to alleviate anti-Catholic suspicions. Though the son of Mary Queen of Scots, he did not share his mother's Catholic faith. The Gunpowder Plot of 1605, a Catholic conspiracy to blow up the Houses of Parliament, led to a traitor's death for Guy Fawkes and his fellow conspirators and a renewed period of persecution for English Catholics.[9] During the 1630s, by contrast, a handful of Catholics enjoyed royal favor under Charles I (1625–1649) and his Catholic French wife Henrietta Maria. Among them was Caecelius Calvert, the second Lord Baltimore, to whom the king gave a founding charter for the colony of Maryland. It was England's first American colony to have a sizable Catholic population and to practice religious toleration. By contrast the zealous Protestant founders of the Massachusetts Bay Colony, farther north, ordered that any Catholic priest found in their

6. E. I. Watkin, *Roman Catholicism in England from the Reformation to 1950* (London: Oxford University Press, 1957), 28.

7. Two converts wrote biographies of the Jesuit martyr: Richard Simpson, *Edmund Campion: A Biography* (London: Williams and Norgate, 1867); Evelyn Waugh, *Edmund Campion* (1935; Boston: Little, Brown, 1946).

8. J. C. H. Aveling, *The Handle and the Axe: The Catholic Recusants in England from the Reformation to Emancipation* (London: Blond and Briggs, 1976), 74–75. See also John Bossy, *The English Catholic Community, 1570–1850* (London: Darton, Longman, and Todd, 1975), 77–107.

9. Alan Haynes, *The Gunpowder Plot: Faith in Rebellion* (Dover, N.H.: A. Sutton, 1994).

colony "shall be deemed and accounted an incendiary and disturber of the publick peace," be imprisoned for life, and if he tried to escape, "he shall be punished with death."[10]

Charles I's favor cemented English Catholics' loyalty to the crown but renewed Protestant fears. "In the winter of 1641–2," writes John Kenyon, "the country was in the grip of hysterical fear at the prospect of a Catholic uprising—so much so that many landowners put their houses and estates in a posture of defense and turned out the local militia."[11] In the event, the first English Civil War broke out in 1642. Most English Catholics fought on the king's side, and they paid a heavy price in lives and fortunes for supporting his losing cause, even though the Puritan-dominated Commonwealth and Protectorate of the 1640s and 1650s practiced more religious toleration than the preceding regime. The Restoration of 1660 brought the Stuart family back to the throne.[12]

Charles II (1660–1685), Charles I's elder son, was closely allied to Louis XIV of France and sympathized with Catholicism but was shrewd enough to disguise his sympathies from a rabidly anti-Catholic population. It remained an act of high treason to convert an English man or woman to Catholicism, and any priest entering England or any Englishman sheltering a priest was liable to capital punishment. The laws were not stringently enforced, but they acted as a permanent deterrent to potential converts and a constant threat to the Catholic remnant in the population, many of whom (the "Church Papists") hedged their bets by periodically attending Anglican services. "Popery" remained bitterly unpopular, and wild fears of a popish plot to blow up the banks of the River Thames, flood the city of London, and kill the king, led to a renewed wave of executions and imprisonments for Catholics between 1678 and 1683.[13]

Charles II converted to Catholicism on his deathbed in 1685. His imprudent brother, James II, had converted earlier and now mounted the throne as England's first Catholic monarch since "Bloody Mary." His political folly in trying to force an abrupt Counter-Reformation on England and his alienation of all domestic allies led to the rapid dissolution of his authority. He was forced to flee in 1688, carrying the Catholic cause down to another ruinous defeat. His grimly Protestant successors, William III and Mary II, wafted from Holland to England by what their supporters saw as a providential "Protestant wind," supervised a new round of anti-

10. James Hennesey, S.J., *American Catholics: A History of the Roman Catholic Community in the United States* (New York: Oxford University Press, 1981), 37.

11. John P. Kenyon, *The Popish Plot* (London: Heinemann, 1972), 3.

12. Aveling, *Handle and Axe*, 164–79.

13. Kenyon, *Popish Plot*, 5–15.

Catholic legislation in Britain.[14] In Maryland religious toleration for Catholics, under assault since the Civil War era, now came to an end and the colony was confiscated from the Baltimore family proprietors until one of them converted to Anglicanism in 1713. Catholics there lost the right to vote or to hold public office and were compelled (like their English cousins) to attend Anglican services or pay "recusancy" fines.[15] Catholicism was again linked directly to treason in the minds of most Britons on both sides of the Atlantic.

In 1715 James II's son, the "Old Pretender," with papal encouragement, raised a rebellion in Scotland and tried to seize the throne rather than see it pass to the Protestant Hanoverian dynasty at the death of Queen Anne. He was defeated, as was his son, the "Young Pretender" (Bonnie Prince Charlie), in 1745, but the reaction to these two uprisings kept alive the equation of Catholicism with treason in the minds of British Protestants through its second centenary.[16] British acquisition of French Canada by the Treaty of Paris, 1763, which ended the French and Indian Wars, brought a large Catholic population under British control. The government pragmatically offered them religious freedom in the Quebec Act of 1774, which enraged settlers in the British colonies farther south. The colonists saw this toleration of Canadian popery as the entering wedge of tyranny, and it was one of the escalating sequence of grievances (the Intolerable Acts) which sparked the American War of Independence in 1775.[17]

Ironically, in view of this background, the War of Independence benefited the Catholics of both nations, affording them in each case a broader religious freedom than they had hitherto enjoyed. By 1778 Britain was fighting a war on two fronts, in Europe and America, and in order to encourage military recruitment in Catholic districts such as the Scottish Highlands, Parliament passed the first of a series of Catholic Relief Acts. It exempted Catholic soldiers from the Protestant "Attestation Oath" and cautiously extended Catholics' right to worship and to purchase and inherit land.[18] At the same time American Catholics' active part in the Revolutionary War, at the urging of their leader Charles Carroll of Mary-

14. Aveling, *Handle and Axe*, 222–37, 238–52.
15. Jay P. Dolan, *The American Catholic Experience: A History from Colonial Times to the Present* (Garden City, N.Y.: Doubleday, 1985), 84.
16. Bruce Lenman, *The Jacobite Risings in Britain, 1689–1746* (London: Eyre Methuen, 1980).
17. Edmund S. Morgan, *The Birth of the Republic, 1763–1789* (Chicago: University of Chicago Press, 1956), 61, 118.
18. Christopher Hibbert, *King Mob: The Story of Lord George Gordon and the Riots of 1780* (London: Longmans, Green, 1958), 19.

land, won them toleration in most new state constitutions even though most American Protestants still viewed their religion with grave suspicion.[19]

Government toleration certainly did not mean social harmony, especially in England. War against Catholic France nurtured rumors, such as the belief in Southwark, London, that the city's flour supplies had been poisoned by Benedictine Monks in disguise and that bread would have to be tested by dogs, or the rumor that Jesuits in a network of tunnels were undermining the Thames and preparing to inundate London.[20] This popular backlash against Catholic relief culminated in the Gordon Riots of 1780, when an enraged Protestant mob surrounded Parliament, terrorized its members, intimidated the lord mayor of London into complete inaction, burned several Catholic chapels to the ground, and fought pitched street battles against London Irishmen. The death toll was 285, and 21 others were later executed for their part in the affray.[21]

English anti-Catholic passions were never quite so fierce again. The French Revolution's attack on the church a decade later brought fifty-five hundred refugee priests to England by 1797 and promoted a more benign view of Catholicism in the British upper classes. "The Catholic Church," says H. T. Dickinson, "once despised and feared by Protestants, was now seen as a valuable bulwark against revolutionary principles."[22] In 1788 an association of Catholic lords and gentlemen, the Committee, drew up an agreement, the Protestation, in which they undertook not to break their oaths of allegiance to the monarchy, and they collaborated in drafting a further Catholic Relief Act in 1791.[23] King George III's refusal to grant further relief led to the resignation of his ministers in 1801 and 1807, delaying further progress on the issue until 1829. The Catholic Emancipation Act of that year, which was the prime minister's (the duke of Wellington's) response to the threat of civil war in Ireland, marked another breakthrough. It entitled Catholics to take seats in Parliament, sit on the judicial bench, and hold crown administrative appointments (with certain

19. Margaret Mary Reher, *Catholic Intellectual Life in America: A Historical Study of Persons and Movements* (New York: Macmillan, 1989), 1–8; Dolan, *American Catholic Experience*, 96–97.

20. Hibbert, *King Mob*, 19–20.

21. J. Paul de Castro, *The Gordon Riots* (London: Oxford University Press, 1926); see also Hibbert, *King Mob*.

22. H. T. Dickinson, ed., *Britain and French Revolution* (New York: St. Martin's Press, 1989), 19.

23. Aveling, *Handle and Axe*, 331–32.

enumerated exceptions).[24] It also raised the fascinating possibility that Catholic politicians might one day be in the position to decide the fate of the Anglican Church.[25]

Despite these reforms, popular suspicions and prejudices persisted far into the nineteenth century, especially when Catholicism appeared in European garb. When an Italian priest, Dominic Barberi, visited Stone, Staffordshire, in 1841, "crowds soon began to assemble in the streets to watch him pass, to shout coarse insults, throw stones at him, and cover him with mud. A great scar remained on his forehead till his death, where one heavy stone had hit him."[26] The novelist Charlotte Brontë mixed her disdain for foreigners with contempt for Catholicism when she wrote in 1842 that any Protestant thinking of turning Catholic should visit Belgium and there "attend mass regularly for a time to note well the mummeries thereof also the idiotic, mercenary, aspect of *all* the priests, and *then* if they are still disposed to consider Papistry in any other light than a most feeble childish piece of humbug let them turn papists at once that's all."[27]

The Catholics themselves, fully aware of these suspicions, always insisted on their loyalty to the nation, and nationalism usually made a stronger claim on them than the supranational ideals of their faith. Even at the height of the sixteenth-century religious wars most English Catholics rejoiced at the defeat of the Spanish Armada, including the young men studying for the priesthood at the English College in Rome.[28] They were loyal to the crown through the revolutions of the seventeenth century, and few English Catholics joined the Jacobite uprisings of 1715 and 1745. Similarly, in America, nationalism prevailed over the transnational claims of faith; the Catholic minority, much of it clustered in Maryland, had no wish to inflame its neighbors. Catholics fought side by side with Protestants in the Revolutionary War, and one among them, Charles

24. Derek Beales, *From Castlereagh to Gladstone, 1815–1885* (London: Thomas Nelson, 1969), 25–26, 81–83.

25. Denis Gwynn, *A Hundred Years of Catholic Emancipation, 1829–1929* (London: Longmans, Green, 1929), 13. On the political atmosphere of Catholic emancipation, see Sheridan Gilley, *Newman and His Age* (Westminster, Md.: Christian Classics, 1990), 81–82. The act, introduced by a Tory administration against the wishes of King George IV, was supported by Whig radicals and Utilitarians. Ironically, it provoked sharp opposition from Newman and other Anglicans who were later to become Catholics themselves, because they resented political intervention in Anglican Church affairs.

26. Gwynn, *Hundred Years*, 57. Barberi was the priest who in 1845 received Newman into the Catholic Church.

27. Margot Peters, *Unquiet Soul: A Biography of Charlotte Brontë* (New York: Atheneum, 1986), 109.

28. Watkin, *Roman Catholicism*, 48.

Carroll, signed the Declaration of Independence. They hoped their fidelity to the revolutionary cause would calm the anti-Catholic fears that had fueled colonial resentment of Britain in the decade before the fighting began.[29]

The disestablishment of all American churches in the decades after the Revolutionary War and the rapid spread of religious toleration, underwritten by the First Amendment to the Constitution, helped Catholics establish their churches more widely in the new republic. Relief from legal penalties and prohibitions did not end anti-Catholic sentiment, however. The 1830s and 1840s bore witness to a succession of violent anti-Catholic demonstrations, such as the burning of an Ursuline convent in Massachusetts in 1834. Two years later Maria Monk's *Awful Disclosures of the Hotel Dieu Nunnery of Montreal* (1836) became a Protestant best seller. It described the sexual debauchery supposedly taking place in a convent to which innocent girls were dragged forcibly. Lecherous priests would impregnate them, then strangle the resulting babies after baptizing them, said Monk. She depicted Catholic life as sheer tyranny, with no glimmerings of democracy.[30] Further attacks on Catholic churches ensued in the 1840s, including the burning of a Philadelphia convent, a Catholic library, and two churches in 1844 and street fighting with muskets and even a cannon which killed thirteen and wounded fifty.[31] Anti-Catholicism was central to the politically influential Know-Nothing Party of the 1850s. In that decade one of the founders of the Republican Party, George William Curtis, described American civilization as "historically, the political aspect of the Reformation" because it was "a permanent protest against absolutism."[32]

From the sixteenth to the nineteenth centuries, in sum, British and North American Catholics faced recurrent persecution and accusations of treason, along with a torrent of religious invective, charging them with idolatry and blasphemy, alleging vicious habits among priests, monks, and nuns, and depicting the papacy as a bastion of arbitrary, tyrannical power. To describe the unchecked powers of an English newspaper, Anthony Trollope found a ready metaphor in the papacy:

29. Dolan, *American Catholic Experience*, 97.

30. Ray Allen Billington, *The Protestant Crusade, 1800–1860: A Story of the Origins of American Nativism* (New York: Macmillan, 1938); Barbara Welter, "From Maria Monk to Paul Blanshard: A Century of Protestant Anti-Catholicism," in Robert Bellah and Frederick Greenspahn, eds., *Uncivil Religion: Interreligious Hostility in America* (New York: Crossroads, 1987), 43–71.

31. Hennesey, *American Catholics*, 122–23.

32. Curtis, quoted in Eric Foner, *Free Soil, Free Labor, Free Men: The Ideology of the Republican Party before the Civil War* (New York: Oxford University Press, 1970), 228.

From here [the editorial office of the *Jupiter*] issue the only known infallible bulls for the guidance of British souls and bodies. This little court is the Vatican of England. Here reigns a pope, self-nominated, self-consecrated— ay, and much stranger too—self-believing!—a pope whom, if you cannot obey him, I would advise you to disobey as silently as possible; a pope hitherto afraid of no Luther; a pope who manages his own inquisition, who punishes unbelievers as no most skillful inquisitor of Spain ever dreamt of doing—one who can excommunicate thoroughly, fearfully, radically; put you beyond the pale of men's charity.[33]

The passage nicely conveys the mood of English anti-Catholicism. "Self-believing" suggests the common English view that the actual pope was knowingly hypocritical. In *Barchester Towers* (1857), Trollope introduces an Anglican divine named Francis Arabin, remarking that he was "a high churchman at all points; so high indeed that at one period of his career he had all but toppled over into the cesspool of Rome."[34] Trollope himself was too urbane to use this language without an ironic turn, but his Church of England novels, littered with such passages, give a good sense of the dismay and loathing many Anglicans felt for Catholics.

These were not the ideal conditions in which to nurture a literary culture, and most Catholic works in English from the Reformation to the nineteenth century are either polemics against Protestant accusations or devotional, consoling the bearers of a hard burden on unfriendly soil. The literary landscape discloses an occasional Catholic landmark, including the poets Richard Crashaw, John Dryden (both converts), and Alexander Pope, but such eminences were few and far between. From the sixteenth to the nineteenth centuries, Catholics were barred from the learned professions and from the colleges and universities. Catholic parents who sought a good education for their sons were obliged to send them abroad, usually to France, Italy, or Belgium. Those who joined the priesthood wrote as often in Latin, French, or Italian as in English.[35]

The social structure of Catholicism also inhibited the development of anglophone intellectual life. Throughout most of these three centuries, Catholicism in Britain was led by a small group of aristocrats and gentlemen, with their dependent tenants usually following the landlord's religion. Well into the late eighteenth and early nineteenth centuries there

33. Anthony Trollope, *The Warden*, 108, in *"The Warden" and "Barchester Towers"* (1855, 1857; New York: Bantam, 1984).
34. Trollope, *Barchester Towers*, 275.
35. Aveling, *Handle and Axe*, 146. As Aveling notes, the sons of temporizing "church papists" were able to enjoy an English education but those more zealous for their faith were less likely to make the necessary concessions to Anglicanism.

was virtually no Catholic middle class, and when the Catholic population began to swell it was mainly because of the immigration of poor Irish families in search of work or in flight from famine.[36] Similarly, in the United States a small elite was surrounded by a poor working population. There, too, the rise in Catholic population in the early decades of the nineteenth century was mainly due to immigration, chiefly from Ireland and Germany.[37] Throughout the nineteenth and well into the twentieth century, the Catholic population of both Britain and the United States would be made up of a small group of "Old Catholics," a large number of recent immigrants and their descendants (Irish, Polish, Italian, German, and Slavic), and a small but very articulate and influential group of Anglo-Saxon converts. Intergroup tensions and Anglo-Irish animosities would often play a role in shaping anglophone Catholicism, with further complications arising later in the United States as new immigration brought greater ethnic and linguistic diversity.

Even before the Irish migration transformed it, the English Catholic community was internally divided, as is so often the way among beleaguered minorities remote from power and influence. The divide lay between Ultramontanes and Cisalpines. Ultramontanes looked past the Alps, in other words, to Rome, from which they desired a strong lead. Their favored instrument was the Jesuits, who had brought Roman writ to England ever since the Elizabethan persecution. Among Protestants "Jesuit" was a byword for intrigue, sinister power, and Machiavellianism. Not only among Protestants, indeed. In 1773, under pressure from King Charles III of Spain, who blamed it for fomenting popular unrest in his kingdom, Pope Clement XIV suppressed the Society of Jesus altogether,[38] and not until 1814 did Pius VII restore it. Even during the hiatus, its subterranean efforts could be felt, and Bishop John Milner, vicar apostolic of the Midland District from 1803 to 1826, supported its policy of Romanizing British Catholicism.[39] The Ultramontanes also published Britain's first successful Catholic periodical, the *Orthodox Journal*, which flourished between 1813 and 1820. Its editor, William E. Andrews, said

---

36. Bossy, *English Catholic Population*, 182–84. Bossy discusses the conceptual problem involved in trying to count England's Catholic population, whether to assume that at the moment of the Reformation everyone was a Catholic or that no one was. He emphasizes that an English Catholic in 1600 has to be thought of in a quite different light from a member of the English church (which was then Catholic) in 1500.

37. J. P. Dolan, *The Immigrant Church: New York's Irish and German Catholics, 1815–1865* (Notre Dame, Ind.: University of Notre Dame Press, 1983).

38. J. H. Pollen, "Society of Jesus," *Catholic Encyclopedia* (New York: Appleton, 1912), 14:96–100.

39. Aveling, *Handle and Axe*, 339–42; Bossy, *English Catholic Community*, 334–37.

that his "sole motive" in creating the journal "was to aid the cause of the Catholic Church and to caution my Catholic brethren against the workings of a party, who have entailed more disgrace upon the Catholic name by their casuistical policy, than by all the calumnies raised against it by our enemies since the Reformation."[40]

The "party" that Andrews had in mind included much of the lay Catholic aristocracy and gentry, who favored a "Cisalpine," or this-side-of-the-mountains, strategy. The Cisalpines sought to adapt their religion to the exigencies of British life, trying to minimize friction in contacts with their fellow Britons, eschewing the baroque devotions of southern Europe, and turning a jaundiced eye on the Jesuits. Laity rather than clergy dominated, after working out their practical compromise with the civil power.[41] Between the Catholic Relief Act of 1791 and the restoration of the Catholic hierarchy in 1850, tensions between Ultramontanes and Cisalpines hindered their joint quest for full religious, political, and social emancipation and diminished what influence they might have had on society. Meanwhile, as E. I. Watkin later wrote, "Liberal Europe went forward with triumphant assurance, confident in its own enlightenment, in reason, freedom, and progress, and failed to notice that its heart was a void."[42]

Despite these problems, the early nineteenth century witnessed the beginnings of a Catholic literary revival in England, though its steps were hesitant until the era of conversions began in earnest with Newman's turn to Rome in 1845. Edward Norman maintains that in the 1840s "the converts tended to exaggerate the humble attainments of existing Catholic learning," but even he admits that standards among the born Catholics were low.[43] Three English Catholic writers from the early and middle nineteenth century—John Lingard, Nicholas Wiseman, and John Acton—illustrate both the strengths and the limits of the church's indigenous resources. Each of these born Catholics was a gifted author and what we would now call a "public intellectual." Lingard and Acton in particular stand squarely in the center of the British historiographical tradition, fig-

---

40. Andrews, quoted in Edward R. Norman, *The English Catholic Church in the Nineteenth Century* (Oxford: Clarendon Press, 1984), 289.

41. Gwynn, *Hundred Years*, 4, 10–12.

42. Watkin, *Roman Catholicism*, 153. Watkin, simplifying for dramatic effect, describes the nineteenth century as "the Maccabean age of the Christian dispensation, when Catholic forces intellectual and spiritual are engaged in a desperate struggle to beat off from the beleaguered fortress of their faith the advancing hosts of a liberal and secular rationalism. The result was a profound gulf between the Church and the Liberal society and civilization of Western Europe. Neither side understood or attempted to understand the language of the other. The few Catholic exceptions, such as Newman, raised their voices in vain" (153).

43. Norman, *English Catholic Church*, 288.

ures of national intellectual importance; Wiseman, also a competent author, is remembered more for his administrative achievements as first archbishop of Westminster. All three were educated in part abroad and owed heavy debts to their continental teachers; they could not have learned in England what they did in France, Italy, and Germany. But they also form something of a domestic genealogy, in the sense that Lingard taught Wiseman, who in turn was one of Acton's teachers. All three deplored the feeble condition of English Catholic literary life, and all believed that the accession of well-educated converts was the surest way to elevate their church's position in the nation. As writers they dedicated themselves to raising scholarly standards, avoiding polemics, and seeking the sympathetic attention of Protestant readers.

Lingard (1771–1851) came from an Old Catholic family in Winchester, England.[44] He was at Douai, France, training for the priesthood when Revolutionary troops occupied the seminary in 1793 and obliged the seminarians to flee. The French Revolution brought to England many other seminarians, priests, and bishops—English, French, and later pan-European refugees from Napoleon's conquests. The recent Catholic Relief Act permitted them to establish schools and church buildings relatively unmolested, which would have been impossible a few years before. Lingard was ordained in 1795 and soon rose to the position of vice-president of the new Catholic college at Crook Hall, County Durham, in the northeast of England. The college moved to nearby Ushaw in 1808, but after three years there, Lingard retired to the Lancashire village of Hornby. He devoted the latter forty years of his life to writing a ten-volume history of England (1819–1830), which is remarkable for its exacting use of original sources, its freedom from polemic, and its judicious, evenhanded tone, unmatched by any other Catholic work from its time. Lingard began it with the object of writing a school textbook for Catholic boys, but it soon grew into a much larger project.[45]

Lingard had studied the great eighteenth-century histories in English, Edward Gibbon on the decline of Rome and David Hume on England. His work was an attempt to counter their philosophic assumptions and

44. The following passage on Lingard is based on Donald Shea, *The English Ranke: John Lingard* (New York: Humanities Press, 1969); Joseph Chinnici, *The English Catholic Enlightenment: John Lingard and the Cisalpine Movement* (Shepherdstown, W.Va.: Patmos Press, 1980); Edwin J. Ryan, "Lingard," in Peter Guilday, ed., *Church Historians* (New York: P. J. Kennedy, 1926); G. P. Gooch, *History and Historians in the Nineteenth Century* (1913; New York: Peter Smith, 1949); T.C., "Lingard," in *Dictionary of National Biography* (Oxford: Oxford University Press, 1960), vol. 11.

45. John Lingard, *History of England from the First Invasion of the Romans* (1830; Dublin: James Duffy, 1893).

biases while matching them in erudition and literary art. No English Catholic before had made such an attempt, and as one biographer remarks of his history, "its temperate tone, especially on religious topics, commended the work to the attention of Protestant readers, who seemed surprised to find a Roman Catholic ecclesiastic treating controverted questions in a spirit of candour and truthfulness."[46] This reaction was just as he had hoped; he had written to a friend that he wanted to "defend the Catholics but not so as to hurt the feelings of the Protestants. Indeed my object has been to write such a work, if possible, as should be read by Protestants, under the idea that the more it is read by them, the less Hume will be in vogue, and consequently the fewer prejudices against us will be imbibed from him."[47]

Lingard, influenced by the German historians Barthold Niebuhr (1776–1831) and Johann Gatterer (1727–1799), was a pioneer among English historians in the use of primary sources, and he lamented the way in which apocryphal anecdotes or inaccurate stories were often passed down from one historian to another when original documents were available. "In the pursuit of truth," he wrote, "I have made it a religious duty to consult the original historians. Who would draw from the troubled stream when he may drink at the fountainhead?"[48] He researched in Rome and Milan as well as England and persuaded Robert Gradwell, rector of the English College in Rome, to keep him supplied with Vatican documents once he had returned to Hornby. A talented linguist, he also collected reports written by foreign ambassadors at the courts of England's kings and queens, using them to get an outsider's view of British life in a way which had not previously been tried.

Lingard made no comprehensive remarks about the Reformation, inevitably the most contentious area of study between Catholics and Protestants. Instead, he chronicled its events and personalities one by one, offering cautious, modulated judgments. This approach stood in marked contrast to that of the antireligious Hume, who had done his best to dismember the churches with sweeping strokes of the pen. "Few ecclesiastical establishments have been fixed upon a worse foundation than that of the Church of Rome," Hume had written of the Catholics, "or have been attended with circumstances more hurtful to the peace and happiness of mankind." Hume had explained the progress of the Reformation against the "pious frauds" of Pope Leo X as the result of ill-thought-out popular enthusiasm: "The rapid advance of the Lutheran doctrine, and the

46. T.C., "Lingard," 1200.
47. Lingard, quoted in Shea, *English Ranke*, 28.
48. Ibid., 25.

violence with which it was embraced, proved sufficiently that it owed not its success to reason and reflection."[49] Lingard patiently reasserted the legitimacy of Catholicism, described papal and monarchical actions in the kind of detail Hume rarely achieved, and assigned praise and blame even-handedly. He declared that Queen Mary's persecution of the Anglican bishops was "the foulest blot" on her character, but mitigated that judgment with the reminder that "the extirpation of erroneous doctrine was inculcated as a duty by the leaders of every religious party."[50] He could understand Queen Elizabeth's persecution of Edmund Campion and the other Jesuit priests because they did not disavow the papal deposition, but he added that Elizabeth's suspicions "could not justify their execution for an imaginary offense." Rather, he proposed in the Cisalpine spirit, "the proper remedy would have been to offer liberty of conscience to all Catholics who would abjure the temporal pretensions of the pontiff."[51]

Lingard's cool and detached style did not signify a lack of imagination; indeed, his biographer Donald Shea argues persuasively that he required much self-control to disguise his feelings. By contrast with his history, Lingard's correspondence "fairly brims with caustic contempt and ridicule."[52] Many reviewers admired the history, but despite his conciliatory approach, he had to endure some vintage specimens of anti-Catholic rhetoric. In *Blackwood's Edinburgh Magazine*, for example, an anonymous reviewer declared: "[Lingard] is a thorough papist, and of course his work is in the thorough spirit of his blinded and unhappy faith—venomous with the most sanctified appearance of impartiality. . . . Dr. Lingard is a man of some ability and some reading, of course a wonder in the general ignorance and dullness of the Popish writers of his time. His style is that of the cloister, monotonous, creeping, and cold" (70). Despite its nagging animosity the review came close to the truth in declaring most "Popish writers" of the time ignorant and dull and in finding Lingard's existence among them a "wonder." What is so striking about him is his isolation, both literal and intellectual. He founded no school of history, lived largely alone as Catholic vicar in a remote part of England, and was visited as much by local Protestant gentry as by his fellow Catholics. And despite his service to English Catholics he did not win their undivided admiration. The vituperative Bishop Milner, in particular, resented his Cisalpine spirit

---

49. David Hume, *The History of England from the Invasion of Julius Caesar to the Revolution in 1688* (Boston: Little, Brown, 1863), 28, 31.
50. Lingard, quoted in Shea, *English Ranke*, 91.
51. Lingard, *History* 6:343.
52. Shea, *Lingard*, 34.

and regarded the work as unsound, "a bad book . . . only calculated to confirm Protestants in their errors" (76).

Lingard was one of a kind, but he had a shrewd sense that his coreligionists needed more people like himself to bestow an intellectual credibility on Catholicism. In a statement that anticipated almost to the letter the ideals of many subsequent converts, Lingard declared, "Our great object should be to extend the Catholic religion among us, and for that purpose I hold it necessary to make converts among the higher of the middle classes of society. . . . If this be the case we are bound in conscience to eliminate everything unnecessary that is calculated to indispose such persons from joining us, or to augment their antipathy to us" (79). Lingard's example showed members of the Oxford Movement in the 1830s and 1840s that Catholicism was compatible with high intellectual standards, and some historians have seen him as an inspiration to Newman's generation of converts.[53]

As a schoolboy Nicholas Patrick Wiseman studied at Ushaw and took classes from Lingard.[54] Born in 1802 to an Irish trading family in Seville, Spain, Wiseman learned Spanish before English and later, like Lingard, became conversant with all the western European languages. In 1818 after school at Ushaw he moved to the English College in Rome, which was then just reopening at the end of the Napoleonic era. In Rome he enjoyed unbroken academic success, distinguishing himself in languages, ancient history, and the natural sciences. He was ordained in 1825 and published his doctoral dissertation on Syrian biblical manuscripts in 1827, winning widespread scholarly recognition (in England as well as Rome) and appointment to the Royal Society of Literature.[55] He was also elected professor of oriental languages at the Pontifical University. At the age of just twenty-six Wiseman became head of the English College, a position which brought him into contact with most of the leading Catholic intellectuals of Europe and made him a familiar figure at the Vatican.

Although he had spent no time in Britain since his schooldays, Wiseman agreed in 1831 to contribute to a new journal, the *Catholic Magazine*, dedicated to spreading the faith in England. Published in the wake of Catholic emancipation, it promised a "liberal and enlarged" outlook on

53. Ryan, "Lingard," 286–87; Gooch, *History and Historians*, 290–92.
54. The following passage is based on Richard Schiefen, *Nicholas Wiseman and the Transformation of English Catholicism* (Shepherdstown, W.Va.: Patmos Press, 1984); and S. W. Jackman, *Nicholas Cardinal Wiseman: A Victorian Prelate and His Writing* (Dublin: Five Lamps, 1977).
55. Michael E. Williams, *The Venerable English College, Rome: A History* (London: Associated Catholic Publications, 1979), 93–109.

Catholics' role in English life. A perceptible tension soon developed between the two most luminous contributors, Wiseman and Lingard, over how to preach Catholicism in England. Lingard belonged to the Cisalpine and Enlightenment tradition, whereas Wiseman lived and breathed (literally) the Ultramontane air of Rome. "The basic disagreement," writes one Wiseman biographer,

> was between those who, educated in the Enlightenment tradition of the eighteenth century, saw the need for the Church to adapt to the times in a clear, well-reasoned manner, especially suitable to the English temperament, and those who, influenced by the romantic revival, stressed the emotional appeal of Catholic devotional life, advocating Latin forms as the ideal. . . . Lingard represented the older model, Wiseman the newer.[56]

Lingard wrote one article for the magazine deploring the introduction of the Litany of Loreto in England and another doubting whether claims about the liquefaction of Saint Januarius's blood (a relic in Naples) should be believed without scientific verification. Strangely enough in view of future developments, Lingard wrote his Loreto articles under the pseudonym "Proselytos," posing as a recent convert from Protestantism who was deterred by the superstitious Mediterranean flavor of the litany. Wiseman was annoyed by these articles, which he believed might disturb the confidence of faithful Catholics in miracles, and he refused to contribute any further articles to the journal.[57]

In his own way, nevertheless, Wiseman was intellectually alert to contemporary developments. A series of lectures on natural science from the mid-1830s, delivered at the English College, show that he was familiar with the most recent scholarship on biology and geology, the two scientific fields that were to cause the bitterest controversy among Christians in the ensuing decades. The lectures also give evidence of a judicious mind at work, aware of the strengths of empirical science but watchful for philosophical question-begging. One lecture is devoted to refuting polygeny, the theory that the different races of human beings had different origins. Of one French polygenist, Julien-Joseph Virey, Wiseman noted: "Not content with attributing to the negro a different origin from the European, he goes so far as almost to suspect a certain fraternity between the Hottentot and the baboon." Wiseman recognized the need to offer an explanation of the differences among individuals without resort to poly-

56. Schiefen, *Wiseman*, 38.
57. Chinnici, *English Catholic Enlightenment*, 139–40.

geny, and his proposal anticipated at least some elements of Darwin's later
synthesis:

There is a perpetual tendency, I might say a striving, in nature, to raise up in
our species varieties, often of a very extraordinary character, sometimes
approximating, in a marked manner, to the peculiar and specific distinctives
of a race different to that in which they arise; and secondly, that these
peculiarities may be communicated through successive generations, from
father to son. A strong presumptive evidence is thus obtained, that the
different families or races among men, may owe their origin to some similar
occurrence, to the casual rise of a variety which, under the influence of
favorable circumstances—the isolation, for instance, of the family in which
it began and its consequent intermarriages—became fixed and indelible in
succeeding generations.[58]

    Yet, though he felt that obvious human variation needed an explanation,
Wiseman, unlike Darwin, did not draw the further conclusion that these
variations might also be the basis of species development. He was familiar
with the evolutionary theory of Lamarck, Darwin's predecessor, who had
"attempted to point out the steps whereby nature proceeds, or in former
times did proceed, towards gradually developing one class of beings from
another," but he dismissed it as a "degrading theory" (113). After accurately summarizing Lamarck's theory of the inheritance of acquired characteristics, Wiseman looked to historical evidence in making his refutation.
"Egypt, which . . . has preserved for us a museum of natural history not
only in its paintings but in the mummies of its animals, presents us every
species, after three thousand years, perfectly unchanged" (114). Today, of
course, the Egyptian case counts for naught in the evolution debate, but
most scientists of Wiseman's generation had no notion that the earth's age
should be reckoned in millions of years. They thought of ancient Egypt as
the civilization that had flourished when the world itself was young. The
existence then of species identical to those of the scientists' own day,
accordingly, seemed like an effective basis for rebutting the first evolutionists.

    When Wiseman compared the civilizations of the ancient world with the
"savages" encountered by European explorers in his own age, he took the
contrast as empirical support for the idea of the Fall. Far from evolving
from a "lower" to a "higher" state, as Lamarck and progressive evolutionists believed, Wiseman thought that all the evidence supported the Bible

---

58. Nicholas Wiseman, *Twelve Lectures on the Connexion between Science and Revealed
Religion* (Andover, Mass.: Gould and Newman, 1837), 124, hereafter cited in the text.

by showing how human beings had degenerated since their expulsion from the Garden of Eden and dispersal from Babel. Closing the lecture with an elegiac passage, Wiseman remarked that the degeneration theory was "more consoling to humanity than the degrading theories of Virey or Lamarck, and yet there is intermixed therewith some slight bitterness or humiliation. For if it was revolting to think that our noble nature should be nothing more than the perfecting of the ape's maliciousness, yet it is not without some shame and sorrow that we see that nature anywhere sunk and degraded from its original beauty till men should have been able plausibly to suggest that odious affinity" (126–27).

The degeneration view remained strong among Catholic scientists through the nineteenth century, and as we shall see, the first Catholics to challenge it, moving over to the evolutionary standpoint, were converts. The significant issue here, however, is not that Wiseman in the mid-1830s was no evolutionist but that he should have been so well versed in the scientific literature and controversies of his day and so willing to take their evidence seriously. Far from fearing that science might shake the foundations of revelation, he insisted on their full compatibility: "It has been the malice of superficial men, who had not patience or courage to penetrate into the sanctuary of nature, that has suggested objections from her laws, against truths revealed" (158). His successors would not be quite so self-assured.

Wiseman favored the establishment of a Catholic college, and for a time in the 1830s worked to create one with Bishop Peter Baines of the Western District, at his Prior Park estate. Personality clashes and philosophical differences with the autocratic Baines stalemated the project. It was the first of many occasions when English Catholics failed to create institutions of higher education.[59] On a visit to England in 1836 Wiseman, who had been away for eighteen years, since well before Catholic emancipation, said that the Catholics "had just emerged from the catacombs" but added that "their shackles had been removed, but not the numbness and cramp which they had produced."[60] To combat the numbness he helped establish the *Dublin Review*, a journal that was to play a central role in English-language Catholic intellectual life for the next century, compensating in part for the lack of a university. At first Wiseman himself edited the journal, but it soon passed into the hands of a historian, Mark Tierney. Within ten years it would be dominated by converts.[61]

59. Jackman, *Wiseman*, 18; Schiefen, *Wiseman*, 40–41.
60. Gwynn, *Hundred Years*, 18.
61. J. J. Dwyer, "The Catholic Press, 1850–1950," in George Beck, ed., *The English Catholics, 1850–1950* (London: Burns and Oates, 1950), esp. 475–78.

Wiseman was one of the first English Catholics to realize the signifi-cance of the Oxford Movement, which had begun to generate heated controversy at the Anglican universities and in London. He wrote a suc-cession of articles for the *Dublin Review* in the late 1830s and the early 1840s on the continuing differences between Catholics and Anglicans. Uncompromising in his defense of Catholicism, he was at the same time conciliatory to the Anglicans, hoping that he might show them how near they already were to affirming the doctrines of the Roman church.[62] In a letter to a friend in Rome he wrote prophetically that the fortunes of Catholicism in England depended on an influx of these talented converts:

Let us have but even a small number of such men as write in the Tracts, so imbued with the spirit of the early Church, so desirous to revive the image of the ancient Fathers. . . . let even a few such men, with the high clerical feeling which I believe them to possess, enter fully into the spirit of the Catholic religion, and we shall be speedily reformed, and England quickly converted. I am ready to acknowledge that, in all things, except the happi-ness of possessing the truth, and being in communion with God's true Church, and enjoying the advantages and blessings that flow thence, we are their inferiors.

He ended by declaring, "If the Oxford divines entered the Church we must be ready to fall into the shade, and take up our position in the background."[63]

Meanwhile, one of Wiseman's articles, on Saint Augustine and the Do-natists, which appeared in the *Dublin Review* in 1839, was having a stun-ning effect on Newman, making him doubt the validity of his efforts to depict the Anglican Church as genuine heir of the early Christian commu-nity.[64] In fact Wiseman was almost the only Catholic contemporary who contributed to Newman's conversion; his analysis of the church Fathers was the main catalyst. Nevertheless, Wiseman, despite his erudition, was not a brilliant man or an original thinker. One of his most partisan biogra-phers admits, "Regretfully but truthfully it must be realized that Wiseman did not have either a very supple or a very original mind."[65] Even New-man, despite his intellectual debt, wrote later that Wiseman was "too busy to be strenuous about anything. He was a man of large views and full of resource and suggestion, but he lived for the day, and every fresh event

62. Jackman, *Wiseman*, 48–53.
63. Wiseman, quoted in Gwynn, *Hundred Years*, 45.
64. Wiseman's article was "Anglican Claims of Apostolical Succession," *Dublin Review* 7 (August 1839): 139–80.
65. Jackman, *Wiseman*, 64.

seemed to wipe out from his mind those which preceded it."[66] His greatest achievements were to be administrative rather than academic.

After twenty-two years in Rome, Wiseman began to consider moving back to England, where his talents were widely appreciated in the Catholic community. A course of lectures on Catholicism which he had given in London during his 1835–1836 visit had made him a minor celebrity; he was the first Catholic priest to address a mixed audience of English Protestants and Catholics on the nature of the Catholic faith.[67] Among his admiring visitors in Rome during the 1830s were William Gladstone, the future prime minister, Thomas Macaulay, the historian, and Newman himself. From England also Augustus Welby Pugin, a recent convert and Gothic revival architect, pleaded with Wiseman to resign from Rome and come home: "Of what service would your great talents and eloquence be in this country where unfortunately the great body of those who profess the true faith are lamentably deficient in this respect."[68] In 1840 Wiseman acceded to such requests and to his own inclination. His intellectual contributions diminished thereafter as his administrative responsibilities increased. First he worked as president of Oscott College in Birmingham, before inheriting the bishopric of the Midlands district.

In 1850 Pope Pius IX decided to restore the full Catholic hierarchy in England and Wales (Scotland in 1878) and chose Wiseman to be the first Catholic primate since the Reformation, appointing him cardinal archbishop of Westminster. Wiseman got carried away at his new elevation; his perfervid declaration of Catholic triumph in a pastoral letter, "From the Flaminian Gate," was a tactless way to begin and it set off a storm of protest in England and another round of anti-Catholic rioting. Anti-Catholic sermons rang from Anglican pulpits, Queen Victoria said her throne was under attack, and the prime minister, Lord John Russell, fanned the flames by denouncing the "papal aggression." Russell's letter to the *Times* ended with a summary declaration of the Protestant view: "The liberty of Protestantism has been enjoyed too long in England to allow of any successful attempt to impose a foreign yoke upon our minds and consciences. No foreign prince or potentate will be at liberty to fasten his fetters upon a nation which has so long and so nobly vindicated its right to freedom of opinion, civil, political, and religious."[69] Charlotte Brontë,

66. Newman, quoted in Shane Leslie, *Henry Edward Manning: His Life and Labours* (1921; Westport, Conn.: Greenwood, 1970), 103.

67. Jackman, *Wiseman*, 66.

68. Pugin, quoted in Schiefen, *Wiseman*, 90.

69. Russell, quoted in Edward Norman, *Anti-Catholicism in Victorian England* (New York: Barnes and Noble, 1968), 160.

daughter of a staunchly anti-Catholic Anglican vicar, was indignant too, but she could not resist the temptation to go and see Wiseman preaching in 1851. She penned a memorable caricature in a letter to her father:

He is a big portly man. . . . He has not merely a double but a treble and quadruple chin; he has a very large mouth with oily lips, and looks as if he would relish a good dinner with a bottle of wine after it. He came swimming into the room smiling, simpering, and bowing like a fat old lady, and sat down very demure in his chair, and looked the picture of a sleek hypo-crite. . . . A bevy of inferior priests surrounded him, many of them very dark-looking and sinister men. The Cardinal spoke in a smooth whining manner, just like a canting Methodist preacher. The audience looked up to him as to a god. A spirit of the hottest zeal pervaded the whole meeting.

Elizabeth Gaskell, her biographer, thought that this and other spiteful passages in Brontë's writings, were designed to compensate for a subterra-nean attraction she felt toward Catholicism.[70]

Lingard, always alert to English xenophobia, lamented the bombastic Romanizing idiom of his former student, so different from his own cir-cumspect style, learned in the days of the penal laws. But for all their differences, Wiseman, who spent the first months of his primacy trying to repair the damage his pastoral had caused, admired Lingard and recog-nized the importance of his work. "Be assured of my affectionate gratitude to you," he wrote to the aging historian in 1850, "for the great, impor-tant, and noble services which you have rendered to religion through life, and which have so much contributed to overthrow error, and give a solid historical basis to all subsequent controversy with Protestantism."[71]

When Wiseman revived the English Catholic hierarchy his own former pupil John Acton was sixteen years old, and already showing evidence of superb intellectual powers. Acton is more nearly than any other figure the exception to the rule that the Catholic intellectual revival was a convert phenomenon. In his own lifetime his reputation spread beyond the bounds of the Catholic community, which can be said of few other born Catholics of his day. Prime Minister Lord Rosebery recognized his genius and crowned his career by appointing him Regius Professor of History at Cambridge in 1895.[72]

70. Peters, *Unquiet Soul*, 334.
71. Wiseman, quoted in Shea, *English Ranke*, 81.
72. Biographical information on Acton is based on Gertrude Himmelfarb, *Lord Acton: A Study in Conscience and Politics* (Chicago: University of Chicago Press, 1952); David Math-ew, *Lord Acton and His Times* (University: University of Alabama Press, 1968); Josef L.

Born in 1834, Acton was related to the British, German, and Italian aristocracies. His stepfather, Lord Leveson, helped launch his English political career, and an uncle, Cardinal Charles Januarius Acton, wielded considerable influence for the family at Rome, so the young man enjoyed formidable advantages and connections. He went to school at Oscott, Birmingham, studying there from 1843 to 1848. Among his teachers, Wiseman was born a Catholic, but nearly all the others, George Spencer, Augustus Pugin, Bernard Smith, John Brande Morris, Sir Peter de Page Renouf, and Henry Logan, were recent converts from the Church of England. Despite his high birth and good connections, Acton's application to Cambridge University was denied on grounds of his religion, and he spent eight years abroad instead, studying under Ignatz Dollinger in Germany, and making visits to Rome and the United States. Dollinger was the premier Catholic historian of his age, eager to keep pace with the historiographical revolution of his era, merciless in cutting away superstitions and dogmatic obstacles from Catholic history, and receptive to the developmentalist hypothesis flowing through European intellectual life. Gertrude Himmelfarb, Acton's best biographer, shows that Dollinger's influence over Acton's formation as a historian was decisive. Each of them emphasized the need to rely on the testimony of original sources and to explain historical changes without recourse to the supernatural. "Historians have not to point out everywhere the hand of providence, but to find out all the natural causes of things," wrote Acton. "Enough will always remain that cannot be explained."[73]

His early historical writings bore witness to the influence of Edmund Burke's political ideas as well as Dollinger's methods. He emphasized the organic character of society, the danger of dramatic interruptions of political life, and the need for incremental social change. Like Lingard, he cultivated at first a detached and neutral style, avoiding judgments that would reveal his personal moral convictions. And like Lingard and Wiseman, he was confident that science and faith were fully compatible. "Science . . . was hostile to Catholics only when they rejected it and permitted it to be usurped by their enemies."[74]

As he matured, however, and as his work with the convert Richard Simpson on the liberal Catholic magazine the *Rambler* led to official condemnations, Acton shifted his ground. He was working, he complained in an 1860 letter to Newman, "in the midst of a hostile and

---

Altholz, *The Conscience of Lord Acton* (Houston, Tex.: University of St. Thomas, 1970); Hugh Tulloch, *Acton* (London: Weidenfeld and Nicolson, 1988).

73. Acton, quoted in Himmelfarb, *Acton*, 41.
74. Ibid., 40.

illiterate episcopate, an ignorant clergy, [and] a prejudiced and divided laity," none of whom he considered intellectually trustworthy.[75] He was shocked to discover in the 1850s and early 1860s that the Vatican discouraged and sometimes prevented free historical inquiry and often used or omitted historical truths from pragmatic considerations. As a result of these discoveries, he became an outspoken historical and political moralist, refusing to turn a blind eye to unscrupulous but politically expedient conduct. Popes, he declared, had no excuse for deviating from historical truth, which was for him inseparable from God. This view in turn persuaded him that the higher the station of a leader, the less excuse he had for acting immorally in any way. He became intolerant of historians who tried to take a position of objective neutrality in describing and analyzing history's persecutors. Instead, Acton insisted, the historian must make inflexible moral judgments against the great men of the past, who were nearly always (as he came to think) bad. This was a far cry from Lingard's cool detachment, and trying to enact his program all but paralyzed Acton, who never finished any major historical project.[76]

Acton came to believe that his church was one of the worst offenders against truth and one of the great persecutors in European history. He was enraged by Pope Pius IX's decision in 1867 to canonize Pedro de Arbues, the ferocious Spanish inquisitor of the late fifteenth century, and by a widespread reluctance among Catholics to condemn the Catholic role in the Saint Bartholomew's Day Massacre of 1572. He led English and American opposition to the declaration of papal infallibility at the First Vatican Council in 1869 and 1870 as an affront to historical intelligence, and he publicized "leaks" from the debates, which he gleaned from sympathetic English, German, and American participants. With Dollinger's help he published news of the Vatican deliberations in the *Allgemeine Zeitung* under the pen name of "Quirinus." Far from fortifying the church, as the infallibilists intended, he believed they would undermine it by suggesting Catholicism's refusal to come to terms with its own past. As "Quirinus" he wrote: "The predilection for the Infallibilist theory is in

75. Acton, quoted in Gilley, *Newman*, 309
76. Altholz, *Conscience of Acton*, 13–15. Altholz shows how Acton was unable to live up to his own requirements in his lectures on the French Revolution. The thing itself was justified, but not the means. "The right of resistance to authority in the name of conscience, and even the ultimate appeal to arms, were inescapable conclusions from his principles. Yet revolution involves force and violence, the killing of men for the sake of an abstract cause. When that killing had been done in the name of religion, Acton had stigmatized persecution as nothing more than murder; how then could he justify killing for the sake of political principles? The same morality which required revolution also condemned the acts which necessarily accompanied it. This was a dilemma which Acton was never able successfully to resolve" (15).

precise proportion to the ignorance of its advocates."[77] He was angry with Newman and other opponents of the declaration for hiding behind the "inopportunist" label—that is, for claiming that they opposed the timing rather than the content—instead of coming out into the open as downright foes of the idea.[78] In the same way he opposed the continued temporal power of the papacy at a time when it was a virtual litmus test of Catholic loyalty.

Acton, clearly, was no ordinary Catholic. His opposition to the direction of the church and his prominence in English public life (Gladstone ennobled him just before the council began) vexed Pope Pius IX. "Feeling ran so high against Acton," writes Himmelfarb, "that for a time he feared assassination at the hands of the Jesuits, which makes it possible to credit the rumour that he sometimes thought it prudent to move about Rome in disguise."[79] His old teacher Dollinger refused to accept the council decrees and suffered excommunication. Acton narrowly escaped excommunication himself and was obliged to write an equivocal letter of submission to his bishop. By the 1880s, so disenchanted was he with the moral standards of Catholicism that he warned Anglicans that converting to Catholicism might be a *backward* step, that "the moral risk entailed in embracing Catholicism was greater than the dogmatic risk in remaining an Anglican."[80]

The later years of Acton's life were in many ways disappointing, even though he scored a symbolic triumph in being awarded the nation's highest post for a historian at the same university that had denied him an undergraduate place. Despite massive preparations and an unparalleled erudition, he never succeeded in writing his great projected "History of Liberty," of which only drafts and fragments survive. Instead, he helped Mandell Creighton found the *English Historical Review*, edited the *Cambridge Modern History*, and wrote dozens of articles and reviews. Similarly he never managed to be appointed British ambassador to Berlin, despite his apparent conviction in each of the four Gladstone ministries that the post was about to be offered to him. Like his American contemporary Henry Adams (1838–1916), Lord Acton had about him the air of a man too fastidious for the dirty world of politics, one whom a bustling world had decided to pass by.[81]

77. Acton, quoted in Himmelfarb, *Acton*, 102.

78. John N. Figgis and Reginald Laurence, eds., *Selections from the Correspondence of the First Lord Acton* (London: Longmans, Green, 1917), 85–91.

79. Himmelfarb, *Acton*, 106.

80. Acton, quoted ibid., 163.

81. On Adams, see Ernest Samuels, *Henry Adams* (Cambridge: Belknap of Harvard University Press, 1989).

Much of Acton's life and work is interwoven with the convert generation, and he plays a central role in the following chapters. But it is worth
pausing for a moment to witness Acton, still only a teenager, visiting the
United States of America in 1853 with Lord Ellesmere. Among the American Catholics he found few to admire except the convert Orestes Brownson and Archbishop John B. Fitzpatrick, the man who had received
Brownson into the church. He talked with Brownson for two hours about
writers they both admired and about the works of Newman. "I was the
more eager in conversation that I was uncertain whether I should see him
again," said Acton, though later in his visit he caught up with Brownson
again at Emmitsburg, Maryland, and carried on the discussion. Of
Fitzpatrick he remarked, "I found him a real specimen of a kind of men
who . . . without mingling in public life or gaining literary reputation,
possess greater abilities and wisdom than those who do."[82] Acton's judgments on this trip show him to have been a rather censorious nineteen-
year-old—he declared Harvard contemptible. So these expressions of enthusiasm were high praise indeed. Acton mentioned no other Catholic
writers. Subsequent historians have been forced to admit that American
Catholicism prior to the 1840s had few intellectual ornaments. In her
recent history of American Catholic intellectual life Margaret Mary Reher
attests to the thinness of Catholic intellectual life in America before the
conversion of Brownson in 1844 and Isaac Hecker in 1845.[83]

In the early nineteenth century most American writers had an ambiva-
lent attitude toward Britain. As citizens of a new democratic nation that
had broken free of British rule in the Revolutionary War, they wanted to
assert their own distinct identity. But their literary traditions, like their
language, made perpetual reference to British models. The first American
literary successes, James Fenimore Cooper, Washington Irving, and a little
later Edgar Allan Poe, all made their reputations by gaining acclaim *in
England*, which in turn validated them in their compatriots' eyes. The
same would be true among American Catholics, who were, in effect,
marginalized twice over, once by being part of a British cultural offshoot,
and again by belonging to a disfranchised and despised religion.

82. Acton, quoted in S. W. Jackson, *Acton in America* (Shepherdstown, W.Va.: Patmos
Press, 1979), 78.
83. Reher, *Catholic Intellectual Life*. Her first chapter, "Enlightenment and Episcopal
Leadership," concentrates on the work of John Carroll, first archibishop of Baltimore, and
John England, bishop of Charleston, both of whom wrote mainly on church affairs and
church-state relations. She also mentions (15–16) the work of Matthew Carey, an Irish
Catholic immigrant and founder of the first American cultural magazine, the *American
Museum or Repository of Ancient and Modern Fugitive Pieces, etc., Prose and Poetical,* in 1787.
The next two chapters of her book (six chapters in all) move straight to the converts
Brownson and Hecker.

The intensity of anti-Catholic prejudice and the insubstantiality of Catholic intellectual life together suggest that there was no material enticement for British and American intellectuals who contemplated conversion. Three men—Lingard, Wiseman, and Acton—however gifted, did not make up a tradition; they were in fact remarkable anomalies. At the Reformation, moreover, all the great church buildings in Britain had passed into Anglican hands, so that worshipers in pursuit of the beauty of holiness were much more likely to find it by staying with the Anglicans. To join the Catholic Church meant to put up with rough, makeshift churches and chapels and the company of uncouth Irish laborers. For convert clergymen, at least those who were married, the turn to Rome also meant the loss of livelihood. Nevertheless, in many cases religious and intellectual conviction won out, and a flow of conversions to Rome began in both countries which continued through the rest of the nineteenth century and well into the twentieth.

# III

# LOSS AND GAIN
## *The First English Converts*

ENGLISH AND AMERICAN CONVERTS to Catholicism in the early nineteenth century usually came from the Anglican or Episcopal Church. Since the Reformation one strand of Anglicanism had remained similar to Catholicism, being sacramental, ritualistic, and hierarchical. But the compromise embedded in the Thirty-nine Articles, by which the Anglican communion defined itself, also offered accommodation to thoroughly Protestant participants. The compromise had had political advantages in sixteenth-century England, but it also laid the foundations for centuries of wrangling. Puritans within the church always hoped to line it up more closely with the Calvinist tradition, whereas High Church Anglicans tried to create an Anglican branch of Catholicism, as similar as possible to the Roman version but without the pre-Reformation abuses and without papal supremacy.[1]

From the early seventeenth century to the Tractarian Movement of the 1830s and 1840s, Oxford was the home of the High Church tradition. Cambridge University, by contrast, had a more puritan-evangelical tradition, and yet a small "Cambridge Movement" of Catholic conversions preceded the more influential Oxford Movement.[2] In the years between 1825 and 1830 three young Englishmen, all from Trinity College, Cambridge, and all admirers of medieval England, converted to Catholicism

1. On the High Church tradition, see Peter B. Nockles, *The Oxford Movement in Context: Anglican High Churchmanship, 1760–1857* (New York: Cambridge University Press, 1994). Nockles's first chapter is a superb essay on the historiography of the Oxford Movement itself.

2. The following passage is based on Kevin Morris, "Kenelm Digby and English Catholicism," *Recusant History* 20 (May 1991): 361–70; Morris, "The Cambridge Converts and the Oxford Movement," *Recusant History* 17 (October 1985): 386–98.

and then took upon themselves the role of missionaries to convert their Protestant brethren. They were Kenelm Digby (1796–1880), George Spencer (1799–1864), and Ambrose Phillipps (1809–1878). Spencer, already an Anglican clergyman at the time of his conversion, was obliged to resign his well-endowed parish and his livelihood; he is alleged to have remarked, "There goes three thousand pounds."[3] He was the first of many Anglicans who would make large economic sacrifices for their convictions. Not that he had ever been acquisitive: he had always lived frugally and given everything he could to the poor. He trained for the priesthood in Rome, renamed himself Ignatius, and later became head of the Passionist Fathers in England who worked for conversions, tramping the countryside in shabby habits and begging for alms.[4]

Phillipps, a far wealthier man who had no need to work, was optimistic about bringing the whole of Britain back into the Catholic fold. He added "de Lisle" to his name for medieval effect. A staunch patriot, he favored corporate reunion, a negotiated settlement between Canterbury and Rome, but the project made little headway. He founded the Association for the Promotion of the Unity of Christendom in 1857, wrote frequent letters to Vatican officials assuring them that the day of reunion was at hand (they remained skeptical), and meanwhile donated land in Charnwood Forest, Leicestershire, for the foundation of the first Cistercian (Trappist) monastery in England since the Reformation.[5]

Kenelm Digby, third of the Cambridge converts, was an admirer of the European reactionary theorists Joseph de Maistre and Louis de Bonald. His *Broad Stone of Honour* (1822) argued for the enlightened rule of Catholic aristocrats, and his massive *Mores Catholici*, published in eleven bulky volumes beginning in 1831, was a eulogy to the glory of the high Middle Ages, "ages of the highest grace to men; ages of faith; ages when all Europe was Catholic." Circuitous and wordy, *Mores Catholici* was nevertheless important in its day for the scale of its polemic. It moved step by step through Protestant criticisms of Catholicism, refuting every charge and then demonstrating, at least to Digby's satisfaction, that the Middle Ages were a Catholic golden age, exempt from modern vices. The medieval era was intellectually and aesthetically alive, peace loving, charitable, and honest. "Englishmen, it is true, at present, are not such as adored at Calvary when they followed Richard [the Lion-Heart] to the Holy Land;

3. Edward R. Norman, *The English Catholic Church in the Nineteenth Century* (Oxford: Clarendon Press, 1984), 208.
4. Urban Young, *Life of Father Ignatius Spencer* (London: Burns, Oates, and Washburn, 1933).
5. Norman, *English Catholic Church*, 207–16, 220.

their manners are not those of the beatitudes," Digby lamented, but still he thought large numbers of conversions to Rome were possible. Knowing the Anglican faith from within, he believed that the best Anglicans (like himself in former days) were often close to Rome in spirit, capable of high Catholic thought, if only they could admit it and overcome their prejudices:

Never did Catholics write more eloquently on things pertaining to the true discipline than those illustrious [Anglican] men, when they pleased; but let them pass by a chapel where its holy rites were still observed; and then, as a troop of maskers when they put their vizors off look other than before, the counterfeited semblance thrown aside, so these returned to those habits of vituperation, which others, in every respect besides unlike them, cultivated, muttering against Rome in tokens of their spite.[6]

The Cambridge converts' luxurious medievalism, coinciding with the romantic vogue for Shelley, Byron, and Walter Scott, struck a resonant chord among many of their non-Catholic contemporaries, including the poet William Wordsworth, the Pre-Raphaelite artist Edward Burne-Jones, and the critics John Ruskin and William Morris, who also liked to cast longing glances back to an idealized Middle Ages but without taking the drastic step of conversion. There was in the 1820s, 1830s, and 1840s a growing romance with the aesthetics of Catholicism throughout Britain and the United States.[7]

One of Phillipps's closest friends and a fellow medievalist was Augustus Welby Pugin (1812–1852), an architect who played a central role in the Gothic revival movement.[8] Son of a French immigrant and an English mother who belonged to the evangelical side of the Anglican Church, Pugin showed exceptional intellectual gifts early on and was a precocious teenager. When he was only fifteen, his father, an architectural draftsman, entrusted him with the important commission of making some Gothic-

6. Kenelm Digby, *Mores Catholici, or Ages of Faith* (London: C. Dolman, 1847), 3:801–2.

7. On the American vogue for Catholicism, see in particular Jenny Franchot, *Roads to Rome: The Antebellum Protestant Encounter with Catholicism* (Berkeley: University of California Press, 1994).

8. The standard biographies of Pugin, on which the following passage is based, are Phoebe Stanton, *Pugin* (New York: Viking, 1971); and Michael Trappes-Lomax, *Pugin: A Medieval Victorian* (London: Sheed and Ward, 1933). There has been a revival of interest in his work in the 1990s, culminating in an exhibition at the Victoria and Albert Museum, London, in the summer of 1994. For the most recent studies, see Paul Atterbury and Clive Wainwright, eds., *Pugin: A Gothic Passion* (New Haven: Yale University Press in association with the Victoria and Albert Museum, 1994).

style furniture for King George IV. Pugin matured quickly and became increasingly convinced by the claims of the Catholic faith, to which he converted at the age of twenty-two, in 1834. John Ruskin later claimed that Pugin had converted for aesthetic reasons—"blown into a change of religion by the whine of an organ pipe; stitched into a new creed by the gold threads on priests' petticoats."[9] Pugin's conversion certainly had an aesthetic element but his own explanation was fuller and more convincing than Ruskin's. He had been brought up, he recalled, "thoroughly imbued with all the popular [anti-Catholic] notions of racks and faggots, and fires, idolatry, sin-purchase, etc., with all the usual tissue of falsehoods so industriously propagated throughout the land." But his love of England's medieval churches and cathedrals, which he toured extensively, had led him to study the reasons for their original building:

With what delight did I trace the fitness of each portion of those glorious edifices to the rites for whose celebration they had been erected. Then did I discover that the service I had been accustomed to attend and admire was but a cold and heartless remnant of past glories, and that those prayers which in my ignorance I had ascribed to reforming piety, were in reality only scraps plucked from the solemn and perfect offices of the ancient Church. Pursuing my researches among the faithful pages of the old chronicles I discovered the tyranny, apostasy, and bloodshed by which the new religion [Protestantism] had been established, the endless strifes, dissensions, and discords that existed among its propagators, and the devastation and ruin that attended its progress: opposed to all this, I considered the Catholic Church; existing with uninterrupted apostolical succession, handing down the same faith, sacraments, and ceremonies unchanged, unaltered through every clime, language, and nation.

For upwards of three years did I earnestly pursue the study of this all-important subject; and the irresistible force of truth penetrating my own heart, I gladly surrendered my own fallible judgment to the unerring decisions of the Church, and embracing with heart and soul its faith and discipline, became an humble, but I trust faithful member.[10]

For Pugin, as for his Cambridge friends, conversion hampered the fulfillment of his ambitions. England's Gothic churches had all been in Anglican hands since the Reformation; conversion denied him the chance of participating in their restoration. Meanwhile he was obliged to join England's tiny Catholic population in their makeshift chapels, most of them

9. Ruskin, quoted in Trappes-Lomax, *Pugin*, 55.
10. Pugin, quoted ibid., 57, 58.

quite devoid of architectural merit. They were, he wrote, "inferior to many Wesleyan meeting houses, and with vestments and altar-furniture that would hardly have been admitted among the properties of a travelling [theater] manager."[11] Pugin made it his life's work to provide England's Catholics with Gothic churches of their own. His Byronic eccentricities— he sometimes posed as a poor sailor and at other times swaggered about in billowing homemade capes—were a self-conscious effort to make himself a larger-than-life representative for the traditionally modest and self-effacing Catholic community. No wonder he became an object of suspicion to ordinary citizens. When a lady seated near him on a train saw the recent convert ostentatiously cross himself, she cried out in alarm: "You are a Catholic, Sir! Guard, guard, let me out—I must get into another carriage!"[12]

Among Pugin's most important architectural work was his part in rebuilding the Houses of Parliament. The old houses burned down in 1834, the year of his conversion. One of the competitors for designing the new houses was Edward Barry, and Pugin "ghosted" a set of designs for him. When Barry won the commission, the two men collaborated on the new Parliament buildings. In the century and a half since then, Catholic and Protestant historians have disputed the extent of Pugin's dominance behind the scenes.[13] Pugin also worked at an incredible pace to build more than fifty new churches, supported and generously financed by John Talbot, the Catholic earl of Shrewsbury, and by Ambrose Phillipps de Lisle, his two most generous patrons. Among them were Phillipps de Lisle's Cistercian monastery, Saint Bernard's, the superb church in Cheadle, Staffordshire, and the new Catholic cathedrals of Birmingham and Southwark. In addition he designed vestments, metalwork, tiles, murals, wallpaper, and all the repertoire of the visual, ecclesiastical arts, in Gothic style. His projects were hamstrung by lack of funds—many of the churches had to be far plainer and smaller than he would have liked—and often brought him into conflict with patrons anxious to get as much as they could for the smallest possible sums. Nevertheless, the churches rose, gained influential admirers throughout Britain, and made Gothic the characteristic style of Victorian public building.

Pugin was a polemicist for the Gothic, or "pointed," style as well as a

---

11. Ibid., 104.

12. Kenneth Clark, *The Gothic Revival: An Essay in the History of Taste* (1928; London: Constable, 1950), 170.

13. Trappes-Lomax, a Catholic champion, argues that Barry was in the embarrassing position of having to pose as the designer while covertly relying on Pugin's genius. Trappes-Lomax, *Pugin*, 85–86.

zealous practitioner. His books *Contrasts* (1836) and *Apology for the Revival of Christian Architecture* (1843) maintained that sound building coincided with sound faith and that the Catholic Middle Ages, Digby's "age of faith," had been the greatest era of building in history.[14] Gothic buildings, he believed, were Catholic truth distilled in stone. They revealed their own structure and created a morally exalted blend of form and function, whereas classical and baroque architecture depended on what seemed to him the morally inferior techniques of disguise and cloaking.[15] He scorned nearly all Counter-Reformation Catholic building, which seemed to him more pagan than Christian, directing men's thoughts to earthly self-glorification rather than leading their eyes and minds up to heaven. The art historian Kenneth Clark attributes to Pugin two of the distinctive ideas of Victorian aesthetics: that "the value of a building depends on the moral worth of its creator; and [that] a building has a moral value independent of, and more important than, its esthetic value."[16]

No place was more paganized, in Pugin's view, than Rome itself, whose Renaissance and baroque churches he detested. He described Saint Peter's, which he visited in 1847, as "a humbug, a failure, an abortion, a mass of imposition, and a sham constructed even more vilely than it was designed." He hated the sensual statues and wrote a friend that in the Gesu he had tried in vain to pray: "I looked up, hoping to see something which would stimulate my devotion. But I saw only *legs* sprawling over me. I expected them to kick me next, and rushed out." Pope Pius IX gave him a gold medal in gratitude for his services to Catholicism, but Pugin was not mollified. He reciprocated by pressing a copy of his Gothic manifesto *Contrasts* into the pontiff's hands.[17]

Pugin was tactless and often made enemies when he could have used friends. One historian remarks aptly enough that he "acquired enemies with reckless abandon."[18] Like many subsequent converts, Pugin never shied away from criticizing contemporary Catholicism. As a result he won the enmity of influential English Catholic bishops such as Peter Baines,

14. Augustus Welby Pugin, *Contrasts*, ed. H. R. Hitchcock (1836; New York: Humanities Press, 1969); Pugin, *An Apology for the Revival of Christian Architecture in England* (London: J. Weale, 1843).

15. Andrew Saint, "The Fate of Pugin's True Principles," in Atterbury and Wainwright, *Pugin*, 272–82. Saint points out that Pugin's style of argument about "truth" and "deception" in architecture persists into the twentieth century, even in the work of the otherwise utterly dissimilar Le Corbusier (281).

16. Clark, *Gothic Revival*, 202.

17. Trappes-Lomax, *Pugin*, 112.

18. Guy Williams, *Augustus Pugin versus Decimus Burton* (London: Cassell, 1990), 108. This book describes Pugin's rhetorical war against Burton, a leading exponent of classical architecture.

vicar apostolic of England's Western District, who opposed his Gothic principles. Baines may have been responsible for reporting Pugin to the Office of Propaganda in Rome, criticizing him for making unauthorized "innovations" and drawing on him a warning from the Vatican. Pugin indignantly denied the charge and declared that he was *restoring* the genuine Catholic style, rescuing it from worldly debasements. He had a low opinion of bishops in general and remarked in a later pamphlet that in Henry VIII's day nearly all the English Catholic bishops had surrendered to the king's will rather than put up a spirited fight against his apostasy.[19]

"Everything glorious about the English churches is Catholic, everything debased and hideous, Protestant," he declared in one characteristic rhetorical flight, adding that to judge from their buildings, the English Catholics had been infected since the Reformation by the Protestant virus: "A fine old Catholic church used for Protestant service is indeed a melancholy sight, but scarcely less melancholy is it to see modern Catholics with their own hands polluting and disfiguring, by pagan emblems and theatrical trumpery, the glorious structures raised by their ancestors in the faith."[20] The characteristic style of worship caused him physical pain. "Since Christ himself hung abandoned and bleeding on the Cross of Calvary," he wrote in the *Apology*, "never has so sad a spectacle been exhibited to the afflicted Christian as is presented in many modern Catholic chapels, where the adorable Victim is offered up by the Priests of God's Church, disguised in miserable dresses intended for sacred vestments, surrounded by a scoffing auditory of protestant sight-seekers who have paid a few shillings a head to grin at mysteries which they do not understand, and to hear the performances of an infidel troop of mercenary musicians, hired to sing symbols of a faith they disbelieve, and salutations to that Holy Sacrament they mock and deny."[21] At the opening ceremonies for one of his churches, Saint Marie's in Derby, he drove off in a huff when he found that the choir was going to sing operatic music rather than the Gregorian chant he had specified.[22]

Pugin is a central figure in British architectural history and his vast influence on the associated fields of design, ceramics, metalwork, and dress are now being explored. For example, Megan Aldrich, in her history of Gothic revival, shows that Pugin argued for flat designs on flat surfaces. On his highly patterned tiles, wallpapers, and carpets, he eschewed per-

19. The pamphlet was *Earnest Address on the Establishment of the Hierarchy* (1851), cited in Trappes-Lomax, *Pugin*, 261–63.
20. Pugin, *Contrasts*, 51.
21. Pugin, *Apology*, 24–25.
22. Trappes-Lomax, *Pugin*, 106.

spectival illusions. "This," says Aldrich, "is a highly significant idea in the history of Western art, as it represents a turning away from the whole system of pictorial perspective. . . . By rejecting this tradition in favor of the use of flat pattern, Pugin helped to promote the development of abstraction that was to become so characteristic of twentieth century art and design."[23] Pugin's premature death at the age of forty in 1852, apparently brought on by overwork and exhaustion, shocked even his architectural rivals. Obituaries recognized the importance of his innovations. Even the London *Times*, no friend to Catholics at that time, admitted that "with all his crotchets, and with an absurd attachment, not merely to the spirit, but to the letter of medievalism, he has perhaps done more for architecture than any of those who run him down. He it was who first exposed the shams and concealments of modern architecture, and contrasted it with the heartiness and sincerity of medieval work." It added, with a characteristically Victorian turn, that "it was he who first showed us that our architecture offended not only against the laws of beauty, but also against the laws of morality."[24]

Ironically Pugin's theories proved more influential among Protestants than Catholics, and in the following decades dozens of Anglican churches were built or refashioned along lines he had laid down. To compound the irony, many of the most memorable Victorian Gothic buildings were factories, railway stations (such as Gilbert Scott's incomparable London Saint Pancras), or even the Staffordshire Water Works—manifestations of the very industrialism against which the medievalists were in revolt. Pugin was disappointed in his hope that Gothic building and Catholic conversions would spread together across the land.

The architectural historian Kristine Garrigan notes many striking similarities between Pugin and John Ruskin (1819–1900), though the two men never met. Both despised postmedieval architecture, particularly the Renaissance and baroque, and both believed that "only pious men in a healthy society can build good buildings." Garrigan adds that "the very turn of mind of the two men—their assurance, enthusiasms, and inconsistencies—was similar, even to the disabling madness in which each tragically closed his life." Pugin was the earlier of the two, however, and Ruskin was often accused of plagiarizing from his work. He denied it, attacking Pugin's writings and buildings with "savage, tasteless vehemence" because of Pugin's Catholicism, which stood in stark contrast to

23. Megan Aldrich, *Gothic Revival* (London: Phaidon, 1994), 153, 155.
24. *Times*, quoted ibid., 176.

his own religion.[25] Not only did Ruskin *not* convert, he littered his works on the Gothic, such as *The Stones of Venice*, with anti-Catholic asides and, in effect, made the Gothic style safe for Anglicans while trying to undermine the Catholic foundation on which Pugin believed it to rest.[26] It was a source of recurrent annoyance to Catholic converts to find their ideas taken up by Protestant or secular readers but separated from their religious sources—or even turned against them—rather than swallowed whole. Pugin's example shows that a convert's work would not necessarily have the religious consequences he desired and might even invigorate antagonists.

The Oxford Movement would have the same effect as the Pugin-Ruskin controversy, leading some adherents to Rome but then, in reaction, intensifying anti-Catholic feeling among many others.[27] It began in the 1830s when, according to one later historian, "Oxford was the sacred city of Anglicanism, into which nothing common or unclean could enter, and where neither popery nor Dissent could gain a foothold. . . . it was inefficient, cumbersome, out of date. But it was beautiful; more beautiful perhaps than any other place in an England which was still rich in beauty; and consequently it could still inspire loyalty and affection."[28] The leading figures in the early days of the movement, John Keble (1792–1866), Newman (1801–1890), and Hurrell Froude (1803–1836), were unconcerned with questions of architecture, medievalism, or ritual. The central issue for them was authority. They wanted to clarify, first, the Church of England's claim to wield dogmatic authority and, second, the nature of its

25. Kristine O. Garrigan, *Ruskin on Architecture: His Thought and Influence* (Madison: University of Wisconsin Press, 1973), 19, 20.
26. John Ruskin, *The Stones of Venice* (New York: John Wiley, 1860).
27. The literature on the Oxford Movement is extensive. The following passage is based on the work of its Anglican and Catholic historians. From the Anglican side: C. P. C. Clark, *The Oxford Movement and After* (London: A. R. Mowbray, 1932); Owen Chadwick, ed., *The Mind of the Oxford Movement* (London: Adam and Charles Black, 1960); Eugene Fairweather, ed., *The Oxford Movement* (New York: Oxford University Press, 1964)—a document collection with commentary; Geoffrey Rowell, *The Vision Glorious: Themes and Personalities of the Catholic Revival in Anglicanism* (Oxford: Oxford University Press, 1983); Owen Chadwick, *The Spirit of the Oxford Movement: Tractarian Essays* (New York: Cambridge University Press, 1990); Nockles, *Oxford Movement in Context*. From the Catholic side: Christopher Dawson, *The Spirit of the Oxford Movement* (New York: Sheed and Ward, 1933); Shane Leslie, *The Oxford Movement, 1833–1933* (London: Burns, Oakes, and Washbourne, 1933); Marvin O'Connell, *The Oxford Conspirators: A History of the Oxford Movement, 1833–1845* (New York: Macmillan, 1969); Ian Ker, *John Henry Newman: A Biography* (Oxford: Clarendon Press, 1988); David Newsome, *The Convert Cardinals: John Henry Newman and Henry Edward Manning* (London: John Murray, 1993).
28. Dawson, *Spirit of Oxford Movement*, 86–87.

relationship to the British government. They hoped to show that the Anglican Church stood in a continuous line of descent from the early church Fathers, by tracing a lineage through Roman Catholicism but separating from it when it became incurably corrupt. They placed great emphasis on the principle of apostolic succession, the ordination of each bishop and priest by his predecessors, in continuous unbroken line from Jesus' first charge to Peter right down to the present.

On the second issue, the Oxford theologians opposed the principle of erastianism, that the church should be dependent on and governed by the state. Paradoxically, in light of later events, one of the issues around which the movement took shape was opposition to Catholic emancipation in 1829 and the suppression of several Anglican dioceses in Catholic Ireland. These Tory High Churchmen did not like the idea that the British government could tamper at will with the constitution of the church: the action made all too plain the church's subordination to the state.[29] Keble, wrote Christopher Dawson, brooded on this affair "until he felt that silence was a criminal acquiescence in an act of rebellion against God. The abolition of the Test Act and the suppression of the Irish sees seemed to him to destroy the solemn covenant between God and the English nation which was the justification of the Anglican Establishment. It was an act of national apostasy."[30] His 1833 sermon "National Apostasy" is the event by which most historians have marked the beginning of the movement.

The Oxford Tracts, which gave the movement its nickname, "Tractarianism," attacked erastianism on the "right" but dealt equally hard blows to the puritan-evangelical side of Anglicanism on the "left," presenting the church as a supernatural society and offering the principle of apostolic succession as a challenge to both. In the course of the 1830s Newman developed his idea of the *via media*, depicting Anglicanism as the preserver of original Christian doctrine, steering a "middle way" between Catholic idolatry and puritan-evangelical iconoclasm. While Keble relied largely on evidence and writers from earlier Anglican history, Newman moved far back in history to make an intensive study of the early

---

29. John L. Morrison, "The Oxford Movement and the British Periodicals," *Catholic Historical Review* 45 (July 1959): 137–60. Morrison emphasizes that the Oxford Movement was judged by the periodicals according to party affiliation, getting the most sympathetic attention from the Tory *Blackwood's Magazine* and the least sympathy from the nonconformist *British Quarterly Review*. Morrison concludes: "Usually the Movement has been presented by Catholic historians as a vehicle for the spiritual career of Cardinal Newman, and by Protestant writers as the story of spiritual rebirth within the Anglican church. . . . Viewed externally, as political and intellectual factions saw the tractarians, it was the political implications of their theology which seemed paramount" (158).

30. Dawson, *Spirit of Oxford Movement*, 88.

church Fathers. His close friend, Froude, upset the normal Anglican view of religious history by denigrating the sixteenth-century reformers. "They despised tradition, they had no reverence for the past, they fawned on the secular power and they attacked the most sacred mysteries of Catholic worship with scurrilous invective."[31] Froude discouraged Newman's early tendency to venerate the reformers and urged him to tone down his own marked anti-Catholicism, but at this stage, the mid-1830s, minimizing the reputation of the reformers was not enough to push Newman toward Rome.

Neither their stress on authority and doctrine, however, nor their intellectual intensity should be taken to imply that the Tractarians were deficient in spiritual ardor or that their movement was merely academic. Their vision of an invigorated and independent Church of England was a godly rebuke to the lethargic Anglicanism of their era. As the church historian Alec Vidler said, "It was as if the Tractarians were declaring that on the drab, dirty, and distempered walls within which English churchmen were accustomed to worship or doze, there were wonderful pictures that, when uncovered, would transform the whole building into something mysterious and sublime."[32] The movement reached a crisis with Newman's publication of Tract 90 in 1841, an attempt to prove that the Thirty-nine Articles, when read straightforwardly rather than in light of conventional Protestant prejudices, were compatible with Catholic doctrine as enunciated in the early church and codified at the Council of Trent in 1565. The tract caused an outcry among the Oxford divines, who formally condemned it, prompting Newman's resignation from the pulpit of Oxford's university church, Saint Mary's, and from his Oriel College fellowship.[33]

When the Cambridge converts heard about these developments in Oxford they tried, not surprisingly, to suggest that Rome was the logical destination for anti-Protestant Anglicans like Newman. George Spencer had met Newman the year before, but though his doubts about Anglican legitimacy were fermenting, Newman gave him a chilly reception, intimating that the Catholic Church was seeking to destroy Anglicanism. "This confrontation," says Kevin Morris, "shows that the Tractarians were basically indifferent to, and even fearful of, Catholic advances, the feeling being that the Catholic 'ecumenists' were, by their attentions, drawing

31. Froude, quoted ibid., 48.

32. Alec Vidler, *The Church in an Age of Revolution* (New York: Penguin, 1971), 51. See also Chadwick, "Mind of the Oxford Movement," in his *Spirit of Oxford Movement*, esp. 1–4.

33. Newman did not think highly of his own logic in Tract 90, and most later historians have agreed. See, for example, Newsome, *Convert Cardinals*, 138–42.

unnecessary fire on a very fragile and vulnerable movement."[34] In a reciprocal way Kenelm Digby was suspicious of the Tractarians (he called them "religious antiquarians"). Nevertheless several Oxford Movement men admired his *Mores Catholici*, notably Richard Waldo Sibthorpe (1807– 1891), first of the Tractarians to convert to Catholicism. The emotion aroused by religious controversy at this time can be seen in an incident of 1842. Sibthorpe visited Digby in Southampton to discuss Catholicism, and the day after he left, Digby's house burned to the ground in what Digby believed to be a religiously motivated arson attack.[35]

Ultimately, against all his inclinations, Newman was forced to admit that his own studies of the church Fathers, combined with a well-timed push from one of Wiseman's *Dublin Review* articles of 1839, undermined the plausibility of his *via media*. The months and years of agonizing over his religious position which followed are vividly recreated in his *Apologia Pro Vita Sua*, written more than twenty years later but packed with letters written to him and by him in the late 1830s and early 1840s.[36] Froude had annihilated his original esteem for the reformers, but he was still left with the problem of justifying aspects of Catholic doctrine for which he could find no sanction in the Bible or the Fathers. Further study of the Fathers ensued, along with help in clarifying Catholic dogma from Charles Russell, president of Maynooth Seminary in Ireland.[37] The outcome of these years of anguish was Newman's *Essay on the Development of Christian Doctrine* (1845), his last preconversion work, in which he argued that the original desposit of faith, though complete, was not always fully elaborated in the early church, and that full unfolding of doctrines often required the challenge of subsequent historical crises. In this way the *apparent* contrast between the Catholic Church in the fourth and the nineteenth centuries could be resolved, since both rested on the same dogmatic foundations.[38]

Newman's strong sense of duty and the emotional ties of Oxford, all his former life, still held him back from conversion between 1841 and 1845, and some of his more ardent friends and admirers preceded him into the Catholic Church. He clearly did not relish the prospect of conversion, but in the last resort he was convinced by his own doctrinal and historical arguments. He finally "went over to Rome" in 1845, causing a sensation in British public life. Renowned as one of the foremost Anglican writers,

34. Morris, "Cambridge Converts and Oxford Movement," 391.
35. Ibid., 389. Sibthorpe converted in 1841. He reverted to Anglicanism in 1843 but converted for a second time in 1865.
36. John Henry Newman, *Apologia Pro Vita Sua* (1864; New York: Image, 1989).
37. Newsome, *Convert Cardinals*, 165.
38. John Henry Newman, *An Essay on the Development of Christian Doctrine* (1845; New York: Longmans, Green, 1949).

preachers, and controversialists, he had a wide following, and his conversion brought many of his admirers in his train. "After many mental struggles, and an agony of doubt which may well be surmised," wrote Anthony Trollope, in his superb fictional transfiguration of the era, "the great prophet of the Tractarians confessed himself a Roman Catholic. Mr. Newman left the Church of England and with him carried many a waverer."[39]

His life as a Catholic was not to be an easy one. He trained for the priesthood in Rome at the College of Propaganda. On an earlier visit to Italy he had been delighted by Sicily but not by Rome itself or its inhabitants. "One is struck at once," he wrote during this second visit, "with their horrible cruelty to animals—also with their dishonesty, lying, and stealing, apparently without any conscience—and thirdly with their extreme dirt."[40] He was bitten by bedbugs before moving to better accommodations. The Roman Jesuits responsible for his reeducation were another disappointment: they neglected Aristotle and Saint Thomas Aquinas, and he soon realized that they were his intellectual inferiors.[41] Even his meeting with Pope Pius IX began badly when, bending to kiss the pontiff's foot, he misjudged his distances and butted the papal knee. He tried to ease his homesickness in Rome by writing a novel, *Loss and Gain*, which was published anonymously in 1848.

*Loss and Gain* follows Charles Reding, an Oxford undergraduate, son of an Anglican clergyman, through a religious quest that ends in Catholic conversion. The external details were changed but the sensibility was Newman's. Satirizing the various Anglican parties, high, low, and "broad church," Newman also, like his convert predecessor Pugin, made a few jabs against Rome itself. One of his clergyman dons declares: "Anyone who is inclined to Romanize should go abroad. . . . Such heaps of beggars in the streets of Rome and Naples; so much squalidness and misery; no cleanliness; an utter absence of comfort; and such superstition. They push and fight while Mass is going on; they jabber their prayers at railroad speed. . . . Their images are awful and their ignorance prodigious."[42] Reding admits that these matters, though incidental, will be a cross to bear. More harrowing is his mother's sense that her own son has betrayed her, and his friends' sense of abandonment. Even his closest friend, Shef-

---

39. Anthony Trollope, *Barchester Towers*, 327–28, in *"The Warden" and "Barchester Towers"* (1855, 1857; New York: Bantam, 1984).

40. Newman, quoted in Ker, *Newman*, 326.

41. Ibid., 327, 331.

42. Newman, *Loss and Gain* (1848; New York: Garland, 1975), 159. He did not reveal his authorship until 1874.

field, describes a convert as a man "swallowing, of his own free will, the heap of rubbish which every Catholic has to believe! In cold blood, tying a collar round his neck, and politely putting the chain into the hands of a priest. . . . How an Englishman, a gentleman, a man here at Oxford, with all his advantages, can so eat dirt, scraping and picking up all the dead lies of the dark ages—it's a miracle."[43] The novel vividly portrays the convert's dismay at the social consequences of his act and the disgust his conversion generates in friends and family.

Theological motives predominated among most of the Oxford converts, but they sometimes blended imperceptibly with aesthetic and moral issues. Trollope's fictional High Churchman Francis Arabin, who "at Oxford . . . sat for a while at the feet of the great Newman," felt the pull of the Catholic way of life:

The ceremonies and pomps of the Church of Rome, their august feasts and solemn fasts, invited his imagination and pleased his eye. His flesh was against him: how great an aid would it be to a poor, weak, wavering man to be constrained to high moral duties, self-denial, obedience, and chastity by laws which were certain in their enactments, and not to be broken without loud, palpable, unmistakable sin! . . . Some great deed, such as that of forsaking everything for a true church, had for him allurements almost past withstanding.[44]

Real-life Arabins who succumbed to the temptation included William George Ward, Richard Simpson, Bernard Dalgairns, and F. W. Faber, leading Oxford churchmen, whose conversion was a source of acute embarrassment to their High Anglican colleagues. It laid them open to the charge that they were halfway into heresy themselves, and they often felt betrayed. Arabin's colleague, the head of "Lazarus College," Oxford, is himself a High Churchman, but "he felt no sympathy with men who could not satisfy their faiths with the Thirty Nine Articles. He regarded the enthusiasm of such as Newman as a state of mind more nearly allied to madness than to religion; and when he saw it evinced by very young men, was inclined to attribute a good deal of it to vanity" (329). Accordingly, the conversions did nothing to quiet anti-Catholic prejudices, nor did they bring the two branches of Christianity closer together. Quite the opposite. In Lytton Strachey's memorable words: "The University breathed such a sigh of relief as usually follows the difficult expulsion of a hard piece of matter from a living organism, and actually began to attend to education.

43. Ibid., 106–7.
44. Trollope, *Barchester Towers*, 328.

As for the Church of England, she had tasted blood, and it was clear that she would never again be content with a vegetable diet."[45]

After Newman's departure, the other leaders of the Oxford Movement, Keble and Pusey, were careful to insist that they were loyal Anglicans to the end, as indeed they proved to be. But subsequent events showed a continuing Catholic temptation to other Oxford clergymen. The Gorham case of 1850–1851, like the emancipation and Irish sees controversy of 1829, reminded High Church Anglicans that they belonged to an erastian church, over which the civil government held the whip hand. G. C. Gorham was appointed vicar of the Anglican parish of Bramford Speke, but the diocesan bishop, Henry Phillpotts of Exeter, refused to install him, because Gorham held a Calvinist view of innate human depravity and denied the power of baptismal regeneration. The Anglican courts upheld the bishop's decision, but on appeal the Judicial Committee of the Privy Council, an executive committee of the British government, overruled them and ordered Gorham's installation. The case showed with unmistakable clarity that the Anglican Church was a branch of the state, that its ultimate point of authority was the government, not God. Dismayed by this display of state power over the church another group of Anglican clergy converted to Catholicism, of whom the best known then, and the best remembered now, was Henry Manning.[46]

Manning and Newman, who had been friends and intermittent correspondents, led, in some respects, parallel lives.[47] Both went to Oxford as undergraduates. Both had wealthy fathers who went bankrupt in the volatile economy of the early Industrial Revolution. Both became Anglican clergymen and drew the favorable attention of their religious superiors, who marked them out for preferment. Both were powerful and persuasive writers; Manning's *Unity of the Church* (1842) won him a reputation

---

45. Lytton Strachey, *Eminent Victorians* (1918; London: Chatto and Windus, 1948), 46.

46. Newsome, *Convert Cardinals*, 180–84.

47. Biographical information on Manning in the following passage is based on Newsome, *Convert Cardinals*; and on Shane Leslie, *Henry Edward Manning: His Life and Labours* (1921; Westport, Conn.: Greenwood, 1970). Newsome shows in his excellent dual biography that the two convert cardinals have fared very differently at the hands of the historians. Newman has enjoyed an almost unbroken succession of sympathetic and laudatory biographers, whereas Manning's first biographer, Edmund Purcell, was sharply critical, and compounded his harsh judgments by causing part of the documentary record to disappear. Worse was to follow when Lytton Strachey singled out Manning as one of his four subjects in *Eminent Victorians* (1918). Brilliantly written and sharply satirical, it aims to debunk the Victorians' complacency and high-mindedness, with the result that Strachey magnifies Purcell's indictment. Newsome, in redressing this balance, remarks: "The abuse of his original biographer has saddled Manning with a reputation too bad to be wholly credible, while the tendency to panegyric in the biographical treatment of Newman over the last fifty years has served to make of him a figure rather too good to be true" (21).

almost equal to Newman's when they were both still Anglicans. And both of them shocked the Anglican establishment by converting to Catholicism, where they both rose to the eminence of the cardinalate. In other ways, however, their lives were a study in opposites. Newman was always primarily an intellectual, immune to worldly temptations but touchy and awkward, whereas Manning, despite intellectual and literary gifts, was an ecclesiastical statesman, shrewd, imposing, and ambitious. Manning always agonized in prayer before accepting a higher station in life but usually accepted it when it came to the point.

After Oxford he became a country curate rather than a don, and married while Newman remained celibate. His diligence, administrative skill, and preaching ability led to early promotion and in 1840 he was made archdeacon of Chichester. He read the Oxford Tracts (and was a minor contributor to the series) and found their vigorous argumentation persuasive, but he was determined after Newman's apostasy of 1845 to stay loyal to the church of his birth, and he preached a critical sermon about Newman's conversion. Even so he was forced to admit in letters to his friends that he found Roman claims hard to refute and Newman's arguments on the development of doctrine persuasive.[48] Aptly enough, in view of their contrasting characters, whereas Newman's conversion was the result of theological and historical research, Manning's came in response to the politically charged Gorham case. His longtime friend and confidant William Gladstone (subsequently the Liberal prime minister) took Manning's conversion as a betrayal and declared that it hurt as much as if he had "murdered my mother." He broke off their friendship but resumed it, more guardedly, ten years later after a chance meeting in the streets of London.[49]

Manning's wife had died in 1837. He was therefore eligible for the Catholic priesthood, which he entered at once. His conversion coincided with the restoration of the Catholic hierarchy and the furor caused by Wiseman's pastoral letter "From the Flaminian Gate." Manning soon befriended Wiseman and introduced him to many of his own prominent friends, beginning the work of edging the Catholic hieararchy into the British establishment and laying the foundations of Catholic influence in national affairs. Until then England's few remaining Catholic aristocrats, such as the duke of Norfolk and Pugin's patron the earl of Shrewsbury, had maintained a privileged position in British life, but the priests and bishops, often men of humble birth, had lacked friends in high places and

48. Newsome, *Convert Cardinals*, 169–79.

49. Leslie, *Manning*, 98. See also David Newsome, *The Parting of Friends: The Wilberforces and Henry Manning* (1966; Grand Rapids, Mich.: Eerdman's, 1993), 363–67.

the chance to influence the course of national politics. Manning's friendship with politicians certainly did not mean that he wanted to establish formal links between the Catholic Church and the British government. Quite the opposite. He championed a forceful Ultramontane policy and was to advocate papal infallibility at the First Vatican Council in 1870, one of many issues which set him at odds with Newman. What he feared, said Manning was "an English Catholicism of which Newman is the highest type. It is the old Anglican, patristic, literary, Oxford tone .transplanted into the Church. . . . It is worldly Catholicism." What he wanted, by contrast was "downright, masculine, and decided Catholics—*more* Roman than Rome, and more Ultramontane than the Pope himself."[50] In light of the Gorham case it is easy to see why. For Manning, building up transnational papal power was the surest way of enhancing church authority as a counterweight to the civil power. Protestants looked on papal power as repressive and tyrannical, but for antierastians like Manning it could seem very liberating. Nevertheless, he was too shrewd a politician to forgo the advantages of having friends among the "great and the good."

Manning also dedicated himself to seeking new converts, and he had dozens of correspondents and aspirants. Among the most distiguished was Florence Nightingale, who shared Manning's objections to state domination and recognized that Catholicism offered women the prospect of useful working lives. Nightingale wrote to Manning that joining the Catholic Church would be no sacrifice to her. On the contrary, "all my difficulties would be removed. . . . She would give me daily bread. The daughters of St. Vincent [de Paul] would open their arms to me." In another letter she underlined the anomalous condition of the Anglican Church. "In Germany . . . they know why they are Protestants. I never knew an Englishman who did, and if he inquires, he becomes a Catholic!"[51] In the event, the outbreak of the Crimean War (1854–1856) gave her the opportunity to begin a nursing career without taking the drastic step of conversion.

These two waves of converts, Newman's in 1845 and Manning's in 1851, met a mixture of enthusiasm and resentment from England's Old Catholics, some of whom doubted the Oxford men's sincerity. "They could not believe," says Edward Norman, "that the traditional antipathy of the Protestant Church could so easily be exchanged for genuine Catholicism. Lingard always felt like that and warned Wiseman against trusting the Oxford divines."[52] Wiseman himself feared that the Old Catholics

50. Manning, quoted in Adrian Hastings, *A History of English Christianity, 1920–1990* (London: Collins, 1986), 147.
51. Leslie, *Manning*, 109, 111.
52. Norman, *English Catholic Church*, 211.

would be discouraged by the newcomers' dominance of the Catholic press, and in 1846 he wrote to C. W. Russell, editor of the *Dublin Review*: "It is of great importance that the Catholic element of the *Review* should be kept together as much as possible, and as strong an infusion of old Catholicism as possible be kept in it. This I mean for the sake of keeping up confidence from the Catholic body, which will be jealous of seeing the *Review* pass too much into neophyte hands."[53] Before long, however, Wiseman became an eager supporter of the converts, and his patronage facilitated Manning's rapid rise through the Catholic ranks.

Ambrose Phillipps de Lisle, one of the Cambridge converts, was indignant at the cool reception offered to Newman and his associates by most English Catholics. He wrote to his friend Charles, comte de Montalembert, in France: "The English Catholics *as a body* are utterly unprepared and unfit for the great occasion. . . . It is impossible to conceive a set of men more stupidly perverse than they in general are—instead of meeting the Catholick movement of our Anglican Brethren with courtesy, charity, or tact, they indulge in the bitterest sneers." It was a source of lasting woe to Phillipps, moreover, that so many of his coreligionists, with whom he was now obliged to rub shoulders, should belong to "that wretched and untameable race" of the Irish; cultivated gentlemen like Newman and Manning seemed to him a far more palatable alternative.[54]

53. Introduction to "The Dublin Review," in Walter Houghton, ed., *The Wellesley Index to Victorian Periodicals, 1824–1900* (Toronto: University of Toronto Press, 1972), 2:13.

54. Phillipps de Lisle, quoted in Norman, *English Catholic Church*, 211, 218.

# IV

# TRACTARIANS AND TRANSCENDENTALISTS IN AMERICA

T HE OXFORD CONVERSIONS echoed throughout the English-speaking world and found an answering call among American Episcopalians. With the waning of anti-British sentiment fifty years after the Revolutionary War the Episcopal Church was enjoying a period of steady growth in the 1820s and 1830s. Membership often connoted high social and economic status, and the church offered a refuge to Americans who disliked the emotional evangelical revivalism of the Second Great Awakening which was the religious staple of the era.[1] In the United States the Episcopal Church, like all others, was completely disestablished. Erastianism, state control of the church, was therefore not an issue on the western shores of the Atlantic and the High Church faction never had to fear political manipulation. "In other words," wrote an Episcopal historian, "the Episcopal Church needed the Oxford Movement less than did the Church of England and for that reason it produced . . . less extreme results."[2] John Henry Hobart, the Episcopal bishop of New York, was a familiar figure on both sides of the Atlantic. A persuasive High Churchman, he had met Newman in 1824, and Newman later paid tribute to his influence, suggesting that the

1. On the changing character of American religious life in the early nineteenth century, see Nathan Hatch, *The Democratization of American Christianity* (New Haven: Yale University Press, 1989). On the growth of Episcopalianism in this era, see James Thayer Addison, *The Episcopal Church in the United States* (New York: Scribner's, 1951), 139–50.

2. Addison, *Episcopal Church*, 156.

61

flow of ideas, even at this stage, did not move entirely from Britian to the United States.[3]

Episcopal priests and seminarians read the Oxford Tracts with eager interest, however, and the arrival of Newman's famous Tract 90, in which he argued that the Thirty-nine Articles could be read in a spirit compatible with Catholic orthodoxy, sparked as much controversy in America as in England. The bishop of Quebec said that he heard the tracts discussed more ardently in three days in New York than during a year's stay in London.[4] Several High Church bishops accepted Newman's reasoning, but in rebuttal an angry Bishop Charles McIlvaine of Ohio, from the evangelical wing of the Episcopal Church, wrote *Oxford Divinity*, declaring that any Anglican who denied the Protestant principle of justification by faith alone belonged in the Roman, not the Anglican, communion.[5] Another bishop said that "the Tractarian movement was of Rome, the work of Satan," and that "condemnation and even force must be brought to bear to silence these advocates of the Dark Ages and followers of the Scarlet Woman."[6] At their 1844 convocation the American Episcopal bishops composed a pastoral letter in which they stated: "We feel it our duty to declare that no person should be ordained who is not well acquainted with the landmarks which separate us from the Church of Rome; and being so, who will not distinctly declare himself a Protestant, heartily abjuring her corruptions, as our Reformers did."[7]

Nevertheless, a group of seminarians at the General Theological Seminary in New York was enthusiastic about the tracts. One among them, Arthur Carey, born in England in 1822, was a childhood immigrant to America. He graduated early from Columbia College, moved quickly through the seminary course, and had to wait a year for ordination because he had not yet reached the necessary minimum age of twenty-one. When he came before his examiners for ordination in July 1843 Carey said that he understood the Thirty-nine Articles in the light of Newman's Tract 90, in other words, as consonant with Catholic teaching from the Council of Trent. This answer split his examiners, but he was allowed to proceed to ordination. When the moment of Carey's formal investiture arrived, two

---

3. David O'Brien, Introduction to Clarence Walworth, *The Oxford Movement in America*, ed. O'Brien (1895; New York: U.S. Catholic Historical Society, 1974), vi–viii.

4. E. Clowes Chorley, *Men and Movements in the American Episcopal Church* (New York: Scribner's, 1950), 198.

5. Charles P. McIlvaine, *Righteousness by Faith: A New and Revised Edition of Oxford Divinity* (Philadelphia: Protestant Episcopal Book Society, 1862).

6. Quoted in Chorley, *Men and Movements*, 203.

7. Addison, *Episcopal Church*, 159.

bishops ostentatiously jumped up and stormed out of the church. Carey, a spellbinder, preached for a few months and seemed all set to convert to Roman Catholicism but then, already weak with a heart condition, succumbed en route to a "cure" in Havana, and died at sea aged only twenty-two. Like Hurrell Froude in the English Oxford Movement, he took on, for the friends who outlived him, the mantle of a martyr to fearless religious truth seeking.[8]

On a visit to England the next year, Carey's close friend and admirer at the seminary, James McMaster, went to see Newman and urged him to write Carey's biography. Newman knew about Carey, listened sympathetically, but answered that an American writer must take on the task. So reported the American who did ultimately write Carey's life, Clarence Walworth, another Episcopal seminarian. The son of a wealthy and influential Presbyterian family in Saratoga, New York (his father was chancellor of New York State), Walworth had graduated from Union College in Schenectady, passed the bar, and become a lawyer in Rochester. But after a religious experience in 1839 he converted to Episcopalianism, and resolved to join the clergy. Walworth, like Newman, was convinced that his religion, to be worthy of serious devotion, must be based on doctrinal certainty, but as an Anglican seminarian, he recalled, "no questions had been put to me as to what I believed. I found myself in the Anglican Church with apparently the full liberty to believe what I liked and to change my beliefs unquestioned." He presented a striking analogy:

Americans who remember Barnum's museum or his menageries will understand what I mean when I say that the Anglican Church constitutes what Barnum would have called "A Happy Family" in religion. A happy family, according to Barnum's phraseology, was a group of various animals, by nature most hostile to each other, shut up in one cage and obliged perforce to keep peace. A dog was made to dwell in apparent harmony with a cat, a cat with a mouse and a bird.[9]

The works of Newman, Ward's *Ideal of a Christian Church*, Keble's *Christian Year*, and then the series of lives of the early English saints which Newman's friends were writing, all circulated at the New York seminary and finally brought a group of the students to the point of Catholic conversion. Another group of six American Episcopalians, earlier graduates of the same seminary, established an Anglican monastery at Nashotah, Wisconsin, then converted together in 1844. The anxious authorities at

8. Walworth, *Oxford Movement in America*, 34–63.
9. Ibid., 66, 13, 39.

the seminary became convinced that Jesuits in disguise were corrupting the students one by one, and they reacted by suspending several students, including Walworth. Walworth also experimented with Episcopal monasticism in a tiny Adirondack farmhouse. Most of the time the monastery consisted solely of himself and another enthusiast, Edgar Wadhams.[10] Both men soon converted to Catholicism; Wadhams went on to become Catholic bishop of Ogdensburg, and Walworth an early Paulist mission priest.

Not all the American converts of the 1840s came from the Episcopal Church. The two who were to make the heaviest imprint on history, Orestes Brownson (1803–1876) and Isaac Hecker (1819–1888), were restless religious seekers whose last stop before Catholicism lay on the border between Unitarianism and Transcendentalism.[11] Brownson described his long road to Catholicism in *The Convert* (1857), which was in part a tract urging other Protestants to follow him into the Catholic fold and in part a criticism of Catholic evangelizing techniques. He declared quite frankly that the usual Catholic method of trying to gain converts was almost certain to fail because it did not correct Protestant misapprehensions about Catholic intolerance. He stressed that up to the last moment before conversion he had disliked the Catholic faith and people: "I should sooner have thought of turning Jew, Mahometan, Gentoo, or Buddhist."[12] The Catholic controversial works he had tried to read were written in "a dry, feeble, and unattractive style and abounded with terms and locutions which were to me totally unintelligible. Their authors seemed to me ignorant of the ideas and wants of the non-Catholic world, engrossed with obsolete questions, and wanting in broad and comprehensive views" (267). Brownson through his own studies had concluded, nevertheless, that Catholicism was intellectually liberating, the perfect religion for self-confident citizens of the American republic. The convert's job was to make this openness more apparent. An intelligent Catholic's mind, he said, "is no more restricted in its freedom by the authoritative definitions of an infallible church than the cautious mariner by the charts and beacons that guide his course" (v). If some Catholic immigrants seemed intolerant, it was not because of their faith but because that they had recently escaped the dominion of European tyrants (319). Certainly the English and Amer-

10. Ibid., 137, 114–16.
11. The following passage is based on Thomas P. Ryan, *Orestes Brownson: A Definitive Biography* (Huntington, Ind.: Our Sunday Visitor, 1976); Arthur Schlesinger Jr., *Orestes A. Brownson: A Pilgrim's Progress* (Boston: Little, Brown, 1939); and Theodore Maynard, *Orestes Brownson: Yankee, Radical, Catholic* (New York: Macmillan, 1943).
12. Brownson, *The Convert* (1857; New York: D. and J. Sadlier, 1877), 12, hereafter cited in the text.

ican traditions of liberty provided fertile soil for this free man's religion, and Brownson said he was heartily glad that England had prevailed over the Spanish Armada and that the duke of Marlborough had crushed French power at Blenheim, for whatever their religious aspect, these were victories for liberty (328–29).

A twin, born in Vermont and raised partly there and partly in the fervently religious climate of New York's "burned over district" Brownson had memorized nearly all the Scriptures by the age of fourteen. All the family were ardent religious seekers, rather than steady devotees of any one church. His brother Oren later became a Mormon. Brownson passed through Presbyterianism in the early 1820s but said that it required him to deny his own convictions and that "the most rigid Catholic ascetic never imagined a discipline a thousandth part as rigid as the discipline to which I was subjected" (17). Leaving the Presbyterians because they demanded unquestioning faith in revelation at the expense of reason, he tried for several years to depend on reason alone, despite what seemed to him its obvious insufficiency. He joined the Universalist ministry in the later 1820s but became convinced that the Scriptures did not in fact teach universal salvation. Next, under the influence of Robert Owen and Fanny Wright, Brownson became a utopian socialist and constructed a purely secular creed based on honesty, benevolence and self-improvement. For a while in the early 1830s he was an active member of the New York Workingmen's Party and wrote a scorching denunciation of industrial capitalism even though, as he admitted, he was "not naturally a radical or even inclined to radicalism" but was motivated by "a deep sympathy with the poorer and more numerous classes" (102). Throughout the 1830s and early 1840s he was an outspoken opponent of laissez-faire, "the system which gives the supremacy to trade and manufactures. . . . I regarded, and still regard [it], as worse than the serfdom of the middle ages, and worse even than slavery as it has existed or can exist in any Christian country" (103).

In the 1830s Brownson befriended William Ellery Channing and began to preach in Unitarian pulpits. At the same time he undertook a serious study of French and German philosophy, and discovered the work of Benjamin Constant, an early theorist of the idea of progress. Under Constant's influence, and seeing himself as the John the Baptist of a progressive church of the future, he preached in Boston's Society for Christian Union and Progress between 1836 and 1843, aiming to take what was best from Catholicism and Protestantism and merge them in a higher synthesis. In 1838 he founded a quarterly review, in which he hoped "to startle." He "made it a point to be as paradoxical and extravagant as I could without doing violence to my own reason and conscience" (147). He was convinced that most of his contemporaries simply did not think carefully and logically about their religious or political convictions but contented themselves with moving through life observing cold, lifeless forms. Perhaps he could shake them up. "Alas! I did not know then that men act from habit, prejudice, routine, passion, caprice, rather than from reason; and that, of all people in the world, Englishmen and Americans are the least disturbed by incongruities, inconsistencies, inconsequences, and anomalies—though I was beginning to suspect it!" (189).

The election of 1840 marked a turning point in Brownson's life. The Whig party distributed thousands of reprints of his article "The Laboring Classes," alleging that this condemnation of wage slavery was a manifesto of the Jacksonian Democrats. They in turn scrambled to dissociate themselves from its radicalism. Until then Brownson had thought of himself as a Democrat, but the party's repudiation of his ideas, which years later he continued to believe had been "honest, undisguised, fearless" (171), destroyed his faith in democracy. "I became henceforth a conservative in politics . . . and through political conservatism I advanced rapidly towards religious conservatism" (200).

In the early 1840s close study of Victor Cousin and Pierre Leroux, and their theory of communion, brought Brownson for the first time the conviction that he might be able to be an orthodox Christian, holding faith in revelation, without doing violence to his reason. "I drew from Leroux the conclusion that man is not and cannot be in himself progressive, and that his progress depends on the objective element of life, or in other words, on his living in communion with God" (218). He was now able to conceive of God as "superior to humanity, independent of nature, and intervening as Providence in human affairs" (219); this new conception explained to him (as Constant's secular progressive theory could not) why Jesus lived not in Athens or Rome, "progressive" centers of their day, but in "a by-corner of the world, in an obscure hamlet, in the person of an obscure peasant, followed by humble fishermen and despised publicans" (226). He worked out this insight in detail in a series of review articles titled "The Mission of Jesus." Always before he had assumed that God was bound by the laws of nature. Realizing he was not "threw a heavy burden from my shoulders and in freeing God from his assumed bondage to nature, unshackled my own limbs and made me feel that in God's freedom I had a sure pledge of my own" (237). When he found Catholics responding warmly to his essays on Jesus, it dawned on him that their church might be his destination and that it alone, blending reason and revelation, authority and freedom, represented "the true Church or living body of Christ" (266).

Brownson was formally received into the Catholic Church in 1844 by Archbishop John B. Fitzpatrick of Boston, who urged him to forget his philosophical learning up to that point and adopt, instead, the scholastic method. Obediently, Brownson made what was for him a difficult switch and for a while wrote just the kind of apologetics he had deplored before his conversion. Seeing this swerve, many of his old friends and colleagues belittled Brownson's conversion as just one of the more erratic steps in the life of a restless spirit, rather than the culmination of a long process of careful thought. In the 1850s, however, Brownson recovered his intellectual confidence. As his biographer Theodore Maynard notes, *The Convert* was in effect his "declaration of independence" from Fitzpatrick and scholasticism, and his own *Apologia*.[13]

Isaac Hecker, an admirer and follower of Brownson, also moved out of Transcendentalism and into Catholicism in 1844, after an anguished youth of religious doubt.[14] The son of German Lutheran immigrants, Hecker was born in 1819 and grew up in New York City with intense religious anxieties. In 1842 he had a series of profound religious experiences, the sense of being in the company of a protecting angel.

I saw a beautifull angelic pure being, and myself standing alongside of her feeling a most heavenly pure joy and it was as if it were that our bodies were luminous and they gave forth a moonlike light which I felt sprung from the joy that we experienced. We were unclothed pure and unconscious of anything but pure love and joy and I felt as if we had always lived together and that our motions actions feelings and thoughts came from one centre and when I looked towards her I saw no bold outline of form but an angelic something I cannot describe but in angelic shape and image . . . this vision continually hovers o'er me and prevents me from its beauty of accepting any else.[15]

He had met Brownson in 1841; they began a correspondence, and under Brownson's tutelage Hecker began to read Cousin, Constant, German philosophy, and the Oxford Tracts, though his own path to conversion was to be more affective and less cerebral than either Newman's or Brown-

13. Maynard, *Brownson*, 257.

14. The following passage is based on David O'Brien, *Isaac Hecker, an American Catholic* (New York: Paulist Press, 1992); Joseph McSorley, *Father Hecker and His Friends: Studies and Reminiscences* (St. Louis: Herder and Herder, 1953); Martin J. Kirk, *The Spirituality of Isaac Thomas Hecker: Reconciling the American Character and the Catholic Faith* (New York: Garland, 1988); Patrick Allitt, "The Meanings of Isaac Hecker's Conversion," *Journal of Paulist Studies* 3 (1994): 9–29.

15. Isaac Hecker, *The Diary: Romantic Religion in Antebellum America*, ed. John Farina (Mahwah, N.J.: Paulist Press, 1988), 105–6.

son's. Hecker spent a few weeks at Bronson Alcott's vegetarian commune, Fruitlands, and several months at George Ripley's Transcendentalist commune, Brook Farm. Although he decided against these forms of community life for himself he continued to think highly of Brook Farm after his conversion. It was, he wrote later, "the greatest, noblest, bravest dream of New England" and "the realization of the best dreams [its founders] had of Christianity." But as his biographer David O'Brien relates, Hecker "had none of the Transcendentalist disdain for institutions, though he shared their desire to get at the spirit behind the form."[16] When he later created his own religious community, the Congregation of Saint Paul, it was based on dogma rather than questioning, but like Brook Farm, it placed full confidence in the wisdom and maturity of its members.

Hecker was in Concord, Massachusetts, studying Greek with George Bradford and conversing regularly with Henry David Thoreau when he heard that Brownson was going to join the Catholics. He decided to do the same and ultimately preceded Brownson into Catholicism. But as O'Brien shows, it was a very Transcendentalist sort of conversion: "Transcendentalists argued that each person must harken to the voice within, the voice of 'reason' as opposed to understanding, intuition rather than logic. Hecker identified the inner voice of the spirit with the spirit who spoke through the Roman Catholic Church."[17] Like his mentor Brownson, Hecker soon found that the Catholic Church in America left a lot to be desired, especially in intellectual matters. "As for [the Catholics'] philosophic basis," he wrote in a letter to Brownson, "they seem to me profoundly ignorant." He also found them personally unpleasant and was shocked that they took snuff "even in the midst of that holy awful sacred Sacrafice [sic] the Mass." Also like Brownson and the English converts, Hecker declared himself ready and willing to put things straight. "These men have done well to keep and preserve the Church but a new generation must take their place if Catholicism is to be re-established in the World."[18]

Hecker joined Clarence Walworth and James McMaster, two of the New York Episcopal Seminary converts, on an expedition to Europe in 1846. The three new Catholics planned to study for the priesthood with the Redemptorist order. Hecker and Walworth persisted in this ambition, preparing for ordination in Belgium; McMaster decided against ordination but stayed with his new faith, later becoming a combative and fearless

16. O'Brien, *Hecker*, 47, 59.
17. Ibid., 71.
18. Joseph F. Gower and Richard M. Leliaert, eds., *The Brownson-Hecker Correspondence* (Notre Dame, Ind.: University of Notre Dame Press, 1979), 105.

newspaper editor at the helm of the *Freeman's Journal*.[19] As a seminarian Hecker enjoyed recurrent mystical experiences, flagellated himself, and practiced so many bodily mortifications that he alarmed his superiors. Nevertheless, he was acceped into the order and ordained in 1849 by none other than Bishop Nicholas Wiseman in London. Hecker and Walworth spent the next two years in England, preaching to Irish famine victims, many of whom had fled to England in the foregoing decade, and they witnessed the furor over the "Catholic Aggression" when the hierarchy was restored in 1850. Following their return to America in 1851, they worked hard in missions and enjoyed a massive response. When a mission came to town, wrote another convert Redemptorist, "the church is frequently filled two hours before the time of service. The porch, the steps, the windows even are crowded and hundreds go away disappointed. . . . I have seen at least four thousand persons congregated in the streets adjacent to the New York Cathedral, besides the crowd inside."[20] As Catholics they practiced their own version of the revivalism that was so marked a feature of Protestantism in that era.[21]

Eager to gain middle-class Anglo-Saxon converts, whom he saw as his special vocation, Hecker wrote *Questions of the Soul* (1855). O'Brien, describes it as "an almost perfect expression of contemporary American self-culture. It was filled with the confused excitement of that American sense of innocence of the past and openness to the future."[22] Aimed at the well-educated American Protestant or Transcendentalist, it was crammed with quotations from Carlyle, Wordsworth, Byron, Goethe, Channing, Hawthorne, and Emerson. Hecker said that thousands of young Americans were adrift, full of religious aspirations but without a sure religious harbor. "The desire after a more spiritual life is one of the chief characteristics of the American people," wrote Hecker, and he aimed to show that it could be satisfied only in the sacramental, dogmatic world of Catholicism.[23] A church should be like a mother, he went on, "upon whose loving bosom we can lay our wearied heads, and from her breasts of divine truth

19. Sister Mary Augustine Kwitchen, *James Alphonsus McMaster: A Study in American Thought* (Washington, D.C.: Catholic University Press, 1949), esp. 60–69. As Kwitchen shows, McMaster became a champion of the Irish immigrant community. A fervent Democrat, his outspoken anti-Union posture during the Civil War led to several months of imprisonment.

20. Augustine Hewit, *Life of the Rev'd Francis A. Baker* (New York: Catholic Publication House, 1865), 124.

21. Jay P. Dolan, *Catholic Revivalism: The American Experience, 1830–1900* (Notre Dame, Ind.: University of Notre Dame Press, 1978), esp. 43–44.

22. O'Brien, *Hecker*, 105.

23. Isaac Hecker, *Questions of the Soul* (New York: Appleton, 1855), 55, hereafter cited in the text.

and love draw, like babes, sweet nourishment for our thirsting souls" (114). Unfortunately, Protestantism was not "a true, kind, and loving mother, from whose breasts her children can draw copious streams of truth and love," but rather "a step-mother, heartless, cold," with "breasts of stone" (128). Because it entrusted interpretation of Scripture to each individual, Protestantism had no proper doctrinal principle, and when "the youth of our land rise up and ask in all earnestness for true guidance to the fulfillment and realization of the divine inspirations of their hearts," the Protestant church simply "stands and listens to their appeals, stony, heartless, and unconcerned as a sphinx" (136).

After disposing of Protestant claims with a great deal more of this vivid imagery, Hecker examined Catholic claims and vindicated them one by one. The pope was not a tyrant, for he was subject to Catholic doctrines like everyone else; the church encouraged "perfect equality," which "gives security, repose, and peace to the heart; elevates, ennobles, and gives freedom to the mind" (171). Confessing one's sins to a priest was laudable, superior to the American alternative of confessional popular literature with all its "filthy and disgusting details," which polluted the minds of innocents (184). The priest preserved the seal of the confessional, while administering divine forgiveness to penitents; society and the individual soul both benefited. Monasticism was an option for those who sought to free themselves from the bondage of the self; mortification prompted charity; chastity and poverty nourished holiness; and the cult of the saints gave earthly glimpses of heaven. Hecker, dealing with his literary contemporaries and eager to avoid caustic polemics, apportioned praise and blame carefully, admitting, for example, that Emerson had done a fine job of shaking off "the false and narrow dogmas, the hollow forms, and the hollower cant of Protestantism" (277) but regretting that he had not taken the next step of sanctifying the nature in which he placed his trust, with supernatural grace. Hecker closed with a rousing call to the youth of America to convert to Catholicism, declaring that "all men, so far as their nature is not perverted, are Catholics, and if they but knew their real wants they would have to do violence to themselves not to enter the Catholic church" (288). The book sold widely but did not bring in the flood of converts Hecker would have liked. A sequel, *Aspirations of Nature* (1857), as we shall see, would bring Hecker into the unwelcome glare of theological controversy.

His German-American Redemptorist superiors wanted Hecker, Walworth, and their fellow converts to spend more time ministering to the German Catholic population in the United States and less time seeking new converts from among the Anglo-Saxon middle classes. In 1857 this difference led to a fracture, and Hecker was expelled from the Redemptorists after setting out to Rome without his superiors' approval. He visited Newman in England en route and after prolonged negotiations at the Vatican, where he used his charm to maximum effect, won official approval to create a new order, the Congregation of Saint Paul, in 1858.[24] Its first home was the house of Hecker's long-suffering brother George, a businessman and fellow convert who throughout his life stood ready to fund brother Isaac's projects. In the following years the Paulists built a church and residence in New York, began an arduous round of missions to gather converts, and in 1865 launched a journal, the *Catholic World*, which remained one of the two or three principal journals for American Catholic intellectuals until it closed down in 1996. (The other two most influential Catholic journals, *Brownson's Quarterly Review* and the *Freeman's Journal*, were also edited by converts, and when the *American Catholic Quarterly Review* began publication in 1876 it too was guided by a German-American convert, George Dering Wolff.)

All the early Paulist priests were converts, among them three English immigrants, Robert Tillotson, who had come over from Newman's Birmingham Oratory, Alfred Young, who had migrated as a child, grown up in the United States and graduated from Princeton, and George Searle, a professor of astronomy at the U.S. Naval Academy. Among the American-born Paulists was a former Congregationalist, Augustine Hewit (born 1820) who, like Clarence Walworth, had arrived at Catholicism via Episcopalianism. In Baltimore Hewit met and befriended Francis Baker, a Methodist convert to Episcopalianism, and together these two earnestly religious young men began to explore the religious life of the city. "The remarkable movement led by Dr. Pusey and Mr. Newman was then at its height," Hewit recalled later. "In this country we were somewhat behindhand and were following at some distance in the wake of the most advanced English leaders, so that the later developments [i.e., Newman's conversion] rather took us by surprise."[25] Several Episcopal clergy in the city, including Baker's brother Alfred, were High Churchmen and admirers of Newman. Alfred Baker "followed him, like so many others, to the verge of the Catholic Church but drew back, startled and perplexed, when he passed over" (22). This was not surprising, said Hewit, because "we all had imbibed such an intense prejudice from our early education against

24. O'Brien, *Hecker*, 131–46, 167.
25. Hewit, *Life of Baker*, 36, hereafter cited in the text.

the Roman Catholic church that we were appalled at the thought of joining her communion" (38). Baltimore's Episcopalians were amazed by the event:

I remember well the startling effect produced by the news of Mr. Newman's conversion. Whatever his modesty may induce him to say in disclaimer he was the leader, the life, and the soul, of the Oxford movement; his genius had acquired for him in this country, as well as in England, a sway over a multitude of minds such as is seldom possessed by any living man. . . . I heard it from Bishop Whittingham, one evening, after I had been to prayers in St. Paul's. I passed him on the steps and went out, and heard him say in a sorrowful tone, "Newman has gone." It went to my heart as if I had heard of my father's death.[26]

Only gradually did Hewit see through "the mists of misrepresentation, prejudice, and ignorance which obscured the Catholic Church and her doctrines" (40). He was ordained an Episcopal priest in 1845 and, despite his inclinations, obeyed an order by Bishop William Whittingham to read no Catholic literature; "so it was Anglican books which brought us onward toward the Catholic Church" (60). He converted to Catholicism in 1846 and became a priest in 1847. His old friend Baker, by then a prominent Episcopal clergyman in Baltimore, followed him seven years later, and his conversion made "a great sensation" (111). Some of his parishioners were dismayed; some decided to convert with him; and a few wrote sharply reproachful letters. Baker took Hewit as his confessor, studied for the Redemptorist priesthood, and was ordained in 1856, and then both men volunteered to join Hecker's Paulists in 1858.

Within the Paulist Fathers Hewit saw his vocation as the conversion of Americans from Calvinist backgrounds like his own. He was careful to appeal to them in their own idiom. He used the King James Bible in his sermons and writings, rather than the English translation of the Douai Bible familiar to most Catholics, and he held that all the positive elements of Protestant creeds were good, if incomplete. "I have never lost any thing or been required to abdicate any thing which I had previously acquired in the intellectual or spiritual life, by embracing Catholic doctrine, but have only added to it that which makes it more integral and complete."[27] He agreed with Calvinists that the Bible stood at the center of Christianity,

26. Ibid., 67. Recall Gladstone's reaction to Manning's conversion. "It was as though he had murdered my mother." Quoted in Shane Leslie, *Henry Edward Manning: His Life and Labours* (1921; Westport, Conn.: Greenwood, 1970), 98.
27. Hewit, *Life of Baker*, 144.

but insisted that on its own it could not drive back infidelity. Rather, it needed the support of the church. Echoing one of Hecker's favorite themes, that the diversity of Protestant groups indicated the imminent dissolution of them all, Hewit added: "For the coming generation, the alternative of the Catholic faith or no religion is certain, imperative, and inevitable."[28]

Not only in his preaching did Hewit draw on his earlier life. He stood squarely in the American Protestant tradition of praising rural and deprecating urban life, the lot of most Catholics. The life of a farmer, he believed, "is incomparably more wholesome, more happy, and more favorable to virtue and piety than the feverish, comfortless, and unnatural existence to which the mass of the laboring class are condemned in large cities." It had the further advantage of fostering "sobriety, industry, and prudence," and Catholic rural settlement, he believed, would "enrich both the country and the Church."[29] The dangers of urban life came home with special force when his friend Francis Baker, on an urban mission, caught typhus and died in 1865, aged forty-five, being the first Paulist to die.[30]

The phenomenon of conversion is central to American religious history, and from its earliest days the European population of the American colonies and states spoke a language of new beginnings, personal transformations, and conversions from darkness into light. Americans also placed great faith in individual initiative and the priority of conscience over organization or authority. Conversion from one religion to another is more characteristic of the United States than of Britain, with its suspicion of religious enthusiasm, its centripetal establishment, and its venerable class system. In light of this contrast it is no surprise to find that many American converts to Catholicism in the nineteenth century later reverted to Protestantism when they found aspects of their new faith abrasive. The same happened in England, but less often. One American example is John Murray Forbes, an Episcopal priest from New York City who followed the lead of Brownson and converted to Catholicism in 1849. His intellectual eminence and organizational skills prompted Catholic Archbishop John Hughes of New York to send him to Rome, where he helped organize the American College. But in 1859 Forbes reverted to his Anglican allegiance, telling Hughes in a letter:

28. Augustine Hewit, *The King's Highway, or The Catholic Church as the Way of Salvation* (1874; New York: Catholic Book Exchange, 1893), 290–91.
29. Hewit, *Life of Baker*, 179.
30. O'Brien, *Hecker*, 188.

When I came to you it was, as I stated, with a deep and conscientious conviction that it was necessary to be in communion with the See of Rome; but this conviction I have not been able to sustain in face of the fact that by it the natural rights of man and all individual liberty must be sacrificed—and not only so, but the private conscience often violated, and one forced by silence at least, to acquiesce in what is opposed to moral truth and justice.[31]

What a contrast to Hecker's encomiums. It is perhaps impossible to say whether Catholicism was *really* spiritually or intellectually liberating. Some found it so; others not. Individual temperament and particular experiences seem to have decided the issue for each convert. The Episcopalians, delighted to win this assent to their anti-Catholic outlook, welcomed Forbes back despite his decade-long deviation, and by 1869 he was dean of the General Theological Seminary of the Episcopal Church.

Newman in England and Brownson in the United States were much more eminent than their predecessors as converts, and their jump caused a splash that sent out a widening circle of ripples for decades. In some ways they were comparable. Both men converted not in response to Catholic proselytizing but in the light of what they had read and the conclusions they had drawn from it. For neither man was the writing of recent Catholic apologists significant. Newman had studied the church Fathers intensely but most of the more recent authors to seize his imagination were Anglicans; he was an admirer of Dr. Johnson and even of the skeptic Edward Gibbon, whose historical method he took as a model for his own.[32] Brownson was a member of the Transcendentalist Club in Boston, a friend of Emerson, Thoreau, Channing, and Theodore Parker, and was much better read in the literature of Unitarians and Universalists than that of Catholics. This point deserves emphasis: from the outset they *thought* their way into Catholicism by other means and, finding their new faith intellectually impoverished, undertook to enrich its patrimony. Brownson wrote that for centuries in Catholic Europe, "education declined, free thought was prohibited, and it is hard to find a literature tamer, less original and living than that of Catholic Europe all through the eighteenth century down almost to our own times."[33] Later generations of converts could

31. Forbes, quoted in O'Brien, Introduction to Walworth, *Oxford Movement in America*, xvi.

32. Thomas Bokenkotter, *Cardinal Newman as an Historian* (Louvain: Publications Universitaires de Louvain, 1959), 12; Sheridan Gilley, *Newman and His Age* (Westminster, Md.: Christian Classics, 1990), 90.

33. Brownson, *Convert*, 328–29.

and did read Newman and Brownson but these two were, in effect, pioneers in conversion.

Nor in this intellectually barren landscape did they find much ready companionship. In the days that led up to his conversion Newman was surrounded by other Anglican friends also in transition to Catholicism and remote from England's few islands of Catholic community. Likewise for Brownson. The growing number of Catholic immigrants to America from Ireland and Germany had small traditions of scholarship, and Catholic education was then largely confined to seminaries and a few raw new colleges (the University of Notre Dame, founded in 1842, was then just a log hut in the Indiana woods).[34] Brownson, who already ran his own subscription journal, *Brownson's Quarterly Review*, was able, like Newman, to leap into instant prominence as the best-known Catholic controversialist of his day and the only one with a large non-Catholic audience.

Brownson and Newman were also alike in trying to separate Catholicism from what seemed to them the Cambridge converts' and Pugin's unwholesome obsession with the Middle Ages. They both maintained that to link the Catholic Church with one particular time and place was to imply that it was *out* of place in other ages. They would not concede that point, Brownson declaring: "We have the same church which our ancestors had . . . as dear to us as she was to the medieval knights and monks, as good, as wise, as powerful, as young, as fresh, as beautiful, as vigorous, as she was in the Dark Ages."[35] Newman agreed that the Middle Ages should not be condemned out of hand (as they sometimes were by Protestant historians) but added that Pugin's indiscriminate adoration of medievalism was unbalanced, one-sided, and ultimately destructive: "He has the great fault of a man of genius, as well as the merit. He is intolerant and, if I might use a stronger word, a bigot."[36] The later Middle Ages—the fourteenth, fifteenth, and early sixteenth centuries—Newman said, had been no golden age but "the most disastrous and melancholy in the internal history of the church of any that can be named . . . that miserable period which directly prepared the way for Protestantism."[37] When he

34. Edward J. Power, *A History of Catholic Higher Education in the United States* (Milwaukee: Bruce, 1958). On the poor quality of faculty and the harsh rules imposed on them, see esp. 89–96. On the ethnic issue, see Philip Gleason, "American Catholic Higher Education: A Historical Perspective," in Robert Hassenger, ed., *The Shape of Catholic Higher Education* (Chicago: University of Chicago Press, 1967), esp. 21.

35. Orestes Brownson, *The Works of Orestes Brownson*, collected and arranged by Henry F. Brownson (Detroit: Nourse, 1882–1908), 10:240.

36. Newman, quoted in Phoebe Stanton, *Pugin* (New York: Viking, 1971), 7.

37. John Henry Newman, *Historical Sketches* (London: Basil Montagu and Pickering, 1873), 2:139.

became a priest, Newman attached himself to the Oratory of Saint Philip Neri, which had not been founded until the age of the Counter-Reformation and had no medieval traditions.

Nevertheless, these similarities of Newman and Brownson should not be exaggerated; the two men's differences are equally significant and serve to illustrate Anglo-American contrasts. Newman, as Anglican vicar of Saint Mary's, Oxford, had intended to revive a moribund Church of England, to demonstrate its distinguished place in the lineage of Christendom and its freedom from servility to the state. His tracts indicated a deep learning in early Christian history and theology. Newman had remained celibate, sheltered in the life of an Oxford don before conversion. Brownson, by contrast, had lived the strenuous life of a traveling lecturer, minister, and editor, constantly struggling to keep his large family fed and ceaselessly on the move. Largely self-educated, Brownson had worshiped and preached in half a dozen churches and moved through a succession of political and intellectual enthusiasms before approaching Catholicism. Whereas Newman was familiar with the European capitals, including Rome, Brownson never left the United States, and like many Americans of his generation, for whom the War of Independence was a quite recent memory, he enjoyed "twisting the lion's tail" and criticizing all things British. Even the Oxford converts he generally looked upon with suspicion, treating them as men who had converted for aesthetic rather than genuinely religious reasons.[38]

Continuities from before conversion are apparent in the Catholic writings of both men. As an Anglican, Newman treasured the works of the church Fathers and his interpretation of them had brought him all the way to Rome. His last preconversion work, *An Essay on the Development of Christian Doctrine* (1845), attempted to explain the contrast between the beliefs and actions of Christians in the fourth century and the nineteenth.[39] These ideas, matured in Anglicanism, harmonized with Newman's Catholicism, and he remained satisfied with much of his preconversion historical-theological work throughout his later life. Brownson's case is a little different. As we have seen, Bishop Fitzpatrick of Boston, who supervised his instruction in Catholicism, was uninterested in the course of Brownson's reading and reflection prior to joining the church. He simply required his new convert to adopt the outlook of orthodox Catholicism, lock, stock, and barrel, and to master as quickly as possible the methods of scholastic disputation and apologetics. At first

38. Schlesinger, *Brownson*, 198–200.
39. John Henry Newman, *An Essay on the Development of Christian Doctrine* (1845; New York: Longmans Green, 1949).

Brownson did so, and his articles from 1844 until about 1847 suggest an abrupt rupture from the work that had gone before, but before long, elements of his former thinking reemerged, and by the 1850s he was in the thick of a "Catholic liberalism," which, with its faith in intuition, showed appreciable similarities to his earlier Transcendentalism. *The Convert* showed Brownson fully aware of his own intellectual history and happy to vindicate, rather than traduce, much of his earlier life's work.

Soon after conversion the two men's paths crossed. In the first fervor of his conversion, Brownson wrote a harsh review of Newman's *Essay on the Development of Christian Doctrine*, arguing that Newman's "development" was really a mask for the heretical claim that new doctrines emerged over time while old ones changed.[40] Newman was stung by the accusation that his book violated Catholic orthodoxy, especially since he had written it before becoming a Catholic, with a view to helping other Anglicans come to terms with difficulties he had faced. One of Newman's fellow Oxford converts, William George Ward, rebutted on his behalf in the *Dublin Review* and an exchange between Ward and Brownson ensued. Bishop Fitzpatrick, Brownson's mentor, was annoyed by Newman and Ward, and made the classic remark about converts, variants of which would repeatedly be uttered during the following century: "I really think that these gentlemen have not come into the fold by the right and proper door. . . . in their reading they have followed a wrong principle for guide: the principle of private judgment. . . . they have read [the church Fathers] as Protestants read the Bible."[41] For the moment Fitzpatrick regarded Brownson as a "sound" convert but their honeymoon was not to last long. Brownson regretted that his review had caused ill feeling, especially as he studied and admired Newman's subsequent writings and got his own conversion into better perspective. He was also pleased to learn that Saint Edmund's Hall, the English Catholic college in which Ward taught, subscribed to *Brownson's Quarterly Review*.[42] Ward, too, was pleased by Brownson's general sharpness, especially in comparison with the low standards he found in English Catholic education. "The whole philosophical fabric which occupies our colleges is rotten from the floor to the roof," he wrote. "No one who has not been mixed up practically in a seminary would imagine to what an extent it intellectually debauches the students' minds."[43]

40. Orestes Brownson, "Newman's Development of Christian Doctrine" and "Newman's Theory of Christian Doctrine," both in *Works* 14:1–28, 28–74.
41. Fitzpatrick, quoted in Ryan, *Brownson*, 368.
42. Ibid., 376.
43. Ward, quoted in Frank Sheed, *The Church and I* (Garden City, N.Y.: Doubleday, 1974), 94.

Newman and Brownson almost met, and for a while planned to live and work together in Dublin. John Acton met Brownson on his American tour in 1853 and recommended him to Newman as a possible professor for the Catholic University of Dublin, which Newman, as first rector, was then trying to organize. Newman was eager to appoint Brownson and wrote a letter of invitation. He also arranged accommodations for himself and for Brownson's family in the same house. He is supposed to have remarked at this time that Brownson "is by far the greatest thinker America has ever produced."[44] Brownson was flattered to get the invitation but decided against accepting it because it would entail closing down his own journal; he answered: "I have neither the manners nor the learning you have a right to demand in a University Lecturer. I am a plain, untutored backwoodsman, wholly overrated both as to my talents and as to my acquisitions in both your country and my own." He reiterated his regret about their earlier dispute, adding: "I am most anxious that the bonds between English and American Catholics should be drawn as close as possible."[45]

Newman, undeterred, renewed the request with more favorable terms; this time Brownson accepted, but then his decision was blocked in an unforeseen way. The Catholic bishops in Ireland, and those of Irish descent in the United States, were uneasy at the prospect of so large an Anglo-Saxon presence in the new Catholic University. Newman, an Englishman and a convert, was bad enough, but Brownson in addition seemed intolerable. He had angered Irish Americans by defending the U.S. public school system and by urging Catholics to assimilate quickly, become loyal citizens, and recognize the high merits of the American republic. The Irish American bishops, irritated by Brownson's blunt high-handedness, which they interpreted as support for the anti-Irish Know-Nothing Party, now retaliated by scheming against him, and obliging Newman to cancel his invitation.[46] In consequence, Brownson and Newman never met. Irish dislike of Anglo-Saxons would be an important dimension of the history of convert intellectuals for much of the ensuing century.

Newman and Brownson both recognized that the Catholic populations with which they now lived must be better educated if their hopes for intellectual influence were to be realized. They each wrote extensively on education, and on the superiority of Catholic scholarship, properly undertaken, to its Protestant and secular counterparts. But they also recognized that Protestant scholars, whatever their ultimate shortcomings, had much

44. Ryan, *Brownson*, 509.
45. Ibid., 503.
46. Ibid., 506–9.

of proximate usefulness to teach Catholics, and they tried to incorporate these lessons in their analysis of Catholic education and its needs. Newman's classic statement was *The Idea of a University*, which began as a series of lectures given in Dublin in 1852 and laid him open to the complaint that he was really intent on creating a Catholic version of Oxford. Brownson argued the educational issue in many of his quarterly essays, making claims similar to Newman's, suitably adapted to the American environment.

First, each man realized that Catholic literature, history, and science would win favorable notice outside the church only if Catholic scholars felt untrammeled in their work and if they had nothing to fear from intrusive ecclesiastical censorship. While stressing the centrality of theology to a complete education, Newman insisted that a liberal education is an end in itself and needs no ulterior religious justification. Each of the disciplines has its own autonomous sphere, he argued, and, if well taught in balance with the others, can contribute to forming the mind of a gentleman.[47] There need be no harm in using books written by Protestants or skeptics, so long as they were not designed to undermine faith. After all, "the gravest Fathers recommended for Christian youth the use of pagan masters" (10). There need be no hesitation in using Isaac Newton's *Principia*, for example, or the teachings of Benjamin Franklin on electricity, even though these authors were well known as personal foes of Catholicism (264). Newman noted that a liberal education, for all its merits, could not guarantee a young man's virtue or even his orthodoxy, however much it might tend to restrain his worst passions and liberate him from ignorant bigotry. "Quarry the granite rock with razors, or moor the vessel with a thread of silk; then may you hope with such keen and delicate instruments as human knowledge and human reason to contend against those giants, the passion and the pride of man" (107). Education might guide and constrain the will but could never conquer it.

Brownson was equally sure that education in many of the disciplines was separable from religious questions—hence his willingness to see Catholic children attending public schools at a time when the Catholic hierarchy in eastern cities was campaigning against them. Until good parochial schools were ready, said Brownson, the public schools were admirable substitutes and would go far to teach Catholic children necessary lessons in honesty and patriotism in addition to literacy and numeracy. Brownson declined several offers to teach at U.S. Catholic colleges; they never attracted him

47. John Henry Newman, "Knowledge Its Own End," Discourse 5 of *The Idea of a University*, ed. Charles Harrold (1853; New York: Longmans Green, 1947), 89–109, hereafter cited in the text.

in the way that Newman's university had done.[48] He considered them overregimented and intellectually stifling rather than liberating, overhung with a thick air of clerical defensiveness and reluctant to grant the disciplines their proper autonomy. "They practically fail to recognize human progress," he wrote in an essay of 1862, "and thus fail to recognize the continuous and successive evolution of the idea in the life of humanity." Moreover, "they tend to repress rather than to quicken the life of the pupil, to unfit rather than to prepare him for the active and zealous discharge either of his religious or his social duties."[49]

Agreed on the need for education, for autonomy in the disciplines, and for higher standards, Brownson and Newman differed in their response to the intellectual upheavals taking place around them in the mid-nineteenth century. First, the Bible, long taken throughout Christendom as a source of revealed truth, was now being treated by some critics as simply one among many historical texts, to be subjected to historical scrutiny without privilege—a method with potentially immense intellectual consequences. Second, in geology, Charles Lyell's *Principles* (1837) had pushed back the probable date of creation by millions of years and thrown into jeopardy the venerable belief that Genesis described actual events. Third, in biology, Darwin's *Origin of Species* (1859) was challenging the ancient assumption that species were fixed once and for all by the divine act of creation. Darwin claimed not only that different species had common ancestors but also that mutations were random, rather than the progressive fulfilment of a divine plan. Every Christian intellectual felt challenged to respond in some way to these events. Newman and Brownson took quite different approaches.

It is possible to see Newman's theory of the development of doctrine as consonant with the evolutionary hypothesis, attuned to the nineteenth-century recognition of *process* in history, as in biology and geology. In 1863 he remarked in a letter to a friend that he was "willing to go the whole hog with Darwin." He was never agitated about it, and noted that the church had always avoided making categorical statements as to how the Genesis story should be interpreted or on the antiquity of the earth.[50] In his view the seeming conflict between theology and the new sciences was more apparent than real, because each discipline had its proper sphere, and points of contact between them were few. Theologians, whose disci-

48. Power, *Catholic Higher Education*, 103–4.
49. Brownson, "Catholic Schools and Education" (1862), in Alvan S. Ryan, ed., *The Brownson Reader* (New York: P. J. Kennedy, 1955), 139.
50. Newman, quoted in Brian Martin, *John Henry Newman: His Life and Work* (London: Chatto and Windus, 1982), 144.

pline was essentially deductive, based on reasoning drawn from the fixed deposit of revelation, should avoid trespassing into the realm of natural philosophy (what we now think of as natural science), he said, just as scientists, whose method was strictly inductive, should keep out of the theologians' territory. Although there would be times when the two *seemed* to be in conflict, patience and close reasoning would sooner or later resolve antinomies since each was capable of truth, and truth came from God, who could not be self-contradictory. He added that every scientist was familiar with seeming contradictions and should not balk at the idea of truths seeming to be inexplicable. "Such for instance is the contemplation of space; the existence of which we cannot deny, though its idea is capable in no sort of posture . . . of seating itself . . . in our minds. For we find it impossible to say that it comes to a limit anywhere; and it is incomprehensible to say that it runs out infinitely."[51]

Newman's historical works also showed his developmental assumptions. He argued that civilizations developed from primitive beginnings, had an inner dynamic of progress, and tended to advance from simpler to more complex forms. This did not mean that continuing or inevitable progress could be assured, however, and it certainly did not mean that Catholics had always acted rightly in the past and always been a force for good, as Catholic apologetics often implied. Newman, impressed since his childhood by Edward Gibbon's *Decline and Fall of the Roman Empire*, knew that empires can fall and civilizations crumble, though he made a neat inversion of Gibbon by claiming that the *lack* of Christianity in Rome's foundations had enabled the barbarians to destroy the empire. By contrast, he argued, Christianity had been built into the civilization that succeeded Rome right from the start, giving it, despite its many shortcomings, a greater dynamism and vigor. Newman was not so whiggish as his great contemporary Thomas Macaulay (whose history of England makes benign progress an intrinsic historical force), and his religious sense that the world is our provisional rather than our ultimate home restrained him from attributing to worldly civilizations any ultimate destination or transcendent significance. Newman believed, rather, that the events of history were the playing out of a divine plan, that an inscrutable divine providence supervised the events of history, and that they were of deep (if not ultimate) significance. For example, the Battle of Lepanto, 1571, was not to be explained simply as a victory of the Holy Roman Empire over the Turks, he said, but as an event of supernatural significance. Hence in his account he found it appropriate to devote more pages to describing Pope

51. Newman, "Christianity and Scientific Investigation," in *Idea of University*, 339.

Pius V's agonized days of prayer as he awaited news of the battle than to the maneuvering of the contending admirals.[52] Newman's extensive historical writings, like his theology, were saturated with developmentalist assumptions and showed him at home with his historiographical contemporaries, most of whom also saw historical development as a partnership between God's providence and the force of progress. Soon, however, a generation of positivist historians would arise to deny that providence had any role to play.

Brownson likewise assumed that God was working in history, and like Newman and Lingard, he was determined to avoid simpleminded declarations that Catholics were and invariably had been right and their antagonists wrong. Rather, he was alert to the complexities and paradoxes of history and to mundane factors in historical causation. In an 1855 essay on the Reformation, for example, he argued that Luther and the other reformers had not created but given voice to a widespread, preexisting heretical tendency. Resisting, like Newman, the temptation to idealize the Middle Ages, Brownson noted that heresy had flourished in Christian Europe for centuries. "We agree with Protestant historians," he added, "that society in the sixteenth century was in a most wretched state" and added that the Catholic response had at first been ineffective.[53] Slyly doing what he said he must never do, Brownson evaluated the early conciliatory policy of Pope Adrian VI, "which, if we were to judge the policy of the vicar of Jesus Christ after human modes of judging, which we do not allow ourselves to do, proved so disastrous" (471). It was the rise of the absolutist nation-state which gave Protestantism its chance, he went on, and not the work of Luther. The willingness of princes to protect heretics against Rome, then, was the chief cause of the Reformation. On their own, said Brownson, Luther's ideas lacked the power to create a movement so immense. Big events had to be explained by big causes. With this argument he could belittle Luther without demonizing him, make him an historical accident rather than an evil genius (478). The article and others like it from the 1850s and 1860s show Brownson's determination to grasp historical complexities and to distinguish the truths of Catholicism from the shortcomings of actual historical Catholics.

On the scientific question, Brownson, like Newman, made a distinction between theology and science, on the one hand, and scientists and theologians, on the other, noting how often opinionated men from one side or the other had stirred up controversy by exceeding the limits of his proper

52. Newman, *Historical Sketches*, 2:155–57.
53. Brownson, "Luther and the Reformation," in *Works* 10:475, hereafter cited in the text.

discipline. He too insisted that there would be no ultimate conflict be-tween science and religion and argued that Catholics should try to become the greatest scientists of their age, rather than turn away from science in fear of its discoveries. "We must go further and meet it [contemporary science] scientifically, with superior science, and refute it, where it errs, on scientific principles, by scientific reasons." Otherwise the church would "come to be looked upon as the enemy of intelligence, as in some sense an institution for the perpetuation of ignorance and diffusion of general stu-pidity."[54]

But unlike Newman, Brownson had no sympathy with developmental ideas, and many of his essays from the last ten years of his life (1866–1876) were devoted to refuting the central assumptions of the scientific revolu-tion of his times. He condemned Lyell, Darwin, Thomas Huxley, and Alfred Russel Wallace less because their theories threatened cherished Christian doctrines than because, when they speculated on the question of origins, they had, in his view, ceased to be scientists. Brownson believed science should keep its nose close to the ground, gather information, describe, classify, and discriminate among natural phenomena. To take a group of observations and spin out a theory of species mutation to ac-count for them seemed to Brownson unscientific. He maintained that only experimental verification entitled a hypothesis to gain scientific status. In the case of species evolution, he thought that the appropriate experiments involved the crossbreeding of animals. Having witnessed many such exper-iments, he said, he had found an inexorable tendency on the part of animals to revert to the stronger of the types from which they were drawn and not to become the founders of new species. By this test the Genesis version, of distinct species created once and for all, seemed to him vindi-cated. Darwin assumed, Brownson added, that domestic animals were the descendants of wild ones, but *he* assumed the opposite, that the wild animals were degenerate versions of animals once placed by God at man's disposal. "In reading Mr. Darwin's books," he summarized, "while we acknowledge the vast accumulation of facts in the natural history of men and animals, we have been struck with the feebleness of his reasoning powers. . . . Patient as an observer, he is utterly imbecile as a scientific reasoner. . . . we could concede all his alleged facts, and still deny in toto his theory."[55] Finally, he thought the Darwinians had made an unwarrant-able assumption in arguing a continuity between men and other animals. To do so they had to suppress, or understate, the central facts of the

54. Brownson, "Science and the Sciences" (1863), in Ryan, ed., *Brownson Reader*, 243–54.
55. Brownson, *Works* 9:488.

human intelligence, reason, and moral faculty, which, in Brownson's judgment, made men and beasts fundamentally dissimilar.[56]

In the same way Brownson had harsh words for his era's anthropologists, philologists, and ancient historians who conceptualized world history as an "ascent" from simple to complex forms of social organization. On the contrary, he said, the "primitive" cultures anthropologists were finding were examples not of the first stage of culture but of the last. They were the degenerate descendants of formerly more civilized peoples whose condition had worsened ever since the Fall. The discovery of the Indo-European language group he took as evidence to support the story of the Tower of Babel; the languages had a common ancestor, he argued, just as the peoples did. Nowhere had anthropologists shown "savages" inaugurating "progress" on their own account, whereas history provided many examples of civilized peoples degenerating: he cited the cases of imperial China and Mughal India.[57] Once again, in his view, the available evidence all pointed away from the developmental hypothesis and toward degeneration.

It would be easy to dismiss these views out of hand as the atavistic blusterings of a Catholic reactionary, but it would also be unfair to do so. The state of biological and historical knowledge upon which the developmental theories were based was at that point still fragmentary. The evolutionary biologists still had no knowledge of genetics, and the fossil record was fragmentary. That their hypotheses gained strong support from subsequent discoveries should not lead us to judge them as self-evidently superior to their rivals in the 1860s when Brownson attacked them. Indeed, what is striking about Brownson's attacks on the developmental hypothesis is their rigorous logic. Once grant his premises, and his conclusions are hard to resist. As he knew, of course, many of the new scientists were reluctant to accept his premises; many were determined not to. For them his claim that Thomas Aquinas was a better scientist than they, because more eager to reconcile natural with supernatural revelation, was wrong. Incidentally, the diametrically opposed views of recent science and the nature of social and historical development which he and Newman were able to hold indicates that Catholic scholars at this period had plenty of latitude for intellectual initiatives. Neither of them encountered official opposition for his writings on science and history.

The middle and late nineteenth century thus witnessed, for the first time, a flourishing literature in English on behalf of Catholicism. It flowed

56. Ibid., 279.
57. Brownson, "Primeval Man" (1869), ibid., 318–32.

largely from the pens of Catholic converts, who continued to use the intellectual baggage brought with them from outside the Catholic Church. The English and American converts' intention was to stimulate other conversions or even heal the Reformation breach, but their inadvertent effect was to arouse antagonism among their new coreligionists and sometimes derision among their former friends. As they tried to move the church *toward* a greater intellectual openness, it reacted to new trends by moving steadily *away* from intellectual freedom and began to set its face more and more doggedly against the entire outside world, creating a seemingly impossible situation for convert scholars intent on reconciliation.

# V

# INFALLIBILITY
# AND ITS DISCONTENTS

B Y 1850 CONVERTS DOMINATED the intellectual life of British and American Catholicism. They wanted to devote their energy to converting more Protestant intellectuals but, in the event, found themselves struggling more among one another and against Old Catholics, Irish immigrants, and the Vatican. Conflicts arose partly because of disagreements over how the church as a whole should respond to modern conditions and partly because converts were often tactless, belittling the Catholic community and seeming to scant its traditions. Lines of alliance became complicated as converts split into two factions, "liberal" and "Ultramontane," neither altogether pleasing to the older Catholic community. Vatican warnings, prohibitions, and condemnations of convert intellectuals' ideas became common, first under Pius IX (1846–1878), abating slightly under Leo XIII (1878–1903), but reaching full force under Pius X (1903–1914). These successive Vatican actions, which culminated in the condemnation of Catholic modernism in 1907, made it ever more difficult for convert intellectuals to convince their neighbors that membership in the Catholic church was compatible with intellectual freedom.

Converts affronted born Catholics in several ways. For example, one of Newman's most famous sermons, "The Second Spring" (1852), describes English Catholicism in the early nineteenth century as no more than a pitiable remnant, rather than the determined organization that had kept the faith alive through centuries of persecution and helped engineer Catholic emancipation. He did not mean to be insulting, quite the opposite, but his words must have sounded condescending to Old Catholics just the same:

One and all of us can bear witness to the fact of the utter contempt into which Catholicism had fallen by the time that we were born. . . . No longer the Catholic Church in the country—nay, no longer, I may say, a Catholic community; but a few adherents of the old religion, moving silently and sorrowfully about, as memorials of what had been. "The Roman Catholics"—not a sect, not even an interest, as men conceived it; not a body, however small, representative of the great communion abroad—but a mere handful of individuals, who might be counted like the pebbles and detritus of the great deluge, and who, forsooth, merely happened to retain a creed which, in its day indeed, was the profession of a Church. Here a set of poor Irishmen, coming and going at harvest-time, or a colony of them lodged in a miserable quarter of the vast metropolis. There perhaps an elderly person seen walking in the streets, grave and solitary, and strange, though noble in bearing, and said to be of good family, and a "Roman Catholic." An old-fashioned house of gloomy appearance, closed in with high walls, with an iron gate and yews, and the report attaching to it that "Roman Catholics" lived there; but who they were or what they did, or what was meant by calling them Roman Catholics, no-one could tell—though it had an unpleasant sound, and told of form and superstition. . . . At length so feeble did they become, so utterly contemptible, that contempt gave birth to pity, and the more generous of their tyrants actually began to wish to bestow upon them some favor.[1]

Newman's intention was to make a vivid contrast with the revived fortunes of Catholics in his own day, but listeners could be excused for detecting condescension in his voice as well as in those of the Anglican onlookers he invoked.[2]

Newman was a paragon of restraint by comparison with his fellow convert Richard Simpson, of whom he remarked: "He will always be flicking his whip at Bishops, cutting them in tender places, throwing stones at Sacred Congregations, and as he rides along the road, discharging pea

1. John Newman, "The Second Spring," in W. S. Lilley, ed., *A Newman Anthology* (London: Dennis Dobson, 1949), 179–80.

2. Sheridan Gilley calls this sermon "the bane of English Catholic historiography" for its misleading picture of Catholic weakness before emancipation. He also shows that the English Catholic bishops, newly gathered for the first time in the Synod of Oscott, praised Newman and that Wiseman was moved to tears. Sheridan Gilley, *Newman and His Age* (Westminster, Md.: Christian Classics, 1990), 272.

shooters at Cardinals who happen by bad luck to look out of the window."[3] Simpson, born in 1820 and raised in the village of Mitcham, Surrey, went to Oxford in 1839 and studied with Newman. Enthralled by Pugin and an early enthusiast for Gothic architecture, he was ordained in 1843 and soon became the Anglican vicar of his home village (his father, lord of the manor, had the right of appointment). He learned of Newman's conversion in 1845 and resolved to follow his teacher's example the next year, even though, as a married man, he would be ineligible for the priesthood. From then on he had to live on a small private income and work as a writer and lecturer. He treated his own conversion almost as an embarrassment. Nurtured in an anti-Catholic environment, said his biographer, "he declared that the conclusions at which he had arrived were repulsive, against his interest, and humiliating to himself and his family. They involved 'loosening of the dearest ties of friendship and relationship—but still, what can I do? I cannot force myself to believe things and to hold principles in virtue of which alone I can continue in my present position.'"[4] He had not known any Catholics previously and he remained unimpressed with his new coreligionists after conversion, remarking later that "our lower orders of Catholics are the most ruffianly set in England, uncivilized barbarians."[5] He was indignant at the English Catholic clergy too. They seemed to be neglecting the opportunity presented by nearly four hundred Anglican clergy converts, whom they did precious little to help. Many Catholic priests, he wrote, apparently thought it "more intolerable to have to suffer the impertinence of a few bumptious converts than to see around them a mass of heathenism on which they feel themselves quite powerless to make any impression."[6]

In 1848 Simpson met Isaac Hecker, who was in Europe preparing for ordination. The two became firm friends, and each followed the other's career closely in the ensuing years. Hecker wrote in 1857: "When my mind recurs to England . . . no event gives me so much pleasure as my acquaintance with you and your most amiable wife."[7] Simpson looked favorably on American democracy and, like Hecker, was willing to trust its ordinary citizens. "In those countries where the government is most democratical," Simpson wrote, "where the people feel themselves of most

3. Newman, quoted in Damian McElrath, *Richard Simpson, 1820–1876: A Study in Nineteenth-Century Liberal Catholicism* (Louvain: Publications Universitaires de Louvain, 1972), xi. The following passage is based on this work.

4. Ibid., 36.

5. Simpson to Hecker, September 10, 1859, in Hecker Papers, Paulist House of Studies, Washington, D.C.

6. Simpson to Hecker, December 5, 1857, Hecker Papers.

7. Simpson, quoted in McElrath, *Simpson*, 46.

importance, where the dignity of human nature is recognized under the beggar's rags, there the Church progresses most rapidly."[8] The United States therefore had much to teach England. He asked Hecker to send American political news for the *Rambler* after joining its editoral board in 1856, and he later urged Hecker to establish a branch of his Paulist fathers in England because "we sadly want an order whose rule has been fashioned under other external influences than reign in Italy."[9]

In 1856 Hecker read one of Simpson's articles on original sin and wrote to say that it coincided almost exactly with themes from his forthcoming book. "What right have you to steal my thunder? Have you been looking over my shoulder, or I yours?" He outlined the sequel he was writing to *Questions of the Soul*, adding, "I shall not forget to adapt it to the American people and their institutions also. Our institutions are based on the maxim 'trust the people.' This is Catholic. Protestantism says the contrary: human nature is worthless. I shall not fail to draw my conclusions."[10] In the event Hecker's superiors condemned his new book, *Aspirations of Nature*, because it went too far in praising the "natural" man:

Original sin did not efface the image of God stamped upon the soul. Reason and free will remained, their essence unimpaired, uncorrupted, uninjured. It did not despoil man of any of his merely natural faculties, capacities, or powers. All the rights which absolutely belonged to man's nature, he possessed after the Fall. Man, by original sin, lost absolutely nothing necessary to his nature—since he only fell back into the simply natural state in which he had been originally, or might have been, created.[11]

As we shall see, the argument was indeed similar to Simpson's in "On Original Sin as Affecting the Destiny of Unregenerate Man" (1856).

Eager to convert more Americans in order that the United States—"the country of the future" (48)—could rise to heights of greatness, Hecker gave his countrymen every possible benefit of the doubt in *Aspirations of Nature*, which reads like a Catholic version of Jacksonian democracy. "Here we have men enlightened by reason, free for the most part from false religions, and open to the conviction of Truth. What a noble prospect for the triumph of true Religion!" (44). Protestant fragmentation, he said, especially the breakup of the old Calvinist orthodoxy, was a demonstration of weakness, and he praised Channing and Emerson for exposing Protes-

8. Simpson, quoted ibid., 44.
9. Simpson to Hecker, September 10, 1859, Hecker Papers.
10. Hecker to Simpson, June 1856, Hecker Papers.
11. Isaac Hecker, *Aspirations of Nature* (New York: James B. Kirker, 1857), 197, hereafter cited in the text.

tant flaws. He elaborated the point he had made to Simpson, that the Protestant view of human nature was totally opposed to the basis of the American republic: "The foundations of our political fabric do not suppose Reason imbecile, nor human will enslaved; they rest on the maxim of man's capability of self-government, and this presupposes the possession and exercise of Reason and Free Will" (185). Catholicism had to be suitably adapted to American conditions, Hecker believed, and he tried to soft-pedal what seemed to him its European rigidities. Our age, he said "demands a Religion which unites reverence for God with a profound respect for the divinely gifted intelligence and the heaven-born freedom of man" (28). He expressed what was more a pious hope than a contemporary reality, claiming that no other religion so warmly encouraged intellectual pursuits:

The Geologist may dig deep down into the bowels of the earth till he reaches the intensest heats, the naturalist may decompose matter, examine with the miscroscope what escapes our unaided nature . . . the historian may consult the annals of nations, and unriddle the hieroglyphics of the monuments of bygone ages . . . and Catholicity is not alarmed! Catholicity invokes, encourages, solicits your boldest efforts; for at the end of all your earnest researches you will find that the fruit of your labors confirms her teachings, and that your genuine discoveries add new gems to the crown of truth which encircles her heaven-inspired brow. (202)

Hecker concluded that "the most intellectually gifted and independent minds of the age" in England and America, Newman and Brownson among them, had "cast off Protestantism and embraced Catholicity" because they recognized its ideal blending of spiritual and intellectual life (212).

U.S. Catholic bishops did not see independent minds as an unmixed blessing. When *Aspirations of Nature* appeared, Hecker was at odds with his Redemptorist superiors over the direction of his mission work. He wanted to work for converts among Protestants. The American Redemptorist superior, George Ruland, wanted him to concentrate on keeping German Catholic immigrants true to their faith. Ruland disliked the book, particularly its emphasis on the power of reason and its minimal account of original sin. He preferred to emphasize that human beings were so sinful that they must first submit to authority and use reason only to satisfy themselves of the need for submission.[12] Hecker, hoping to resolve the controversy and supported by his fellow converts, traveled to

12. See David O'Brien, *Isaac Hecker, an American Catholic* (New York: Paulist Press, 1992), 119.

Rome without Ruland's permission in 1857. This act, coupled with suspicions about his theology, led to his expulsion from the Redemptorists. In 1858, after seven anxious months in Rome, he won papal assent to create the Congregation of Saint Paul.[13]

Hecker was upset to learn, while in Rome, that his friend Orestes Brownson also objected to his book's optimistic tone. Brownson's review article created a breach between him and Hecker which never entirely closed.[14] Brownson's criticism was originally a lot harsher than the version that appeared in print but Hecker's friend and fellow convert Redemptorist George Deshon heard about it, visited Brownson, and after "battling back and forth for three hours," persuaded him to tone down his objections.[15] Even so Hecker was stung by the article, which made it clear that Brownson did *not* believe America was ripe for conversion. On the factual point Brownson was of course right. American conversions were slow and hard won, as he said, because there was "scarcely a trait in the American character as practically developed that is not more or less hostile to Catholicity."[16] Even so Richard Simpson was indignant on Hecker's behalf, and wrote him from England that Brownson's real motive had been to restore himself in the good graces of John Hughes, archbishop of New York, after a dispute about Irish immigrants. Simpson, who had earlier praised *Brownson's Quarterly Review*, now declared that Brownson "has turned Irishman"; given his view of the Irish as barbarians, that was a piercing condemnation.[17]

Simpson was becoming more influential among English Catholics after gaining editorial control of a lay Catholic journal, the *Rambler*, along with his friend John Acton. The *Rambler*'s founder, John Moore Capes, another convert of 1845, had believed "that it was my function to devote myself to promoting that general culture of the English Catholic body in which, as I soon found, they were grievously deficient."[18] Capes was always sensitive to how non-Catholic readers would interpret his journal, which showed an abiding admiration for American democracy and religious freedom and brought news of Hecker and Brownson to England. Like Simpson, one of his regular contributors, Capes was apt to provoke the

13. Ibid., 151–67.
14. Ibid., 246.
15. Quoted in Thomas P. Ryan, *Orestes A. Brownson: A Definitive Biography* (Huntington, Ind.: Our Sunday Visitor, 1976), 543.
16. Brownson, quoted in O'Brien, *Hecker*, 122.
17. Simpson to Hecker, Dec. 5, 1857, Hecker Papers.
18. Capes, quoted in Josef L. Altholz, *The Liberal Catholic Movement in England: The "Rambler" and Its Contributors* (London: Burns and Oates, 1962), 9.

authorities and, sometimes, the Old Catholics. He shocked them with an early article, "Four Years' Experience with the Catholic Religion," in which he wrote that at the time of his conversion "the balance of probabilities was decidedly in favour of Rome" and that he had "embraced the more probable of two alternatives." This line of reasoning implied that the Catholic claims could not be *proved* and that religion should be decided as a matter of personal experience and preference and led to some private criticism of Capes for substituting theological "probabilism" for the traditional Catholic teaching of the *certainty* of faith.[19]

Capes was ill and experiencing religious second thoughts by 1857 when he sold out to Simpson and Lord Acton (he eventually reverted to Anglicanism).[20] Acton, as we have seen, was the great exception to the rule that converts dominated Catholic intellectual life in England. Wide travel and prodigious reading had given him, like Capes, Newman, and Simpson, a low opinion of his fellow English Catholics' intellectual attainments. Like them, he believed in raising intellectual standards and winning more Anglicans to Catholicism. In supporting a more open policy for the training of priests, rather than sequestered seminary life, for example, Acton wrote that English priests ought to be learned enough and skilled enough in debate to convince Protestants that they were in a theologically untenable situation. Let us educate our priests, he wrote in 1860 "with a view to the clever enemy, not only the stupid friend."[21]

Acton and Simpson both favored a historical approach to religion rather than the dominant scholastic tradition, whose ahistorical and syllogistic character seemed to them fatal defects. They were strongly influenced by Acton's German teacher Dollinger and the other European "liberal Catholics," Jean-Baptiste Lacordaire, Félicité Robert de Lammenais, and Count Charles de Montalembert. Simpson was eager to take the offensive in the religious conflict of the era and saw the *Rambler* as an ideal vehicle. It was vital that Catholics not shy away from the difficulties being presented by new developments in historical and scientific research. "It is useless to proclaim that history and science are in harmony with our religion," he warned, "unless we show that we think so by being ourselves foremost in telling the whole truth about the Church and her enemies."[22]

19. Ibid., 22.
20. Capes wrote that "the demand for the absolute submission of the will seemed to him 'the equivalent to a demand for the surrender of my reasoning faculties.'" Ibid., 73. He later wrote two books about the experience, *To Rome and Back* and *Reasons for Returning to the Church of England*.
21. Acton, quoted in Altholz, *Liberal Catholic Movement*, 146.
22. Simpson, quoted ibid., 38.

"Our histories," he wrote elsewhere, "have hitherto been rather guarded (or unguarded) apologies for one side or another, than simple and straightforward statements of all the facts. Such a method of writing is of little use; it teaches no lessons for it owns no mistakes; it reveals no remedies for it probes no wounds, and conceals instead of discovering the symptoms of diseases."[23] He agreed with Leopold von Ranke, the formidable German Lutheran historian, that history should be pursued as a science, with no special pleading or evasion of hard questions, and he remained confident to the end of his life that Catholics had nothing to fear from history and science.[24] In the same vein, Acton wrote that the Catholic scholar "must meet his adversaries on grounds which they understand and acknowledge . . . discuss each topic on its intrinsic merits—answering the critic by a severer criticism, the metaphysician by closer reasoning, the historian by deeper learning, the politician by sounder politics and indifference itself by a purer impartiality. In all these subjects . . . [he] discovers a point pre-eminently Catholic but also pre-eminently intellectual and true."[25] Both men felt sure that such rigorous work could be kept separate from the deposit of faith and failed to anticipate that history and doctrine might come into direct conflict.

Simpson contributed philosophical articles to the *Rambler*, against the British utilitarians and German idealists of his day, defending Catholic claims without recourse to scholastic method. Since Kant, he noted, religion had been relegated to the realm of practical reason, where conscience and feeling held sway, from the realm of pure reason, which logic ruled. His own "psychological metaphysics" was dedicated to overcoming and transcending this separation. Truth, said Simpson, *developed* through history and was not amenable to once-and-for-all formulaic definitions. In a series of articles from 1859 and 1860 he constructed a general theory of knowledge around these insights, finding room for poetry and fiction, not just declarative prose, as vehicles of truthful communication. The theory echoes with insights from Newman's *Essay on the Development of Doctrine* and shares the developmental assumptions of Simpson's scientific contemporaries Lyell and Darwin, but without the strict scientific limits. "Such a

23. Simpson, quoted in Thomas Bokenkotter, *Cardinal Newman as an Historian* (Louvain: Publications Universitaires de Louvain, 1959), 61.
24. Altholz, *Liberal Catholic Movement*, 144. As Altholz says, Simpson has sometimes been regarded as a forerunner of the Catholic modernists of the early twentieth century. But the modernists, notably George Tyrrell and Alfred Loisy, were less confident that doctrine could be partitioned off, uncontaminated by the findings of scientific and historical scholarship.
25. Acton, quoted in Thomas Bokenkotter, *A Concise History of the Catholic Church*, rev. ed. (Garden City, N.Y.: Doubleday, 1979), 322.

theory," writes one interpreter, "has profound implications for literature. Poetry, instead of being dismissed as misrepresentation [as it was] by Bentham, can be seen to be bringing to birth by metaphor and symbol ideas which will in the course of time be defined more clearly and systematically."[26] Simpson regretted that some of the best living authors had acquiesced to the idea that the emotional self was detached from the analytical. His attentiveness to the nature of theological language brought him an insight, already grasped by a few advanced Protestants such as Horace Bushnell but not to be commonplace among Catholics for another hundred years: "The structure of the mind makes the language of theology and philosophy unavoidably metaphorical since . . . no idea, however spiritual, can be projected outwards except by first translating it into the forms of space and time."[27]

Simpson's articles on original sin, published in 1855 and 1856, angered the Catholic hierarchy in Britain, partly because the prelates disliked a layman's writing theology but more because he seemed, like Hecker in *Aspirations of Nature*, to be inching close to the Pelagian heresy, minimizing the "fallenness" of human nature. In one of the articles he declared that original sin was not so much a "positive defilement" as the ordinary human condition.[28] Cardinal Wiseman established a commission to investigate the articles and under its recommendations urged Simpson to desist. Simpson wrote to Hecker that he had agreed to stop out of his sense of obligation to obey the cardinal but was considering trying to get the articles published in the United States, beyond the English bishops' jurisdiction.[29]

The *Rambler* angered Cardinal Wiseman again in 1859 by publishing controversial theological articles, one of which, by Acton, described Saint Augustine as the "father of Jansenism." Newman, still smarting from his disillusionment over the failed Irish university scheme, sympathized with the *Rambler* editors' aim of invigorating Catholic laymen's intellectual life, but he deplored their provocative style and their introduction of theological issues into what had started out as a literary journal. They in turn scoffed at his caution and nicknamed him "Old Noggs" (a reference

26. David Carroll, Introduction to *Richard Simpson as Critic*, ed. Carroll (London: Routledge, Kegan Paul, 1977), 10.
27. Carroll, *Simpson as Critic*, 21. Cf. Horace Bushnell, "Our Gospel a Gift to the Imagination" (1869), in his *Building Eras in Religion* (New York: Scribner's, 1881), 249–85.
28. Altholz, *Liberal Catholic Movement*, 56.
29. Simpson to Hecker, July 28, 1856, Hecker Papers. Simpson ended his letter on a note of defiant rectitude. "I have not been very fairly treated by the authorities here but I owe them obedience and I will pay it—but not out of their limits of authority."

to the character Newman Noggs in Charles Dickens's novel *Nicholas Nickleby*).[30] In another inflammatory article, in January 1859, Simpson's friend Scott Nasmyth Stokes criticized the English Catholic bishops' uncooperative attitude toward a British government commission studying educational reforms. They retaliated by demanding Simpson's resignation. Wiseman asked Newman to step in as interim editor of the *Rambler*, which he did, reluctantly, for the May and June issues of 1859.[31]

Newman was no liberal Catholic and "all his long life had distrusted liberalism and had firmly upheld the dogmatic principle."[32] But he had an inveterate intellectual curiosity and often advanced new theories at unsuitable moments. With insightful exaggeration Lytton Strachey wrote later about the Curial officials who frowned on Newman's work: "It was not the nature of his views, it was his having views at all, that was objectionable."[33] Newman in his turn annoyed Wiseman by publishing in the *Rambler* for May 1859 "On Consulting the Faithful in Matters of Doctrine." By "consulting" he meant observing rather than asking an opinion, just as one might "consult" the barometer for the weather, or the railway timetable to find the times of trains. His choice of verb was certainly open to misinterpretation, however, and a blunt Latin translation, delated to Rome by Bishop Thomas Brown of Newport, flattened out his nuances and made it look worse.[34] Besides, Newman was sincere when he wrote in another article that "we do unfeignedly believe that their Lordships really desire to know the opinion of the laity on subjects in which the laity are especially concerned."[35] Their lordships were not so sure and bristled at Newman's argument that in the Arian controversy of the fourth century the laity had remained faithful to the teaching of the church—the *consensus fidelium*—while the bishops were in schism. A series of misunderstandings inflated the controversy aroused by this article out of proportion and left a festering resentment against Newman among influential officials at Rome.[36]

It would be wrong to imply that in these conflicts of the mid-nineteenth century the converts were on one side and the born Catholics on the other. The cooperation of Acton and Simpson at the *Rambler* on behalf of

30. Altholz, *Liberal Catholic Movement*, 77.

31. Ibid., 90–91.

32. David Newsome, *The Convert Cardinals: John Henry Newman and Henry Edward Manning* (London: John Murray, 1993), 219.

33. Lytton Strachey, *Eminent Victorians* (1918; London: Chatto and Windus, 1948), 81–82.

34. Gilley, *Newman and His Age*, 303–7; Altholz, *Liberal Catholic Movement*, 106–10.

35. Altholz, *Liberal Catholic Movement*, 101.

36. Newsome, *Convert Cardinals*, 222–25.

liberal Catholic ideas shows otherwise. The conservative or Ultramontane side of these disputes also bore witness to an alliance between converts and born Catholics, with converts again playing a prominent role. Edward Manning, a Catholic and a priest since 1851, had won Cardinal Wiseman's special favor for his personal loyalty, his ability to use influence in the high places of British life, and his sympathy for Wiseman's Italianate Ultramontanism. Wiseman had been suspicious of converts at first, but Manning had won him over with loyal and tactful service, to such a degree that Wiseman decided to make Manning, rather than the Old Catholic George Errington, his heir apparent.[37] Among Manning's leading intellectual allies in England were Frederick Faber, leader of the London Oratorians, and William George Ward, both Oxford Movement converts who had deviated from the path of their old friend and teacher Newman in the 1850s. Ward was a high-spirited controversialist with a lofty view of papal powers, who said he would be happy having a new papal bull to read every day at breakfast.[38] He deplored the attitude of the *Rambler* editors, but like them, he held most of the English Old Catholics in low esteem. "At the present time," he wrote, "the Catholic world to the Protestant world is in much the same relation as barbarians to civilized men." And even though he disagreed with Simpson's 1856 articles on original sin, Ward praised the intellectual daring they demonstrated, telling Simpson in a letter that he had "opened the way into a new ground which it is absolutely essential that we Catholics should occupy."[39]

The history of nineteenth-century English Catholicism has more often been told by admirers of Newman than by those of Manning and Ward, and the conflict between them has sometimes been exaggerated for dramatic effect. Manning's first biographer, E. S. Purcell, drew an unflattering portrait, which Lytton Strachey distilled in *Eminent Victorians* (1918). Strachey, a leading figure of the iconoclastic Bloomsbury Group, was a masterful stylist. His mischievous portrait of Manning as an ambitious, worldly, cold-hearted manipulator is still a delight to read. But Strachey had no sympathy for the Victorians and even less for the Catholic Church, imputing the worst motives to both. He described Manning's criticism of Newman's *Apologia Pro Vita Sua* (1864), for example, as the attack of a bird of prey: "It was the meeting of the eagle and the dove; there was a hovering; a swoop, and then the quick beak and the relentless talons did

37. Shane Leslie, *Henry Edward Manning: His Life and Labours* (1921; Westport, Conn.: Greenwood, 1970), 129–38.
38. On Ward, see Wilfrid Ward, *William George Ward and the Catholic Revival* (New York: Macmillan, 1893), on papal decrees, 14.
39. Ward, quoted in Altholz, *Liberal Catholic Movement*, 69, 151.

their work."[40] Manning did not like what seemed to him a morbid dwelling on the past in Newman's *Apologia*, but his reaction was not really that dramatic. His actual response was to write: "I am not, like Newman, a poet or a writer of autobiography, but a priest, and a priest only."[41] He and Ward were sincere, not malicious, and far from being blindly dogmatic, they marshaled formidable arguments on behalf of their own convictions, even when arguing for intellectual self-denial. Whatever the rights and wrongs of their estrangement from Newman and from the liberal Catholics, it is most striking from our point of view to see how converts' voices took the lead on *both* sides of the sundering disputes of the 1860s and 1870s.

One source of these disputes was the Papal States. In the 1860s Pius IX was under attack from Garibaldi and the forces of Italian unification, which aimed to turn these rich lands into the central province of a united Italy. Part of the territory was occupied by Sardinian troops in 1860 and for ten years, before the completion of Italian unification, remained the center of an intense religious-political controversy throughout Europe and America. Manning and Ward urged English Catholics to treat preservation of the Papal States as an issue of almost doctrinal significance, whereas Acton, Simpson, and Newman felt it to be a distinctly secondary matter. Acton's teacher Dollinger hoped that Italy *would* be unified and the pope's double role as secular and religious leader ended. He did not hesitate to add that the Papal States had been misgoverned.[42] Manning's convert friend at Rome, the Ultramontanist Monsignor George Talbot, spread rumors that Newman actively supported Garibaldi and had sent him contributions. The rumors were groundless but further sullied Newman's reputation at the Vatican.[43] This disagreement widened the rift between the two groups of converts.

Another source of concern was growing evidence that the pope feared Catholics' intellectual engagement with their most daring non-Catholic contemporaries. In 1863 Pius IX sent a sharp rebuke, the Munich Brief, to Dollinger for declaring the death of scholasticism and the birth of an era of Catholic intellectual freedom in his lecture "The Past and Future of Theology."[44] In the next year Pius went further and issued the *Syllabus of*

40. Strachey, *Eminent Victorians*, 89.

41. Manning, quoted in Robert Gray, *Cardinal Manning: A Biography* (New York: St. Martin's, 1985), 194.

42. Altholz, *Liberal Catholic Movement*, 163.

43. Newsome, *Convert Cardinals*, 226–27.

44. Bokenkotter, *Concise History*, 322–23. Acton was a participant at the Munich conference where Dollinger made this address. David Mathew, *Lord Acton and His Times* (University, Ala.: University of Alabama Press, 1968), 161–63.

*Errors* and the encyclical *Quanta Cura*, condemning eighty intellectual and political principles, including freedom of religion, freedom of the press, socialism, the idea of progress, and intellectual naturalism. The eightieth and last condemned proposition was that "the Roman Pontiff can and ought to reconcile himself to, and come to terms with progress, liberalism, and modern civilization."[45] As the French liberal Catholic bishop Félix Dupanloup of Orléans hastened to point out, this was no more than a compilation: all eighty had previously been condemned. The particular Italian circumstances that had called forth the repudiation of "progress," for example, made the *Syllabus* a little less drastic than it seemed at first glimpse.[46] Even so, it was a pointed rebuff to liberal Catholics' hopes and ideals.

The *Syllabus of Errors* came as a shock to Isaac Hecker, who also sought ways to minimize its impact.[47] By contrast, Orestes Brownson accepted it as an appropriate rebuke to modern infidelities, even though in the foregoing years his *Quarterly Review* (which he had closed down earlier that year) had sailed very close to several of the condemned propositions.[48] The breach between these two American convert leaders widened when Hecker's Paulist colleague Augustine Hewit published *Problems of the Age* (1866). Hewit took the same view of original sin as had Hecker in *Aspirations of Nature*. Brownson, veering in old age toward a rather irritable conservatism, reacted by reviewing it harshly in the *New York Tablet*. He wrote in a letter to his son the same year: "I diverge more and more daily from Father Hecker's liberalism and virtual rationalism, and I doubt if we shall long be able to get together."[49] And by 1870 Brownson, who had to submit to editorial cutting when he published in the Paulists' *Catholic World*, wrote: "Father Hecker's notion that Democracy is favorable to Catholicity is worse than foolish. Democracy rests on popular opinion and never looks beyond, and no people that makes popular opinion its criterion of right and wrong is or can be Catholic."[50] In one of his last letters to Hecker he even hinted that democracy was demonic: "According to Catholicity all power comes from above and descends from high to low; according to democracy all power is infernal, is from below, and ascends from low to high. . . . Catholicity and it are as mutually antagonistic as the

45. Altholz, *Liberal Catholic Movement*, 220–31.
46. Ibid., 232.
47. O'Brien, *Hecker*, 233, 240.
48. Theodore Maynard, *Orestes Brownson: Yankee, Radical, Catholic* (New York: Macmillan, 1943), 354–55.
49. Brownson, quoted in William Portier, *Isaac Hecker and the First Vatican Council* (New York: E. Mellen, 1985), 19.
50. Brownson, quoted in Maynard, *Brownson*, 367.

spirit and the flesh, the Church and the World, Christ and Satan."[51] Hecker and Brownson remained outwardly on good terms, but Brownson stopped contributing to the *Catholic World* once and for all in 1872.

Meanwhile, in England, the *Rambler*, renamed the *Home and Foreign Review* in 1862, had continued to affront Wiseman and his fellow bishops for its articles on theology, biblical scholarship (Simpson treated the Genesis creation story as primitive mythology and gave Darwin's *On the Origin of Species* a positive review), and other sensitive religious areas. Simpson defended his critical view of the papal temporal power in a letter to his priest: "There is a disposition [among English Catholics] to overlook the lessons of history and the dictates of reason in politics, and to commit oneself blindly to the political guidance of an authority which has no promise of political wisdom. . . . I assert a right to follow my reason in matters of science and experience of the senses and of practical reason and secular prudence."[52] He ran the *Home and Foreign Review* as a competitor to the old English quarterlies, the *Edinburgh* and *Westminster* reviews, and included Anglicans and even a French Jew, Maurice Block, among his regular contributors, being disappointed only in his efforts to get the Liberal prime minister William Gladstone as a contributor. But after vigorously supporting Dollinger against the pope in the Munich briefs conflict, he and Acton felt obliged to close their journal in 1864 rather than disobey the pope's teaching in the *Syllabus of Errors*.[53]

After this setback, from which midcentury liberal Catholicism never recovered, Simpson devoted more time to historical research and writing. He published a biography of Edmund Campion, the Elizabethan Jesuit martyr, in 1867. In an earlier account of Campion's life the English Cisalpine Sir John Throckmorton had treated him unsympathetically, describing him as a martyr only to the papal deposing power and not to the Catholic faith. Throckmorton was passionately opposed to papal intervention in worldly affairs and treated Campion as a papal dupe.[54] John Lingard, in his great history of England, had more accurately observed that Campion did not *support* the deposing power but merely declined to deny it, claiming incompetence to judge so controversial an issue.[55] Simpson took the same approach, but in his hands the story of Campion's demise

51. Brownson, quoted in James Hennesey, S.J., *American Catholics: A History of the Roman Catholic Community in the United States* (New York: Oxford University Press, 1981), 197.
52. Simpson, quoted in Altholz, *Liberal Catholic Movement*, 185.
53. Ibid., 200–202, 207, 222.
54. Ibid., 223.
55. John Lingard, *History of England from the First Invasion of the Romans* (Dublin: James Duffy, 1893), 6:334–37.

turned into an artful polemic against the Ultramontanes of his own day, particularly those who were arguing for papal infallibility and the temporal power. No audience then could have missed the contemporary significance of Simpson's remark, ostensibly about the sixteenth-century English Jesuits: "Those who think themselves infallibly certain that they are infallibly in the right can never profit from the lessons of history."[56] He sympathized with Campion for having been put into a position where the civil authorities were bound to suspect him, but held Campion culpable for not having been readier to disavow the papal deposing power. Ending with a flourish against papal temporal power, Simpson declared: "The divine government of the church was never more triumphantly exhibited than when, in spite of popes, bishops, theologians, religious enthusiasm, popular discontent, foreign intrigues, powerful kings, and invincible armadas, the providential failure of these claims vindicated the purity of the faith from a heterogeneous accretion" (345). As for the Jesuit martyrs themselves, "though a few among them were treasonable busybodies, yet the great mass of them were men of simple characters, pure lives, burning charity, and heroic constancy, who acted and suffered simply for the glory of God" (345). They had been forced to suffer because their superiors declined to separate religious and political affairs. The message for his own day was unmistakable, even though Newman, always more anxious in facing strife, had warned Simpson that this kind of editorializing was liable to get him into more trouble.[57]

The converts' influence on English Catholicism widened when Cardinal Wiseman died in 1865. Pope Pius IX ignored the advice of the Westminster chapter on the question of succession and appointed Manning. By his energetic Ultramontanism Manning had antagonized most of his fellow bishops in the foregoing years. But now, by a display of trust, generosity, and forgiveness toward defeated rivals, he was able to reconcile most of them, even George Errington whom he had displaced in Wiseman's favor. He provided forceful but popular leadership to the church in England for the remaining twenty-eight years of his life, rising to the dignity of cardinal in 1875 and becoming a popular figure in London public life. He was alert to the social condition of the large, poor Irish community and became a hero to the London working classes when he resolved a bitter strike in the dockyard workers' favor. His most sympathetic biographer, Shane Leslie (also a convert), wrote that although the Old Catholics often struck at Manning as he rose to power, "he never struck them, for he remembered

56. Richard Simpson, *Edmund Campion: A Biography* (London: Williams and Norgate, 1867), 341, hereafter cited in the text.
57. Altholz, *Liberal Catholic Movement*, 169.

that whatever the converts could give the Church, they had *not* given martyrs."[58]

In 1869 Pope Pius IX summoned the world's Catholic bishops for a general Vatican Council, the first of its kind since the Council of Trent three hundred years before. Pius and his Curia resolved to make the definition of papal infallibility the council's centerpiece. They designed it partly as a counterstroke to the political attacks then being made against Catholicism in Italy and Germany. Manning issued a pastoral letter to England's Catholics, justifying a lofty view of papal infallibility and fully supporting Pius's aim.[59] He spoke Italian fluently and, unlike Newman, had always enjoyed his visits to the Vatican. (Later, when he took part in the conclave of 1878, Manning was touted as a possible candidate for pope and was flattered to be told by Cardinal Luigi Bilio that "he had been so domesticated in Rome as not to be a foreigner." Despite the temptation Manning declared that the crisis of the times demanded an Italian rather than himself as pontiff.)[60] The council went very much as Manning had hoped. He manipulated the British government's agent at Rome, Odo Russell, into forestalling a planned pan-European intervention against the council and he helped assure passage of the infallibility decree.[61]

Converts were prominent not only among the English-speaking advocates of infallibility but also among its opponents. One English convert, Peter le Page Renouf, a distinguished Oriental scholar, wrote a series of pamphlets just prior to the council reminding Catholics that the sixth-century pope Honorius had made an *ex cathedra* declaration of doctrines which a subsequent council (the Third Council of Constantinople, 680) had formally condemned as heretical. Was he nevertheless infallible?[62] Most antiinfallibilists sailed under the banner of "inopportunism," mitigating their opposition by maintaining that the time was not right, though it is clear that many of them, Renouf included, simply did not believe in it at all.

Isaac Hecker, like Renouf, was unconvinced that infallibility was historically defensible. He accepted an invitation to attend the council as theological adviser to Bishop Sylvester Rosecrans of Columbus and Archbishop Martin Spalding of Baltimore. He sailed from New York via Ireland, En-

58. Leslie, *Manning*, 128.
59. Newsome, *Convert Cardinals*, 272.
60. Ibid., 343. On converts' differing attitudes to Rome, see Patrick Allitt, "America, England, Italy: The Geography of Catholic Conversion, 1840–1960" *Notre Dame Cushwa Center Working Papers*, ser. 26, no. 3 (Fall 1994): 3.
61. Gray, *Manning*, 233, 236–37.
62. Portier, *Hecker*, 31; Gilley, *Newman*, 354. On other antiinfallibilists, see also McElrath, *Simpson*, 127–31.

gland, France, and Germany so that he could visit Simpson, Acton, and Dollinger en route. He had addressed the collected American bishops at the 1866 Plenary Synod of Baltimore, and was now one of the most prominent American Catholics. Dollinger wrote, after meeting Hecker, that "he seems profoundly convinced that the triumph of Ultramontanism would be fatal to the Church in America." Simpson was delighted to hear it. "Hecker as a missionary with a vocation to convert the semi-literary class in the United States puts this truth into the first place—that it is impossible to believe against evidence, and not only impossible but wicked to attempt it."[63]

Hecker disliked Italy, especially Rome. On his earlier visit, in 1857, he had described it as "a crucible in which one's faith either becomes wholly supernatural or disappears entirely," and he depicted the Curia as disreputable procrastinators. The ordinary people were "volatile and impressive . . . more like children and women than men," and full of "ignorance, suspicion, and prejudice" against the United States. This second visit did not improve his impression of Rome. He was shocked by the Curial party's maneuvers to achieve their program and wrote indignantly to his brother George that he was giving up on the place once and for all. "The complete regeneration of Europe," he added, "is to come from the light of the new civilization on the other side of the Atlantic, from the shores of the United States."[64] He was powerless to prevent the swelling support for the definition of infallibility and left Rome before the voting, which took place in a dramatic thunderstorm on July 18, 1870. Later he managed to interpret the definition as providential, but at the time it depressed him.

Newman was no more enthusiastic than Hecker. He believed in the doctrinal infallibility of the church but was too learned in Catholic history to accept the Ultramontanes' claim that they were merely ratifying a *papal* infallibility that had existed for centuries. The declaration seemed to him a violation of the long-established principle of collegiality, and he described the Roman events of 1870 as "a climax of tyranny."[65] He was invited to attend as a theological adviser to the bishop of Newport but declined, disliking the prospect of another visit to Italy and fearing to be either a party to the definition or too prominent an adversary. To his ordinary, Bishop William Ullathorne of Birmingham, Newman wrote during the council that "Rome ought to be a name to lighten the heart at all times, and a Council's proper office is, when some great heresy or other evil impends, to inspire the faithful with hope and confidence; but now we

63. Portier, *Hecker*, 36, 37.
64. O'Brien, *Hecker*, 155, 154, 235.
65. Ian Ker, *John Henry Newman: A Biography* (Oxford: Clarendon Press, 1988), 659.

have the greatest meeting which ever has been, and that at Rome, infusing into us . . . little else than fear and dismay."[66]

While the council deliberated he was hard at work on his *Essay in Aid of a Grammar of Assent* (1870), in which he argued that religious certitude was based on assent to probabilities and that different people inevitably made these assents in different ways because of the variety of their experiences. One could not achieve religious assurance in the way one became sure of a mathematical proof or by syllogistic reasoning. What was most "real" to one person seemed remote and dim to another, and often the decisive moment in coming to faith depended on the "illative" sense, the ability of the mind to jump creatively to truths that exceeded the logical evidence supporting them. The mind, for Newman, was an active agent rather than a passive recorder of experiences and arguments, and he insisted that propositions could not entirely define or contain reality.[67] As with his acceptance of evolutionary theory so with this "probabilistic" argument, Newman showed that he was in the mainstream of the Anglo-Saxon nineteenth century. As Paul Croce has shown, one of the central characteristics of nineteenth-century thought in Britain and the United States was that scientific evidence established probabilities rather than apodictic truths. The *Grammar of Assent* sees Newman working to the same conclusion in religious thought.[68]

Newman had been criticized by his fellow Catholics so often by this time that he dreaded negative Catholic reactions in advance, and the obstacles they would throw in the way of winning new converts. He wrote to his convert friend Henry Wilberforce:

Our theological philosophers are like the old nurses who wrap the unhappy infant in swaddling bands or boards—put lots of blankets over him—and shut the windows that not a breath of fresh air may come to his skin—as if he were not healthy enough to bear wind and water in due measures. They move in a groove and will not tolerate anyone who does not move in the same. So it breaks upon me, that I shall be doing more harm than good in publishing. What influence should I have with Protestants and Infidels, if a pack of Catholic critics opened at my book fiercely?[69]

66. Ibid., 651.
67. John Henry Newman, *An Essay in Aid of a Grammar of Assent*, ed. Ian Ker (Oxford: Clarendon Press, 1985). On this approach to faith, similar to that of Brownson and Simpson, see also Carroll, ed., *Simpson as Critic*, 7–9.
68. Paul Jerome Croce, *Science and Religion in the Age of William James: The Eclipse of Certainty, 1820–1880* (Chapel Hill: University of North Carolina Press, 1995).
69. Quoted in Ker, *Newman*, 632.

The book itself was eagerly awaited in England and sold out on publication day, but Newman was right to fear adverse Catholic reactions. The *Tablet* and the *Month* both noted his deviation from scholastic method and his replacement of certainty with no more than probability. On the other hand, William George Ward (frequently an antagonist) was enthusiastic, as were several High Church Anglican reviewers, though they pointed out what he too recognized as a shortcoming—that one can in fact feel certitude about an idea that turns out to be false and that the illative sense is no certain guide to the truthfulness of one's convictions.[70]

Simpson, like Newman, had often been mauled by Catholic critics, but in 1870 he could not resist joining the public debate surrounding the Vatican Council. He published a long letter in the London *Times*, deploring the illogic and ahistoricity of the decree, then republished it as a pamphlet, later advising Gladstone when he mounted his attack on "Vaticanism" in 1874.[71] In the last years of his life (he died in 1876) Simpson retreated from intra-Catholic controversy into ever-more-intensive study of Shakespeare. Newman had remarked earlier that English was a Protestant language and that the convert intellectuals must find a way to *Catholicize* it.[72] Not necessarily, said Simpson: his way of trying to put Catholicism back into the center of English literature was to prove that England's greatest playwright and poet had *been* a Catholic! By exhaustive analysis of Shakespeare's family history, and the history of Stratford recusancy in the late sixteenth and early seventeenth centuries he built up a plausible case.[73] He had begun this effort with three articles in the *Rambler* in 1858 and extended it, in response to critics, in the late 1860s and early 1870s. Catholicism, he pointed out, would explain the Bard's secretiveness about his personal life. Hence too the existence of such sympathetic characters as Friar Lawrence in *Romeo and Juliet* (quite different from the stereotyped greedy or lecherous friars of Elizabethan and Jacobean drama). Whatever the merits of his theory, Simpson, the first man to advance it, was shrewd in using the new techniques of scientific history in his effort to substantiate the idea—pitching his case on grounds non-Catholic historians would find most persuasive.[74]

70. Gilley, *Newman and His Age*, 416.
71. Altholz, *Liberal Catholic Movement*, 245–47; McElrath, *Simpson*, 137–39.
72. Newman, "English Catholic Literature," in Newman, *The Idea of a University*, ed. Charles Harrold (1853; New York: Longmans, Green, 1947), 271.
73. Unfortunately, his book on the subject was not complete at the time of his death. Another convert and admirer of Simpson, Henry Bowden, published the work as *The Religion of Shakespeare: Chiefly from the Writings of the Late Mr. Richard Simpson, MA* (London: Burns and Oates, 1899). It is not always possible to tell which author is speaking.
74. McElrath, *Simpson*, 104–16.

Simpson's retreat into the study of Shakespeare, Newman's decision to keep out of the Vatican affray, and Acton's brush with excommunication, marked the end of midcentury Catholic liberalism. In the British, American, French, and German Protestant communities, meanwhile, modernism was gathering force. Its most threatening manifestations, from the Vatican point of view, were its unblinking historical method, its shelving of moral and theological questions in the study of biblical literature, its receptivity to the ideas of the new biology, psychology, and sociology, and its willingness to relativize absolute Christian claims. On these rocks a generation of pioneering Catholic converts would come to grief.

# VI

# AMERICA, MODERNISM, AND HELL

T HE CATHOLIC CONTROVERSIES of the 1850s, 1860s, and 1870s, with converts always taking a prominent role, were echoed as the nineteenth century ended. Three episodes underlined the victory of the Ultramontanes, the widening gulf between modern intellectual life and Catholicism, and the anxious position of converts attempting to keep them in contact. The three events were the condemnation in 1899 of the "Americanist" heresy in which Isaac Hecker was implicated, the excommunication of the convert scientist St. George Mivart in 1900, and the excommunication of the convert theologian George Tyrrell in 1906. They were followed by the papal encyclical *Pascendi Dominici Gregis* (1907) which, by prohibiting Catholic priests from evolutionary studies and historical-critical study of Scripture, all but guaranteed the intellectual segregation of Catholicism for the next fifty years.

St. George Mivart (1827–1900) had converted the year before Newman, 1844, and was often touted as Newman's counterpart in the natural sciences, a jewel in the Catholic crown.[1] An anatomist, he specialized in the analysis of primate skeletons. He won the admiration of Richard Owen, founder of London's Natural History Museum, and of Thomas Huxley, Darwin's friend and advocate, who helped to get him appointed professor of comparative anatomy at Saint Mary's Hospital Medical School, London, in 1862. Mivart, like Brownson and Newman, wanted to

1. Biographical information in the following passage is based on Jacob W. Gruber, *A Conscience in Conflict: The Life of St. George Jackson Mivart* (Philadelphia: Temple University Press, 1960).

show the world that Catholics could be good scientists. He was eager to avoid interreligious polemics, and wrote to another scientist convert, Bertram Windle, urging him always to give the benefit of the doubt to non-Catholic scientists. "You and I," he wrote, "know that men may be, very sincerely and honestly, unbelievers. As a matter of justice, then, we ought to be tolerant and, as far as possible, sympathetic, and as a matter of religious policy, doubly so."[2] He too hoped that many more scientists would convert to Catholicism and reconcile a divided Christendom.

Mivart's meticulous research on primate classification led him to agree with Darwin that human beings had evolved from apelike ancestors, but in the 1860s he began to differ from Darwin on several issues. First, he believed that similar traits in different species did not always connote common ancestry; rather, comparable traits could develop in parallel. He also pointed to some questions about evolution with which Darwin himself had struggled inconclusively. For example, how did birds' wings evolve, since in their early stages they cannot have been effective for flying and appear to have given the creature no competitive advantage? And why, in Darwin's ruthlessly competitive world, did species have useless organs, such as the appendix, or men's nipples?[3] It seemed to Mivart unlikely that such diverse organisms as the birds and the mammals had common ancestors, and so, without abandoning the idea of species development, he retreated from the more radical implications of Darwin's theory. Darwin was working on a new edition of the *Origin of Species* at the time and devoted a complete chapter to consideration and refutation of Mivart's attack.[4]

At the philosophical level, Mivart also disagreed with more materialistic Darwinians such as Ernst Haeckel. Mivart could admit the reality of biological evolution but he denied that human intelligence and the capacity for moral judgment had evolved as part of the general physical process. He was shocked by Haeckel's *General Morphology* (1866) which made explicit several themes Darwin had left implicit. "For Haeckel man did not exist apart from the entire organic world; his uniqueness, no matter upon what it was thought to rest, was but a delusion. Intellectual and moral man was nothing but a reflection of physical man."[5] Mivart agreed the body had evolved but believed the soul had been created separately by God.

Gathering his doubts, scientific and philosophic, Mivart published his

2. Ibid., 49.

3. Ibid., 53.

4. Peter Brent, *Charles Darwin: A Man of Enlarged Curiosity* (New York: Harper and Row, 1981), 480.

5. Gruber, *Conscience in Conflict*, 40.

own version of human origins, *On the Genesis of Species* (1871), which appeared on the market in the same year as Darwin's *Descent of Man*.[6] In it he tried to reconcile evolution with Catholicism and included in the text a series of citations from the church Fathers which showed that their views were not incompatible with biological evolution, even if they did not actively support the idea. He followed up his *Genesis*, which sold well, with a critical review of Darwin's *Descent of Man* in the *Quarterly Review*, which infuriated Darwin's circle. From this moment on, many of them turned on him. Huxley in particular assaulted his scientific reputation and even tried to ostracize him socially by excluding him from London clubs. In an article titled "Mr. Darwin's Critics," Huxley reviled his former student and friend. Mivart's biographer summarizes: "Composed in cold anger, Huxley's review was biting, a slashing condemnation not only of Mivart's theological and scientific arguments but of his personal motives as well. It was the public chastisement of the apostate. But it was more. It was a proclamation that between the new science and theology there was— there could be—no middle way, no reconciliation, no middle ground." Huxley added that the Catholic Church was "the vigorous and consistent enemy of the highest intellectual, moral, and social life of mankind."[7]

American Catholics received Mivart's *Genesis of Species* guardedly.[8] Orestes Brownson, as we have seen, was frankly opposed to evolutionary hypotheses, but three other American converts, Augustine Hewit and George Searle, both Paulist priests, and Thomas Dwight, a Harvard professor, were more receptive. Hewit accepted the general evolutionary framework as an explanation for all the "lower" life forms on earth but shied away from accepting it in the case of human beings. His reasoning was that Genesis made no reference to God's *technique* in making the animals, whereas it *did* specify that God had made man in his own image. And he warned that Mivart's willingness to include the human body in the evolutionary pattern might aid the atheists and turn the image of God into a "stupid and vicious beast."[9] Searle and Dwight went further and accepted even the principle of human evolution, though, like Mivart, they were careful to exempt the human soul from the developmental process.

6. St. George Mivart, *On the Genesis of Species* (New York: Appleton, 1871).

7. Gruber, *Conscience in Conflict*, 90, 92. See also John Bowlby, *Charles Darwin: A New Life* (New York: Norton, 1990), 403–5, on Darwin's anxiety over the cogency of Mivart's criticisms.

8. For American Catholic views of evolution, see John Rickards Betts, "Darwinism, Evolution, and American Catholic Thought, 1860–1900," *Catholic Historical Review* 45 (June 1959): 161–85.

9. Hewitt, quoted in Scott Appleby, *Church and Age Unite! The Modernist Impulse in American Catholicism* (Notre Dame, Ind.: University of Notre Dame Press, 1992), 22.

Bolder still was a Milwaukee theology professor, the Reverend John Gmeiner, whose *Modern Scientific Views and Christian Doctrines Compared* (1884) found divine creation through evolution compatible with the Genesis account and declared that this view was actually *taught* in Saint Augustine's theology.[10]

Mivart was never reconciled with his scientific colleagues, and in the later years of his life he continued the polemical battle against them. Darwin's ideas, he said, "tend in the intellectual order to the degradation of the mind, by the essential identification of thought with sensation, and in the political order to the evolution of horrors worse than those of the Parisian Commune."[11] He was also an early opponent of social Darwinism, and in a succession of *Dublin Review* articles between 1874 and 1880, he criticized its leading exponent, Herbert Spencer. If society, like Darwin's nature, was a battle of all against all, he reasoned, only the most pessimistic and wretched outcome of human history could be expected. Mivart saw his own optimistic view, of a changing world presided over by a merciful God, as infinitely more realistic. He knew that many of the social Darwinians were in fact avid "progressives," but he said their philosophy gave the lie to their optimism and they were in effect living contradictions. He, by contrast, had an outlook congruent with his beliefs.[12]

Ironically his emphasis on God's mercy and goodness got Mivart into trouble with the Catholic Church itself. At first the hierarchy had welcomed him, and the success of his books *The Genesis of Man, Contemporary Evolution*, and *Lessons from Nature* prompted Pope Pius IX to award him a pontifical doctorate in 1876.[13] But when he began to argue that the doctrine of free will meant, in effect, complete freedom for every intellect, Catholic reviewers began to challenge him. In an article from 1885, Mivart declared that "no man can be either truly scientific or truly religious who does not set truth pure and simple above every other consideration, whatever it may be." He went on to confront the most famous clash of Catholicism with science: the Galileo affair. Catholic apologists usually maintained that the church had persecuted Galileo not for his scientific investigations but for trying to insist on a doctrinal issue for which he was unqualified. Mivart denied this defense: "Ecclesiastical authority did give a judgment directly affecting physics, and which impeded scientific progress." But Galileo was right and the church was wrong. Sometimes "men

10. Ibid., 22–25.
11. Gruber, *Conscience in Conflict*, 80.
12. Ibid., 123–27.
13. Ibid., 73.

of science may have a truer perception of what Scripture must be held (since it is inspired) to teach than may be granted to ecclesiastical authorities. This is demonstrated by the fact that those who held the very Catholic truth in the Seventeenth Century were not the inquisitors, but those whom they so rashly condemned." He added, more in hope than in expectation, that the long-term consequence of the Galileo case was wholly favorable to scientific freedom. "God has taught us that it is not to ecclesiastical congregations but to men of science that He has committed the elucidation of scientific questions."[14] Mivart hoped that such frank criticism of the Vatican's past errors would have the double consequence of invigorating Catholic scientists and drawing new converts into the church.

Increasingly impressed by developmental ideas and by the growth of humanitarianism, Mivart next turned his attention to the doctrine of hell in a series of articles for *Nineteenth Century* in 1892 and 1893. The traditionally lurid depiction of everlasting, burning hellfire, which contributed to the current unpopularity of Catholicism, was not to be taken literally, he said. It was just a symbolic way of expressing the vast difference between the natural happiness men would experience in hell and the inexpressibly more marvelous supernatural happiness they would enjoy in the beatific vision of heaven. "God has, with infinite benevolence, but with inscrutable purposes, created human beings the overwhelming majority of whom, being incapable of grave sin, attain to an eternity of unimaginable natural happiness."[15] He even speculated that the ideas and feelings of the condemned might *evolve* toward a reconciliation with God. After all, "it is of faith that a process of evolution takes place in Purgatory, and justice and reason seem to demand that it should also have its place in Hell."[16] A flurry of angry letters in the Catholic press criticized Mivart's views, and a Jesuit priest, Richard Clark, rebutted in *Nineteenth Century*, denying that the church Fathers gave any reason to hope for "progress" in hell and alleging that Mivart had misused his sources. He seemed to have forgotten that "the fear of Hell is a powerful deterrent to many . . . and many a sin would be committed were it not for the wholesome dread of eternal misery before the sinner's eyes."[17] The Catholic bishop of Nottingham

14. St. George Mivart, "Modern Catholics and Scientific Freedom," *Nineteenth Century* 17 (July 1885): 32, 40, 41.
15. St. George Mivart, "Happiness in Hell," *Nineteenth Century* 32 (December 1892): 918.
16. St. George Mivart, "The Happiness in Hell," *Nineteenth Century* 33 (February 1893): 325.
17. Father Richard F. Clark, S.J., "Happiness in Hell: A Reply," *Nineteenth Century* 33 (January, 1893): 84.

issued a pastoral letter affirming the old doctrine that even unbaptized children would suffer eternal punishment, and then Mivart's articles were placed on the Roman Index of prohibited literature.[18]

Mivart and Isaac Hecker had met in Rome at the time of the Vatican Council, and Mivart noted later that they shared the conviction that the church was still developing ("evolving") and still relatively in its infancy.[19] Hecker's last book, *The Church and the Age*, like Mivart's articles, shows that he too liked the taste of his era's intellectual enthusiasms, and was able to bring them to the boil while imparting a distinctive Catholic flavor to them. He was shrewder and more conciliatory than Mivart, partly from temperament and partly because as a priest he was more immediately answerable to authority for his published views. As a result he caused less scandal than Mivart in the short term, and yet his work, especially as interpreted by a sympathetic biographer after his death, was to have explosive consequences for American Catholicism and to contribute to the specter of a heresy called "Americanism" which the Vatican condemned in 1899.

In these essays, as in his earlier books, Hecker praised the U.S. political system, the separation of church and state, the compatibility of Catholicism with the American temperament, and the ideal of intellectual freedom under the guidance of the Holy Spirit. One of the most controversial essays asserted that primacy among the races of the world lay with the Anglo-Saxons. Intellectual predominance was passing from the Latin and Celtic "races" to the Anglo-Saxon, he said, and it ought to be accompanied by a shift in religious dominance. Hence it was appropriate that the Catholic Church, which had been developed by "Latins" in earlier times, should now take its lead from the northern race that had evolved to a higher level in England and the United States. He added that in these countries Protestantism was dying, its endless schisms and its diluted theology betraying its weakness and leaving the field open for the triumphant reemergence of Catholicism. According to Hecker, the genius of Latin and Celtic Catholicism had been to perfect the "outward" forms of the faith, culminating in the Vatican Council. The Saxons, however, had a more "inward" and intellectual approach to religion, which must now be satisfied in order that Catholicism might restore the balance, which had been skewed toward the "outward" ever since the crisis of the Reformation. To achieve this balance the church would have to restore intellectual liberty,

18. Gruber, *Conscience in Conflict*, 185.
19. "While we were at Rome during the Vatican Council we were much interested to find that our belief that we were still in the early ages of the Church was also the conviction of that remarkable American Father Hecker." Mivart, "Happiness in Hell" (1892), 913n.

encourage study of its deepest mysteries, and set forth unshackled on the quest for truth. "By penetrating more deeply into the intelligible side of the mysteries of the faith and the intrinsic reasons for revealed truth and the existence of the church, the strong rational tendencies of the Saxon mind will seize hold of and be led to apprehend the intrinsic reasons for Christianity."[20] The place to do it was of course the United States, the nation whose political institutions accorded best with Catholic tradition and whose first Catholic inhabitants, the original Maryland settlers, had introduced the principle of religious toleration to the New World.[21]

Hecker published this theory just at the time that racism was gaining scientific prestige. Racial prejudice already had a long history in Britain and America but in the last decades of the nineteenth century intellectuals in both countries were trying to substantiate traditional claims about race difference with statistical evidence and supposedly impartial tests. Most of this scientific racism was later discredited by researchers who denied the racists' assumptions, but in its day it established a high reputation in the universities and had such public-policy consequences as the racial segregation of the federal government under Woodrow Wilson and the immigration restriction laws of the 1920s. William Z. Ripley's *Races of Europe* (1899) summarized the scientific racists' view that Europe exhibited several distinct racial types. In general, said Ripley, the farther north the reader looked, the better human material he would find (though he stopped short of granting supremacy to Lapps), whereas to look south was to find "Alpines" and "Mediterraneans" each with their distinctive head shape, intellectual character, and moral defects. Ripley made the argument on purely secular grounds, using an evolutionary pattern to prove that northern white Teutons were the most highly evolved of the races of Europe.[22]

Hecker believed in a European race hierarchy, though for him it was intellectual and religious rather than biological fitness which set the Saxons at the top of the heap. His work, like Newman's and Mivart's, was indebted to developmental assumptions and the theory of progress. God, he said, had created the various races, each to carry out its role in a particular

20. Isaac Hecker, *The Church and the Age: An Exposition of the Catholic Church in View of the Needs and Aspirations of the Present Age* (New York: Catholic Book Exchange, 1886), 49–50.

21. In skillful rhetorical passages, Hecker argues that religiously tolerant Catholics had to face religiously intolerant Protestants in America, that their influence finally prevailed, and that the Declaration of Independence embodied timeless Catholic truths. *Church and Age*, 64–72.

22. William Z. Ripley, *The Races of Europe: A Sociological Study* (New York: Appleton, 1899).

era of Christian history. Now, in the 1870s and 1880s, the Saxon and American moment had arrived! To see Hecker advancing arguments of this kind is to see how close was his outlook to that of liberal Protestants such as Josiah Strong and how skillfully he tried to win new adherents to Catholicism. Hecker pitched his theory on just those grounds most likely to win sympathetic attention in the new universities, among patriotic, up-to-date Americans who were attracted by the new scientific theories but still had religious qualms. Experience soon showed that courting one audience in this way meant losing another.[23]

Hecker's racial argument was tactless. Vatican officials, most of them Italian ("Latin"), and American bishops, most of them Irish ("Celtic"), were hardly likely to enjoy learning that they belonged to the races that had been upstaged by more gifted "Saxons," and they doubtless thought it no coincidence that Hecker should belong to the group that came out on top. The Italians certainly did not share either his racial theories or his fervor for the U.S. political system. In their view, Spain, the European nation least troubled by heresy since the Reformation, was closer to the ideal.

Hecker escaped censure during his life, but when a devoted fellow Paulist, Walter Elliott, published his biography in 1891, three years after Hecker's death, it sparked new controversies.[24] Elliott was a born Catholic but liked to pose as a convert and, wearing ordinary street clothes, give lectures to Protestant audiences on the wholesome, American nature of Catholicism, as Hecker had done. European and American Ultramontanes already suspected some Catholics, particularly the Paulists, of placing too high a value on the U.S. democratic tradition, the separation of church and state, and the appeal to personal experience. They disliked the conciliatory manner of Cardinal James Gibbons of Baltimore (who had led the prayers one morning at the Chicago World's Parliament of Religions in 1893 before an audience of Protestants, Hindus, Buddhists, Jews, Shintoists, and Jains), Archbishop John Ireland of St. Paul, and John Keane, rector of the Catholic University of America, fearing that their friendliness toward members of other faiths could lead to religious "indifferentism." French and German liberal Catholics, on the other hand, admired the American scene, especially the separation of church and state, and they looked to Hecker's Paulists as auguries of a brighter future. One of them,

23. Cf. Josiah Strong, *Our Country: Its Possible Future and Its Present Crisis* (New York: Baker and Taylor, 1885). See also Robert Cross, *The Emergence of Liberal Catholicism in America* (1959; Chicago: Quadrangle Books, 1968).
24. The biography was Walter Elliott, C.S.P., *The Life of Father Hecker* (1891; New York: Arno Press, 1972).

Abbé Félix Klein, a theology professor at the Paris Institut Catholique in Paris, wrote a glowing introduction to the French edition of Elliott's book, portraying Hecker himself as the ideal contemporary Catholic. Hecker became a posthumous celebrity among European liberal Catholics, who adapted parts of his message without doing justice to the full content or context of his work.[25]

Ultramontanes and French royalists responded with polemics against Klein's Hecker and criticized his claim to intellectual freedom under the Holy Spirit and his praise of church-state separation. Charles Maignen, whom a recent Catholic historian describes as a "rabid French monarchist," stated the Ultramontane case in *Le Père Hecker: Est Il un Saint?* [Father Hecker: is he a saint?].[26] When the United States declared war on Spain in 1898, many Vatican officials regarded the Americans as anti-Catholic aggressors and hitherto influential Americans such as Archbishop Ireland found their welcome in Rome much cooler than before.[27] The war and the Maignen version of "Heckerism" were among the factors that prompted Pope Leo XIII's encyclical letter *Testem Benevolentiae* (1899), which condemned "Americanism" and, without actually naming any guilty parties, implied that Hecker and his followers had used undesirable methods. It warned that no point of doctrine should be relaxed for the sake of winning converts, and that Catholics should not be too ready to substitute their own judgment for that of the church.[28]

The effect of *Testem Benevolentiae* was to cast a shadow over Hecker's good name well into the twentieth century. The Paulist house of studies kept its only copy of Elliott's biography of Hecker under lock and key, and later treatments of his life steered away from theological questions altogether. Vincent Holden, C.S.P., who devoted much of his life to studying Hecker and wrote a fine book on Hecker's early years, never continued his biography, probably because he was reluctant to confront the Americanism issue.[29] Post-Vatican II historians, including William Portier, David

25. David O'Brien, *Isaac Hecker, an American Catholic* (New York: Paulist Press, 1992), 380–90; Anthony Rhodes, *The Power of Rome in the Twentieth Century: The Vatican in the Age of the Liberal Democracies, 1870–1922* (New York: Franklin Watts, 1983), 134–45; Richard H. Seager, *The World's Parliament of Religions: The East-West Encounter, Chicago, 1893* (Bloomington: University of Indiana Press, 1995), 54–55, 64–67.

26. William Portier, "Isaac Hecker and *Testem Benevolentiae*," in John Farina, ed., *Hecker Studies: Essays on the Thought of Isaac Hecker* (Ramsey, N.J.: Paulist Press, 1983), 16.

27. Marvin O'Connell, *John Ireland and the American Catholic Church* (St. Paul: Minnesota Historical Society Press, 1988), 441–55.

28. Marvin O'Connell, *Critics on Trial: An Introduction to the Catholic Modernism Crisis* (Washington, D.C.: Catholic University of America Press, 1994), 202–4.

29. See Patrick Allitt, "The Meanings of Isaac Hecker's Conversion," *Journal of Paulist Studies* 3 (1994): 9–29, esp. 21.

O'Brien, and Margaret Reher, have shown quite clearly that in many respects Hecker *was* an "Americanist" but they regard it as a point of pride rather than shame and treat him as an avatar of the Vatican II theological style.[30] As the nineteenth century closed, however, *Testem Benevolentiae* had a chilling effect on American Catholic intellectual life, especially theology. Indeed the Catholic historian James Hennesey describes it as a "deep freeze," adding that American Catholics "now slipped more or less peaceably into a half-century's theological hibernation."[31]

Leo XIII's condemnation of Americanism shocked St. George Mivart, who had thought of Hecker as one of the brightest spirits in the church. Under the influence of men such as Hecker and Cardinal Gibbons of Baltimore he wrote, "Respect for the honest opinions of others is a sentiment which has become deeply rooted in the English mind and certainly no less in that of our cousins across the Atlantic in the present day. It is an admirable kind of 'Americanism'—an 'Americanism' eminently 'Catholic' though profoundly displeasing to 'Curialism.'"[32] Mivart, in other words, saw the condemnation as the work not of the church but a narrow "Curial" faction that was the antithesis of what he called "Catholicity." Now in his seventies, Mivart had developed diabetes and learned from his doctors that he had not long to live. Witnessing the condemnation of Americanism and angered by the French Catholic bishops' dishonorable role in the Dreyfus case, he spoke out more bluntly than ever.[33]

He had not repudiated his views on the Galileo case or the doctrine of hell even though they had been placed on the Index of forbidden books, and he now declared that Catholic intellectuals, if they were to remain plausible to outsiders, must undertake historical-critical study of the Bible in the same rigorously scientific spirit as German Protestant scholars such as Albrecht Ritschl and Adolf von Harnack. Leo XIII's encyclical *Providentissimus Deus* (1893) had disappointed him by arguing for the divine inspiration of all the Scriptures. In his view the Old Testament was largely a collection of ancient oriental folk tales, with neither historical nor moral value. "We have the revolting treachery of Jacob and his mother rewarded with a divine blessing . . . [and] the vile examples of Jael and Judith set

---

30. Margaret Mary Reher, *Catholic Intellectual Life in America: A Historical Study of Persons and Movements* (New York: Macmillan, 1989), 83–86; O'Brien, *Hecker*, 376–96; Portier, "Hecker and *Testem Benevolentiae*."

31. James Hennesey, S.J., *American Catholics: A History of the Roman Catholic Community in the United States* (New York: Oxford University Press, 1981), 203.

32. St. George Mivart, "The Continuity of Catholicism," *Nineteenth Century* 47 (January 1900): 56.

33. St. George Mivart, "The Roman Catholic Church and the Dreyfus Case," *Times* (London), October 14, 1899, 13–14.

before us with praise, and the pusillanimous and deceitful conduct of both Abraham and Isaac with respect to their wives."[34] Just as much of Scripture was historically false, he concluded, so was the notion of Catholic "continuity" from Christ's day to the present. He admitted that the church had enjoyed continuity in the sense of changing its doctrines only gradually, rather than in a dramatic shift like the Reformation, but he insisted, nevertheless, that the church was not at all what it had been in the first century. Reminding his audience that the church was an abstraction, he demonstrated that only by averting their eyes from all the evidence could traditionalists deny that they stood at the end of a long process of transformation.[35]

Mivart's esteem for modern scientific method had by then led him to look upon Catholic tradition as a source not of strength but of weakness, and this view put him at diametrical odds with his more orthodox contemporaries. "Newman has clearly shown Christians," he said, borrowing the prestige of the convert cardinal, now dead, "that they should look rather to the future than to the past, in order to obtain the clearest and fullest religious knowledge. However much we venerate 'the Fathers' it is their very remote descendants to whom we must have recourse for the fullest knowledge and best interpretation of the writings of their remote predecessors."[36] Newman, despite this tribute, would almost certainly *not* have endorsed Mivart's idea that doctrine evolved. He had insisted, to the contrary, that the deposit of faith was laid down once and for all but was worked out ("developed") over the course of time. Mivart now took the more radical position that doctrines themselves had steadily shifted over the course of church history, so that propositions once denounced as heretical had later been affirmed as infallibly true.

British and American Catholic journals joined in denouncing Mivart; some, such as the London *Tablet*, added ferocious ad hominem attacks.[37] His old antagonist, Father Clark, made a fearlessly ahistorical rejoinder in *Nineteenth Century*, maintaining that the church, far from being an abstraction, was the living body of Christ. Its doctrines were exactly the same now as when they were originally laid down and "so mutually dependent on each other, so completely bound up one with the other into one harmonious and perfect whole, that if any one of them swerved in the

34. St. George Mivart, "Scripture and Roman Catholicism," *Nineteenth Century* 47 (March 1900): 437.

35. St. George Mivart, "What Church Has Continuity?" *Nineteenth Century* 46 (August 1899): 203–12.

36. Ibid., 210.

37. Gruber, *Conscience in Conflict*, 210.

faintest or slightest degree from the truth, the whole edifice would be destroyed thereby."[38] Writing in the United States for *Catholic World*, James J. Fox also repudiated Mivart's claims, declaring that this once-great apologist of Catholicism had distorted Newman's idea of development and made himself an enemy of the faith.[39] George Searle, a Paulist priest, convert, and scientist, chided Mivart more gently with a reminder that application of scientific method could hardly be expected to solve every religious mystery. Perhaps the old man "did not fully realize the consequences which would necessarily follow from the adoption of his principles."[40] After a heated exchange of letters with Cardinal Herbert Vaughan of Westminster, all causing scandal to "pious ears" by being aired in the columns of the London *Times*, Mivart refused to sign an orthodox profession of faith and was excommunicated early in 1900. He died later that spring, unreconciled.[41]

Mivart's most outspoken defenders in England were themselves converts. One, Robert Edward Dell, mourned the excommunication and noted that by this action "the Church loses the only scientific man of repute that it could count among its adherents in England." Mivart, moreover, was "the last of the race of great converts whose influence on English Catholicism during the last half century has been so remarkable."[42]

Mivart had first been "Indexed" for his articles on hell. George Tyrrell, S.J., another convert, published a controversial article of his own on the subject of everlasting torment, "A Perverted Devotion" (1899), which began his own descent into controversy and ultimate disgrace. Tyrrell (1861–1909), says one of the many historians of Catholic modernism, was "a truly religious thinker, with something . . . of the spirit of Luther in him. . . . He was never the man for half-measures or discreet adjustments. An Irishman from Dublin, he was a born fighter whose pugnacity sometimes disturbed his best friends and well-wishers."[43] Tyrrell was the son of Irish evangelical Anglicans. His father, a controversial journalist, had passed on his disposition to his son but did not live long enough to see him

38. Father R. F. Clark, S.J., "Dr. Mivart on the Continuity of Catholicism," *Nineteenth Century* 47 (February 1900): 249, 252.

39. James J. Fox, "Dr. Mivart on the Continuity of the Church," *Catholic World* 70 (March 1900): 725–36.

40. George Searle, "Dr. Mivart's Last Utterance," *Catholic World* 71 (June 1900): 353.

41. Gruber, *Conscience in Conflict*, 212–13.

42. Robert Edward Dell, "A Liberal Catholic View of the Case of Dr. Mivart," *Nineteenth Century* 47 (April 1900): 669.

43. Bernard M. G. Reardon, *Roman Catholic Modernism* (London: Adam and Charles Black, 1970), 37.

born, so that Tyrrell's restless widowed mother, with three children to keep, lived in genteel poverty.[44]

As an intellectually precocious teenager, Tyrrell endured a period of religious skepticism before converting to Anglo-Catholicism. With Robert Dolling, later a major figure in Anglo-Catholicism, he went to London in 1879 at the age of eighteen and began attending Roman Catholic services, where at first he thought he had found a "continuity that took one back to the catacombs." Ritualistic Anglo-Catholicism in the long aftermath of the Oxford Movement exhibited what seemed to Tyrrell a staginess, whereas in the Roman church "there was no suspicion of pose or theatrical parade; its aesthetic blemishes were its very beauties for me in that mood."[45] Within two weeks of his arrival in England, he was received into the Catholic Church. Looking back on his conversion from the age of forty, he remarked that he had "drifted into the Church for a thousand paltry motives . . . much as an ignorant and drunken navigator gets his vessel into the right port by a mere fluke."[46]

Almost at once, fired with a convert's enthusiasm, he joined the Jesuits in London and, after a trial year at Jesuit schools in Cyprus and Malta, did his formal training at Manresa near London, Stonyhurst in Lancashire, and Saint Beuno's in Wales. The intellectual narrowness of his novice master at Manresa disappointed Tyrrell, as did the timidity of his fellow novices. Having read romantic hagiographical tales of the Jesuits' early days he was hoping for extravagant convert-seeking zeal and the chance for dramatic self-sacrifice rather than the orderly schoolteaching duties that appeared to await him. Moreover, he recalled later, the other novices regarded him "not as one who had courageously embraced a more difficult and somewhat paradoxical position, in lieu of an easier and more obvious one; but rather as a drunkard who had come to his senses—a repentant fool, if not a repentant rake."[47] Quelling early doubts, he returned to Stonyhurst in 1894 to teach philosophy but soon got into trouble for preferring the study of Thomas Aquinas's own works to the later, formalized scholasti-

44. Biographical information in the following passage is based on Nicholas Sagovsky, *On God's Side: A Life of George Tyrrell* (New York: Oxford University Press, 1990); Maud Petre, *The Autobiography and Life of George Tyrrell*, 2 vols. (London: Edward Arnold, 1912); Ellen Leonard, *George Tyrrell and the Catholic Tradition* (London: Darton, Longman, and Todd, 1982); David Schultenover, S.J., *George Tyrrell: In Search of Catholicism* (Shepherdstown, W.Va.: Patmos Press, 1981). The general crisis of Cathlic modernism is very well explained in O'Connell, *Critics on Trial*.

45. Tyrrell, quoted in Schultenover, *George Tyrrell*, 19.

46. Tyrrell, quoted in Leonard, *Tyrrell and Catholic Tradition*, 10.

47. Tyrrell, quoted in Schultenover, *George Tyrrell*, 22.

cism of Francisco Suarez. Tyrrell saw Aquinas as a brilliant improviser, adaptable, intellectually creative, everything his Jesuit contemporaries were not. He idolized Saint Ignatius Loyola, founder of the Jesuits, and saw in him the same ability to adapt Catholicism to new conditions. In a letter of 1899 Tyrrell referred to Ignatius as "the sixteenth century Hecker," and elsewhere he expressed high praise for the American.[48] Tyrrell was also a devoted admirer of Newman, and praised his theology and his alertness to non-Catholic intellectual developments. In a letter of 1893 he said that the study of Newman "would tend to unbarbarize us and enable us to pour Catholic truth from the scholastic into the modern mould without losing a drop in the transfer."[49]

His uneasy superiors moved him in 1896 to Farm Street, London, where in the late 1890s he led retreats and wrote for the Jesuit journal the *Month*. He was a popular spiritual director and confessor, gathering many followers, with whom he had an immense correspondence. In 1897 he met Baron von Hugel (1852–1925), an Anglo-Austrian scholar who, like Lord Acton, had a private income and an inexhaustible intellectual appetite for Catholic theology and history. Under von Hugel's guidance Tyrrell began to study the works of controversial continental theologians and historians: Adolf Harnack, Johannes Weiss, and Albert Schweitzer, all Protestants, and their Catholic counterparts Maurice Blondel, Lucien Laberthonnière, and Alfred Loisy. He was also invited by Wilfrid Ward, son of Newman's old adversary William George Ward, to join the Synthetic Society, a debating club made up of leading intellectuals from all of Britain's churches, which kept him in closer touch with Protestant ideas and developments than most of his more "ghettoized" Catholic contemporaries. When rumors began to circulate that Tyrrell was giving unorthodox ideas to Catholics who consulted him about their "difficulties" and when his 1899 article "A Perverted Devotion" criticized the doctrine of hell as untenable to modern minds, the Jesuits removed him from the *Month* and sent him to a remote Yorkshire parish at Richmond-in-Swaledale.[50]

Tyrrell's challenge to official church teachings, which emerged in his writings after 1899, was based partly on historical study and partly on his attitude toward theology. First, he immersed himself in the historical-critical study of Scripture and early church history pioneered by German

48. Letter quoted in Petre, *Autobiography and Life* 2:73. Speculating on the deplorable rigidity of the Jesuits, he told a correspondent in 1900: "I should allow a Hecker to gather a band of fellow-spirits as long as he was alive to keep up the first fervour. After his death they should die out ruthlessly" (78).
49. Letter to Ward, in Mary Jo Weaver, ed., *Letters from a Modernist: The Letters of George Tyrrell to Wilfrid Ward, 1893–1908* (Shepherdstown, W.Va.: Patmos Press, 1981), 3.
50. Sagovsky, *On God's Side*, 96–100.

liberal Protestants, much of which already lay under the restriction of the Index. He was impressed by the Germans' methods, which convinced him, like Mivart, that the present Catholic Church had "evolved" from simpler antecedents. Historical study showed, for example, that the bishop of Rome had at first been one among equals—centrally placed in the Roman Empire but having no special authority over his brother bishops elsewhere. Only with the passage of centuries, the forgery of decretals alleging early papal dominance, and temporal princes' manipulation of the church, had the idea of the pope as Catholic primate emerged. He saw in Loisy's work *L'évangile et l'église* (designed as a rebuttal to Harnack) a not-to-be-missed opportunity for the Catholic Church to reconcile itself with historical-critical method and retain intellectual plausibility in the eyes of non-Catholics: "The conclusion will soon be drawn for us by outsiders and we shall find ourselves with no *modus vivendi* if we now burn the boats that [Loisy] has prepared for our escape," he told von Hugel in 1902.[51]

Tyrrell lamented the declaration of papal infallibility at the Vatican Council. It was, in his view, a declaration of historical ignorance which bespoke contempt for history by reading a new idea back into earlier epochs. He noted that as recently as 1800 "the Catholics of England and Ireland read in their approved catechism (Keenan's Catechism) that the doctrine of papal infallibility was the invention of Protestant calumniators."[52] The view that an ecumenical council of bishops was the highest source of church authority was more defensible on historical grounds.

Second, and closely related to history, was Tyrrell's theology. The Thomistic revival since Leo XIII's encyclical *Aeterni Patris* dismayed him because it was increasingly ahistorical, deductive, and detached from personal experience. By the early years of the twentieth century Tyrrell was sure that theology had to start from the personal *experience* of revelation, rather than from sterile intellectual premises that were often remote from it. Closely attuned to the turn-of-the-century philosophical mood expressed in the work of Henri Bergson, and in William James's *Varieties of Religious Experience* (1902), Tyrrell argued that the church's role was to guide Catholics in interpreting their religious experiences in light of its accumulated wisdom but not to impose doctrines on them under threat of punishment. Faith must come first. "For all the service theology may render to faith, we may find a maximum of faith consistent in certain

51. Tyrrell, quoted in Schultenover, *George Tyrrell*, 252.
52. George Tyrrell, *Medievalism*, ed. Gabriel Daly (Tunbridge Wells, Kent: Burns and Oates, 1994), 50.

circumstances with a minimum of theology."[53] Attuned also to the evolutionary idiom, he assumed that in different ages religious experience itself gained in complexity and refinement and that doctrine must be modified to fit each new era: "The understanding is subject to a process of rapid transformation from generation to generation. According as the results of experience, observation, and inquiry accumulate, new arrangements, new systems of classification, new methods are requisite to deal with this tangle of matter and get it into serviceable shape and order."[54] Like Mivart, he was trying to push further arguments that Newman had outlined in *On the Development of Doctrine*.[55]

These historical and theological views, expressed in a succession of books, brought Tyrrell a reputation for dangerous controversy, first in England and later in Rome. Several of them, including *The Church and the Future* (1903), which urged a transformation of the church from an authoritarian institution to "an art-school of Divine Majesty," were published privately and under pseudonyms (in that one he was Hilaire Bourdon).[56] But his style was so distinctive and his arguments so hard-hitting, that none of these incognitos provided adequate cover for long. Baron von Hugel admired Tyrrell but warned him of the need for circumspection, especially in view of the severity of the new pope, Pius X. Maud Petre, a Catholic admirer who was in love with him and with whom he had a vast correspondence, pleaded with him to mollify the authorities who were moving reluctantly to condemn one of their most brilliant scholars. (Despite her love, she had no wish to make him compromise or betray his vows and indeed took her own vow of chastity. Tyrrell depended on her love and support but often treated her cruelly and dismissively.)[57]

Tyrrell was combative in most of his personal dealings, always ready to argue and reluctant to back down. He made it too evident that he regarded most of his fellow Jesuits as his intellectual inferiors. He did nothing to build up a party of sympathizers to intercede for him or to soften his fall. In 1906 an Italian newspaper, *Corriere della Sera* got hold of the "confidential letter to a professor of Anthropology" that he had written in 1903 and published some spectacular extracts, such as that "the positions of conservative Catholics can only be maintained by force of systematic or

53. George Tyrrell, *A Much-Abused Letter* (London: Longmans Green, 1906), 32.
54. Ibid., 29.
55. Reardon, *Roman Catholic Modernism*, 45. Reardon notes that Newman had had a profound effect on Tyrrell earlier but that Tyrrell had outgrown him, telling a correspondent: "I do not think his [Newman's] effort to unite the conception of development with the Catholic conception of tradition was successful or coherent; but it has given an impulse to thought which may issue in some more successful effort."
56. Sagovsky, *On God's Side*, 158.
57. Ibid., 202–14.

wilful ignorance."[58] Tyrrell's superiors drew from him the admission that he was the author and demanded a retraction, but he refused. Instead, he published the complete text of the letter, along with a commentary. He denied that it was heretical, insisting, rather, that it was "medicinal," containing strong passages only because the man he had been advising felt severely threatened by the conflict between science and Catholic doctrine. (He was being disingenuous: there was no "professor of anthropology.") His method, he said, "assumes that if a man is absolutely and practically sincere to whatever little measure of religious and moral truth he still holds, he is bound to advance to whatever fuller measure of truth may be necessary for him. It assumes that nothing short of conscious and deliberate wickedness of some kind or other can separate a man from communion with Christ and His Church." The current generation of Vatican theologians, whom his "friend" found troublesome, he added, were sincere men of goodwill, but then so were the Jewish scribes and Pharisees who condemned Jesus and who, *by their reckoning*, were right to do so! The object of his letter was not to attack theology "but to thrust it down to its proper place at the footstool of Faith." When he refused to renounce these views, the Jesuits expelled him.[59]

In April 1907 Pius X issued a decree, *Lamentabili Sane Exitu*, enumerating the "modernist" ideas, methods, and principles that were to be added to the Index, among them the application of evolution and historical-critical method. Pius elaborated five months later with an encyclical letter, *Pascendi Dominici Gregis*, which banned Catholics from all these elements of intellectual life, categorized them collectively as "modernism," and threatened excommunication for transgressors.[60] A. L. Lilley, an Anglican commentator sympathetic to Tyrrell, wrote that "this supposed Modernist system is but a perverse figment of the imagination of the clever and inveterately scholastic theologian to whom Pius X entrusted the drafting of the encyclical," and most historians since then have agreed that modernism was not a coordinated movement.[61] In 1910 Pius added a stipulation, in *Sacrorum Antistitum*, requiring priests to take an anti-modernist oath and all Catholic teachers to renew their oath each year—a rule that remained in force until 1967. Many Catholic historians today remember this episode as one of the most shameful in their history. One writes:

58. Tyrrell, *Much-Abused Letter*, 3.
59. Ibid., 28, 101; Sagovsky, *On God's Side*, 201–2.
60. O'Connell, *Critics on Trial*, 338–54.
61. Lilley, quoted in Alec Vidler, *The Modernist Movement in the Roman Catholic Church: Its Origins and Outcome* (Cambridge: Cambridge University Press, 1934), 4.

The encyclical *Pascendi* . . . inaugurated a period of ecclesiastical Mc-Carthyism when "modernists" were hunted down with a zeal that was as pathological as the paranoia that fed it. . . . Vigilance committees met in solemn conclave to determine who was guilty, or at least suspect, of this newest and most nebulous of heresies. Career-oriented priests denounced their colleagues. A climate of fear prevailed throughout the Church.[62]

Cardinal Joseph Mercier, the archbishop of Malines, Belgium, offered the former Jesuit Tyrrell a position as secular priest in his diocese in 1907, on condition that Tyrrell submit all his writings to the archbhishop's censor before publication. Tyrrell declined. He also refused to revert to Anglicanism despite the urging of old friends. That Catholic officials were now persecuting him, he declared, did not change his belief that the Catholic Church was the sole guardian of true Christianity. He treated them as an impertinent crowd of innovators trying to uproot an old tradition of church consensus rather than as the legitimate heirs of Saint Peter and insisted that he must remain a Catholic for the sake of coreligionists in the same situation. "I feel that my work is to hammer away at the great unwieldy carcase of the Roman Communion and wake it up from its medieval dreams. Not that I shall succeed, but that my failure and many another may pave the way for eventual success."[63]

Cardinal Mercier, under Vatican disapproval for his offer of clemency, gave up on Tyrrell. In 1908 he wrote a Lenten pastoral letter condemning modernism in general and naming Tyrrell as its foremost exponent, as a way of righting himself in the eyes of the Curia. In Tyrrell's work, wrote Mercier, "we often find . . . the parent-idea of Protestantism. Little wonder, for Tyrrell is a convert, whose early education was Protestant."[64] Tyrrell, like Newman, Simpson, Hecker, and Mivart before him, was discovering that the fact of his being a convert could seem ominous to his born-Catholic adversaries. R. F. Clark, S.J., had said of Mivart that he was one of those converts who "never made in their heart the necessary act of complete intellectual submission to [the church's] teaching." Having entered the church precincts, such converts "bring their private judgment with them . . . instead of bidding it farewell on the threshold. They continue to act on their private judgment just as they did before. . . . Thus they are *in* the Church but not *of* it."[65]

Learning of Mercier's pastoral, Tyrrell wrote a furious and satirical re-

62. Gabriel Daly, Foreword to Tyrrell, *Medievalism*, 10.
63. Tyrrell, quoted in Reardon, *Roman Catholic Modernism*, 47n.
64. Mercier's Lenten Pastoral is reprinted in Tyrrell, *Medievalism*, 21–34; I quote from 26.
65. Clark, "Dr. Mivart on the Continuity of Catholicism," 254.

buttal, *Medievalism* (1908), which crystallized his attitudes and placed him outside the Catholic pale once and for all. On theology Tyrrell wrote that Mercier had misrepresented him, falsely implying that he had opposed its value altogether:

I believe firmly in the necessity and utility of theology; but of a living theology that continually proceeds from and returns to that experience of which it is the ever tentative and perfectible analysis. . . . What I deny is a theology that draws ideas from ideas, instead of from experience; that gives us shadows of shadows instead of shadows of reality; that wanders further and further from facts along the path of curious and unverified deductions; that makes itself the tyrant instead of the servant of religious life.

It was not he who had betrayed church tradition, but the "new theologians," that is, the current generation of Vatican authorities, who aimed to make "ornamental nonentities of the bishops; and to substitute, as the rule of faith, the private judgment of the Pope instead of the public judgment of the whole Church as represented by the entire episcopate." Glancing over his shoulder in the way of many converts, Tyrrell asked, "Can you wonder if Protestants speak of 'Papolatry' or of the Pope as the anti-Christ who sets himself up as God in the temple of God?"[66] The fiery challenges thrown out in *Medievalism* he followed up more temperately in *Christianity at the Crossroads* (1909) the next year, showing that for all his criticisms and conflicts, his Christian faith was burning as strongly as ever.[67] Adrian Hastings describes it as "perhaps the finest apologetic vindication of Catholicism ever written in English."[68] But by the time of its publication Tyrrell had died of Bright's disease, at the age of only forty-eight. Dying excommunicate and unreconciled, he was denied burial in consecrated Catholic ground and so was laid to rest in the Anglican churchyard of Storrington, Sussex. Only one English Catholic priest, the convert Basil Maturin, attended. Hastings comments that "no other English Christian of the twentieth century has been so harshly treated, none other privileged to share so utterly in the condemnation and lonely death of the Saviour."[69]

The chief exponents of modernism were English and French, but there was also, as the historian Scott Appleby expresses it, a modernist "spirit" in American Catholicism, expressed by a group of priests and scientists at Notre Dame, Saint Joseph's Seminary in Dunwoodie, New York, and in a

66. Tyrrell, *Medievalism*, 54, 50, 73.

67. George Tyrrell, *Christianity at the Crossroads* (London: Longmans Green, 1909).

68. Adrian Hastings, *A History of English Christianity, 1920–1990* (London: Collins, 1986), 155.

69. Ibid., 155.

short-lived journal, the *New York Review*. Leading spirits were the Notre Dame chemistry and physics professor John Zahm, whose *Evolution and Dogma* (1896) was an attempt, in the spirit of Mivart, to reconcile the church to the new biology; and William Sullivan, a biblical critic impressed by the cogency of Tyrrell's historical-critical approach. As Appleby says, "Their work was largely derivative in that they drew upon, and developed for their own audiences, the insights of European Catholic modernists such a Alfred Loisy, George Tyrrell, and St. George Mivart." Although they "did not match their European counterparts in boldness of vision and sophistication of argument," he adds, they tried to expand on the work of Hecker and add a scientific dimension to Americanism in the years before its prohibition.[70] When Leo XIII condemned Americanism and then Pius X prohibited modernism, these Americans were faced with the choice of retracting their views or repudiating the church altogether. Zahm and Mivart had been regular correspondents, but whereas the convert had faced up to excommunication, the priest withdrew his book from circulation under threat of condemnation by the Index.[71] Sullivan left the church in disgust and wrote one of the most trenchant condemnations of the antimodernist Vatican.[72]

Tyrrell was the last of the English or American converts to argue that the Catholic Church was an intellectual pioneer. In the new century the church would continue to win converts of the highest intellectual stature, but henceforth they would generally steer away from theology and find the church's strength in its *resistance* to intellectual novelties and its deference to an enduring tradition and a strong authority principle. The condemnation of modernism therefore marks a watershed. Convert intellectuals remained dominant in the English and American Catholic churches for the next fifty years but no longer as theological pathfinders. Most from then on were, to the contrary, pillars of orthodoxy, willing to accept the lessons of the Vatican Council and *Pascendi* and to act as apologists in their defense. Only very gradually would Tyrrell's memory find a later generation of convert intellectuals willing to resume his challenge to neoscholastic theology and imperious Vatican authority.

70. Appleby, *Church and Age Unite!* 2, 4.
71. Ibid., 49–50.
72. William Laurence Sullivan, *Letters to His Holiness Pope Pius X* (Chicago: Open Court, 1910).

# VII

# THE LOWLINESS
# OF HIS HANDMAIDENS
## *Women and Conversion*

T HE MOST FAMOUS CONVERTS to Catholicism in Britain and America between 1840 and 1960 were men, but many women were also attracted to Rome. In some respects the women's situation was comparable to that of male converts. They were generally of Anglo-Saxon rather than Irish or southern European origin, better educated than born Catholics, more articulate, wealthier, and better connected socially, intellectually, and politically. These qualities gave them the opportunity to wield influence in their new community, and they pioneered in several areas of Catholic life. The first woman to win Notre Dame's Laetare Medal was a convert (Eliza Allen Starr), as were the first woman to get a doctorate from Villanova University (Elizabeth Kite), the first woman columnist in a Catholic journal (Katherine Burton), and the first woman president of a Catholic scholarly association (Eva Ross). But their gender made a crucial difference in the strongly patriarchal Catholic environment, whose traditions encouraged them to play the role of self-effacing wives and mothers. Catholic notions of woman's place and their own self-limitation muted both their influence and the range of their work.

To our eyes, therefore, women converts seem to have been simultaneously privileged by comparison with their born coreligionists, yet fenced in by the ideals of their new faith and by its low status in non-Catholics' eyes. In their own eyes, of course, conversion meant the *removal* rather than the creation of barriers, and several of them gladly suffered the loss of social and material benefits to put on the Roman yoke. They were all convinced that they had found their true spiritual home in Catholicism, and I can find no convert women who overtly criticized the church until the very end of this period, except on aesthetic questions.[1] Nevertheless, it is possible to trace in their work some of the stresses and paradoxes of conversion. Becoming Catholics out of religious conviction, they at once joined a community that shared a range of ideas and beliefs on many other issues quite at odds with their own. Some adapted their ideas to their new faith; others remained culturally "Protestant" in most respects.

They nearly all struggled with conflicting feelings about their role as Catholic women. The circumstances of their own lives demonstrated that realities did not conform neatly to the Catholic ideal of submissive wife and mother. In almost every case they became writers *instead* of marrying or after their marriages had ended with their husbands' deaths or else in separation. They were not antagonistic to men, however, and most avowed a natural complementarity between the two sexes, with men dominant and themselves subordinate. In fact, the memoirs and letters of nearly all convert women writers show them soliciting the guidance of priests and male friends before taking important decisions.

Women's historians of the last three decades have documented the "separate spheres" ideology of late nineteenth-century Britain and the United States—the idea that the two genders had different and complementary roles to play, rather than a large measure of interchangeability and equality. Marriage and motherhood were central to the role of women in the "cult of true womanhood." Even reformers who advocated a larger political role for women often justified it in domestic terms, arguing, for example, that women should be involved in "national housekeeping," bringing their superior moral capacities to bear on public as well as private questions. More often, of course, the ideology kept women out of public life, higher education, and professional careers.[2]

1. Ellen Gates Starr asked a Paulist priest to admit her to the Catholic Church but he resisted at first, suspecting that she was drawn to it solely for aesthetic reasons. She wrote: "I smiled interiorly . . . at the assumption that the attraction towards the Catholic Church could ever have been, for me, in my own country, an aesthetic one; the almost uniform ugliness of American Catholic churches and their appointments, decorations, and articles of devotion being one of the trials which a Catholic of taste and education has to endure with what fortitude he may in this land. . . . And not less painful is the horror of operatic music, and modern religious tawdriness." Ellen Gates Starr, "A By-path into the Great Roadway," *Catholic World* 119 (May 1924): 186.
2. Nancy Cott, *The Grounding of Modern Feminism* (New Haven: Yale University Press, 1987), 115–43. On women's higher education and professional careers, see Ellen Fitzpatrick, *Endless Crusade: Women Social Scientists and Progressive Reform* (New York: Oxford University Press, 1990). For Catholic dimensions, see Mary Jo Weaver, *New Catholic*

Articulate Catholics were as convinced as their Protestant neighbors that emphasizing gender differences confirmed natural realities. Meanwhile, the Catholic symbol of the Virgin Mary pointed to motherhood as an elevated vocation. Protestants frowned on the cult of Mary as a form of idolatry, but converts to Catholicism frequently dedicated their devotional lives to the Virgin and found her a consoling and rewarding figure. Mary represented the two virtues of virginity and motherhood simultaneously, an impossible blend for ordinary women! By giving as much weight to her virginity as to her motherhood, however, the church implicitly conferred a high dignity on unmarried women. At times it seemed to laud virginity even more strongly than motherhood. Catholic women who took the veil certainly enjoyed an honored place in the church, and at least until Vatican II Catholic moral theology treated married life as a slightly inferior status, allotted to those who could not live up to the rigorous higher ideal of celibacy. Moreover, a long tradition of glorifying Mary as the queen of heaven suggests a female symbol of greater power than anything Protestantism could offer. As the historian Colleen McDannell has shown, this empowering aspect of Mary caused devotees of domesticity some unease; they often compensated by depicting Mary as a submissive Nazareth housewife.[3]

In the mid-nineteenth century nearly all Catholic women who broke into print were converts. Later, born Catholics played a larger role in Catholic literary life, though even then they were often the daughters of converts. At first many of the converts shrank from public notice, publishing their work anonymously or under male pseudonyms. The American novelist Pearl Craigie (1867–1906), for example, who enjoyed a spectacular success in England in the 1890s, wrote as John Oliver Hobbes and kept her identity secret.[4] Similarly, Frances Tiernan (1846–1920), another prolific American novelist, wrote as Christian Reid, and her peer Mary Agnes Tincker (1831–1907) came before the public as "M.A.T."[5] In the early twentieth century converts were less bashful. The apologetic content of

*Women: A Contemporary Challenge to Traditional Religious Authority* (1986; Bloomington: University of Indiana Press, 1995), 1–36.

3. James Kenneally, "Eve, Mary, and the Historians," in Janet W. James, ed., *Women in American Religion* (Philadelphia: University of Pennsylvania Press, 1980), 191–206; Kenneally, *The History of American Catholic Women* (New York: Crossroads, 1990); Colleen McDannell, "Catholic Domesticity," in Karen Kennelly, ed., *American Catholic Women: A Historical Exploration* (New York: Macmillan, 1989), 48–80.

4. On the life and work of John Oliver Hobbes, see Margaret Maison, *John Oliver Hobbes: Her Life and Work* (London: Eighteen Nineties Society, 1976).

5. On Frances Tiernan, see Sister Luce Marie, O.P., "Christian Reid," in *The Book of Catholic Authors*, 4th ser., ed. Walter Romig (Grosse Pointe, Mich.: Walter Romig, 1948); Kenneally, *History of Catholic Women*, 27–30.

# CATHOLIC CONVERTS

their work became less strident and their willingness to challenge or refine Catholic social and intellectual traditions increased. Eva Ross (born 1903), who converted in 1927, for example, was an outspoken critic of Catholic racism, and Katherine Burton (born 1890) reproached the bishops for denigrating working women. Dorothy Day (1897–1980), who is by now the best known of the American women converts, espoused strict religious orthodoxy, yet challenged conventions in society and the Catholic Church by working as a radical lay leader without clerical guidance. Clare Boothe Luce (1903–1987), the American playwright, congresswoman, and ambassador, never shrank from publicity, and her 1946 conversion at the hands of Monsignor Fulton Sheen was a media event. Luce took advantage of her privileged social position to bend the church's rules to her advantage: she was a divorcée but took no steps to discard her second husband, Henry Luce, to whom, in the church's eyes, she was not legally married.[6] As these examples suggest, convert women in the twentieth century became willing to test rules and to act in what for Catholics were unconventional ways.

A central theme of this book is that converts played a large part in creating an English-language Catholic literature and intellectual life in the nineteenth and twentieth century, giving it an indigenous form and character for the first time after the long post-Reformation hiatus. Newman, Ward, Brownson, Hecker, Tyrrell, and other convert men, all gifted controversialists, wrote extensively on theology and played an active role in the theological disputes of the era, particularly the debate over papal infallibility, which came to a head at the first Vatican Council and the debate over Catholic modernism at the turn of the century. Their concern with theology is hardly surprising since intense theological concerns had induced them to change their religion in the first place. By contrast, women converts never wrote on theology, and so far as I can tell, none of them even remarked on this omission, though they had as much reason as the men to be seriously interested in theological questions. Theology may have been the queen of the sciences, but her ladies in waiting were, without exception, men. Only in the 1960s in the work of Rosemary Ruether and Mary Daly would come the first budding of a Catholic women's theology. Women converts wrote novels, poetry, and history, and on art, literature, social reform, and sociology. Since they stayed away from doctrinally sensitive matters, none fell afoul of official displeasure, and what-

6. On Clare Boothe Luce, see Stephen Shadegg, *Clare Boothe Luce: A Biography* (New York: Simon and Schuster, 1970); Wilfrid Sheed, *Clare Boothe Luce* (New York: Dutton, 1982).

ever censure they suffered came from unfavorable press notices or from their own consciences, not from church officials.

Like their male counterparts they aimed at two audiences: Catholics, on one side, and other potential converts, on the other. With this dual audience in view, various writing strategies were possible. Some nineteenth-century novelists, including Frances Tiernan and Anna Dorsey (1815–1890) favored a heavy-handed didacticism as though they thought they could cajole Protestants into submission to Rome. Many of their novels consist of organized processions of Protestants turning from falsehood to Catholic truth, converting in response to their Catholic friends' syllogistic persuasions.[7] Later generations of convert women chose a less didactic tone and tried to make a favorable intellectual impression on potential converts. Incrementally, they hoped, successive generations would follow them by converting to the one true church.

The tensions involved in the position of an early woman convert can be appreciated in the life of the art historian and teacher Eliza Allen Starr, who presided over a Chicago salon, wrote seven books on Catholic art, and founded the art department at Saint Mary's College, South Bend, Indiana. She had a "majestic theory" that "the Catholic Church will give a crowning grace to the art and literature of America."[8] She was also one of the founding members of the Catholic Women's League, which established day-care centers, helped working women find jobs, and advocated votes for women. Her detachment from Protestantism and her adherence to Catholicism both came in response to male authority figures. In 1846, aged twenty-two, she heard the preaching of the Boston Unitarian Theodore Parker. "I was prepared for an intellectual and spiritual banquet," she wrote later, "which would mark an era in my life. It certainly did so mark it, but in a way how different from that which I had anticipated! For as sentence after sentence came from the lips of the renowned preacher, first a tremor, then an actual chill came over me, as with smoothly flowing language, but irresistible logic, I found him demolishing every foundation-stone of my religious faith, and even hope."[9] For the following nine years Starr endured a prolonged crisis of religious faith, and it was only under the guidance of Francis Kenrick, archbishop of Baltimore, and of

---

7. See, for example, Christian Reid [Frances Tiernan], *Nina's Atonement and Other Stories* (New York: Appleton, 1873); Anna Dorsey, *Ada's Trust* (Baltimore: John Murphy, 1887); Dorsey, *The Old House at Glenaran* (Baltimore: John Murphy, 1887).

8. James J. McGovern, ed., *The Life and Letters of Eliza Allen Starr* (Chicago: Lakeside, 1905), 270. This book is also my source for biographical information on Starr.

9. Ibid., 34.

her cousin, George Allen, a University of Pennsylvania professor of classics and himself a convert, that she finally became a Catholic in 1854. Having made up her mind to it, she became intensely fervent and applied for admission to a convent but was discouraged because of her poor health. In the event she lived (to the age of seventy-seven) as a member of the Third Order of Saint Dominic, staying in "the world" but attending mass every day and living a life of mortification and self-denial. She never published her books, poems, and articles before getting her cousin's approval.

In the mid-nineteenth century, interfaith hostilities were at their most intense. The mass immigration of poor Irish Catholics had caused a Protestant backlash that found organized expression in the Know-Nothing Party. Rebecca Reed's *Six Months in a Convent* (1835) and Maria Monk's lurid *Awful Disclosures* (1836) became anti-Catholic best sellers in the 1840s and 1850s.[10] Protestant families nourished on these and similar anti-Catholic tracts often reacted in horror to the conversion of their daughters, who faced the paradox of introducing discord into a family life that their new religion taught them to hold sacred. This was the atmosphere in which the convert novelists Dorsey and Tiernan proposed a mirror image of the Know-Nothing view, demonizing Protestant characters and boosting Catholic characters to a condition of eerie sanctity. Eliza Allen Starr, endowed with a large fund of Yankee common sense, disliked the polemical war and tried to improve interfaith relations. Having lived on both sides of the divide, she was convinced that it was created by fear and misunderstanding rather than malice. Straightforwardness would put things right. In August 1866 a Methodist family visited her, and one of them noticed the photograph of a Catholic bishop above the fireplace. She "asked me abruptly about it," Starr recalled:

I knew then that she was a Catholic, but how could it be with old Mr. M. . . . for a grandfather? He had handed my brother such awful books against Catholics, so bad my brother would not read them. After a little time the other ladies strolled out to see the flowers, and in three minutes we understood each other. I took her to my room, to my little altar. . . . We said some Aves and the litany and the Salve Regina together, and I think she

10. Maria Monk, *Awful Disclosures of the Hotel Dieu Nunnery of Montreal* (1836; Hamden, Conn.: Archon Books, 1962); Rebecca Reed, *Six Months in a Convent* (1835; Boston: American Citizen, 1893). On the persistence of Protestant anti-Catholicism, see Barbara Welter, "From Maria Monk to Paul Blanshard: A Century of Protestant Anti-Catholicism," in Robert Bellah and Frederick Greenspahn, eds., *Uncivil Religion: Interreligious Hostility in America* (New York: Crossroads, 1987), 43–59. See also Ray Alan Billington, *The Protestant Crusade, 1800–1860: A Story of the Origins of American Nativism* (New York: Macmillan, 1938).

felt as much better as I did for a little Catholic sympathy. . . . When we returned to the parlor I spoke of everything as a Catholic naturally would. The ladies were charmed to find they were not treated as outsiders. I showed them pictures, explained them, and to explain them was to explain much that was in the Church. I even showed them my rosary and crucifix, said an Ave for them; one could see they were dying of curiosity. After tea I quietly asked the aunt to my room, and there before the little altar she promised not to believe, or appear to believe, about Catholics what she now knew to be false. . . . They left in fine spirits, and mine were restored.[11]

Starr could reproach Catholics as well as their antagonists and never emulated apologists who saw all the faults on the Protestant side. In the American agrarian tradition she thought it shameful that most Catholics huddled in cities rather than becoming settlers and farmers in the healthful western countryside, adding: "I wonder why all our priests cleave to the city as they do, with its squalor and misery, instead of coming of their own free will to these airy places where there is such a field for Christian labor?" To her, as to her English counterpart Augustus Pugin, it seemed "monstrous" to find most American Catholics totally indifferent to their religion's rich artistic, musical, and literary heritage. She noted that the revival of Gregorian chant, exquisite ancient Catholic music, was taking place in *Episcopalian* churches, "while Catholic congregations grumbled over its reintroduction to our choirs. They are not satisfied unless they can have a polka to come out of church by."[12]

Starr's contemporary Mary Agnes Tincker, who converted in 1855, also wanted to reduce intercommunity tensions and recognized that no religious group in America had a monopoly of virtue. Her novel *Grapes and Thorns* (1874) illustrates her views. The plot pivots on a murderer's confession to Father Chevreuse that he is responsible for the murder of Chevreuse's own saintly mother. Not only is the priest bound by his vows to keep this confession secret, he also has to watch an innocent man be convicted of the crime through circumstantial evidence and condemned to death. The innocent man is Jewish, the real murderer a Catholic. Through a sequence of melodramatic developments and coincidences, the Jew's innocence is established just as he mounts the gallows. He is so impressed by the patience and goodness of another unprejudiced Catholic woman who has believed him innocent throughout the ordeal that, once set free, he converts to Catholicism and they marry. Meanwhile the culprit, once a vain, dandified gambler and rake, is brought to judgment by his own

11. McGovern, *Life and Letters of Starr*, 259–60.
12. Ibid., 294, 275–76.

conscience and spends his last years as a self-mortifying poor laborer in Rome, shadowed by his adoring wife who has repudiated her own vanity (and money) and risen to greatness through suffering.[13]

Tincker was emphatic that salvation comes only within the church, but she knew that Catholicism was anything but synonymous with goodness. *Grapes and Thorns* depicts many of the Catholic townsfolk as violently anti-Semitic: one woman believes that "every Jew is a Judas. That he could be moral, that he could adore his creator, and pray earnestly for forgiveness of his sins, she did not for an instant believe. The worst criminal, if nominally Catholic, was in her eyes infinitely preferable to the best Jew in the world." Conversely Tincker spells out good interfaith gestures from the town's Protestants. When Father Chevreuse is robbed of two thousand dollars, which he had collected for his church building fund, "some wealthy Protestants . . . made up for Father Chevreuse the money he had lost, and thus soothed their regret for the loss which they could not repair to him."[14] In her own life Tincker had witnessed interreligious hostilities when a Jesuit priest in her home town of Ellsworth, Maine, was tarred and feathered by a Know-Nothing mob, and she made the incident central to her first, semiautobiographical novel, *The House of Yorke*.[15]

Neither of these advocates of conciliation, Eliza Allen Starr nor Mary Agnes Tincker, ever married. Elizabeth Kite (1864–1954), another Catholic convert, took a vow of chastity after discovering that the man she loved, a sun-bronzed geologist in Colorado, was already married. Kite was born and raised a Quaker and spent much of her twenties and thirties as a girls' schoolteacher in Philadelphia and Nantucket. She converted to Catholicism at the age of forty, after a series of religious experiences in London. Just as Starr faced a crisis of faith in response to a preacher's sermon, so too did Kite. Feeling intellectually and spiritually dissatisfied after flirting with socialism, Hinduism, and theosophy around the turn of the century, she attended a sermon in Westminster Abbey, only to find the preacher dispensing the cold comfort of the historical-critical method:

I was a starving soul begging imploringly for the bread of life. But all the minister had to offer were *stones, stones, stones,* or rather baked clay tablets from old Babylon, with which he frittered away the whole Gospel narrative as an absurd myth. . . . It seemed to me that Almighty God had permitted

13. Mary Agnes Tincker, *Grapes and Thorns* (New York: Catholic Publishing Society, 1874).

14. Ibid., 39, 73.

15. Mary Agnes Tincker, *The House of Yorke* (New York: Catholic Publishing Society, 1872). See also Kenneally, *History of Catholic Women*, 38–42.

me to hear the very worst this evidently popular speaker could do in the way of giving a so-called higher criticism interpretation of the Christian religion, so that never again would I turn to the Church of England when in search of spiritual food.[16]

After that she began to visit a Catholic church. She found herself there on Holy Thursday, 1904, joining a procession to kiss the feet of the crucified Jesus. As she did so she experienced an intense psychological or spiritual sensation:

As I rose the corpus as it were came alive and as I gazed, a glance from under the partly closed lids struck to the inmost center of my being cleaving me in twain. For I, from above the feet, distinctly saw myself, even to the dress I wore that day, with head bowed and downcast eyes, join the retreating line of worshippers. At the time I did not understand, but I now see that what had happened was the miracle of *Belief*—a pure gift from the divine heart of Jesus. (352)

Within a few weeks she had taken instruction and was confirmed in the Catholic faith. Unlike many converts of the previous generation, Kite did not have to suffer rebukes or reproaches from her relatives. Indeed, "since that time there has never been an incident where anything but the kindest feelings and pleasantest associations have existed between me and my Quaker relatives and friends."[17] In the following decades Kite persuaded fifteen members of her extended family to follow her example and convert.[18]

Elizabeth Kite was an effective and capable woman, but at the same time, she was self-effacing, preferring to shelter behind strong male figures and to give them credit for much of the work she had done. She spent the second half of her ninety-year life working in two distinct careers, one of which was fully consonant with her new religion, the other bizarrely contradictory. The first of these careers she chose during the same momentous midlife London expedition on which she converted, inspired by the teaching of Emil Reich, a Hungarian Jewish professor. His lecture on the confrontation of Emperor Henry IV and Pope Gregory VII in the snowy Alps

16. Elizabeth Kite, "A Conversion Story: From Quakerism to the Catholic Church" (typescript, Kite Papers, Rutgers University Archives), 3. This manuscript, the only source I have found for her biography, is jumbled. It contains one long section with sequentially numbered pages and, in addition, a series of short chapters each numbered from 1. Parenthetical figures in the text here represent page numbers from the long section.

17. Kite, "Conversion Story,"" chap. 7, p. 5.

18. An anonymous introduction to the "Conversion Story" makes this claim about the fifteen converts.

had an effect on Kite almost as profound as had her religious conversion. "That lecture was to have a definitive effect upon my entire future career. . . . [It] roused my historical imagination so that it became an instrument capable of being used in all future studies to which I devoted myself" (322). Reich's description of a moment when the pope enjoyed a great victory over the temporal power showed Kite Catholicism in a new light, as a great *historical* religion, the "miracle of the ages," which combined "perfect democracy with perfect authority."[19] History became for her a quasi-religious vocation.

Under Reich's tutelage and inspiration and with the full approval of her new confessor, Kite now began to research and write the history of France's role in the American Revolutionary War. She aimed to show that American independence had been made possible through the aid of a Catholic power and that French aid had been based on religious feeling as well as balance-of-power considerations. Her research took her back and forth among London, Paris, and Washington, and for the last three decades of her life she was an almost permanent fixture in the Library of Congress, where she helped reform the library's holdings in French diplomatic history and became a founding member of the Institut Français de Washington. Her research was meticulous and painstaking, eventuating in seven books and dozens of articles, all of which can be summarized thus: without the aid of Catholic France and its pious king, Louis XVI, the United States would never have become independent. "It goes without saying that up to the present the part played by Catholics, as Catholics, in the great drama of the war of American Independence has been consistently ignored by historians," she wrote in one characteristic article, adding that she was now telling the story in its full dimensions and setting the record straight.[20] Aware that the most famous French volunteer for the Revolutionary cause, the marquis de Lafayette, had been a freethinker, Kite denigrated his role in the Revolution while exalting those played by good Catholics, notably Louis Duportail, the artillery commander, and Pierre-August Caron de Beaumarchais, the supervisor of covert aid in the early revolutionary years.[21] Through the 1920s, 1930s, and 1940s, Kite doubled as archivist and librarian of the Catholic Historical Society of

19. Elizabeth Kite, "Dr. Emil Reich, as he appeared to an Americane [*sic*] in 1904–1906," (typescript, Kite Papers), n.p.
20. Elizabeth Kite, "Hard Money for Colonial Soldiers at Valley Forge Given by Catholic France," *National Catholic Welfare Conference Editorial Sheet* 8 (September 1927): 4.
21. Her histories include *Beaumarchais and the War of American Independence* (Boston: R. G. Badger, 1918), *Brigadier-General Louis Lebegue Duportail* (Baltimore: Johns Hopkins University Press, 1933), and *The Catholic Part in the Making of America* (Philadelphia: Dolphin Press, 1936).

Philadelphia, contributing regularly to its journal and becoming a distinguished and honored elder stateswoman among Catholic historians.

Coming from a venerable American Protestant family, Kite made it her mission to force honest patriots to admit that the nation—antipopery prejudice notwithstanding—owed its genesis to the selfless work of *Catholics*. Other convert scholars in the early twentieth century worked along similar lines. The historians Gaillard Hunt, Ross Hoffman, and Carlton Hayes, for example, all argued that the U.S. Constitution embodied the wisdom of the "great tradition" of natural law political philosopy which traced its roots back through the pagan-Christian synthesis in Aquinas to the principles of Augustine's *City of God*. All denied that its intellectual origins could be traced to John Locke. Kite's work on Franco-American relations contributed a new dimension to this wide-ranging effort to "Catholicize" American history.

Kite's other postconversion career also put her historical research and French-language skills to good use, but in a very different direction, to which nearly all born Catholics and the church hierarchy were hostile. It serves as a reminder that for Kite, a fervent Catholic faith existed side by side with a sustained interest in the "progressive" experiments she had studied in her pre-Catholic days. She was, between 1909 and 1920, a psychological researcher at the Training School for the "feebleminded" in Vineland, N.J., under the guidance of Henry H. Goddard, a leading eugenicist. Eugenics later took on the ugly flavor of Nazism but in the early twentieth century it seemed to its exponents a progressive scheme for the improvement of the population. Liberals of the era generally favored eugenic reforms: Catholics generally opposed them because eugenicists seemed to be trespassing on God's sacred ground, attributing greater value to some lives than others, rather than according a spiritual equality to all. (Catholic opposition to eugenics in the early twentieth century was a direct forerunner of Catholic opposition to abortion in more recent decades.) The typical Catholic view was voiced by the Jesuit editors of *America*, who deplored proposed laws in several states which would limit marriage to those granted a eugenic health certificate by the state. "Herein lies the crux of the whole eugenic question from the Catholic point of view," they wrote in 1913:

Marriage is a sacred institution established and sanctified by God Himself for the propagation and proper rearing and education . . . of the human family. . . . If man is not merely the nobler brother of the brute, but a being of an essentially higher order, with an origin and a destiny infinitely beyond that of the irrational world; if he can work out the lofty purpose of his

137

existence in spite of a diseased body and a "eugenically defective" mind, then must we cry "Halt!" to the ill-advised enthusiasts who would tamper with the sacred institution and obligations of conjugal life in violation of the laws of nature and of nature's God.[22]

Laws permitting the sterilization of the mentally defective, then progressing through many state legislatures, seemed to these editors evidence that "eugenists are doing more than their share to cast us into the abyss" and that they were turning the United States into a "most tyrannous despotism."[23] Kite, by working with Goddard, was not actually violating the tenets of her religion: there was no infallible Vatican pronouncement against eugenics. But eugenics was certainly alien territory to almost all her Catholic contemporaries.[24]

Goddard aimed to sequester the "feebleminded" at training schools such as Vineland and prevent their reproduction, while encouraging the accurate diagnosis of feeblemindedness at an early stage. The most influential method of quantifying intelligence (after phrenology and head-size measurement had been discredited in the late nineteenth century) was the intelligence quotient (IQ) test, invented by the French psychologist Alfred Binet. Elizabeth Kite, an expert French speaker, made the first English translation of Binet's books *The Development of Intelligence in Children* and *The Intelligence of the Feeble-Minded*, which she considered masterpieces, and on which Goddard based his diagnostic tests.[25] The Catholic journals, by contrast, condemned IQ tests and their widespread use as further signs of encroaching eugenism, denouncing the tests' advocates as "the host of faddists, experimenters, and latter-day scientists who are in places of trust where their theories can be worked for the unhappiness of those committed to their keeping," adding that they "lack[ed] . . . a sense of responsibility . . . to the body politic."[26]

Goddard's famous book *The Kallikak Family* (1913) appeared under his name alone, but Elizabeth Kite was the author of its long central chap-

22. Editorial, "Wildcat Eugenism," *America*, August 30, 1913, 495.
23. Untitled editorial, *America*, July 4, 1914, 287.
24. On the history of the eugenics movement, see Daniel Kevles, *In the Name of Eugenics: Genetics and the Uses of Human Heredity* (1985; Cambridge: Harvard University Press, 1995); Mark Haller, *Eugenics: Hereditarian Attitudes in American Thought* (1963; New Brunswick, N.J.: Rutgers University Press, 1984); and Stephen Jay Gould, *The Mismeasure of Man* (New York: Norton, 1981).
25. Alfred Binet, *The Development of Intelligence in Children*, trans. Elizabeth Kite (Lincoln, Ill.: Courier, 1912); Alfred Binet, *The Intelligence of the Feeble-Minded*, trans. Elizabeth Kite (Baltimore: Williams and Wilkins, 1916).
26. Untitled editorial, *America*, July 29, 1916, 388.

ter.[27] She was as eager to give credit to Goddard for her work in eugenics as to Reich in her historical studies. *The Kallikak Family* is an investigation of Deborah Kallikak, an inmate at Vineland, whom the staff tried to educate between the ages of eight and twenty-two, with little success. She was, said Goddard, an example of the "high-grade feeble-minded person, the moron, the delinquent." If she left the asylum, "she would at once become a prey to the designs of evil men or evil women and would lead a life that would be vicious, immoral, and criminal" (12). To find out more about Kallikak's family, Kite set out to trace Deborah's relatives and, if possible, her ancestors. Taken in one sense, her work in reconstructing the history of the Kallikak family can be seen as a pioneering piece of social history, but taken in another, it is a tendentious assault on human dignity, with glaring methodological deficiencies.

According to Kite the entire family could be traced to one Martin Kallikak, an upright young man who volunteered to fight in the War of Independence. On campaign he succumbed to sexual temptation and during a brief affair impregnated a young feebleminded woman. Later he married a smart young Quakeress and sired a legitimate family. As a result, Kite claimed, it was possible to trace the two bloodlines descending from this one man and the two women who bore his children. From the union of Martin and the feebleminded girl Kite traced a line of criminals and delinquents, thieves, prostitutes, and drunkards. From the legitimate side descended a succession of solid citizens, judges, professors, and burgesses of the highest probity (81–94). This case history demonstrated, Kite and Goddard concluded, that heredity outweighed environment in the transmission of desirable traits and showed that when a normal man and a feebleminded woman mated, feeblemindedness would dominate their offspring. "Now that the facts are known, let the lesson be learned . . . let it be impressed upon our young men of good family that they dare not step aside even for a moment," sermonized Goddard (103). Neither Kite nor Goddard adequately addressed the point that six generations had passed since the Revolution and that Deborah Kallikak had sixty-four great great great great grandparents rather than the one couple Kite had singled out as the central actors in this pseudodrama of heredity. Neither did Kite and Goddard, as devotees of accurate science, explain how the alleged feeblemindedness of the tavern girl could be established, since she predated Binet and his tests by more than a century.

27. Henry H. Goddard, *The Kallikak Family: A Study in the Heredity of Feeble-Mindedness* (New York: Macmillan, 1913), hereafter cited in the text. In the preface Goddard praised and thanked his fieldworkers, "especially Elizabeth Kite, to whom I am also indebted for practically all of Chapter IV" (xi).

Kite met several of Deborah Kallikak's living relatives, some in cities, others in the countryside of the New Jersey Pine Barrens, and all of them, she claimed, were feebleminded. Her own remarks demonstrate that her methods often fell short of the ostentatiously "scientific" claims she and Goddard were making, however, and sometimes her analysis was based on no more than a first visual impression. Of a girl she interviewed in one household Kite remarked: "She was pretty, with olive complexion and dark, languid eyes, but there was no mind there. Stagnation was the word written in large characters over everything" (73). And of a man she met a few days later, Kite confidently declared: "A glance sufficed to establish his mentality, which was low" (78). She went on, mixing observation with judgment and policy speculation:

In this house of abject poverty, only one sure prospect was ahead, that it would produce more feeble-minded children with which to clog the wheels of human progress. The laws of the country will not permit children ten years old to marry. Why should they permit it when the mentality is only ten? These and similar questions kept ringing through the field worker's mind as she made her way laboriously over the frozen road to the station. (78)

Kite confined her remarks to generalizations of this kind. Goddard went further, regretting that public opinion ruled out wholesale sterilization of the feebleminded. He believed that the "asexualization" of all feeble-minded people in one generation would bring the rapid elimination of the trait thereafter, but he was never able to persuade the New Jersey state government to adopt his plan (107).

Unfortunately, Elizabeth Kite's papers, now at Rutgers University, contain none of her personal correspondence or diaries from the period of her work with Goddard; so we cannot learn whether she was aware of the tension between her work and her adopted faith. At no time does she appear to have repudiated eugenics, and the eugenics journals continued to refer positively to her contributions after she left Vineland to devote herself solely to history. Her story is a reminder that even the most dedicated of Catholic converts carried into their new faith an array of attitudes and convictions developed earlier and that they often did not conform to the full worldview of their new religion. Or, to state it more positively, Kite shows us that the Catholic laity, particularly converts, did not simply fall in with all the opinions expressed by the church hierarchy on nondoctrinal matters and that they were levering open the doors of the Catholic "ghetto" as they entered.

Kite was a Third Order Franciscan, one who lives in the world but observes most elements of the Franciscan rule. In her autobiography she described her decision not to marry as a "victory." She received her first marriage proposal at the age of fifteen but rejected it, recalling that after dismissing her suitor, "I found myself lifted up to a clearer self-understanding and with increased objective interest in life and in study. A victory, indeed, had been won over the emotional side of my nature, a victory that left me immune from like disturbances for ten years and more."[28] Even the great emotional crisis of her life more than a decade later she attributed to "the rapturous loss of self-consciousness that accompanied my first experiences amid lofty mountain solitudes in central Colorado," which "left me quite off my guard" (58), implying that at sea level she would never have been so carried away. When she found that the man with whom she recognized a "soul union," a geologist, was already married, "I could take it as nothing less than God's will, now that the real facts of the case became known to me in a way so strikingly directed by Him, that it was intended for me to lead a single life. And from that moment I so accepted it, though the struggle that night lasted for hours" (120). Kite elsewhere wrote about the need to "conquer" the "lower" side of one's nature in order that other work could be accomplished. Still, she was in no way isolated from family life, and like Starr and other unmarried female scholars, she honored the rhetoric of female dependence, wifeliness, and motherhood. She personally raised *two* sets of nephews and nieces whose parents, her brother and her sister with their respective spouses, had all died prematurely. Apparently it was the physical and relational character of marriage rather than the practical details of household life that seemed to her an impediment.

Several other woman writers who converted to Catholicism also described single life as a positive vocation, providing an opportunity for work that would otherwise have been impossible, and in this attitude they emulated such born-Catholic writers as Agnes Repplier (1855–1950) and Louise Imogen Guiney (1861–1920).[29] For example, Katherine Bregy, a Philadelphian from a High Church Episcopalian family, channeled her emotional energy into the church itself and wrote about her approach to conversion in the language of romantic love. As a teenager, "my secret visits to singularly unattractive Catholic bookshops and above all my shyly

28. Kite, "Conversion Story," 58, hereafter cited in the text.
29. On Repplier, see George S. Stokes, *Agnes Repplier, Lady of Letters* (Philadelphia: University of Pennsylvania Press, 1949); and John Lukacs, *Philadelphia: Patricians and Philistines* (New York: Farrar, Straus, and Giroux, 1981). On Guiney, see Henry George Fairbanks, *Louise Imogen Guiney* (New York: Twayne, 1973).

wistful prayers before the tabernacle in nearby Catholic churches, began to take on the romance of a clandestine if supernatural love affair." A priest whom she idolized, the Paulist John Burke, received her into the church; she described him as "a tall and dreamy young Galahad" (525) and added that her infatuation with the church led her into "the bad habit of falling in love with the most ineligible people in sight," which may be a cryptic way of saying, with priests.[30] She too never married.

Bregy became a regular and prolific contributor of prose and poetry to Catholic journals in Britain and America, and said her life was dedicated to "an appreciation of Catholic poetry as the beauty of holiness."[31] What Kite had attempted for American history, Bregy attempted for English and American literature, arguing that its explicitly Protestant character was really no more than a thin covering over sturdy Catholic timbers and that all the really inspiring elements of post-Reformation literature could be traced to the old faith. Following convert critics such as Richard Simpson, who had devoted the last two decades of his life to proving that Shakespeare was a Catholic, Bregy maintained that *Pilgrim's Progress*, though undeniably the work of a Protestant, owed what strengths it had to Bunyan's familiarity with the great Catholic tradition: "In the light of present-day vagaries the Catholic reader is often surprised to note the orthodoxy of these seventeenth century dissenters—their hold upon Christ, upon the Holy Trinity, and many cardinal points of faith." Even so, she emphasized, the Reformation had impoverished the tradition of Christian allegory, so that "one turns back with a sigh to the wholesome, unstudied sanity of pre-Reformation standards."[32] In the mid–1920s Bregy won a *Commonweal* competition prize of a thousand dollars for a five-thousand-word essay on Dante, befriended many of the poetic luminaries of the interwar years, and was elected president of the Catholic Poetry Society of America in 1939. She also helped revive the poetry of the convert and priest Gerard Manley Hopkins, who had been largely forgotten since his death in 1889, and treated his conversion and dedication to Jesuit austerity with breathless reverence.[33]

Not all convert women were celibates, of course. Many were married,

30. Katherine Bregy, "Of Poets and Poetry," *Catholic World* 148 (February 1939): 524, 525, 528.
31. Ibid., 525.
32. Katherine Bregy, *From Dante to Jeanne d'Arc* (Milwaukee: Bruce, 1933), 105, 110.
33. The Dante essay is reprinted as "Dante's Dream of Life," in Bregy, *From Dante to Jeanne d'Arc*, 2–27. On Hopkins, see Katherine Bregy, *The Poet's Chantry* (St. Louis: Herder, 1912), 70–88. On the Catholic Poetry Society, see Arnold Sparr, *To Promote, Defend, and Redeem: The Catholic Literary Revival and the Cultural Transformation of American Catholicism: 1920–1960* (Westport, Conn.: Greenwood, 1990), 23–27.

but often it was the *failure* of the marriage which led them into their life's work. For example, an American woman, Cornelia Connelly (1809–1879), founder of the Society of the Holy Child Jesus, an educational order for English Catholic girls, began this work only after her husband, Pierce, had decided to leave her and their three children to become a priest. They had been married when he was an Episcopal minister, to whom marriage presented no career obstacles, and they had converted to Catholicism together. At first she begged him not to leave her and the children, but she finally gave her consent when he convinced her that it was God's will. Later he changed his mind, apostatized, began writing scurrilous anti-Catholic pamphlets, and sued his wife for recovery of the children he had abandoned a few years before. The case, *Connelly v. Connelly*, caused a scandal in Britain and harmed the reputation of the reviving Catholic Church there, but it led ultimately to Pierce Connelly's defeat. Cornelia Connelly remained true to her new vocation in the face of great personal and political difficulties.[34]

Similarly, the *end* of marriage prompted Rose Hawthorne Lathrop (1851–1926) to begin an independent career. Daughter of the novelist Nathaniel Hawthorne, she and her husband, George Lathrop, converted together in 1891. At first he was the dominant figure in the partnership, working as assistant editor of the *Atlantic Monthly* and writing the first critical biography of her father while she stayed at home. But Lathrop became an unstable alcoholic after the death of their only child, and Rose Hawthorne left him in 1893. She devoted the rest of her life to caring for incurable cancer victims. She lived until 1926 and through skilful administration and fund raising built up a complex of cancer hospices in the New York area. Lathrop, by contrast, went into a rapid decline and died of cirrhosis in 1898. At first Rose Hawthorne Lathrop and her assistant, Alice Huber, lived semimonastic lives as Third Order Dominicans and advertised their ancestry by calling themselves "Daughters of the Puritans." Later, as they attracted new recruits, they formally organized themselves into a religious order with their bishop's approval, becoming the Servants for the Relief of Incurable Cancer under formal Dominican rule.[35]

Neither Connelly nor Lathrop was primarily a writer, but a similar pattern of work after the end of marriage can be seen in the lives of many

34. On Connelly, see Kenneth Woodward, *Making Saints: How the Catholic Church Determines Who Becomes a Saint, Who Doesn't, and Why* (New York: Simon and Schuster, 1990), 253–79.

35. On Rose Hawthorne Lathrop, see Katherine Burton, *Sorrow Built a Bridge: A Daughter of Hawthorne* (New York: Longmans Green, 1937); and Theodore Maynard, *A Fire Was Lighted* (Milwaukee: Bruce, 1948). Both biographers, Burton and Maynard, were also converts.

women convert intellectuals. Perhaps the most striking was Martha Moore Avery, who was also born in 1851, the same year as Rose Lathrop, and raised a Unitarian in Maine. Avery did little intellectual work while married, but after her husband's premature death in 1890, she became interested in Marxian socialism. She joined the Socialist Labor Party of Boston in 1891 and founded the Boston School of Political Economy in 1896, where she taught classes on the works of Marx to students and radical trade unionists. The depression of the 1890s saw a succession of bitter strikes and the rapid spread of Socialist ideas in the union movement with Avery playing an active role and contributing regularly to the socialist press. Meanwhile, however, she had sent her daughter to a Catholic convent boarding school in Canada, where the girl converted to Catholicism, later becoming a nun. She bombarded her mother with literature about the Catholic faith, and Avery followed her child's example, converting in 1903.[36]

Popes and bishops discouraged Catholics from joining socialist organizations. Pope Leo XIII, in his 1891 encyclical *Rerum Novarum*, condemned socialism as an atheist and materialist system, which violated the natural law principle of private property. But as the contemporaneous example of Elizabeth Kite's work in eugenics showed, official disapproval was not always enough to deter a strong-minded convert. Besides, a handful of American Catholic priests, notably Edward McGlynn, Thomas J. Hagerty and Thomas McGrady, were themselves advocating socialism.[37] In the year of her conversion, nevertheless, Avery broke away from the new American Socialist Party in a way that shows that for her issues of family and motherhood remained paramount. The catalyst for her resignation was not papal or episcopal disapproval but a notorious divorce case in the ranks of the Socialist leaders.

George Herron was a talented Congregationalist minister of strong socialist views, married and with five children, who had won the patronage of one Elizabeth Rand, a wealthy philanthropic widow. Rand endowed a chair at Grinnell College, Iowa, for teaching the social and economic philosophy of Jesus, specifying that Herron should occupy it. He began a love affair with his patroness's daughter, Carrie Rand, then divorced his wife and married her, remarking: "I do not believe that the present mar-

36. Owen Carrigan, "Martha Moore Avery: Crusader for Social Justice," *Catholic Historical Review* 54 (April 1968): 17–38; Debra Campbell, "Reformers and Activists," in Kennelly, *American Catholic Women*, 152–81. On Avery and other Boston convert women, see also Paula Kane, *Separatism and Subculture: Boston Catholicism, 1900–1920* (Chapel Hill: University of North Carolina Press, 1994), 181–99.

37. Debra Campbell, "David Goldstein and the Rise of the Catholic Campaigners for Christ," *Catholic Historical Review* 72 (January 1986): 35.

riage system is sacred or good. . . . Love must be set free and liberty must be trusted." The scandal led to his expulsion from the Congregationalist pulpit, but by then Herron's star was rising in the Socialist Party, many of whose members regarded his union with the ardent socialist Carrie Rand as entirely defensible. When a Socialist editor declared at a 1903 conference that Herron was a second Jesus Christ, Martha Moore Avery stood up and denounced Herron, saying that, on the contrary, he was immoral and that attempts to justify his conduct brought the institution of marriage into disrepute.[38]

Many women converts, as we have seen, looked to strong older men for guidance; Avery's partner was a strong *younger* man, David Goldstein, with whom she appears to have had a mother-son relationship. Goldstein (1871–1954), an immigrant from a British Jewish family, was twenty years her junior, but they found each other compatible fellow workers, especially when Goldstein followed her example and became a Catholic. Together they wrote a book, *Socialism: The Nation of Fatherless Children* (1903), in which they elaborated their condemnation of Herron's marital misconduct, and threw in the further example of Karl Marx's daughter Eleanor, whose unsuccessful "socialist marriage" with Edward Aveling had led to her suicide. The whole book indicted socialism for its affront to marriage and the family. After all, said Avery and Goldstein, socialists saw all social institutions as conditioned by the relations of production. Logically they were forced to deny that marriage was anything but an institution contingent on a particular set of economic relations, that it was in no way sacred, and that, as August Bebel and other socialist theorists had already declared, it would be displaced by voluntary unions based on "sex fondness" in the socialist future. According to Avery and Goldstein, however, marriage is a divinely instituted sacrament and the family is the basic unit of society, regardless of economic relations. If the socialists triumphed, they concluded, marriage would evaporate and every child would be, as their title put it, a fatherless orphan, condemned to "the social barracks and the infant farm."[39]

American socialism never showed the militant atheism and anticlericalism of its European parent. Indeed, claims that Jesus was himself a socialist were commonplace in the first decade of the twentieth century. Ministers such as Herron and Norman Thomas played a large role in the party's

38. On George Herron's background and work, see John Cort, *Christian Socialism: An Informal History* (Maryknoll, N.Y.: Orbis, 1988), 236–40. On the divorce case, see David Goldstein and Martha Moore Avery, *Socialism: The Nation of Fatherless Children* (Boston: Union News League, 1903), 256–94.

39. Goldstein and Avery, *Socialism*, 248, 207–9, 218.

development and its first leader, Eugene Debs, wrote a biography of Jesus the working carpenter and union man titled *The Supreme Leader.*[40] Avery and Goldstein, therefore, made a special point of denying that Christianity and socialism were compatible:

How often is the statement made, by those new converts whose ardor outstrips their knowledge, that socialism is identical with Christianity. In "green" socialist papers and in "literature for beginners," one may frequently read the statement that "the ethics of Christianity and socialism are identical," when an investigation will conclusively prove that the ethic of socialism is as directly opposite to the ethics of Christianity as the positive is from the negative pole of human activity.

The authors insisted that in detaching themselves from the socialist movement they were *not* abandoning the cause of the suffering proletariat and were not trying to endorse the industrial status quo, whose flagrant injustices were "a stench in a true man's nostrils."[41] Rather they wanted to aid the working class while conforming to the sound and constructive principles laid down by Leo XIII in *Rerum Novarum.* Their pro-union, anti-socialist politics led to endorsements from President Theodore Roosevelt and Samuel Gompers, first head of the American Federation of Labor. Goldstein and Avery continued to work actively in the trade union movement; the school of political economy stayed open (with a suitably revised curriculum), and Avery later became founder and president of the Boston Common Cause Society, an organization of Catholic laypeople dedicated to economic justice.

Starting in 1917, Goldstein and Avery also collaborated in the Catholic Truth Guild, driving a modified Ford Model T painted in the papal colors, yellow and white, preaching prolabor Catholicism on street corners in working-class districts and speaking against suffrage for women as a latently socialist assault on the family. They also wrote a condemnation of the Russian Revolution, *Bolshevism: Its Cure* (1919), which declared that the great conflict in the world now lay between communism, "the Red International," and Catholicism, "the Black International," and that the way for America to avoid bolshevism was to establish a thoroughgoing welfare state.[42] As the historian Owen Carrigan notes: "Martha Moore Avery was

40. On the Christian element in American socialism, see Nick Salvatore, *Eugene Debs: Citizen and Socialist* (Urbana: University of Illinois Press, 1992), 62–65, 310–12, 316–17.
41. Goldstein and Avery, *Socialism,* 23, 7.
42. David Goldstein and Martha Moore Avery, *Bolshevism: Its Cure* (Boston: School of Political Economy, 1919), 9, 35. They also said that it was no coincidence that Marxism began in Germany or that the "flood" of bolshevism "swept over the land of Luther where

one of the few laymen of any prominence in the Church actively engaged in spreading the social teachings of Leo XIII. . . . Her own views were stated well before the American hierarchy made any official pronouncements on a social program."[43] Later endorsement of Leo's program by the National Catholic Welfare Conference (NCWC) made her seem a prophet.

The example of Avery demonstrates that women who converted to Catholicism were not necessarily social conservatives. Passionate defense of the traditional family led in her case to criticism of industrial capitalism because, under the prevailing impersonal economic system, workers were subject to the vagaries of the business cycle, putting *families* in constant economic jeopardy. Avery therefore echoed Leo XIII's call for wages high enough to permit the raising of a family with sufficient money left over to allow workers to gather savings against illness and old age.[44] At the same time, her militant opposition to women's suffrage—often repeated in public speeches—in the belief that it would accelerate the breakup of the family, does carry conservative connotations.

The same mixture of radicalism and conservatism could be found in other convert women writers, among them Ellen Gates Starr (1859–1940), niece of Eliza Allen Starr. She and her old schoolfriend Jane Addams founded Hull House settlement in 1889. For more than thirty years the two friends worked together in the west-side slums of Chicago to alleviate the problems of recent immigrants from the countryside and from central Europe.[45] Like her aunt, Ellen Starr romanticized the Middle Ages, and her condemnation of capitalism carried the antiquarian flavor of William Morris, John Ruskin, and the Arts and Crafts Movement. She taught Hull House classes on Dante, Shakespeare, and Browning, and read George Eliot aloud to a women's reading circle. She even spent a year in England learning to bind books by hand and set up a hand-bindery at Hull House, believing that the recovery of such skills was the antidote to soulless industrialization.[46] Neither she nor Addams ever married but

---

the false principle of Higher Criticism had long since ripened into the atheist assent that right is the creature of might." Ibid., 5.

43. Carrigan, "Martha Moore Avery," 28.

44. Goldstein and Avery, *Bolshevism*, 35.

45. Jane Addams, *Twenty Years at Hull House* (1910; New York: Penguin/Signet, 1981), 73–75, 79, 261, 299. On Addams, see also Christopher Lasch, *The New Radicalism in America, 1889–1963* (1965; New York: Norton, 1986), 3–68.

46. Allen F. Davis, "Ellen Gates Starr," in Edward James et al., eds., *Notable American Women: A Biographical Dictionary* (Cambridge: Belknap of Harvard University Press, 1971), 350–53. On the Arts and Crafts Movement in America and the influence of Ruskin and Morris, see T. Jackson Lears, *No Place of Grace: Antimodernism and the Transformation of American Culture, 1880–1920* (New York: Pantheon, 1981), 66–83.

both described their work in familial terms and devoted much of their energy to helping working women, providing day care for children, and lobbying for "domestic" reforms in the city. Hull House was far from popular with the Catholic Church. Early in the century the Chicago diocesan newspaper *New World* described its workers as "hysterically emotional, childless female slummers," as "feminine busybodies who neglect their own homes in order to indulge in a little sentiment or gain notoriety by attempting to pauperize whole neighborhoods."[47] Not until 1920, when she was sixty, did Starr, a Socialist Party member, finally convert to Catholicism, and only when she was sure that the Catholic Church in America was following a "progressive" social policy consonant with her Hull House work. In a letter just before her conversion she complained about what had earlier seemed to her Catholicism's "reactionary attitude . . . in the matter of social and political progress, its organized and authoritative opposition to socialism, and its obstructive policy toward social reform movements." She said she was very glad to learn of the new NCWC policy, "which, if followed up, will remove this obstacle for me and for others who meet with this difficulty."[48] Having become a Catholic, she soon became convinced that the church was the most dedicated social justice organization in the country, though few impartial observers would agree with this estimate.[49]

The most radical Catholic social justice organization, the Catholic Worker Movement, began in New York at the nadir of the Great Depression. It too was the creation of a convert and writer, Dorothy Day, and bore the stamp of her preconversion experiences as a labor radical and pacifist. She converted to Catholicism in 1927, founded her newspaper, the *Catholic Worker*, in 1933, and the first House of Hospitality in 1934.[50]

47. *New World*, quoted in Kenneally, *History of Catholic Women*, 101.
48. Starr, "A By-Path into the Great Roadway," *Catholic World* 119 (May 1924): 177–90; (June 1924): 358–73.
49. See, for example, Aaron Abell, *American Catholicism and Social Action: A Search for Social Justice, 1865–1900* (Garden City, N.Y.: Doubleday, 1960); David O'Brien, *American Catholics and Social Reform* (New York: Oxford University Press, 1968). Abell and O'Brien show that the NCWC program encountered widespread opposition and resistance from Catholics through the 1920s and 1930s and that one of its central principles, the abolition of child labor, ran into organized opposition from inside the church.
50. Principal sources for the biography of Dorothy Day, used here in summarizing her life and work, are Dorothy Day, *The Long Loneliness: The Autobiography of Dorothy Day* (1952; Chicago: Thomas More Press, 1989); William D. Miller, *Dorothy Day* (New York: Harper and Row 1982); Mel Piehl, *Breaking Bread: The Catholic Worker and the Origin of Catholic Radicalism in America* (Philadelphia: Temple University Press, 1982); Robert Ellsberg, *By Little and by Little* (New York: Knopf, 1985); Robert Coles, *Dorothy Day: A Radical Devotion* (Reading, Mass.: Addison Wesley/Merloyd Lawrence, 1987); James Fisher, *The Catholic Counterculture in America, 1933–1962* (Chapel Hill: University of North Carolina

As with Rose Hawthorne and Martha Moore Avery, it was the breakdown of her married life which inaugurated the convert's vocational work. And like the other converts, Day, who had a low opinion of many born Catholics, proved fearless in standing up for her beliefs against Catholic critics.

Day was born in Brooklyn in 1897 and traveled around the country with her family, led by their hard-drinking father, a sportswriter and aspiring novelist. She struggled as an adolescent against what one historian calls her "flinty Protestant-American inheritance,"[51] indulging a taste for gestures of self-mortification and literary romance and coming to identify with the victims of injustice. After two years at the University of Illinois she moved to the Lower East Side of New York, to work for the Socialist newspaper the *Call* and later did a two-year stint on the Communist *Liberator* in Chicago. In New York she gained a reputation as a Greenwich Village bohemian. She befriended Eugene O'Neill, Max Eastman, Floyd Dell, Mike Gold, and other radical writers and recalled later that O'Neill's recitation of Francis Thompson's poem "The Hound of Heaven" gave her an early premonition of her conversion: "Sooner or later I would have to pause in the mad rush of living and remember my first beginning and my last end."[52] It was among the Village radicals that she learned her pacifism, and she worked as a volunteer with the Anti-Conscription League during the First World War. Later she would scandalize her coreligionists by introducing pacifism to an American Catholic population that saw bellicose nationalism as the ideal medium of Americanization.[53]

She had an abortion after an unsuccessful love affair with Lionel Moise, a cynical fellow journalist, and may even have attempted suicide.[54] Then, on the rebound, she impulsively married a literary promoter, Barkeley Tobey, but separated from him in the space of a few months while living among the American expatriate writers in Paris. Her common-law marriage with a biologist, Forster Batterham, worked better than these early relationships, at least for a time, and led to the birth of a daughter, Tamar Teresa, in 1925. But Batterham, an anarchist and atheist, was horrified by Day's decision to baptize the child in the Catholic faith and then to follow suit by converting. He refused to have anything to do with her maturing

---

Press, 1989); and June O'Connor, *The Moral Vision of Dorothy Day: A Feminist Perspective* (New York: Crossroads, 1991).

51. Fisher, *Catholic Counterculture*, 15.

52. Day, *Long Loneliness*, 108.

53. Catholic bishops, eager to quiet nativist allegations of disloyalty, urged young men to volunteer for military service in wartime and led their dioceses in wartime fund raising. See, for example, Edward Kantowicz, "Cardinal Mundelein of Chicago and the Shaping of Twentieth-Century American Catholicism," *Journal of American History* 68 (June 1981): 64.

54. Fisher, *Catholic Counterculture*, 13.

religious convictions. They broke up as she entered the church. In her autobiography she wrote that he was right to feel jealous of her new lover, Christ, into whose mystical body she had entered.[55]

She had begun reading the novels of the Belgian convert Joris Karl Huysmans in the preceding year and was drawn to his Catholic vision of decadence, mystical spirituality, and suffering. At the same time, aware of her tendency to self-dramatization, Day feared she might be making no more than another romantic gesture and later described her self-interrogation:

One part of my mind stood at one side and kept saying, "What are you doing? Are you sure of yourself? What kind of affectation is this? What act is this you are going through? Are you trying to induce emotion, induce faith, partake of an opiate, the opiate of the people?" I felt like a hypocrite if I got down on my knees, and shuddered at the thought of anyone seeing me. (178)

But if Catholicism was tainted by affectation at first, it soon became a deep conviction, which guided her in the remaining fifty-three years of her life. She had already published an autobiographical novel, *The Eleventh Virgin* (1924), and was working on more fiction. She even got a short-term contract as a screenwriter in Hollywood but soon abandoned it in favor of a trip to Mexico, where she turned to religious writing and reportage for the Catholic journals *Commonweal* and *America*.

Like Ellen Gates Starr, Dorothy Day did not seek out Catholic friends and "after three years of Catholicism . . . I still did not know personally one Catholic layman" (197). She found much to deplore in the U.S. Catholic Church—"the scandal of businesslike priests, of collective wealth, the lack of a sense of responsibility for the poor, the worker, the Negro, the Mexican, the Filipino" (179). In 1930 she followed a convoy of unemployed hunger marchers from New York to Washington, reporting for *Commonweal* but motivated by her Communist friends, who had organized it. As she watched the marchers, she wrote later, she felt "joy and pride" in their courage but also "bitterness . . . since I was now a Catholic with fundamental philosophical differences. . . . I could write, I could protest, to arouse the conscience, but where was the Catholic leadership in gathering bands of men and women together, for the actual works of mercy that the [Communist] comrades had always made part of their technique in reaching the workers?" (195). She created the *Catholic Worker* and the Houses of Hospitality to fill these gaps, offering practical

55. Day, *Long Loneliness*, 178–79, hereafter cited in the text.

and philosophical Catholic help to the unemployed. Uptown in Harlem the colorful Russian émigrée and convert Catherine de Hueck created a similar settlement, Friendship House, which offered charity and preached Catholicism to the local black population.[56]

The vast majority of her Catholic contemporaries sought upward social mobility and social assimilation. Day, by contrast, cherished the hard doctrines of her new faith, the burden of suffering, and the elements of Catholicism that made it resistant to assimilation. And with the same confidence as her fellow converts, she did not wait for episcopal approval but took her own initiatives, supporting strikers, agitating for union recognition, and laying the foundations of Catholic pacifism. She infuriated Catholic bishops and editors by refusing to take sides in the Spanish Civil War (most Catholics were fervently pro-Franco) and precipitated a split in her own movement when she greeted even the Second World War with an uncompromising pacifism.[57] The impecunious *Catholic Worker* tried to support a Catholic conscientious objectors' camp in New Hampshire, but the federal government broke it up in 1943 after discovering that the men were all malnourished. According to archdiocesan legend the archbishop of New York, Francis Spellman, disliked Day and her radical and pacifist ideals but dared not stop her for fear that she might turn out to be a saint.[58]

Despite her independence and charisma, however, even Dorothy Day claimed that her religious ideas and guidance came from a man, the wandering French philosopher Peter Maurin. She said she found spiritual sustenance in his cryptic utterances, and she tried to put into practice his plan for antiindustrial communes. As the historian Mel Piehl points out: "It was personally comforting to Day, as well as strategically useful to her as a woman leading a social movement in the sexually conservative Catholic Church, to be able to point to the male co-founder of the movement and to emphasize that she was merely carrying out Maurin's program."[59]

56. Thomas Merton, after his conversion, worked at Friendship House for a while before moving into the Trappist monastery, and he recorded the scene in his spiritual autobiography, *The Seven Storey Mountain* (New York: Harcourt, Brace, 1948), 340–48. Wilfrid Sheed, who visited de Hueck with his father, the publisher Frank Sheed, comments; "She was wonderful window-dressing for her group . . . but a pain in the neck to those within. Bored to madness with dailiness, she was forever planning new branches and whole new approaches for her movement to take." Wilfrid Sheed, *Frank and Maisie: A Memoir with Parents* (New York: Simon and Schuster, 1985), 163.

57. On the Spanish Civil War, see Piehl, *Breaking Bread*, 192–93, and on World War II, 199–204.

58. John Cooney, *The American Pope: The Life and Times of Francis Cardinal Spellman* (New York: Times Books, 1984), 90.

59. Piehl, *Breaking Bread*, 65.

Like Day, Maurin had a vision of sanctification through suffering and failure.

The *Catholic Worker*, the rural communes, and the Houses of Hospitality, to which Day devoted the rest of her life, were chaotic, shabby, and anarchic. They did nothing to change the American economic system and acted largely as emergency sources of food and shelter for derelicts. They contained something to displease everybody. Many Catholics saw the movement as "a potential Trojan Horse for Communist infiltration," while Commuists and some trade union activists regarded it as "a tool of clerical fascism."[60] The movement's greatest impact was probably on the minds and consciences of the young Catholics who volunteered to work for it: it forced them to ask whether their striving for success was not a betrayal of their religion's ideals. As James Fisher says, "Day's genius resided in her ability to reverse the trajectory of the conventional American conversion narrative. . . . Day offered deconversion, or breakdown, as a permanent state of grace."[61]

Maurin, like Day, was an outsider to American Catholicism; he had failed in his vocation to the priesthood and become a mendicant sage. This odd partnership of outsiders could ask the most radical questions of American Catholicism, ones its own brood had not thought to raise. Day's assumption of a Christ-like poverty and her uncompromising pacifism made her a radiant figure to the Catholic Left and pacifists of later generations. The historian David O'Brien called her in an obituary "the most significant, interesting, and influential person in the history of American Catholicism."[62] The study of her life and work has now become an academic subfield in itself. In view of her current high profile, it is worth emphasizing that during much of her lifetime the majority of American Catholics knew little or nothing of Dorothy Day, and many of those who had heard her name regarded this convert as at best a deluded, unpatriotic crank. Her near contemporary and friend Katherine Burton is less well remembered today but was far more widely read and more influential between 1930 and 1960.

Katherine Burton (née Kurz) was born in 1890 and raised in Cleveland.[63] After dabbling in social work and schoolteaching she married an

---

60. Fisher, *Catholic Counterculture*, 1.

61. Ibid., 32.

62. O'Brien cited in George Weigel, *Tranquillitas Ordinis: The Present Failure and Future Promise of American Catholic Thought on War and Peace* (New York: Oxford University Press, 1987), 148–49.

63. For the following biographical summary I am indebted to Rob Carbonneau, C.P. for his unpublished article, "Katherine Kurz Burton's Quest for Catholic Feminine Identity in a Male Dominated Church: 'Woman to Woman' in *Sign Magazine.*"

ambitious journalist, Harry Burton, who became editor of *McCall's* magazine in New York City. Between the ages of eighteen and thirty she had little religious life and joined the local Episcopal church in Garden City, New York, more as a neighborly act than from religious conviction. She met Selden Delany (1874–1935), an Episcopal priest who was struggling with the issue of whether to convert, and through his influence her religious life intensified. Her husband's rapid rise and workaholic habits, meanwhile, led him to a nervous breakdown (and eventually suicide). After trying in vain to help him, she went one day into a Catholic church, seeking solace.

As I knelt I was suddenly aware of a new sensation. For weeks and weeks I had had the feeling of falling and falling nowhere. Now of a sudden something seemed to be holding me up. It too came from outside; it was not anything I had conjured up to comfort myself. Somehow I had been caught and lifted high above my own pain and loss. They were still there, heartbreakingly real, but the sense of being alone with them was gone.[64]

From this time on, she followed her mentor Delany first to Anglo-Catholicism, then into Roman Catholicism. His book *Why Rome?* provided the final necessary arguments.[65]

Meanwhile separation from her husband put Burton and her three young children in economic hardship. To support the family she went to work as a writer, first for women's magazines, then as a biographer of figures—often strong women—in U.S. Catholic history. In 1933 (the inaugural year of Day's *Catholic Worker*) the editor of the Passionist Fathers' magazine, *Sign*, invited Burton to write a women's column for his journal.[66] The column, "Woman to Woman," ran every month for the next thirty-six years, ending only with Burton's death in 1969. It was the first women's column in the history of American Catholic journalism.

Burton, like her fellow converts, wrote enthusiastically of marriage and motherhood as the central and highest vocation of a Catholic woman. At the same time she reminded readers that contemporary realities—marital breakdown or economic hardship—forced large numbers of women to work, and that work in no way demeaned them. Working women needed all the support and sympathy they could get because "breadwinning is a serious task and requires a concentration that often makes difficult the

64. Katherine Burton, *The Next Thing: Autobiography and Reminiscences* (New York: Longmans Green, 1949), 98.
65. Selden Delany, *Why Rome?* (New York: L. MacVeagh/Dial Press, 1930); Burton, *Next Thing*, 127, 143.
66. Burton, *Next Thing*, 177.

rearing of children." Juggling the two was sure to be "a little breathless, a little hurried, a little uneasy and unsatisfactory." But she insisted that it had its compensations. "The most terrific discovery such women can make is that they can run the ship without a man, that they can hold the helm straight, that the children will not drown."[67]

Burton was as ardent in support of women's suffrage and political rights as Martha Moore Avery had been in opposing them, maintaining a view she had held in the pre–World War I days when she had joined prosuffrage demonstrations and marched with a "Votes for Women" banner. She disliked many aspects of the official Catholic attitude toward women in the interwar years and at times pointedly contradicted it. For example, she wrote an enthusiastic book, *According to the Pattern*, about Agnes McLaren and Anna Dengel, who campaigned for a change in the rule that prohibited nuns from training as doctors. She was jubilant when the Vatican revoked the prohibition in 1935.[68] She also tried to spread information about the rhythm method of contraception following the discovery of the fertile and infertile periods of the menstrual cycle in the 1920s, only to be ordered by her bishop to desist.[69] And she bridled when a prominent priest, Father Leonard Feeney, spoke patronizingly about nuns, calling them "dear little women." To the contrary, said Burton, "they are fearless women, intelligent women, happy women, hardworking women, and they have many other qualities, but I have never yet met one whom I would characterize as a 'dear little woman.'"[70] The picture she drew of nuns and sisters, in her columns and books, was of decisive, capable, hard-headed women, never women of unthinking docility.

Burton's columns and biographies were written for a (Catholic) mass audience, but during the interwar years, a generation of Catholic women was seeking doctoral degrees and university careers. For them acknowledgment by their non-Catholic peers was the avenue to advancement. The career of Eva Ross is a case in point.[71] Whereas Elizabeth Kite never gained a permanent academic job and was largely self-taught, Ross (born 1903), forty years her junior, was one of the first Catholic laywomen to

67. Ibid., 111.
68. Katherine Burton, *According to the Pattern* (Toronto: Longmans, Green, 1946). Burton describes its inception and execution in *Next Thing*, 235.
69. Burton, *Next Thing*, 179–80.
70. Ibid., 238.
71. Biographical information on Eva Ross is based on "Eva Ross," in Walter Romig, ed., *The Book of Catholic Authors: Informal Self-Portraits of Famous Modern Catholic Writers* (Detroit: Walter Romig, 1942), 224–28; "Eva Jeany Ross," in Matthew Hoehn, O.S.B., ed., *Catholic Authors: Contemporary Biographical Sketches* (Newark, N.J.: St. Mary's Abbey, 1948), 651–52.

become an academic professional. Born and raised in Ireland and England and dreaming of literary success, she studied modern languages at Bedford College, London, but a financial disaster in her family forced her to abandon college and go to work. She became an executive secretary, working in London and Paris for an American investment company. In 1930, after converting to Catholicism, she abandoned business and emigrated to the United States, where she taught sociology, anthropology, and economics at a succession of Catholic women's colleges. During this period the Catholic colleges still employed many teachers without higher degrees but were trying to emulate the professionalization of secular universities.[72] In order to keep pace Ross worked for a sociology master's at St. Louis University, then switched over to the secular universities, gaining a Yale doctorate in 1937. She became a prolific author on sociology, anthropology, and economics, a founding member of the American Catholic Sociological Association, and its president in 1943.

Ross aimed to have her work taken seriously both within and beyond the Catholic academic community, without compromising her Catholic integrity. She believed that the scientific study of sociology and anthropology confirmed rather than contradicted the basic postulates of Catholicism and the natural law, including monotheism and monogamy, and that close, unbiased, empirical study would refute the evolutionary metaphors that had come to dominate those fields. In her books and articles Ross paid close and respectful attention to the work of major contemporaries— Franz Boas and Alfred Kroeber in anthropology, Sigmund Freud in psychology, Max Weber and Emile Durkheim in sociology—and gave accurate summaries of their methods and findings. Then she tried to chip away at the edifice of *their* orthodoxy by close deductive reasoning and by pointing out their omissions and non sequiturs. In the introduction to her book *Social Origins* (1936), for example, Ross explained her method and voiced her conviction that, sooner or later, secular social scientists would *have* to listen to the Catholics. The study of social origins

enables us better to understand the fundamental operations behind our major culture-patterns. It enables us to meet on their own ground those sociologists who still propound unilinear evolution. These theorists take scanty account of history, and they will not listen to philosophical disquisition, or to religious revelation. They ignore the existence of a Creator, and of an intelligently created and planned world, whose inhabitants have a destiny beyond the grave. If, however, we can show them the obviously false

72. Philip Gleason, *Contending with Modernity: Catholic Higher Education in the Twentieth Century* (New York: Oxford University Press, 1995), 58–60, 184–88, 202–4.

inferences which they have drawn from the culture of those very primitives whom they have professed to study scientifically and with an unbiased mind, surely then they can hardly fail to take at least some cognizance of our claims.

She gave examples of evidence that had been forced into preconceived theoretical structures, emphasized that influential political philosophers such as Hobbes had written persuasive fictions rather than history, and showed that the available historical and anthropological evidence supported the Catholic claim that private property and the state were "natural" rather than artificial phenomena.[73]

Ross was eager not to be thought a mere Catholic fundamentalist and made frequent concessions to her antagonists, admitting, for example, the probability of biological evolution. The Darwinians were not wrong; they were simply conceptually unable to tell the whole story because they had excluded from their worldview the whole spiritual side of humanity, treating it instead as a purely material phenomenon. Thus "even if evolution of the material universe and of the body took place, nevertheless at some time in the history of the world this evolution must have ceased, and God must then have infused into the evolved body a human soul." Similarly the Fall might not have been quite the event described in Genesis, but it remained a lively possibility, a hypothesis deserving of further scrutiny in light of the available empirical data.[74] Her academic work is peppered with reminders to non-Catholic readers that they must not beg the philosophical question and reminders to Catholic readers (and fellow researchers) that they must not rely on faith alone but rather improve the quality of their empirical work to make their arguments sustainable without appeal to revelation.[75] A near contemporary of John Tracy Ellis, whose appeal for a higher quality of Catholic scholarship energized Catholics in the 1950s, she called for the same kind of unblinking methodological rigor that he demanded in history.

In the 1930s Ross was an anomalous figure, one of very few Catholic women publishing in her several academic fields, severe in her style and in her strictures on method. But she also represented an augury of things to come. After the Second World War women in the American Catholic professoriate, earning the Ph.D. and adhering to the canons of the academic disciplines, became increasingly common, and by the 1950s many

73. Eva Ross, *Social Origins* (New York: Sheed and Ward, 1936), 9, 54–55.
74. Ibid., 21.
75. See, for example, Eva Ross, "Do Primitives Fill a Gap in History?" *Central Blatt and Social Justice* 31 (January 1939): 301–4, and *Social Justice* 31 (February 1939): 339–42.

of them were born rather than converted Catholics. They took to heart the message Ross and other converts had preached: that to gain respect they must appeal to non-Catholic readers on the strength of their research and reasoning. In 1964 this new generation changed the name of the journal she had helped found from the *American Catholic Sociological Review* to *Sociological Analysis*. By then, most Catholic sociologists preferred to emphasize their scientific credentials rather than their faith, and they opened the journal to all comers—a reform Ross might not have endorsed. She had never meant to compromise or disguise the explicitly Catholic provenance of her work. As the educated Catholic population mushroomed at a massive array of universities and colleges, its distinctiveness steadily diminished, as did its sense of being a community set apart.

It would be difficult to claim of any of the women described here, apart from Dorothy Day, that they were major figures in either American or Catholic history. Moreover, they were the kind of women most likely to be ignored in the recent development of women's history as it grew out of the feminist movement. None but Burton fits the usual definitions of feminism, and the rest of them, subservient to men, deferential, self-effacing, sometimes antisuffrage, would seem the least enticing and least likable to historians seeking avatars of modern gender-role transformations. Certainly none but Day has yet won the attention of a biographer, and the sources on their work remain scattered and diffuse, full of tantalizing gaps. Still, taken together they are worthy of investigation. They show that the limited intellectual world open to women in English-language Catholicism was predominantly a *convert* world, drawing as much from its members' Protestant and secular experiences as from the Catholic tradition. They also show that, like their male counterparts, convert women writers tried to pull Catholicism as a whole toward greater intellectual engagement with the rest of the world while drawing more non-Catholics into the embrace of the church. Examples of cultural dissonance, such as Kite's eugenics and Burton's feminism, are reminders of Catholic diversity and pointers to the Catholic conflicts of the 1960s, when a group of more dissatisfied and more militant women would take up where their convert forerunners had left off.

# VIII

## THE BRITISH APOLOGISTS' SPIRITUAL AENEID

A MERICAN INTELLECTUALS drew much of their inspiration from Europe, particularly Britain, in the second half of the nineteenth century. Lyell, Darwin, Huxley, and Spencer had immense influence on geologists, biologists, sociologists, and historians.[1] George Bernard Shaw, Sidney and Beatrice Webb, Edward Bernstein, Max Weber, and Wilhelm Dilthey, influenced a generation of American social democratic and progressive reformers as they debated the problems of industrial society.[2] Among Protestant theologians and historians the same was again true, this time with Germany leading the way. Historical-critical study of the Bible and the interpretation of comparative religions were refined in German universities by such scholars as Ernst Troeltsch, Julius Wellhausen, and Adolph Von Harnack, whose work had an immense impact on American theology.[3]

It is not surprising to find a similar situation among Catholic intellectuals. The American Catholics relied on European, particularly British, inspiration and guidance in the late nineteenth century and continued to draw on this resource far into the twentieth century. The relative poverty of U.S. Catholics, their undereducation, and their lean intellectual accomplishments made them dependent on Britain until almost the eve of the

1. See, for example, Robert V. Bruce, *The Launching of Modern American Science, 1846–1876* (Ithaca: Cornell University Press, 1987). On Lyell in particular see Robert Silliman, "The Hamlet Affair: Charles Lyell and the North Americans," *Isis* 86 (December 1995): 541–61.
2. See James T. Kloppenberg, *Uncertain Victory: Social Democracy and Progressivism in European and American Thought, 1870–1920* (New York: Oxford University Press, 1986).
3. See the essays in Nathan Hatch and Mark Noll, eds., *The Bible in America: Essays in Cultural History* (New York: Oxford University Press, 1982).

Second Vatican Council. There were exceptions to this rule, such as Brownson and Hecker, but whereas many British Catholic writers made an impression in the United States, few U.S. Catholics managed to ship their ideas east across the Atlantic prior to 1950.

Among the English Catholics whose work was widely read in America in the late nineteenth and early twentieth century, nearly all were converts. Hilaire Belloc, a born Catholic, was the one major exception to prove the rule. A succession of converts wrote much of the Catholic literature of both countries, and many of them went to live and work for a time in the United States or Canada. Among the best known of this group were Basil Maturin (1847–1915), Bertram Windle (1858–1929), Robert Hugh Benson (1871–1914), G. K. Chesterton (1874–1936), Alfred Noyes (1880–1958), Arnold Lunn (1881–1974), Shane Leslie (1885–1971), Christopher Dawson (1889–1970), Theodore Maynard (1890–1956), and Christopher Hollis (1902–1977). Maturin lived in Philadelphia for ten years before his conversion in 1897. He returned to the United States as a Catholic priest to make lecture tours in 1913 and again in 1915, and died when the *Lusitania*, on which he was traveling home, was sunk by a German U-boat. Windle spent the last ten years of his life, 1919–1929, as a professor of anthropology at Saint Michael's College, University of Toronto. Chesterton, Lunn, Leslie, and Hollis each spent semesters teaching at the University of Notre Dame in Indiana during the 1930s and gave lecture tours in other parts of the United States. Maynard emigrated to the United States in 1920 and spent the rest of his life there, writing, teaching at Catholic colleges, and becoming one of the premier historians of Catholicism in America. Noyes was a professor of English at Princeton from 1913 to 1925 and frequently returned to the United States after his 1927 conversion to Catholicism, and Dawson became the first professor of Catholic studies at Harvard in 1958. Others from their generation, notably C. C. Martindale (1879–1963) and Ronald Knox (1888–1957), never visited America but sold as many books there as in England and became familiar landmarks on the American Catholic scene. Another influential convert, the artist Eric Gill (1882–1940), worked as an illustrator, sculptor, and woodcut maker. His decorations, woodcuts, and typefaces became the distinctive hallmark of interwar Catholic literature and journalism in England and the United States. He was, besides, a vigorous controversialist, a critic of industrial society who played the same sort of role for Catholics that William Morris had played for Anglicans fifty years before.[4]

4. Peter Faulkner, *William Morris and Eric Gill* (Salisbury, Wiltshire: William Morris Society, 1975).

This generation of converts, the subject of this chapter and the next two chapters, was equally important for Catholic developments on both sides of the Atlantic. They gave poise and assurance to Catholic literature and presented Catholicism as an attractive religious option for the growing literate middle classes. Newman had set high literary standards, but here was a group whose members, at their best, were able to live up to them. Trained in the classics at English public schools, they knew how to blend intellectual refinement, accessibility, and rhetorical drama. Living in the shadow of *Pascendi*, they avoided theology and, as the historian Adrian Hastings says, "accepted the current Roman Catholic position in doctrine and practice as almost unquestionably right in all its details."[5] Quite unlike George Tyrrell, who had found the Catholic tradition, as currently interpreted at the Vatican, more and more irksome, they were drawn to its dogmatism and celebrated it as a sure refuge in a chaotic world.

Several of these men (and they were all men) achieved fame and distinction in British life. Chesterton was widely recognized in his day and since as a master of English prose, and he gave to this convert generation much of its distinctive voice and mood. He was famous not only for his religious writing but as a political and literary journalist, an outspoken opponent of the Boer War (1899–1902), and a passionate anti-German in the First World War (1914–1918). By the time of his conversion to Catholicism in 1922 he was the most famous fat man in England, and his regular newspaper columns almost certainly made him Britain's most widely read journalist throughout the whole population. Bertram Windle was a distinguished scientist, a university president and a fellow of the Royal Society; he and Noyes were both knighted for their services to Britain. Arnold Lunn, also knighted, was captain of the English alpine ski team in the (long ago) days when it could compete seriously at the Olympic level, and Hollis was an economist and a member of Parliament. But despite these distinctions, they saw themselves first and foremost as Christians who had turned to Rome and aimed to make their readers do likewise.

They were quite different from most of their fellow British Catholics, 80 percent of whom at the start of the century were Irish immigrants.[6] Four prominent converts, Knox, Hollis, Benson, and *Dublin Review* editor Algar Thorold (1866–1936), were the sons of Anglican bishops; all came from the upper middle class and shared many of its attitudes. They offered a model of the compatibility of Catholicism with polite society. But they formed a minority within a minority, and there was something

---

5. Adrian Hastings, *A History of English Christianity, 1920–1990* (London: Collins, 1986), 279.

6. Ibid., 134.

cliquish about their closely interwoven relationships. Knox and Hollis, for example, born fourteen years apart, were both sons of Anglican bishops; both went to Summer Fields preparatory school, then to Eton, then to Balliol College, Oxford, became president of the Oxford Union, and converted to Catholicism in their twenties! Knox was first attracted to Catholicism by reading the convert Hugh Benson's *Light Invisible* in 1903. He was received into the Catholic Church in 1917 by another convert, C. C. Martindale, author of the standard biograpy of Hugh Benson, who was also the son of an Anglican bishop. Other members of the group established a kind of conversion genealogy, noting one after the next that reading rather than personal contact had drawn them to Catholicism, that Newman and Chesterton had been their chief literary inspiration, and that they were received into the church by fellow converts who had become priests, such as Knox and Martindale.[7]

Conversion did not necessarily bring them close to the everyday life of ordinary British Catholics or change their low opinion of their new core-ligionists. Evelyn Waugh wrote of Ronald Knox, for example, that "he became a Catholic in violation of all his tastes and human sympathies, in obedience to his reason and in submission to what he recognized as the will of God. He asked from the Church only priestly orders and the right to do her bidding, but in many ways he knew less than the average well-informed Protestant layman of her physical life."[8] Waugh, as we shall see in a later chapter, could have said the same of himself; he regarded most of the ordinary Catholics he met after his own conversion as insufferable. The social penalties of conversion were less by the early twentieth century than they had been in Newman's day. No one ostracized them, and only those who were Anglican clergymen, such as Maturin and Knox, stood to lose their livelihoods. Conversion did not, in most cases, estrange them from their former friends.

Why should anyone want to become a Catholic? In the last resort these apologists had no hesitation in saying: Because it is the one true religion. They took doctrine seriously and identified the Catholic Church as doctrinally right. The erastian Church of England, by contrast, waffled for the

---

7. Francis "Sligger" Urquhart (1864–1934) was a popular Catholic don at Oxford whom they nearly all knew and admired. Knox wrote in an obituary to him that Urquhart "was so closely identified with the whole return of Catholicism to Oxford that the tale would be too long in the telling." Educated at Stonyhurst, he had been granted special permission to attend Oxford in 1890 (most Catholics were excluded before 1896) and had influenced Catholic undergraduate life for the next four decades. See Ronald Knox, "Francis Urquhart," *Dublin Review*, no. 392 (January 1935): 148–53.

8. Evelyn Waugh, *The Life of the Right Reverend Ronald Knox* (London: Chapman and Hall, 1959), 176–77.

sake of inclusiveness. All shared the view that human beings without a dogmatic teaching church and a definite principle of religious authority were too vulnerable to their passions, prone to idolatry, and likely to turn to fearsome political psuedoreligions such as nazism and communism, which were rising around them. They also became convinced that Catholicism, the traditional faith of their civilization, was its binding force. A dogmatic church would protect them—first, spiritually and, by extension, politically—from the chaotic forces loose in the twentieth-century world.

But they knew better than to start out with blunt dogmatic propaganda. Instead, they introduced a note quite absent from Catholic apologetics until this point. Be a Catholic, they said, because it is fun! Life is richer, the world more beautiful, sex more rewarding, family life happier, food and wine tastier, literature fuller, art and the landscape more beautiful, the sun more brilliant for people who understand that all good things come from God and that God's promises are guaranteed by Christ's sacrificial death. Catholic apologetics until then had been somber. Now it glittered. In Chesterton's telling, being a Christian was a stroke of the purest good luck, a gift from God which anyone would want to share. Ronald Knox deflated the Calvinist theology of predestination not with laborious syllogisms but with a jolly limerick:

> There was a young man who said "Damn:
> I have suddenly found that I am
> A creature that moves
> On predestinate grooves;
> Not a bus, as one hoped, but a tram!"[9]

Chesterton knew how to turn every epithet to his advantage without losing his good humor.

As an apologist I am the reverse of apologetic. So far as a man may be proud of a religion rooted in humility I am very proud of my religion; I am especially proud of those parts of it that are most commonly called superstition. I am proud of being fettered by antiquated dogmas and enslaved by dead creeds. . . . I am very proud of what people call priestcraft; since even that accidental term of abuse preserves the medieval truth that a priest, like every other man, ought to be a craftsman.[10]

9. Knox, quoted in Penelope Fitzgerald, *The Knox Brothers* (London: Macmillan, 1977), 96.

10. G. K. Chesterton, *Autobiography* (London: Hutchinson, 1936), 80.

These converts warned traditional apologists away from the old fire and brimstone and reminded other Catholics, as well as potential converts, that if the church made a severe rule, such as that priests must be celibate, it was not because it disliked sex but rather because it found sex so wonderful that voluntarily sacrificing it became the ideal gesture of sincerity and commitment. "It is precisely because sex is good," wrote Arnold Lunn, "that celibacy is a worthy offering to the creator of all good things."[11] Not that they all renounced it: one biographer has discovered that Eric Gill took his own enjoyment of sex to the opposite extreme.[12] Life, death, sin, procreation, and salvation were dramatic human issues, and here was a group willing to dramatize and humanize them to the fullest.

But if Catholicism was fun, it was also the last remaining lifeboat for the citizens of a foundering world. The rise of materialism, militant nationalism, and total war convinced these converts that the price of progress was too high and that humanity was destroying itself. Only by turning back to God and accepting the guidance of the one church that Jesus had founded, they believed, could they salvage it. Underlying the good humor and whimsy in their writing, therefore, was a serious conviction that they were fighting a battle for the world. By 1945 the deadliest weapons of destruction had been invented, tested, and used in a horrible war. Ronald Knox's *God and the Atom* (1945), written immediately after Hiroshima, bore eloquent testimony to the convert writers' sense of imminent apocalypse and their feeling that the modern world had rebelled against God himself.[13] The clash of good humor and urgent distress in their work seems incongruous at times but heightens its drama.

A third thread running through much of their work, along with fun and danger, was the continuing attempt to reconcile Catholicism and evolution without resort to the condemned principles of modernism. Darwin's generation had left many questions unanswered, including the ultimate origin of life, the relationship between the evolution of the body and that of the soul or spirit, and the nature of reality itself. Two of these British converts in particular, Bertram Windle and Alfred Noyes, tried to integrate evolution into the Catholic worldview without scandalizing the church authorities or the scientists. This reconciliation required delicacy in view of the Roman censors' vigilance after *Pascendi*, but a reader unaware of their situation will hear no defensive notes in their sonorous prose.

11. Arnold Lunn, *A Saint in the Slave Trade: Peter Claver (1581–1654)* (London: Sheed and Ward, 1935), 21.
12. Fiona MacCarthy, *Eric Gill* (London: Faber and Faber, 1989). MacCarthy makes clear, as Gill's earlier biographers had not, that he was sexually promiscuous, a voyeur, and even incestuous with his daughters.
13. Ronald Knox, *God and the Atom* (London: Sheed and Ward, 1945).

A fourth theme was the reevaluation of major figures in history, often to argue that the Protestants were not so benighted as earlier Catholic writers had assumed and that there were strong continuities from the pre-Reformation era into later Protestant literature, rather than a sharp break in history at the Reformation. They wanted to soften the stark antagonism between Protestant and Catholic writers from the past which they believed publicists on both sides to have overdrawn, and we can see them reflecting on their own experience in crossing from the newer to the older form of Christianity. Windle pointed to a religious sensibility even in the great nineteenth-century materialists such as Thomas Huxley and Herbert Spencer; Lunn and Knox admired John Wesley and the first Methodists, and Noyes maintained that Voltaire, properly understood, was less of an anti-Christian than later his vulgarizers had claimed.

The English convert apologists criticized the lack of charity which the Catholic Church in England and the United States showed to non-Catholics in their own day as well as in history. The mutual hostility of the two groups ever since the Reformation, especially when aggravated by Anglo-Irish hostilities, makes this harshness easy to understand, but to converts who had seen the world from both sides of the religious divide it seemed an affront. Hollis wrote that the memory of his father's gracious acceptance of his conversion to Catholicism was "the clearest example which I have ever come across . . . of what true Christian conduct can be, and makes me always very angry when, from time to time, I hear from Catholic lips sweeping and uncharitable denials of the existence of true Christian feeling or of the love of truth among Anglicans."[14]

It was a cardinal point for these converts that the world's non-Catholics thought of themselves as liberated from old superstitions and yet were more burdened with anxiety than any earlier generation. Whether it was true that everyone else was becoming more anxious and miserable, they certainly *believed* it to be true and used the claim as a way of dramatizing the contrast between the happy Catholic and the wretched outside world. Chesterton was a famous champion of convivial drinking and his fellow converts also saw a more than incidental value in wine and beer, all but implying at times that you had to be a Catholic even to know how to enjoy a drink at the pub. In the United States of the 1920s they beheld Prohibition, an apt symbol of life-denying puritanism, especially when its counterpart was bootlegging and illicit boozing. "Too much drink spoils the party," wrote Christopher Hollis, "but too little drink spoils it even more. Anyone who has had the experience of those frightful American banquets,

14. Christopher Hollis, *Along the Road to Frome* (London: Harrap, 1958), 84.

washed down by ice water, or again of those even more frightful American drinking parties of highballs on an empty stomach, is acquainted with the Scylla and Charybdis of horror."[15] They were champions of moderate self-indulgence and the blending of education, piety, and pleasure. In the name of these principles Arnold Lunn, after his conversion in 1933, arranged religious-cultural cruises around the Mediterranean, stopping at the principal classical and Christian sites en route and getting the Latin- and Greek-speaking geniuses on board (often Father Knox or Father Martindale), to lecture on history in exchange for their free tickets.[16]

One striking contrast between English and U.S. Catholicism in the first half of the twentieth century was that nearly all the most vivid Catholic characters in the United States were authority figures such as Cardinals William O'Connell of Boston, George Mundelein of Chicago, and Francis Spellman of New York, whereas the most vivid English Catholics were these lay writers, who put colorless Cardinal Francis Bourne, archbishop of Westminster, into the shade. "It was the presence of an informed, socially influential laity which had really made Newman's very isolated position in clerical terms a tenable one," writes Adrian Hastings, of this English lay dominance, which persisted into the twentieth century.[17] Wilfrid Sheed, son of the publishers Frank Sheed and Maisie Ward, who met all the major Catholic figures on both sides of the Atlantic in his youth, recalled that "the English view of the clergy was . . . relaxed. Evelyn Waugh, putting it most starkly, claimed that it was the duty of the educated classes to keep the clergy in its place." By contrast, said Sheed, the priests and bishops he met in the United States were "plump know-it-alls," who were granted more servile deference by the laity than they deserved. His parents' publishing house, which published the work of this convert generation, gave American Catholics, for the first time, "permission to think without benefit of clergy."[18] We can see this group of convert intellectuals in retrospect as an augury of the "rising layman," a phenomenon widely discussed in Catholic journals in the 1950s as the United States Catholic middle class gained a sense of self-possession and confidence.[19]

Another contrast between the two countries in the first half of the twentieth century was that the Americans were laboriously building a Catholic university system, to which there was no English counterpart.

15. Ibid., 58.
16. Arnold Lunn's family was in the travel business. See Waugh, *Knox*, 250.
17. Hastings, *English Christianity*, 140.
18. Wilfrid Sheed, *Frank and Maisie: A Memoir with Parents* (New York: Simon and Schuster, 1985), 93–94, 101.
19. On this phenomenon, see Donald Thorman, *The Emerging Layman: The Role of the Catholic Layman in America* (Garden City, N.Y.: Doubleday, 1962).

One of the British converts' motives in going to the United States was to work at these expanding universities and colleges, in a (usually vain) effort to invigorate the thousands of young Catholics studying there. Catholics made up about one-third of the U.S. population by the 1920s, and the ending of free immigration in that decade led to rapid "Americanization" and cultural assilimation. These proved a mixed blessing from the convert intellectuals' point of view since most American Catholic college students, while loyal to their church, aimed to make their mark in the U.S. business world and had little patience with fanciful convert schemes such as economic distributism or the finer points of Catholic cultural studies. The antiintellectualism of the U.S. Catholic universities, on which the convert migrants all commented, became a source of increasing scandal as the century progressed.[20] John Tracy Ellis, who was to blow the whistle on this state of affairs in the 1950s, was in the 1920s a graduate student at Catholic University of America, touted as the jewel in the crown of Catholic education. Disillusioned, he wrote a friend: "The history department here is so poor that it leaves all who touch it petrified with disgust." In the same year Ellis's adviser, Peter Guilday, the department's only ornament, begged the Harvard historian Robert Lord, who had just converted to Catholicism, to join the deparment to "save us from extinction."[21] Lord declined, and the history department staggered on without him. Potentially, nevertheless, these universities bore the seeds of a future intellectual harvest. Britain, by contrast, boasted only a handful of seminaries and private schools, Catholic droplets in a once-Anglican but now increasingly secular ocean.

Bertram Windle was a transitional figure from the world of Newman and Mivart to the quite different era of Chesterton and Knox.[22] Born in 1858, thirteen years after Newman's conversion, and in the same year that Isaac Hecker founded the Paulist order, Windle grew up in the shadow of the evolution debate. He was the son of an Anglican vicar in Ireland, in whose home "it was a sin to go to a theatre or to a dance; it was a sin to play any game on Sunday except that of putting together dissected maps of the Holy Land."[23] He had a conventional Anglican education at schools in Ireland and England (Repton). "It was an axiom" among members of

20. On the growth and characteristics of U.S. Catholic universities, see Philip Gleason, *Contending with Modernity: Catholic Higher Education in the Twentieth Century* (New York: Oxford University Press, 1995).
21. Ellis and Guilday, quoted in Thomas J. Shelley, "The Young John Tracy Ellis and American Catholic Intellectual Life," *U.S. Catholic Historian* 13 (Winter 1995), 7, 10.
22. Biographical information in the following passage is based on Monica Taylor, *Sir Bertram Windle: A Memoir* (London: Longmans, Green, 1932).
23. Bertram Windle, "A Rule of Life," *Catholic World* 103 (August 1916): 582–83.

his family "that the corrupt Church of Rome was composed of a large number of knaves constantly engaged in the deception of a very large number of thoughtless and foolish persons, who idly permitted themselves to be tricked into believing all kinds of nonsense on evidence which could scarce deceive a child."[24]

He was an undergraduate in Dublin and after a distinguished student career became professor of anatomy at the Birmingham Medical School, around which Birmingham University subsequently took shape. As a graduate student he had "an absence of religious belief as complete as that of Sir Arthur [Conan Doyle] himself," but reflection about his research work in human and primate physiology showed him that science had no answer to the question of why things should exist or why the materials of human beings should be infused with life.[25] A period of great religious uncertainty followed until Windle converted to Catholicism in 1883, noting later, like so many other converts, that "most of my Romeward path was trodden amongst books and I had read myself at least on to the threshold of the Church before I ever spoke to a priest or even to any Catholic on the subject."[26] Among the books to influence this step was Newman's *Apologia*—the two both lived in Birmingham and subsequently met. He also corresponded with St. George Mivart, who urged him to demonstrate the compatibility of Catholicism with scientific rigor.[27]

Windle's specialties were embryology and comparative morphology, along with experimental work in the study of musculature (myology) and the study of physiological abnormalities (teratology). He was among the first English scientists to appreciate the importance of Gregor Mendel's genetic work in explaining variation, which filled a gap in Darwin's theory of evolution through natural selection. A distinguished teacher and scholar, he rose over the next twenty years to a senior professorship and then the deanship of the Medical Faculty at Birmingham and was elected a fellow of the Royal Society in 1899.

In 1904 Windle, equally gifted in administration and scholarship, became president of Queen's College, Cork, Ireland, and supervised its transition from a symbol of English and Protestant oppression (the Catholic Church had forbidden Catholic students from attending it for the previous sixty years because of its Anglican character) into a non-

24. Bertram Windle, "Miracles: Fifty Years Ago and Now," *Catholic World* 101 (April 1915), 38–39.
25. Bertram Windle, "The Opportunity of the War," *Catholic World* 108 (February 1919): 582.
26. Bertram Windle, "Some Personal Recollections of Henry Ignatius Dudley," *Catholic World* 94 (March 1912): 809.
27. Taylor, *Windle*, 24–25, 52.

denominational university college with a mainly Catholic student body.[28] At Cork, despite his Anglo-Irish background, Windle came to believe in the cause of Home Rule for Ireland. He helped organize trade conferences to stimulate Irish industry, wrote indignant articles for the American Catholic press about England's commercial policy of prospering at the expense of Ireland, and helped set up an Irish Trade Mark system to encourage the purchase of Irish-made goods.[29] He was made a knight of Saint Gregory by Pius X and later given an honorary doctorate by Pope Pius XI. He also received a knighthood from King George V in 1912 for his services to British education. But like many moderate constitutional Irish Home Rulers, supporters of John Redmond, he found his position becoming untenable after the Dublin Easter Rising of 1916. Supporters of Sinn Fein, the radical Irish revolutionaries, regarded his service on the "Convention" by which prime minister David Lloyd George tried to resolve the crisis and his continued cooperation with Britain a betrayal of the Irish cause. He even feared that his conspicuously moderate position in the midst of a revolution might provoke a firebrand from one side or the other to assassinate him.[30]

It was, therefore, a pleasant surprise for Windle to be invited to a professorship at Saint Michael's College, Toronto. He accepted in 1919, left Ireland with mingled feelings of regret and relief, and spent the last ten years of his life on the western side of the Atlantic, writing, lecturing, and traveling widely through Canada and the United States. He lived long enough to see the early stages of the interwar Catholic literary revival, in which he participated as a contributing editor of a new journal, *Commonweal*, founded in 1924.

Windle was a polymath, vastly learned in the humanities as well as the sciences, and far-reaching in his interests. He was an enthusiastic amateur geologist, archaeologist, and anthropologist—all fields in which he published—and he wrote a guide book to his friend Thomas Hardy's "Wessex."[31] But in one way or another most of his writing aimed to justify and defend Catholic truth; even his books and essays on English fiction and drama (including a guide to Shakespeare) aimed to plumb the deep

28. Michael Maher, "The Conversion of a 'Godless' College: The Irish Catholic University Education Today," *Catholic World* 105 (May 1917): 200–208.

29. See, for example, Windle's harsh criticism of English policy toward Ireland in "The Irish Industrial Revival Movement," *Catholic World* 93 (May 1911): 225–33.

30. Taylor, *Windle*, 256–72.

31. Bertram Windle, *The Wessex of Thomas Hardy* (London: J. Lane, 1902). "Wessex" was one of the seven Anglo-Saxon kingdoms in England and, in Hardy's usage, comprised parts of the contemporary English counties of Dorset, Somerset, Wiltshire, Hampshire, and Oxfordshire.

Catholic wells from which their authors drew.[32] He treated Walter Scott, for example, as a forerunner of the nineteenth-century Catholic converts because he was the first novelist to write in praise of medieval England. Scott's influence was benign, said Windle, because it turned English minds toward the glories of the pre-Reformation era. "The lovely things still remaining after the violence of Henry VIII, Cromwell, and other crowned and uncrowned ruffians cannot but turn the hearts of those who admire them to think kindly of those who constructed them."[33]

The modernism controversy did not silence him as a scientist and philosopher of science. Windle was convinced that at least in its outlines the theory of evolution was right. "To put the matter in a nutshell, evolution *as God's method of creation* is a perfectly tenable hypothesis."[34] He accepted Lyell's evidence for the antiquity of the earth and the view that the fossil record and the morphological connections among members of different species all pointed to common ancestry. Windle made the kind of concession that his Protestant fundamentalist contemporaries strenuously resisted, writing of Genesis that it was not a literal account but what its writer "had to bring before the simple people for whom he wrote in language which they could understand."[35] He cut Darwin down to size, however, by pointing out that he had not explained the origin of the animals that were naturally selected, and that he had not adequately refuted William Paley's *Evidences*, with its defense of a Creator. Treating Darwin as one more in a long succession of "transformism" theorists rather than an intellectual revolutionary, he claimed that Saint Augustine had also been familiar with the idea that new species came into being through successive mutations. In Windle's telling Darwin had added refinements to a long—and largely Catholic—tradition of scientific study.[36]

Windle also believed that the development of culture and civilization could be explained to some extent by using evolutionary metaphors. In his extensive anthropological work, for example, he assumed that the "primitive" peoples of the world were on the lower rungs of a ladder of cultural evolution, and not, as Orestes Brownson had believed, that they were decayed remnants of once more-civilized people scattered by God from

32. Bertram Windle, *Shakespeare's Country* (London: Methuen, 1899).

33. Bertram Windle, "Scott and the Oxford Movement," *Commonweal*, December 3, 1924, 101.

34. Bertram Windle, "The Evolutionary Theory," in *Historical Text Books and Readers: Supplementary Volume* (London: Westminster Catholic Federation, 1928), 1457.

35. Bertram Windle, *The Church and Science* (London: Catholic Truth Society, 1917), 329.

36. Bertram Windle, "A Centenary of Scientific Thought," *Catholic World* 99 (June 1914): 289–308.

Babel.[37] But Windle differed sharply from Huxley and Haeckel's materialist deductions from Darwin. He was a vitalist and insisted on an infinite qualitative distinction between living and inanimate forms, just as Aristotle and the scholastic theologians had done, and he denied that the human soul was itself a product of evolution.[38]

Incurably confident that he was right, a little smug at times, Windle wrote in the first issue of *Commonweal* (1924) that he had lived to see the rise and fall of the evolutionary materialists, the men who had believed there was no difference in kind between a bird and the stone a man might throw at it. Vitalism was now ascendant once more. "The wheel has turned full circle and where has it stopped? . . . at the point where all the time Scholasticism has been standing. The modern theory is that of Saint Thomas six hundred years ago. . . . science has just arrived at the point reached by pure thought centuries ago."[39] Similarly the scholastics had once posed the existence of one basic substance. Robert Boyle had challenged them with the idea of fifty or more distinct elements, but in recent times "chemists and physicists" were coming to realize that "none of these are elements in the old meaning of that word, but . . . all are expressions of one fundamental matter," the discovery of atoms being, in this telling, another belated vindication of the scholastics.[40]

Windle was particularly eager to deny that Catholicism was the enemy of science, an idea central to John Draper's *History of the Conflict between Religion and Science* (1874) and Andrew Dickson White's *Warfare of Science and Theology* (1895).[41] Windle emphasized in successive books and articles that the church had made no dogmatic statement on the question of origins and that, contrary to popular prejudice, there were very few points where religion and science came into conflict. The church, far from being the enemy of science, had been almost its only advocate

37. See Windle's introduction to Edward Tyson, *A Philological Essay concerning the Pygmies of the Ancients* (London: David Nutt, 1894). Tyson, a seventeenth-century writer, had believed the classical authors mistaken in identifying pygmies as people. He argued, instead, that they were chimpanzees. Windle, in his introduction to Tyson's essay, summarized recent anthropologists' and explorers' discoveries of "pygmy" peoples in Africa and Asia.

38. Bertram Windle, *What Is Life? A Study of Vitalism and Neovitalism* (London: Sands, 1908).

39. Bertram Windle, "Science Sees the Light," *Commonweal*, November 12, 1924, 18. Windle's books *What Is Life?* (1908) and *Vitalism and Scholasticism* (London: Sands, undated but about 1922) are histories and justifications of the vitalist view.

40. Bertram Windle, "The Intellectual Claims of the Catholic Church," *Catholic World* 90 (November 1909): 234.

41. John Draper, *The History of the Conflict between Religion and Science* (1874; New York: Appleton, 1916); Andrew Dickson White, *A History of the Warfare of Science with Theology in Christendom* (New York: Appleton, 1895).

throughout the medieval and early modern ages.[42] In a biographical anthology of famous Catholic scientists, published in 1912, Windle declared: "Non-Catholics—some of them, one might perhaps even say many of them—seem to hold the irritating and absurd idea that Catholic men of science are afraid of the hypotheses of their non-Catholic brethren. This ridiculous idea is coupled with another, equally absurd, equally untrue, one may add equally insulting, which is, that the Catholic man of science, if he rejects or hesitates to accept any of these hypotheses, does so, not on scientific grounds, but because he is afraid to accept it on account of its supposed antagonism to religious dogma."[43] As Windle drew him, the Catholic man of science was possessed of great mental stability and infinite patience; he waited to see what the outcome of intellectual fads would be and invariably found in the end no conflict between his faith and his scientific work.

After all, the church had always pointed out that the province of science was limited, that only things susceptible to measurement could be included in it. Windle showed a little epistemological subtlety. He pointed out that scientists no less than Christians have to make an act of faith, first, that the material world really exists and, second, that it acts according to known or at least knowable and predictable laws. Not only an act of faith but also an act of abstraction, because in describing, categorizing, and measuring phenomena scientists are selecting and transforming their original qualities rather than duplicating them. The scientific account of a tree, for example, is a very different thing from the tree itself. Windle also stressed that science works by hypotheses and that a working hypothesis, while essential to every experimental scientist, is likely in time to be discarded, as the history of Western science plainly showed. He admitted that the church authorities had been wrong and Galileo right in his assertion of a heliocentric universe, but both had suffered for lack of the concept of the working hypothesis, which now bestowed, or ought to bestow, an appropriate modesty on practicing scientists. In places Windle's strictures on the history of science and the succession of theoretical paradigms prefigures Thomas Kuhn's *Structure of Scientific Revolutions*.[44]

G. K. Chesterton, the most famous of this generation of Catholic converts, was born in 1874. One of the many paradoxes of his life was that he

42. Bertram Windle, *The Church and Its Relations with Science* (New York: Macmillan, 1929), 39–40.

43. Bertram Windle, *Twelve Catholic Men of Science* (1912; London: Catholic Truth Society, 1923), 242–43.

44. Windle, *Church and Science*. Cf. Thomas Kuhn, *The Structure of Scientific Revolutions* (Chicago: University of Chicago Press, 1962).

wrote his most influential Catholic book, *Orthodoxy* (1908) while still an Anglican, fourteen years before his conversion. Later, as a Catholic, he noted that for him conversion had been an incremental process rather than a sudden shift.[45] His adult sensibility and his mature style were fully formed long before he entered the church in his late forties, and they did not change perceptibly after his Catholic confirmation. It was always tempting for born Catholics to assume that converts had crossed from night into day, but the converts' actual experience rarely bore out that assumption, as Chesterton's life plainly shows.

As a teenager he planned to become an artist and studied at the Slade School in London before shifting to poetry and then journalism. When he was twenty-six he met Hilaire Belloc (1870–1952), then thirty, and they quickly struck up a friendship that was to last throughout their lives. Belloc had a French father and an English mother (herself a convert) and after a brilliant undergraduate career at Oxford, culminating in a first-class degree in history, had expected a college fellowship and life as a don. He was convinced that he was denied the honor because of his Catholic faith, since no Catholic had won a college fellowship since the Reformation, and the disappointment gave him a lifelong hatred of Oxford dons.[46] In 1900 Belloc and Chesterton were both opposed to Britain's role in the Boer War, Chesterton because he was, at that stage, a Christian socialist and saw the war as imperialist bullying of a nation of small farmers, and Belloc because he thought the war was being fought in the interests of a clique of international (largely Jewish) bankers.[47] From Belloc, a hard-hitting controversialist who attacked his targets with pulverizing logic, Chesterton learned of the papal social encyclical *Rerum Novarum*, which offered a Christian and nonsocialist approach to criticizing capitalism and imperialism. He also came to share Belloc's view that a Jewish oligarchy, only partially assimilated to British life, was corrupting the government and Parliament.[48]

In Edwardian London over the next few years Chesterton moved in a

45. G. K. Chesterton, *Orthodoxy* (1908; Garden City, N.Y.: Doubleday, 1959). On the continuities before and after conversion, see Maisie Ward, *Gilbert Keith Chesterton* (London: Sheed and Ward, 1944), 397.

46. A. N. Wilson, *Hilaire Belloc* (1984; London: Penguin, 1986), 62–63. Wilson speculates that he was distracted by the woman he was wooing (and later wed) when he should have been pursuing a college fellowship and that anti-Catholicism was not a factor. C. C. Martindale was offered several Oxford college fellowships a few years later but was obliged as a Jesuit to decline them. See Philip Caraman, *C. C. Martindale: A Biography* (London: Longmans, 1967), 91, 94.

47. Wilson, *Belloc*, 95–97.

48. Ward, *Chesterton*, 227–28; Michael Ffinch, *G. K. Chesterton: A Biography* (London: Weidenfeld and Nicolson, 1986), 153–56.

circle of Anglo-Catholic intellectuals, "a very fine body of men to whom I
. . . shall always feel gratitude," he wrote in his autobiography. He recalled
the paradoxical situation of London's many religious seekers:

Men who believed ardently in altruism were yet troubled by the necessity of
believing with even more religious reverence in Darwinism, and even in the
deductions from Darwinism about a ruthless struggle as the rule of life. Men
who naturally accepted the moral equality of mankind yet did so, in a
manner, shrinkingly, under the gigantic shadow of the Superman of Nietz-
sche and Shaw. Their hearts were in the right place, but their heads were
emphatically in the wrong place, being generally poked or plunged into vast
volumes of materialism and scepticism, crabbed, barren, servile and without
any light of liberty or of hope.[49]

Chesterton wrote *Heretics* in 1905, a critical appraisal of George Bernard
Shaw, H. G. Wells, Rudyard Kipling, and some lesser voices representative
of the skeptical and pop-Darwinian mood of his age, but he was on
bantering good terms with the men whose ideas he most disliked. He
followed up *Heretics* with a defense of traditional Christianity, *Orthodoxy*,
in response to admirers' complaints that hitherto he had said far more
about what he was against than what he was for.

   *Orthodoxy* does not dwell on the issues dividing Anglicans and Catholics. Rather, it is an appeal to reexamine assumptions about what the world
is really like, based on Chesterton's deductions from his own experience.
In the preface Chesterton noted that it was a parallel to Newman's *Apologia* in that he had "been forced to be egotistical only in order to be
sincere."[50] Full of bravura passages on the unexpected and beautiful aspect
of everyday life and the way in which the mundane symbolizes the divine,
*Orthodoxy* reaches its climax in Chesterton's description of how he found
in Christianity an answer to the uncertainties of his youth.

I had been blundering about since my birth with two huge and unmanage-
able machines of different shapes and without apparent connection—the
world and the Christian tradition. I had found this hole in the world: the
fact that one must somehow find a way of loving the world without trusting
it. . . . I found this projecting feature of Christian theology, like a sort of
hard spike, the dogmatic insistence that God was personal, and had made a
world separate from himself. The spike of dogma fitted exactly into the hole
in the world—it had evidently been meant to go there—and then the

49. Chesterton, *Autobiography*, 176.
50. Chesterton, *Orthodoxy*, 6.

strange things began to happen. When once these two parts of the two machines had come together, one after another, all the other parts fitted and fell in with an eerie exactitude. I could hear bolt after bolt over all the machinery falling into its place with a kind of click of relief. . . . Instinct after instinct was answered by doctrine after doctrine.[51]

It is ironic that this description of his intellectual conversion should use mechanical metaphors so well, when Chesterton was a leading opponent of the mechanized view of life, and that it should be the description of his conversion to Anglicanism, not Catholicism. But Catholics valued it because of its stress on the importance of doctrine and the reality of original sin (the "hole in the world") and because of the book's high spirits and dazzling virtuosity. Wilfrid Ward reviewed it enthusiastically in the Catholic *Dublin Review*, and *Orthodoxy* has remained popular among Catholics ever since.[52]

Belloc encouraged in Chesterton the idea that Europe—"Christendom"—had reached its apogee in the High Middle Ages, and since fallen into a despotic oligarchy. Together they criticized the shibboleths of their age, its odd mix of liberal humanitarianism and imperialism, and the capitalist subversion of democracy. "It is a sufficient proof that we are not an essentially democratic state," wrote Chesterton in *Heretics*, "that we are always wondering what we shall do with the poor. If we were democrats we should be wondering what the poor will do with us."[53] In another memorable passage from *Orthodoxy* he argued that tradition and democracy were not at odds with each other as liberals and socialists assumed, but, rightly understood, complementary. "Tradition means giving votes to the most obscure of all classes, our ancestors. It is the democracy of the dead. . . . All democrats object to men being disqualified by the accident of birth; tradition objects to their being disqualified by the accident of death."[54]

Belloc was inexhaustibly prolific. Among his many books written in the first decade of the twentieth century were ten political novels, which Chesterton illustrated.[55] By 1910 the two men's names were so often linked that George Bernard Shaw nicknamed them "the Chesterbelloc." In fact Chesterton had a more philosophical and literary outlook and an irenic style, whereas Belloc emphasized history and politics, and usually

51. Ibid., 79.

52. Wilfrid Ward, "G. K. Chesterton and the Prophets," in his *Men and Matters* (1914; Freeport, N.Y.: Books for Libraries Press, 1968), 105–44.

53. G. K. Chesterton, *Heretics* (London: Bodley Head, 1905), 274.

54. Chesterton, *Orthodoxy*, 48.

55. Ffinch, *Chesterton*, 130–31. Belloc himself came to believe the illustrations were the most valuable part of these books.

wrote polemically. Belloc's ambitions led him to seek a parliamentary seat in the election of 1906. Standing as a Liberal in the largely Protestant constituency of Salford, he won, despite ignoring his agent's advice to soft-pedal his religion. He began one campaign speech like this: "'Gentlemen, I am a Catholic. As far as possible I go to Mass every day. This' (taking a rosary out of his pocket) 'is a rosary. As far as possible, I kneel down and tell these beads every day. If you reject me on account of my religion, I shall thank God that He has spared me the indignity of being your representative!'"[56] After five disillusioning years in Parliament (1906–1910), Belloc concluded that the British party system was a mockery and that the intermarried and interlocked families on the two front benches were virtually interchangeable. In collaboration with Chesterton's brother Cecil, a cantankerous polemical journalist with rhetorical venom to rival his own, who converted to Catholicism in 1913, Belloc wrote *The Party System* and *The Servile State*.[57] This latter book became a vade mecum for English and American Catholic intellectuals in the interwar years for its equally ferocious denunciations of capitalism and socialism, its lament over the "servility" of men forced to live on wages instead of independent landownership, and its advocacy of a Christian, guild-based, "distributist" economy.

Belloc and Cecil Chesterton also founded the *Eye Witness*, a journal dedicated to opposing the political corruption and financial scandals of the age, determined not to be taken in by the Victorian tradition that British politicians operated only from the purest motives. It was, says A. N. Wilson, "a new thing in English journalism. It was, in effect, trying to establish an alternative source of power to that of Westminster, to substitute government by a clique of well-born or wealthy families with government by a posse of journalists."[58] Almost at once they stumbled on the "Marconi scandal," revealing that members of Herbert Asquith's Liberal government had enriched themselves by trading in company shares that were certain to gain value after the (as yet unannounced) award of a lucrative government contract. They exposed Rufus Isaacs, a Jewish senior politician, and David Lloyd George, the chancellor of the exchequer, but in their eagerness to condemn the malefactors, they printed some unsubstantiated allegations which led to their defeat in a libel case. G. K. Chesterton, fully in sympathy with his friend's and his brother's campaign, was a regular contributor to *Eye Witness*. In addition, a wide array of skillful

56. Cited in Wilson, *Belloc*, 133.
57. Hilaire Belloc and Cecil Chesterton, *The Party System* (London: S. Swift, 1911); Hilaire Belloc, *The Servile State* (1912; New York: Holt, 1946).
58. Wilson, *Belloc*, 181.

contemporaries wrote for it, including George Bernard Shaw, H. G. Wells, and Maurice Baring (another Catholic convert). Chesterton commented that the only regrettable part of the *Eye Witness*–Marconi affair was that it familiarized British voters with the idea that their own politicians were corrupt but did not make them rise up in anger. Instead, it just made them a degree more cynical and resigned to an apparently unchangeable fate.[59]

Chesterton is remembered today as the creator of Father Brown, a worldly-wise Catholic priest whose vast experience with human depravity enables him to solve murder mysteries, giving the lie to his apparently simple exterior. Father Brown was modeled on Father John O'Connor of Bradford, whom Chesterton met in the teens of the century. He soon discovered how much O'Connor knew about sin after years of hearing confessions, and the discovery made a lasting impression on him. "I might have sunk more and more into some sort of compromise or surrender of mere weariness" he wrote later, "but for this sudden glimpse of the pit that is at all our feet. I was surprised at my own surprise. That the Catholic Church knew more about good than I did was easy to believe. That she knew more about evil than I did seemed incredible."[60] He began to write Father Brown books while still an Anglican but the encounter with O'Connor, like his friendship with Belloc and his brother's example, was pushing Chesterton toward Rome.

Theodore Maynard, one of Chesterton's many admirers in the early years of the *Eye Witness*, was a religious seeker who read *Orthodoxy* and acted on it by converting to Catholicism sooner than the author himself. Maynard, born in 1890, was to become a central figure in American Catholic life in the interwar years and author of what, at the time, was the best history of American Catholicism ever written.[61] He had grown up in a religious tradition that required conversion of everyone, but certainly not conversion to Catholicism. His parents were English missionaries to India, first with the Salvation Army and later with the Plymouth Brethren. His mother told him: "I would rather see you lying in your coffin than see you a Catholic."[62] "When the years went by and I proved tardy" about experiencing the approved form of evangelical Protestant conversion, he wrote later, "I often had the horrible experience of being prayed at. . . . There grew up in me something morbid and twisted. I knew that I

---

59. Chesterton, *Autobiography*, 210–12.

60. Ibid., 328.

61. Theodore Maynard, *The Story of American Catholicism* (New York: Macmillan, 1941).

62. Theodore Maynard, "Chapters from an Unwritten Autobiography," *Catholic World* 125 (August 1927): 612.

ought to be converted. I knew perfectly well that Hell waited for little boys who died 'unsaved.' But though I tried desperately hard, and even professed conversion at discreet intervals, I could not manage the trick."[63] Bertram Windle had speculated that the horrible psychology of evangelical Protestants like his own parents and Maynard's made an entire generation long to deny God altogether and to embrace atheistic materialism as an alternative.[64]

Maynard's parents' relief was boundless when he wrote them from his English boarding school in about 1905 that he had experienced a religious rebirth in a Baptist chapel. "I was happy like a boy in his first love. . . . Life was transfigured." Looking back on it as a Catholic, Maynard reasoned that "the phenomenon can be accounted for largely on the ground of adolescence—as it is during adolescence that nearly all conversions take place; but though my own experience was not wholly, or even mainly, supernatural, the grace of God did, I am firmly persuaded, avail itself of the psychological (and physiological) moment."[65]

As a teenager, Maynard continued, "my whole being was morbidly exalted, and I began indulging myself in an almost voluptuous surrender to religious emotion."[66] He took a trip to the United States in 1909, aged nineteen, and trained for the Congregationalist ministry at Dwight Moody's Mount Hermon School in Massachusetts. He preached in Vermont but was fired after three weeks for preaching a flippant sermon and then worked at a series of factory jobs before making his way back to England, broke, on a cattle boat. Preaching to English Unitarians and planning to go to college, he came upon Chesterton's *Orthodoxy*: "I was sliding at the age of nineteen from the Calvinist theology in which I had been brought up, into a vague humanitarian skepticism when I read *Orthodoxy*. And that book began in me a reaction which, by the grace of God, three years later carried me into the Catholic Church."[67] From Chesterton he also learned to condemn capitalism and after a short flirtation with socialism turned to the Catholic alternative offered by Leo XIII in *Rerum Novarum*.

Chesterton met Maynard in 1912, saw great promise in him, and wrote

63. Theodore Maynard, "A Chapter from an Unwritten Autobiography," *Catholic World* 125 (July 1927): 461.

64. Bertram Windle, "Some Causes of Theophobia," *Catholic World* 107 (June 1918): 317–22.

65. Maynard, "Chapters" (August), 610.

66. Theodore Maynard, "Chapters from an Unwritten Autobiography," *Catholic World* 125 (September 1927): 777.

67. Theodore Maynard, "The Chesterbelloc, II," *Catholic World* 110 (December 1919): 330.

an introduction to his first book of poetry. Maynard in turn contributed to *Eye Witness* and, desperate for remunerative writing jobs, to the American Paulists' *Catholic World*. "I could not repress a little anti-Catholic shudder," he wrote of his first approach to a Catholic priest, but the priest's friendliness and goodwill soon assured him of an easy entrance into the church. His 1913 reception at London's Brompton Oratory predated Chesterton's conversion by nine years. Writing about it later, Maynard said that apart from the rift with his parents (subsequently healed), the experience had been joyful and painless: "Most converts have bitter spiritual struggles. They have to tear themselves bleeding from the Church of their upbringing and to make appalling sacrifices. I am often disturbed that these experiences have not been demanded of me. I have won the Crown of Faith without having had to bear its Cross."[68]

Eric Gill converted in 1913, the same year as Maynard. He too would be one of the luminaries of the interwar Catholic revival, famous on both sides of the Atlantic. He lived in out-of-the-way parts of Britain, wore homespun clothes, and exalted the virtues of the Middle Ages. Gill was an Anglican clergyman's son. He trained as a stonecutter and woodcarver in turn-of-the-century London. A Fabian socialist, a dabbler in esoteric religions, and a contributor to the *New Age* in the same years as Chesterton, Gill gradually turned to Catholicism as an antidote to soulless commercialism. He became a Dominican tertiary after his conversion and was the nucleus of a Catholic craft community at Ditchling in Sussex, which tried to live out its opposition to commercial capitalism. "There was a considerable amount of splashing of Holy Water and the saying of grace before meals," wrote a visitor to this countercultural scene, "and there was an interminable nightly performance of Compline around a spinet with E. G. taking the part of cantor and singing plainsong in an unmusical voice. . . . Water froze in wash basins, bread and butter were homemade, and eaten off wooden plates; the only lighting was candlelight, and the members of the family were mostly dressed in clothes that had been spun and woven in the colony."[69]

He tried to do for Catholic art what Newman and Chesterton did for Catholic literature and Pugin for architecture: to elevate its standards and give Catholicism aesthetic pride of place in British life. He deplored the sentimental decoration of most English Catholic churches, and he thought that Cardinal Vaughan's showpiece, the recently completed Westminster Catholic Cathedral, represented not the glory of God but "the snobbery

68. Maynard, "Chapters" (September), 783.
69. Spike Hughes quoted in Robert Speaight, *The Life of Eric Gill* (New York: P. J. Kenedy, 1966), 136.

of those who paid" for it.[70] Gill had a love-hate relationship with the cathedral. He won the prestigious contract to carve the stations of the cross in 1914, which he rendered in an austere, neo-Medieval style, and he later added a carved altar in memory of Saint Thomas More, but he kept up a barrage of criticism of the archbishops, first Vaughan and then Bourne, for permitting the installation of statues he considered gaudy and vulgar.[71]

Sex vied with religion and art for Gill's attention. He was constantly involved in sexual affairs with the women around him and loved to draw men and women having sex. One psychologist later diagnosed him as suffering from a phallic fixation. He scandalized even his closest clerical supporter, the Dominican Father Vincent McNabb, when he drew Christ having sex with his bride, the church![72] His obsession with sex was, however, quite different from that of the "sexual revolutionaries" of the 1960s. He regarded it as a religious rite, had no interest in contraception, and reproached himself for his many transgressions during anguished sessions in the confessional with Vincent McNabb or Father John O'Connor, Chesterton's friend.[73]

He also condemned eugenics. As we have seen, the American convert Elizabeth Kite was an anomaly in advocating eugenics *after* her conversion. Most Catholics, born and converted, opposed eugenic interference with life for the same reasons that their descendants opposed abortion in the 1980s and 1990s—that it arrogated to mankind the work of God in giving and denying life and implied that some lives are more valuable than others. Bertram Windle, for example, was horrified by an English eugenicist's suggestion that doctors should have authority to end the lives of defective children. Such a suggestion was "not only immoral but [gave] an opening for the most deadly crimes."[74]

Chesterton agreed with Gill and Windle. He noted that far more harm had been done in the world by people who were too *strong* minded than by the feebleminded and that the whole notion of selective human breeding broke down on the point that no one was entitled to say which qualities should be artificially "selected." If it was really true that healthy men ought not to marry unhealthy or disabled women, and vice versa, he added, the eugenicists "ought to put up statues to the men who deserted

70. Ibid., 78.
71. Ibid., 77–80. Gill carved More's pet monkey hanging onto his robe but it was silently removed after Gill's death in 1940, much to the annoyance of his wife and artistic admirers. Ibid., 286–87.
72. MacCarthy, *Eric Gill*, 163–64.
73. Ibid., 259–63.
74. Windle, "Rule of Life," 583.

THE BRITISH APOLOGISTS' SPIRITUAL AENEID

their loves because of bodily misfortune, with inscriptions celebrating the good Eugenist who, on his fiancée's falling off a bicycle, nobly refused to marry her."[75] He wrote many critical columns on the issue before the First World War, linking eugenics to the mechanized view of life he saw as characteristic of German thought. When the war began Chesterton claimed that this war against "Prussianism" would ensure that "no Englishman would ever again go nosing round the stinks of that low laboratory" of eugenics. Finding after the war that "the ruling classes in England are still proceeding on the assumption that Prussia is a pattern for the whole world," he gathered and republished his earlier articles as *Eugenics and Other Evils* (1922).[76]

Eugenics was closely connected to the cult of the Anglo-Saxons, or Teutons. An influential school of late nineteenth-century historians and sociologists, Edward Freeman in England, Josiah Strong and Herbert Baxter Adams in America, found the "germ" of English and American democracy and freedom in the primeval German woods. They maintained that it had been carried to England by the Anglo-Saxon invaders and had flowered there, later gaining a further lease on life in America. In this account the Anglo-Saxons' displacement of the Celtic peoples and their erasure of the Roman legacy were benign events; they carried obvious implications for contemporary racial attitudes.[77] The First World War offered Chesterton the opportunity to explode this theory as well as the ideals of eugenics, when English soldiers found themselves locked in battle with men who came quite literally from Saxony. Luckily, he wrote, the ordinary British soldier would have no idea what you meant if you called him a "Saxon," and in this instance "the uneducated Englishman is more right than the educated Englishman, as well as more right than the educated German." The Teutonic vogue was, he added, an academic fad of German ("Prussian") philologists and ethnologists which the war ought to destroy once and for all.[78]

Isaac Hecker had found the Anglo-Saxon theory persuasive back in the 1870s and had linked it to his ideas for transforming the church from a

75. G. K. Chesterton, *Eugenics and Other Evils* (London: Cassell, 1922), 7.
76. Ibid., ii.
77. On this historians' fad, see Peter Novick, *That Noble Dream: The Objectivity Question and the American Historical Profession* (New York: Cambridge University Press, 1988), 80–81; John Higham, *History: Professional Scholarship in America* (1965; Baltimore: Johns Hopkins University Press, 1983), 160–62; and Robin Fleming, "Picturesque History and the Medieval in Nineteenth-Century America," *American Historical Review* 100 (October 1995): 1061–1094, esp. 1078–84.
78. G. K. Chesterton, "On Anglo-Saxons and Teutons," April 7, 1917, and "German Philology and Race Theory," April 21, 1917, in Lawrence J. Clipper, ed., *Collected Works of G. K. Chesterton* (San Francisco: Ignatius Press, 1989), 31:69–72, 76–80.

181

"Latin" and "Celtic" body into one dominated by Anglo-Saxons. Hecker
was an exception, because most Teutonists minimized the contribution of
Rome and, implicitly, of Roman Catholicism, in the making of the English-speaking nations. Chesterton's generation of converts, in contrast to
Hecker's, was eager to deny the theory and to reassert the legacy of Rome
in the making of modern Britain. Bertram Windle drew on his archaeological training to emphasize the extent of Roman influence.[79] Chesterton remembered being taught Teutonic theory as a child in the 1870s and
1880s and pointed out its obvious inadequacies:

We were told that our culture came, not from the Cross which everybody
could see, but from the Hammer of Thor, which nobody had ever seen. We
were told that England began her life with the Vikings when it would be
truer to say that she escaped with her life by killing the Vikings. All the
natural flow of tradition from Rome to the rest of the world was blocked
and hidden; and a counter-current set up suggesting that all generous im-
pulses had flowed from the Nordic barbarians, like warm and genial currents
flowing from the North Pole.[80]

By the 1920s Chesterton could have found support among influential
cultural anthropologists such as Franz Boas and Alfred Kroeber, who minimized racial differences, and American historians who had switched their
allegiance from Teutonic germ theory to Frederick Jackson Turner's
"frontier" thesis as an explanation for the development of American institutions.[81]

The First World War did much more than dent Teutonic theorizing; it
had seismic consequences for the British and American Catholic communities. When the war began in the summer of 1914 most Britons jumped
at the chance to fight, whatever their political and religious convictions. A
nation bitterly divided over industrial policy, votes for women, Irish Home
Rule, and the empire could agree that the German invasion of Belgium
was dastardly. Even the rapidly growing Labour Party forgot its pledge, as
part of the Second International, to refuse involvement in imperialist wars.

79. Bertram Windle, "The Roman Legacy to Britain," *Catholic World* 113 (July 1921):
444–51.
80. G. K. Chesterton, *The Resurrection of Rome*, in Robert Royal, ed., *The Complete
Works of G. K. Chesterton* (San Francisco: Ignatius Press, 1990), 21:396.
81. Carl Degler, *In Search of Human Nature: The Decline and Revival of Darwinism in
American Social Thought* (New York: Oxford University Press, 1991), 71–83, 90–100;
Richard Hofstadter, *The Progressive Historians: Turner, Parrington, Beard* (New York:
Knopf, 1969), 50–61, 125–41.

British workers rallied to arms as eagerly as their opposite numbers in Germany, leaving only a forlorn and hated remnant as conscientious objectors.[82]

Chesterton was forty when the war began. Years of overindulgence and overwork had bloated and exhausted him. Just as the war began he collapsed in a coma and was on the brink of death for several weeks. He had resisted joining the Catholic Church out of loyalty to his Anglo-Catholic wife, Frances, although he was convinced by 1911 that it was the right thing to do, and as his life ebbed away, she notified Father O'Connor that he might be needed to effect a deathbed conversion and to administer extreme unction.[83] But the crisis passed, Chesterton recovered, lost weight, and resumed his hectic work schedule. Like Belloc, he saw Germany as an almost wholly mendacious force in world affairs, the embodiment of autocracy and militarism. Britain, with all its faults, he treated as the defender of Christendom and the Christian tradition against the Prussian onslaught. He regarded the conflict as a defensive war, which could not make the world better (he had no Wilsonian illusions) but could prevent it from getting a great deal worse. He held this view both during and after the war and never accepted the later idea—persuasively argued by Hemingway, Dos Passos, Sassoon, Remarque, and other novelists— that it had been futile and insane from the outset.[84]

The view from Ireland was quite different, and Ireland, standing both literally and figuratively between England and America, complicated the issues of the war and the question of loyalties. Irish Catholics had suffered centuries of repression at the hands of England, and few of them were inclined to see Prussia as representing barbarism and Britain as representing Christianity. Many viewed the England of Elizabeth I and Cromwell as itself a symbol of Protestant savagery.[85] The legal disabilities placed on the Catholic Irish had been progressively lightened over the preceding hundred years, and by 1914 a large bloc of Irish Home Rule members sat in Parliament. Prime Minister Asquith's government was on the brink of granting Home Rule when the war began, despite fierce opposition from the Conservative and Unionist forces that represented Irish Protestants. The Catholic Home Rule advocates divided during the war into two camps: those led by John Redmond who believed they could win indepen-

---

82. See, for example, Max Beloff, *Wars and Welfare: Britain, 1914–1945* (London: Edward Arnold, 1984), 15–28.
83. Ffinch, *Chesterton*, 233–34.
84. Chesterton, *Autobiography*, 246–49.
85. R. F. Foster, *Modern Ireland, 1600–1972* (London: Allen Lane, 1988), 101–16.

dence by act of Parliament, and those who rallied to the revolutionary banner of Sinn Fein.[86] Both groups had persuasive advocates, and both were well represented among the huge Irish population living in the United States. The United States was ostensibly neutral between 1914 and the spring of 1917 while the First World War raged in Europe. The British government wanted the Americans to enter the war on their side; most of the Irish Catholics hoped to prevent them from doing so. Into this complicated setting came another eloquent and privileged convert to Catholicism, Shane Leslie, whose circumstances showed in heightened form the awkward mix of loyalties and pressures at work in a convert's mind.

Born in 1885, Leslie came from a prominent Anglo-Irish Protestant family, which divided its time between vast Irish estates at Glaslough and a princely London home. His mother's sister was Winston Churchill's mother; they were the famous and beautiful Jerome sisters of New York, daughters of a millionaire, who had both made fabulous transatlantic marriages on their grand tours. Educated at Eton, Shane Leslie left school in 1901, aged sixteen, to study in Paris, which was then in the throes of the Dreyfus controversy. He followed Emile Zola's funeral cortege, dabbled in the homosexual underworld later recorded by Proust, but began also to attend mass at Notre Dame. "I knelt at the altar rails and kissed the relics of the holy Thorn and a Nail of the Crucifixion . . . [then] returned happier and prouder than if I had kissed the loveliest lips in Paris. Heresy was beginning to leak out of my boots."[87] He also visited Russia, where he met Tolstoy, who inspired him to adopt vegetarianism—though not for long—and Louvain in Belgium, where he studied scholastic philosophy and befriended Cardinal Mercier. Mercier, Leslie recalled, "spoke with yearning sorrow of Father Tyrrell . . . whom he had taken under his robe in a vain attempt to keep him in the Church."[88] As an undergraduate at King's College, Cambridge, Leslie listened to the eloquent preaching of other converts to Catholicism, Robert Hugh Benson and Basil Maturin, and followed their example by converting in about 1906. His conversion horrified his family, as did his decision in 1910 to contest a parliamentary seat against his staunchly Unionist uncle, on behalf of Irish Home Rule.[89]

As a new Catholic Leslie traveled to the United States, where he had rich and influential connections, among whom he spread word of the Gaelic revival and spoke on behalf of Home Rule. He befriended Henry

86. Ibid., 471–93.
87. Shane Leslie, *Long Shadows* (London: John Murray, 1966), 93.
88. Ibid., 118.
89. Ibid., 127–30. He lost the election.

Adams ("the best and finest of the old Americans I ever met"),[90] Woodrow Wilson, Theodore Roosevelt, Cardinal Gibbons of Baltimore, Archbishop John Ireland of Minneapolis–St. Paul, and most of the Irish-American political bosses of the big cities. He also met the young F. Scott Fitzgerald, then a teenager at the Newman School, and one of his teachers, Sigourney Fay (another charismatic convert). Reviewing one of Leslie's books ten years later, Fitzgerald wrote:

He first came into my life as the most romantic figure I had ever known. He had sat at the feet of Tolstoy, he had gone swimming with Rupert Brooke, he had been a young Englishman of the governing classes when the sense of being one must have been, as Compton Mackenzie says, like the sense of being a Roman citizen. Also, he was a convert to the church of my youth and he and another, since dead [Fay], made of that church a dazzling, golden thing, dispelling its oppressive mugginess and giving the succession of days upon gray days, passing under its plaintive ritual, the romantic glamour of an adolescent dream.[91]

In 1918 Fitzgerald sent Leslie draft chapters of his first novel, *The Romantic Egotist,* and Leslie wrote to the publisher Charles Scribner, whom he knew personally, recommending the novel for publication. In gratitude Fitzgerald wrote him: "Did you ever notice that remarkable coincidence— Bernard Shaw is 61 years old, H. G. Wells is 51, G. K. Chesterton 41, you're 31, and I'm 21—All the great authors of the world in arithmetical progression."[92]

Helping the aspiring novelist was incidental to Leslie's main work in America during the First World War. He was a founding editor of *Ireland,* a journal aimed at cultivating Irish-American opinion in favor of Irish Home Rule and support for Britain in the First World War, but against Sinn Fein and revolution. Leslie was Irish enough to resent England's high-handed treatment of Catholic Ireland but English enough to deplore pro-German sentiment among Irish Americans. He urged Irish Americans to join in the war effort against a Germany that he, like Chesterton, regarded as barbaric.[93]

90. Shane Leslie, *American Wonderland: Memories of Four Tours in the United States of America, 1911–1935* (London: Michael Joseph, 1936), 53.
91. Fitzgerald, quoted in Matthew J. Bruccoli, ed., *F. Scott Fitzgerald: A Life in Letters* (New York: Scribner's, 1994), 480.
92. Ibid., 20.
93. Leslie, *Long Shadows,* 128–45. See also his *American Wonderland,* 63. "I made some

Sinn Fein's Easter Rising of 1916 did not lead to revolt throughout Ireland, but when the British government executed the survivors of the Dublin post office siege in the following months, it provoked a wave of anti-British and pro–Sinn Fein feeling throughout Ireland and Irish America.[94] Redmond's position in Parliament as a compromiser and moderate Home Ruler, became more and more marginal. Leslie's book *The Irish Question in Its American Aspect* (1917) shows the complexity of his religious and hereditary loyalties and his conflicting feelings about Ireland, Britain, the United States, and the two contending religions.[95] As the prospect of a constitutional solution faded, the specter of civil war arose, becoming a grim reality between 1919 and 1922. In the short term, however, Leslie was consoled by American entry into the war in the spring of 1917, bringing, as it did, auguries of almost certain victory over Germany.[96]

Another old Etonian and a friend of Shane Leslie's was Ronald Knox, who rivaled Chesterton as a master of paradox and high-spirited Catholic apologetics.[97] Knox was the fourth son of a Low Church Anglican bishop. As a child he read about Newman and the Oxford movement and was excited to discover that "somewhere, beyond the circles I moved in, there was a cause for which clergymen had been sent to prison . . . a cause which could be mine."[98] Despite his father's opposition, he gravitated in his teens to the Anglo-Catholic, "ritualist" side of Anglicanism. As a prizewinning Oxford undergradute and then as an Anglican priest he watched the

---

twelve visits to the White House to help the Irish cause, first for Redmond and after his death for Horace Plunkett and his Convention. But," adds Leslie, "I never hesitated to present the Sinn Fein view when it was obvious that Griffiths and Collins and de Valera represented the resurgence of the Irish soul."

94. George Dangerfield, *The Damnable Question: A Study in Anglo-Irish Relations* (London: Quartet, 1976), esp. 223–64.

95. F. M. Carroll, *American Opinion and the Irish Question, 1910–1923* (London: Gill and Macmillan, 1978): 45, 65, 95–97, 101.

96. Leslie, a frequent visitor to the United States, was guardedly sympathetic to eugenics. Of the American immigration restriction laws of the 1920s he wrote: "Hitherto the employers wanted hands, not brains, to enter the country. Too late America has set out to make the future eugenically safe. But the unknown element in eugenics and race-mixture may set the theories of Stoddard and Madison Grant at a discount." *American Wonderland*, 209. He wrote about African Americans in the stereotypes of the times: "The only solution of the ["negro"] problem, though not edifying, is at least eugenic. Every black quarter is becoming whiter every year. The great negro leaders, Douglass and Booker Washington, had white blood. It stands to reason that white blood will eventually extinguish the black if white men help themselves to dark girls while the converse is punished by death" (ibid., 214).

97. Shane Leslie and Ronald Knox collaborated on a book urging the canonization of King Henry VI of England, founder of their old school: *The Miracles of King Henry VI* (Cambridge: Cambridge University Press, 1923).

98. Fitzgerald, *Knox Brothers*, 64.

Catholic modernist controversy, witnessed its echoes in Anglo-Catholicism, and found himself strongly on the side of the antimodernists. He spent one college vacation with a group of Anglican Benedictine monks on the Isle of Caldey (off the coast of South Wales) who soon afterwards, in 1913, went "over to Rome" en masse, and another vacation with the Catholic don Francis "Sligger" Urquhart in Switzerland.[99] (The temperate Urquhart had won the honor denied to the tempestuous Belloc, of becoming the first Catholic don at Oxford since the Reformation.) Knox took a vow of celibacy in 1912 and was already "Catholic" on all questions other than Roman authority; his dismayed father remarked, "I cannot understand what it is that the dear boy sees in the Blessed Virgin Mary."[100] Knox regarded the Church of England as a "true branch of the Latin Church of the West, which through an accident of history had been partly severed from the trunk. She was feloniously held in bondage by the state" but in time would achieve reunion.[101]

Knox, as chaplain of Trinity College, Oxford, in the early teens of the century, befriended and almost converted Harold Macmillan, a future British prime minister, and led a group of Anglo-Catholic undergraduates. After writing a series of satires against Anglican modernism Knox finally joined the Roman church in 1917. His father's lofty position in the Church of England and his own renown as a defender of Christian orthodoxy led the Manchester *Guardian* to declare that "Rome has landed its biggest fish since Newman."[102] Knox wrote an account of his religious journey, *A Spiritual Aeneid*, and was ordained a Catholic priest in 1919 after being excused on grounds of his accomplishments from having to attend seminary.[103]

Knox welcomed the rocklike certainty Roman Catholicism offered. Far from being repelled by the stifling of theological debate following *Pascendi*, he was glad of it. "Knox's conversion," notes historian Adrian Hastings, "was to a view of Church authority of ultramontane simplicity; no one was less worried by the unmitigated absoluteness of the anti-modernist oath, which he took with positive delight." Hastings adds an apt summary of this generation: "Most intellectual converts for the next forty

99. On the conversion of the Caldey Benedictines, see Katharine Tynan, "The Benedictines of Caldey," *Catholic World* 106 (January 1918): 528–34. Their leader, Aelred Carlyle, was persuaded to take the ultimate step by another convert from Anglicanism, Dom Bede Camm.

100. Fitzgerald, *Knox Brothers*, 103.

101. Waugh, *Knox*, 108–9.

102. Fitzgerald, *Knox Brothers*, 141.

103. Ronald Knox, *A Spiritual Aeneid* (London: Longmans, 1918).

years—and there would be many and brilliant ones—decided upon substantially the same grounds."[104]

Conversion forced Knox to relinquish his position as college chaplain and he spent seven years as a Latin teacher at a minor Catholic boarding school, Saint Edmund's in Hertfordshire. Its obscurity was hardly better than prolonged penance for so scintillating a debater and scholar, but he made the best of it, wrote constantly, and consolidated a reputation for Catholic apologetics in England and America. His *Spiritual Aeneid* in particular struck Catholic critics as a superb accomplishment, to rank beside Newman's *Apologia*. One American reviewer ended with the hope that "this brilliant young convert—he is only thirty"—might "live long to do battle for the cause of the Church of God."[105]

Throughout the first two decades of the twentieth century, meanwhile, Roman Catholics had been watching Chesterton expectantly. He was the subject of admiring articles in the English and American Catholic press throughout the teens of the century, and often contributed articles to it, where his bright idiom enlivened its stolid pages.[106] In 1919 an American Jesuit compared him to Newman and confirmed that *Orthodoxy* was a work of Newmanesque brilliance, adding that the two men had strikingly similiar ideas and sympathies and that Chesterton was "a Catholic at heart."[107] Chesterton's young protégé Theodore Maynard wrote of Belloc and Chesterton in 1919 that "every road they tread leads to Rome."[108] He conceded that Chesterton was still an Anglican but added that his conversion was bound to happen sooner or later. "It will probably be postponed as long as possible, but there is only one end. Has he not assured us, in the monograph on Blake, that every man, if he could live a thousand years, must become either a complete Catholic or a bottomless skeptic?"[109] Maynard was vindicated in 1922 when Chesterton finally took the long-awaited step after a visit to the Holy Land and a promise made before a statue of the Blessed Virgin Mary in Italy.[110]

Conversion brought him closer than ever to Belloc's point of view, but their styles differed in a way which subsequent observers have noted. As

104. Hastings, *English Christianity*, 150.
105. Bertrand Conway, C.S.P., "The Homecoming of Ronald Knox," *Catholic World* 107 (September 1918): 785.
106. See, for example, G. K. Chesterton, "Human Nature and the Historians," *Catholic World* 104 (March 1917): 721–30.
107. Alfred Brickel, S.J., "Cardinal Newman and Gilbert K. Chesterton," *Catholic World* 109 (September 1919): 744–52.
108. Theodore Maynard, "The Chesterbelloc, I," *Catholic World* 110 (November 1919): 146.
109. Maynard, "The Chesterbelloc, IV," *Catholic World* 110 (February 1920): 626.
110. Ward, *Chesterton*, 380–98.

James J. Thompson, one of the editors of his collected works, says, "Belloc's polemics appealed most to the already convinced; his message confirmed them in their faith and steeled them to do battle with the Church's detractors. Chesterton, by contrast, spoke more to those in the opposing camp who might be entertaining doubts about the unalloyed righteousness of their own cause. He understood the mind of the agnostic, the atheist, and the half-believer in a way that Belloc did not, and he sought . . . to pick them off one by one and spirit them into the Church."[111] Like his convert predecessors, he understood the dilemma they felt, and declined his friend's style of dramatic simplification.

By the early 1920s these British converts had laid some of the foundations of a Catholic literary revival. In that decade and the 1930s, Catholics offered, at home and in the United States, an alternative vision of the world to that of their Protestant and secular rivals. They challenged common assumptions on a wide range of political, economic, artistic, and moral issues, often in running debate with the church authorities. Respected and admired by their conservative contemporaries, including T. S. Eliot and Ezra Pound, C. S. Lewis, Paul Elmer More, and Irving Babbitt, they would be scorned by the influential political Left or simply ignored as beyond the pale of serious intellectual life.

111. James J. Thompson, Introduction to Chesterton, *Collected Works* 3:22.

# IX

# REVIVAL
# AND DEPARTURE

THE FIRST WORLD WAR brought the U.S. progressive movement to an end. It also marked the beginning of a Catholic revival, a period of bolder social policy, accelerated institutional growth, and a new concern with intellectual life. U.S. Catholics doubted President Wilson's claim that the First World War was a war to end all wars. As William Halsey notes, "The awakening of Catholic enthusiasm during the war was decisively linked to the waning of enthusiasm among individuals and institutions which had invested the war with any sacred, social, or political mandate. Since Catholicism had made a point of opposing any promises of an earthly paradise, it felt no sting of defeat when the conflict brought more clouded vision than paradise."[1] After the war American Catholics were pulled in two directions, desiring, on the one hand, to promote their church and its distinctive message, but eager, on the other hand, for full assimilation into American life.[2] Their solution to this dilemma, says Halsey, was to pose as guardians of nineteenth-century values, which the war had dented and which a skeptical generation of secular intellectuals challenged. The Catholic revival, as he describes it, was an attempt to use Catholic resources to protect "American innocence."

1. William Halsey, *The Survival of American Innocence: Catholicism in an Age of Disillusionment, 1920–1940* (Notre Dame, Ind.: University of Notre Dame Press, 1980), 31.
2. On these conflicting pressures to assimilate and to remain distinct, see Paula Kane, *Separatism and Subculture: Boston Catholicism* (Chapel Hill: University of North Carolina Press, 1994); and R. Laurence Moore, *Religious Outsiders and the Making of Americans* (New York: Oxford University Press, 1984), 48–71.

Canadian-born Michael Williams (1877–1950), a central figure in this revival, was not technically a convert, though he had spent the first fifteen years of the twentieth century entirely remote from Catholic life. A wandering freelance writer and socialist, he had lived in Upton Sinclair's utopian commune at Englewood, New Jersey, and collaborated with Sinclair on a vegetarian tract.[3] In those years Williams had been "strongly anti-Catholic," seeing the church as an enemy of progress and enlightenment, but he returned to his childhood faith in 1917 after a series of religious experiences, recorded in his spiritual autobiography, *The Book of the High Romance* (1918). He organized a group of enthusiastic New York writers to create a new Catholic magazine, *Commonweal*, which first appeared in 1924.[4] Designed as a lay Catholic rival to the *New Republic* and the *Nation*, it drew jaundiced looks from other Catholic editors at first. For example, Williams's coeditor George Shuster wrote Daniel Hudson, editor of *Ave Maria*, that the atmosphere of *Commonweal* was "slightly too much steeped in 'convert' moods. Converts are of course the best people on earth but it seems to me they need a little seasoning and aging before they set out to interpret Catholic thought." Hudson agreed: "Converts certainly do need seasoning—many of them a great deal of it."[5]

Nevertheless, the first issue carried articles by no less than three British converts: Bertram Windle, G. K. Chesterton, and Theodore Maynard. They and a crowd of other British converts wrote many of *Commonweal*'s articles in the two following decades, with much of the remainder contributed by American converts such as the cofounder Carlton Hayes. Articles were often illustrated with Eric Gill's woodcuts.[6] *Commonweal* aimed to raise literary and intellectual standards among American Catholics, but it steered clear of theological questions. It joined *Ave Maria*, the Jesuits' *America*, the Passionists' *Sign*, and the Paulists' *Catholic World* in its orthodoxy, its faintly Victorian air (Halsey's "innocence"), and its welcoming embrace of the British converts. But unlike its fellows it looked outward into the wider world beyond the Catholic ghetto. On its first anniversary the editors noted that before the appearance of *Commonweal*,

3. Upton Sinclair and Michael Williams, *Good Health and How We Won It* (New York: F. A. Stokes, 1909).

4. Michael Williams, *The Book of the High Romance: A Spiritual Autobiography* (New York: Macmillan, 1918). See also Robert B. Clements, "Michael Williams and the Founding of *Commonweal*," in Edward Kantowicz, ed., *Modern American Catholicism, 1900–1965* (New York: Garland, 1988), 137–47.

5. Shuster and Hudson, quoted in Thomas E. Blantz, *George N. Shuster: On the Side of Truth* (Notre Dame, Ind.: University of Notre Dame Press, 1993), 62.

6. See, for example, the Christmas issue, *Commonweal*, December 23, 1925, illustrated with Christmas scenes by Gill throughout and including an article about him: Henry Longan Stuart, "The Art of Eric Gill," 175–77.

"few organs have addressed themselves to any audience save that of the faithful." Now, however, "among our adversaries and among those who care nothing about religion" there was a new respect "for the opinions and works of the Catholic intellectual classes," a respect that *Commonweal* aimed to foster.[7] Theodore Maynard, though a loyal contributor, found it dull by comparison with Chesterton's *New Witness*, for which he had been writing until then, but he was not surprised: "The fact is that there is no very large body of intellectuals among Catholics in the United States, and its creation is not possible overnight." He did not blame the editors, Williams and Shuster, who had many easily-shocked constituencies to conciliate. "If there is any blame to be given it must fall upon the pious rags that are published in such abundance, and that by reflecting the terribly low average of American Catholic thought and feeling, slow up the progress being made."[8] Bertram Windle, now working in Toronto, reported that the situation in Canada was even worse: "Our Catholic weeklies are simply deplorable. . . . the Church does not seem to envisage the fact that there are non-Catholics, and its awful little weeklies would put any intelligent man off the Church who came in contact with them."[9]

The revival of which *Commonweal* was an element, says Arnold Sparr, was "the awakening of American Catholics to their modern intellectual and cultural heritage as the fruits of the English, French, and German Catholic revivals were communicated to America, but it was also a movement on the part of a self-conscious American intellectual community to stimulate the production of America's own share of modern Catholic thinkers, essayists, poets, and novelists."[10] The editors of *Commonweal* knew that the most influential American intellectuals of the day, such as John Dewey, H. L. Mencken, Alfred North Whitehead, Walter Lippmann,

7. Editorial, "Our Second Year," *Commonweal*, November 11, 1925, 1.

8. Theodore Maynard, *The World I Saw* (Milwaukee: Bruce, 1938), 271.

9. Windle, quoted in Monica Taylor, *Sir Bertram Windle: A Memoir* (London: Longmans, Green, 1932), 336–37.

10. Arnold Sparr, *To Promote, Defend, and Redeem: The Catholic Literary Revival and the Cultural Transformation of American Catholicism, 1920–1960* (Westport, Conn.: Greenwood, 1990), xi. Sparr holds that the Catholic argument with America was more profound than Halsey realized in *The Survival of American Innocence*. "The Innocence model makes the nature of Catholicism's controversy with modernity appear much shallower than it actually was. . . . [Halsey] offers primarily non-creedal, materialistic reasons for the Catholic reaction . . . [but] Catholic thinkers world wide were in revolt against a broad spectrum of modern ideas . . . long before the disillusioned 1920s. Catholic revivalists never seemed to tire of reminding the non-Catholic world that Catholic thinkers as far back as Newman had rebelled against the nineteenth century cult of 'Reason and Progress.' . . . Catholics thus liked to congratulate themselves on the fact that they knew all along what the disillusioned critics of the postwar years were just discovering for themselves—that unlimited progress based upon rationalistic science and unaided human reason was an empty promise" (53).

and Joseph Wood Krutch, thought of Catholicism as a refuge for stunted minds, an enemy of critical thought and broad-mindedness. They also knew, to make matters worse, that several prominent American authors of the era, including F. Scott Fitzgerald, James T. Farrell, and Theodore Dreiser, were ex-Catholics, whose indictment of their childhood religion lent support to the secular critics' ideas. And they knew that these critics were largely right to look down on American Catholics' lean achievements. *Commonweal* coeditor George Shuster admitted in *The Catholic Spirit in Modern English Literature* (1922) that "the great bulk of American Catholic fiction is unintelligent and unreadable" and that, thus far, Catholic America had little of which to boast and was dependent on literary imports.[11]

Williams and Shuster were confident by the mid-1920s that the situation was beginning to change. Williams argued in *Catholicism and the Modern Mind* (1928) that Catholicism, "although generally unacknowledged, or unrecognized, has been and is today a powerful factor in American literature." Moreover, "it is bound rapidly and surely to become a recognized and distinct element of capital importance in our literature" because it alone truly understood the nature of reality. Williams interpreted the crushing attack on "puritanism" by Mencken, Van Wyck Brooks, and other secular critics, as a sign that the Protestant heresy had exhausted its energies. But the glib antipuritans were themselves vulnerable, said Williams, as the criticism of the new humanists, Paul Elmer More and Irving Babbitt, had shown. Catholicism remained "the one force capable of giving what is valid . . . good, true, and beautiful in both Puritanism and anti-Puritanism their full effect." But Williams reiterated the point that Catholics must not be insular. "I repeat . . . that it is important for Catholics to cooperate with non-Catholics in the literary movement now begun by these younger men who are going back to the humanistic tradition for their philosophy."[12]

An example of how one Catholic scholar tried to boost the revival while avoiding insularity can be found in Edward J. Mannix's odd book *The American Convert Movement* (1923), a quirky blend of Catholic theology and contemporary psychology. Mannix saw the steady flow of converts into the church in recent decades as simply the gift of faith from God, but he added that science and faith cannot be at variance, and modern intellec-

---

11. George Shuster, *The Catholic Spirit in Modern English Literature* (1922; Freeport, N.Y.: Books for Libraries, 1967), 312. On the writing of this book, see Blantz, *George Shuster*, 31–33.

12. Michael Williams, *Catholicism and the Modern Mind* (New York: Longmans Green, 1928), 212, 218, 221.

tual methods allow us to probe further and demonstrate the operation of the psychological laws through which God is working. He defended his borrowing of psychological insights from non-Catholic sources to construct a four-stage mental process, in which the individual moved from curiosity to an examination of conscience, then investigation of the church, leading to the fulfillment of faith itself. "Since laws obtain in the supernatural as well as the natural order," said Mannix, "psychology, or the science which investigates the nature, attributes, and activities of the soul or mind of man, has a field to cover, i.e. in ascertaining how these laws react in human nature."[13] When it came to bold generalization about psychological laws, Mannix was as rationalistic as his contemporary John B. Watson (1878–1958), the founder of behaviorism, but the conceptual gulf between the two is apparent when Mannix tries to account for the feelings of depression some converts experience just before their reception into the Catholic faith: "Whether a state of nerves, or a last desperate attempt of the Prince of Darkness to thwart the soul's entrance into Life, it manifests itself in the form of deep discouragement, bordering on despair."[14] *The American Convert Movement* bears witness to a Catholic scholar straining to widen his intellectual horizon but always mindful of scholastic limits and the shadow of *Pascendi*.

How much did the postwar revival really amount to? Sparr shows how a handful of Jesuit publicists, led by Daniel Lord, Francis X. Talbot, and Calvert Alexander, "believed that a Catholic literary emergence could, somehow, be deliberately manufactured in America through inducement, exhortation, and effort."[15] They founded writers' leagues, poetry and drama societies, and even a photographic gallery of "great living Catholic authors," all in the hope of spreading their gospel to parochial school-children, Catholic college students, and the communicant in the pew. Their campaign yielded few immediate results, however, and British and convert support for American Catholic literary ventures remained indispensable throughout the 1920s and 1930s, partly because of the attitude of influential Catholic college administrators and professors. As Philip Gleason has shown, they were building a unified curriculum, based on scholastic philosophy and working from the assumption that all the really important questions in life had already been answered. Gleason quotes the

13. Edward J. Mannix, *The American Convert Movement: Being a Popular Psychological Study of Converts to the Catholic Church in America during the Last Century and a Quarter* (New York: Devin Adair, 1923), 31.

14. Ibid., 97. On the atheist Watson's determination to reduce psychology to physiology, see Clarence Karier, *Scientists of the Mind: Intellectual Founders of Modern Psychology* (Urbana: University of Illinois Press, 1986), 106–58.

15. Sparr, *To Promote*, 32.

warning of a Fordham Jesuit, George Bull, that "Catholic graduate schools could not accept research as their primary aim because research was an activity whose tendency was inevitably destructive of the Catholic intellectual synthesis and the culture it inspired."[16] The revival remained as much pious hope as real event, especially in the matter of achieving massive lay support. Sparr shows that the college courses on the revival drew heavily on the work of the converts, especially Newman and Chesterton, and on the new humanists, but only after careful censorship. Alexander, for example, did not include Newman's essay *On the Development of Doctrine* or his *Grammar of Assent*, two of his most "modern" works, in his syllabus recommendations. He tried to minimize Newman's links to nineteenth-century romanticism and make him sound more like a scholastic philosopher than he had been in fact. "As a neo-scholastic thinker," Sparr notes, "Alexander thought it imperative to dissociate Newman from a movement that posited human sentiment and emotion as the primary guide to truth. The Jesuit wanted no hint of emotionalism or nostalgic medievalism surrounding the rebirth of Catholic letters."[17] But even sanitized like this the revivalists' prominent use of converts was, in a sense, an admission that indigenous intellectual power was still very slight.

One of the Jesuits' expedients in trying to swell the ranks of American "great Catholic writers" was to regard Theodore Maynard as an American as soon as he had taken out naturalization papers. Maynard, an autodidact, had returned to America in 1920 to lecture on poetry, fiction, and Prohibition. After a lecture at the Dominican College of San Rafael in California the college's president offered him a job teaching English literature, even though he had no college education of his own. With a wife and growing family to support (eventually including seven children) he accepted and taught first there, then back east at Fordham and Georgetown. He got his bachelor's degree from Fordham in New York while on its faculty, and his doctorate from Catholic University of America while he was teaching at nearby Georgetown in Washington, D.C. By 1928 he was head of the Engish department there and had switched his literary efforts from poetry to Catholic biography.[18] His studies of the conquistador Hernando de Soto (1929), Saint Francis Xavier (1936), and Saint Vincent de Paul (1939) are well researched and fluently written, marking a dramatic improvement over the hagiographical treatment these figures had suffered

16. Bull, quoted in Philip Gleason, "In Search of Unity," *Catholic Historical Review* 65 (April 1979): 198–99.
17. Sparr, *To Promote*, 69.
18. Maynard, *World I Saw*, 276–81.

hitherto.[19] Pausing in his life of Francis Xavier to discuss the miracles attributed to the saint, Maynard wrote that he believed many of them "are susceptible of a purely natural explanation." He certainly was not denying that God could perform miracles, but he urged readers to reflect that "a good deal of the evidence that formerly passed muster would hardly endure the scrutiny of the papal official named, by a pleasant ecclesiastical joke, the *Advocatus Diaboli*" and that, in history, there should be a strong presumption *against* supernatural explanations.[20]

Maynard found U.S. Catholics religiously observant but complacent. "Few Catholics are so badly instructed as those in this country," he wrote in the mid-1930s, "or more easily fall away from the Church when it suits their convenience, so that one often wonders what would happen to the twenty two millions of them should persecution arise. England, with a Catholic population of only two millions, is much more aware of a vigorous Catholic effort in her midst than is America."[21]

Another key figure in carrying the revival across the Atlantic, was a friend of Maynard's, Frank Sheed. Sheed had been born in 1897 and raised in Australia where, as in the rest of the Anglophone world, the Catholic Church regarded itself as being in a state of siege. Under these conditions, he wrote later, "the defensive doctrines—the Visible Church and its marks, Supremacy, Infallibility, apologetics generally—had first call on the Church's energy" to the neglect of more positive doctrines, "Trinity, Incarnation, Redemption" and the Church as Christ's Mystical Body. His mother was a Catholic, but his paternal grandparents, "and still more their daughters, were of the type who dream of the Pope and wake up in a cold sweat screaming 'Rome!'"[22] He had sharpened his rhetorical skills first in conflict with his father, who had become a Marxist, and later as a street-corner evangelist for the Engish Catholic Evidence Guild. In 1927, forsaking a legal career, he and his wife, Maisie Ward, also a speaker for the Evidence Guild, founded a Catholic publishing company in London, Sheed and Ward, and opened its New York office in 1933. Sheed and Ward

19. Theodore Maynard, *De Soto and the Conquistadores* (New York: Longmans, Green, 1930); Maynard, *The Odyssey of Francis Xavier* (New York: Longmans, Green, 1936); Maynard, *Apostle of Charity: The Life of Saint Vincent de Paul* (New York: Dial Press, 1939). Thanks to Theodore Hendricks for sending me a typescript of his paper "The Historical Works of Theodore Maynard," December 6, 1989.

20. Maynard, *Odyssey of Francis Xavier*, 137n. C. C. Martindale also wrote historical lives of saints in a style that, as his biographer says, "superseded permanently the hagiography fathered on the Catholic public by the Oratorians and others in the Nineteenth Century." Philip Caraman, *C. C. Martindale: A Biography* (London: Longmans, 1967), 139.

21. Maynard, *World I Saw*, 312.

22. Frank Sheed, *The Church and I* (Garden City, N.Y.: Doubleday, 1974), 27, 11.

soon became the publishing arm of the Catholic revival. In 1933 he lectured to the Rocky Mountain Catholic Literature Congress in Denver on the Catholic revival in Europe and listened to fellow speaker Calvert Alexander praise the English converts Chesterton and Ronald Knox.[23]

His cofounder and bride, Maisie Ward, was a daughter of Newman's biographer Wilfrid Ward and granddaughter of the Ultramontane William George Ward, one of the original Oxford Movement converts. The Wards, a prolific family in the biological and the literary sense, nearly all of whose members wrote Catholic apologetics, gave Sheed rapid entrée into British Catholic intellectual life.[24] He was not a particularly creative thinker, but he was a dedicated and determined proselytizer, with formidable gifts as a publicist, publisher, and promoter.

Sheed and Ward, both devout admirers of Newman, were in no doubt about the most serious drawback they faced in making the new publishing company workable in either country: "The absence of a Catholic reading public was our continuing problem. As a businessman the Catholic publisher is a parasite on the reading habits of the public—if they read well he eats well. Like all intelligent parasites we studied the plant to which we had attached ourselves and found it depressingly weedy."[25] Sheed used a variety of marketing devices to expand readership, including making new translations of Catholic classics such as Augustine's *Confessions* and writing tutorial aid programs for study groups. His writers, in English and in translation from French, German, Spanish, and Italian, were mostly converts. "Five of our writers—Belloc, and the four converts Chesterton, C. C. Martindale, Ronald Knox, and Christopher Dawson—spring to mind as having done most for my reshaping. . . . On the key question: What makes Catholics tick? most Catholics tell us little; so dim is their tick that they hardly hear it themselves. There was no dimness in these five. I never knew men more concerned with the Faith or more articulate about it."[26] But Sheed admitted that for all their efforts his stable of writers was not transforming the religious life of either country. His Irish friend Shane Leslie wrote in 1934 that "with all its excellent organization and flow of converts, Rome was never farther from converting England since the coming of Newman."[27]

23. Sparr, *To Promote*, 43–44.
24. On the life and work of Maisie Ward see Dana Greene, *Maisie Ward* (Notre Dame, Ind.: University of Notre Dame Press, 1997).
25. Sheed, *Church and I*, 125.
26. Ibid., 110.
27. Shane Leslie, *The Passing Chapter* (New York: Scribner's, 1934), 205.

G. K. Chesterton was one of Sheed's best-selling authors. He had made a successful lecture tour of the United States in 1920 and contributed regularly to the American Catholic press. Catholic colleges and publicists urged him to return, especially after the success of his most striking postconversion book *The Everlasting Man* (1925). *Commonweal* devoted most of an issue to the book, choosing, characteristically, a pair of British converts— Bertram Windle and Theodore Maynard—to discuss it![28] From then on he was accorded the status of a living saint. Pick up any issue of *America*, *Catholic World*, *Commonweal*, or *Sign* from the 1920s or 1930s and you will not have to turn many pages before finding either an article by Chesterton or else a laudatory reference to him. Gratified by this treatment, he accepted an offer to teach at Notre Dame, the Catholic university in Indiana, in the fall semester of 1930. He gave a series of well-attended public lectures under the golden dome and recalled in his *Autobiography* (1936) that one of them was "an agonizing effort to be fair to the subtleties of the evolutionary controversy." Of the lecture "no record remained except that one student wrote in the middle of his blank notebook, 'Darwin did a lot of harm.' I am not at all certain that he was wrong; but it was something of a simplification of my reasons for being agnostic about the agnostic deductions in the debates about Lamarck and Mendel."[29]

Notre Dame became a magnet for British convert apologists in the 1930s, many of whom followed in Chesterton's broad wake. Another was Arnold Lunn, who, at the time of his conversion in 1933, was already forty-five.[30] Like so many of his fellow converts, he had enjoyed all the advantages Britain could confer on a young man. Born in 1888 in Madras, India, to an English father and an Irish Protestant mother, raised partly as a Methodist and partly as an Anglican, he had attended Harrow and then Balliol College, Oxford, where he had distinguished himself as secretary of the Oxford Union and editor of the university magazine *Isis*. Reading *An Agnostic's Apology* by Leslie Stephen (Virginia Woolf's father) as a schoolboy had led to his loss of faith. He was a pioneering alpine climber, captain of England's Olympic ski team, and the inventor of slalom racing. A gruesome mountaineering accident on the Welsh mountain Cader Idris in 1909, which shattered his leg, had rendered him ineligible for service in the First World War but had not prevented his return to the mountains.

28. Bertram Windle, "Chesterton's Masterpiece," and Theodore Maynard, "The Newman of His Age," *Commonweal*, December 2, 1925, 95–97.

29. G. K. Chesterton, *Autobiography*, (London: Hutchinson, 1936), 310.

30. Biographical information in the following passage is based on Arnold Lunn's autobiography, *Come What May* (London: Eyre and Spottiswoode, 1940).

Lunn built a reputation as a debunking journalist, first with *The Harro-vians*, an irreverent account of his old school and its traditions.[31] He followed it with *Roman Converts* (1924), a skeptical analysis of five converts to Catholicism: Newman, Manning, Tyrrell, Knox, and Chesterton, which argued that each had embraced Catholicism because of ulterior psychological motives. The Catholic Church, Lunn declared in his opening, had for centuries taught "an obscene conception of God" as one who "called into being unnumbered millions with the foreknowledge, and therefore the intention, that they should pass Eternity in excruciating agony." This horrifying teaching "was to disease the whole mind of Europe and in particular to give sanction to the rack and the stake." Catholicism had "caused more unmerited suffering than any other institution in the history of the world." Its intellectual demands were stifling. Why on earth should radiantly intelligent men such as Newman and Chesterton enter it? "I do not pretend . . . to solve the problem but believing that the influences of temperament, heredity, environment, and education are more potent than reason in determining a man's religion, I have chosen five converts of very different types and antecedents, and searched rather for the unavowed influences than for the reasons which they themselves suggest for their change of creed."[32]

Lunn attributed Chesterton's conversion to a sort of wilful perversity, a determination not to fall in with the conventional wisdom of his day. Armed with quotations from an anti-Catholic Cambridge history don, G. G. Coulton, he challenged the accuracy of Chesterton's historical works, and accused him of sheer wishful thinking in his veneration of the Middle Ages and the guild system. As for Knox, Lunn intimated that Catholicism suited his love of party intrigue, and his desire to be thought fascinating and unusual; his new religion gave him "a gratifying feeling of mystery, catacombs, and Jesuitry, combined, of course, with endless opportunities for high-spirited 'rags.'" In the tone of a high-minded Protestant, Lunn concluded: "There is nothing in Knox's writings to suggest that he is writing about Jesus of Nazareth" and far too much of the intolerant sectarian. Knox, as Lunn told it, was more of a church controversialist than a Christian.[33]

Knox was stung by what seemed to him the injustice of Lunn's diagnosis, but restrained himself from writing a hostile response.[34] Scattered

31. Arnold Lunn, *The Harrovians* (London: Methuen, 1913).
32. Arnold Lunn, *Roman Converts* (1924; New York: Scribner's, 1925), 10, 11, 25.
33. Ibid., 244–45, 177, 178. On Coulton's anti-Catholicism, see A. N. Wilson, *Hilaire Belloc* (1984; London: Penguin, 1986), 348–54.
34. Evelyn Waugh, *The Life of the Right Reverend Ronald Knox* (London: Chapman and

references in *Roman Converts* and later works made it clear that Lunn, along with his hostility, had never quite abandoned religion and indeed had glimpsed the appeal of Catholicism.[35] In 1930, after reviewing one of Knox's books sympathetically, Lunn challenged Knox to an epistolary debate on the problems of Catholicism. In the event Lunn found Knox's contribution to the debate, published in 1932 as *Difficulties*, more persuasive than his own![36] He followed the logic of this conclusion and converted, turning, like Saint Paul in the earliest days of Christianity, from persecutor into unflagging evangelist. Evelyn Waugh noted, "Sir Arnold was received into the Church by Ronald in July 1933, less than two years after the last letter was put in the post, and became the most tireless Catholic apologist of his generation."[37]

Like other converts, Lunn, who had Low Church antecedents, was willing to criticize much of what he found in the Catholic Church. He did not like the liturgy of High Mass. "Even as a Catholic I still retain that queer prejudice inspired by the uneasy conviction that I am watching a spectacle rather than assisting in an act of worship."[38] Lunn brought plenty of baggage into the church from his earlier studies. He was more eager than born Catholics to welcome the insights of non-Catholic scholars such as William James, whose *Varieties of Religious Experience* (1902) "gave new courage to timid Christians and was one of the first to disturb the complacency of those who believed that science had dealt a *coup de grace* to Christianity."[39] William James might be wrong on certain doctrinal points, Lunn agreed, but Catholic writers should have been more alert to the constructive theme of his arguments about the efficacy of religious experiences. Lunn never forgot his feelings as a youthful anti-Catholic. He recalled that as a boy he had been horrified and revolted by Catholic hagiography and that it was probably repelling potential converts up to the present: "I was faintly disgusted by these revellings in hospital purulence, these self-inflicted penances and superfluities of devotion."[40]

---

Hall, 1959), 199–200. He declined Shane Leslie's invitation to reply in the *Dublin Review*, of which Leslie was then the editor.

35. "If I do not pretend to be immune from the ancient spell of Rome, or indifferent to the romance of that great Church which for centuries dominated Europe . . ." Lunn, *Roman Converts*, vi-vii.

36. Ronald Knox and Arnold Lunn, *Difficulties: Being a Correspondence about the Catholic Religion* (1932; London: Eyre and Spottiswoode, 1958).

37. Waugh, *Life of Knox*, 236.

38. Arnold Lunn, *Within That City* (London: Sheed and Ward, 1936), 17.

39. Arnold Lunn, *A Saint in the Slave Trade: Peter Claver (1581–1654)* (London: Sheed and Ward, 1935), 3.

40. Ibid., 9.

Effortlessly prolific, Lunn began writing Catholic history, painting with a broad brush and striving always for a maximum of shock, drama, and rhetorical effect. Like Theodore Maynard he wrote in a style that made it plain that he intended to reach as many non-Catholic readers as possible and that he was fully alive to the skepticism he had once felt and they, presumably, felt still. "This brings me," he wrote in his biography of Saint Peter Claver (1935), "to the difficulty which confronts a Catholic who hopes his book may be read not only by those of the Faith but also by non-Catholics." The problem was that his hero really had sucked the poison from his parishioners' festering wounds and that Lunn hardly knew how to express it without inducing the same revulsion and disbelief he had felt in earlier years.[41]

Not that his Catholic audiences objected. Lunn taught at Notre Dame for a semester of each year between 1936 and 1939, and there he indulged his taste for religious drama to the full. Delighted by the story of football coach Knut Rockne's conversion, Lunn remarked in his autobiography that Notre Dame came as a shock "to refined people who think of religion as a discreet emotion to be turned on in church. The spirit of Notre Dame is reactionary," he continued, in what for him was a vein of high praise. "It is out of touch with the modern world for it has its roots in the past. The Olympic Games in Greece and the knightly tourneys of the Middle Ages and the Notre Dame football team have one thing in common: the close association of religion and sport."[42] But he, like Chesterton, had to admit that the students fell short intellectually; he told them in one lecture, "We should aim at producing a team of Notre Dame debaters on fundamental religious issues which would be as formidable and as famous as the Notre Dame football team." The debaters would have to learn every possible argument *against* their faith in order to be able to refute it effectively, just as they would have to learn every argument *for* their greatest foe, communism.[43]

Lunn, a great booster of the Catholic Revival idea, spoke widely in other parts of the United States on each of these visits. He and Frank Sheed met at Hunter College in New York during one of these visits (the college of which *Commonweal*'s erstwhile editor George Shuster was now president) to debate the question whether born Catholics or converts had been of

41. Ibid., 170.
42. Lunn, *Come What May*, 312.
43. "Lunn Lecture," *Scholastic*, October 2, 1936, 7. Lunn founded the Chesterton Club on campus, an organization of impromptu religious debaters. See "Lunn Organizes Chesterton Club," *Scholastic*, October 30, 1936, 3.

greater value to the church. Each chivalrously spoke for the position he did *not* represent, and Sheed wrote about their exchange. "I dwelt especially on what converts had done for the Catholic intellectual revival—they had provided eighty percent of the notable writing. When Lunn's turn came he found it hard to think of anything at all to be said for born Catholics."[44] Sheed and Lunn alike were acutely aware that it was the English converts, supplemented by European writers such as Charles Peguy, Jacques Maritain, and Etienne Gilson who sold most books and kept the company afloat. The reason for their "monstrous articulateness," Sheed believed, was "that converts have studied the Faith as grown-ups," avoiding the often-stultifying Catholic schooling provided to born Catholics in England and America, which, on the evidence, was good at preserving churchgoing loyalty but bad at stimulating deep understanding or any glimmer of creativity.[45]

A third British convert to teach at Notre Dame in the 1930s was Christopher Hollis.[46] He, like Knox and Hugh Benson, was an old Etonian and the son of an Anglican bishop. His 1924 conversion had been a newsworthy event because he was a recent Oxford graduate, a former president of the Oxford Union, and captain of an Oxford debating team that had twice toured the United States, winning every contest. He too had contemplated conversion in light of other converts' experiences: for him also the works of Newman and Chesterton, rather than those of born Catholics, had proved decisive. When he had asked for instruction, he was taught by Monsignor Arthur Barnes, a former Anglican clergyman and old Etonian. Following his conversion, Hollis taught for several years at Stonyhurst, the Jesuit boarding school in the Lancashire hills, until he was recruited by Father John O'Hara, Notre Dame's ambitious president, who pioneered these Atlantic transfusions.

Hollis, like Chesterton and Lunn, was astonished at the low intellectual standards prevalent at Notre Dame, at the priests' intellectual censoriousness, and at the university's preference for sports over academic life. It was a largely immigrant community even then. "American Catholicism for 150 years has had little time for culture" wrote Hollis. "The task of the clergy has been by insisting on strict obligations of the Church, to keep the Catholic body intact. Magnificently have they performed this stark and unbending task but they have—inevitably perhaps—performed it in such

44. Sheed, *Church and I*, 109.
45. Ibid., 97.
46. Biographical information in the following passage is based on Christopher Hollis's autobiography, *Along the Road to Frome* (London: Harrap, 1958).

a way as to make the Church appear as almost defiantly the enemy of culture."[47] Hollis lectured on the history of Anglo-American financial relations and declared: "Most of the freedom you [the United States] won from George III you lost to Alexander Hamilton and his banking reforms. It is certainly true that America was more in the hands of England in the nineteenth century than in the eighteenth."[48]

Shane Leslie, like Chesterton, Hollis, and Lunn, also worked for a while at Notre Dame. He was there in the spring of 1935 and spoke at graduation. He planned and rehearsed a performance of Hamlet in the football stadium using the football team as Fortinbras's army, and in a public speech he echoed Richard Simpson's old idea that Shakespeare might well have been a Catholic.[49] In the fall of 1936 he, Hollis, Lunn, and the English convert philosopher E. I. Watkin were all at Notre Dame together. Leslie arrived after teaching for a year at the much more intellectually demanding University of Pennsylvania, and he too was unimpressed by academic standards at the Catholic university. He pointed out the irony that Robert Hutchins and Mortimer Adler, neither of them Catholic, were teaching scholastic philosophy far more rigorously at the nearby University of Chicago. But he liked the sporting spirit that gave Notre Dame its distinctive élan. "The discipline was twice as strict as in an English university but the American boys knuckle under the rules in their pride of belonging to Notre Dame, whose success they follow with passionate devotion." Leslie, who regularly decried Britain's moral decline, admired this strictness, just as he admired the Catholic Legion of Decency, which he perceived as "far from a protest against free thought or a hindrance to the arts. It simply called for a boycott on the moral destruction of child-life" at a time when Hollywood was teaching that "a divorcing star is the highest career for a girl, and a successful bandit the best for the boys."[50]

Leslie had the knack of appealing to American idealism. His book to commemorate the centenary of the Tractarians, *The Oxford Movement, 1833–1933* (also delivered in lecture form at Notre Dame), emphasized the value of separating church and state in a way his audience was sure to applaud. Placing great stress on the Gorham decision of 1851 and the Bennett case of 1872, Leslie pointed out that in both cases the Church of England had "grovelled to the State." Judges and politicians rather than

47. Ibid., 154–55.
48. Christopher Hollis, typescript of a speech, n.d., Hollis File, Notre Dame archives, UDIS 106/074.
49. "Prof. Shane Leslie Announces Plans for Production of *Hamlet*," *Scholastic* April 5, 1935, 2–3. So far as I can tell from issues of *Scholastic* the play was never actually performed.
50. Shane Leslie, *American Wonderland: Memories of Four Tours in the United States of America, 1911–1935* (London: Michael Joseph, 1936), 177, 253, 192.

churchmen had in effect been left to make the crucial decisions on such questions as biblical accuracy, original sin and the real presence. Leslie showed that the Catholics had maintained religious integrity throughout the nineteenth century, whereas the Anglicans had been forced, as an establishment, to make political compromises. He skewered the Anglican preference for compromise over doctrinal clarity, calling Archbishop Randall Davidson of Canterbury "a very good man without principles, in other words a perfect Anglican Bishop, for he carried compromise to a fine art. . . . His platitudinous pliancy became the strength as well as the weakness of his Communion during the quarter of a century that he ruled. He became a better and better primate while his principles became softer and softer." But like many of his fellow converts, Leslie did not exempt the Catholic hierarchy from criticism. He declared that if only Newman had been allowed to return to Oxford rather than suffer as "a minor schoolmaster in a suburb of Birmingham," he would have made hundreds more converts, since "he alone had the gift of appealing to the Anglican soul in life or in death."[51]

What were the decisive events in English religious life since the onset of the Oxford Movement? All the Anglican factions, high and low, Leslie believed, had been weakened by the rise of modernism, which was itself, indirectly, a fruit of Newman and the Oxford Movement. "The writings of Newman were liable to exquisite misrepresentation and from them Father Tyrrell mistakenly developed his headstrong course, while Christendom watched admiringly at first, before the true nature of the movement had been disclosed, but finally aghast." Leslie openly defended Pius X's excommunication of Tyrrell. Catholics, he insisted, had benefited from having a clear line of authority and a clear papal prohibition on modernism, while the Anglicans' lack of an effective authority principle condemned them to theological confusion.[52]

The steady worsening of the Great Depression in the early 1930s intensified the conviction of many of the converts that capitalism was destructive and useless. A rich connoisseur and collector, Leslie had always before been delighted by the opulence of American life and was shocked by the contrast presented now in the worst years of the Great Depression. He met Dorothy Day in New York and Father Charles Coughlin in Detroit, each of whom preached in a distinctive idiom against soulless capitalism. At this point Coughlin was still supporting the New Deal and had not yet made the anti-Semitic and anti-Roosevelt turn that condemned him in the

51. Shane Leslie, *The Oxford Movement, 1833–1933* (London: Burns, Oates, and Washbourne, 1933), 2, 106–7, 154.
52. Ibid., 103, 102–4.

eyes of his superiors and his liberal admirers. Leslie saw Coughlin as representing "the swing of the Church to the left after feeling herself too long under the pinnacles of Capital." Coughlin seemed to him "a Peter the Hermit in black cloth and bowler hat" whom "the Bishop of Detroit . . . has loosed against the Usurers."[53]

Many of these British converts active in the American Catholic revival preached the benefits of "distributism," a system of political economy developed in England and compatible with Leo XIII's encyclical *Rerum Novarum* (1891) and its sequel, Piux XI's *Quadragesimo Anno* (1931). "The great papal encyclicals . . . deprive Catholics of all excuse for complacently ignoring social evils which should challenge the conscience of all Christian men," wrote Arnold Lunn.[54] Distributism, the brainchild of Chesterton, Belloc, Eric Gill, Father Vincent McNabb, and others, was based on the conviction that capitalism was a depersonalizing system that turned men and work into commodities and gave them all an interchangeable money value. It placed bankers and financiers at the center of society and human spiritual values at the margin. Far from being a system that guaranteed citizens' right to hold private property, said the distributists, industrial capitalism was concentrating property in the hands of a dwindling number of plutocrats. Against the plutocracy distributists—many, though not all, of them Roman Catholics or Anglo-Catholics—favored a dramatic redistribution of land, enabling rootless urbanites to return to the soil as farmers and to feel an organic connection with the actual earth that fed them. They favored decentralization, folk crafts, regional variation and dialect. As one historian says, "Distributists celebrated heterogeneity, just as homogeneity threatened to overwhelm rural England."[55]

Part of the impetus for distributism had come from the convert generation's earlier experiences before they ever heard of papal encyclicals—another of the many cases in which preconversion influences were adapted to the new Catholic setting. Chesterton's and Gill's early economic ideas had been drawn from Christian socialism. At the start of the century, Chesterton had opposed Britain's role in the Boer War because he saw the Boers as a republic of self-reliant small-holding farmers, under threat from a British Empire at the beck and call of gold and diamond merchants. Chesterton, says his biographer Michael Ffinch, "had always seen the Boer

53. Leslie, *American Wonderland*, 138.
54. Lunn, *Saint in the Slave Trade*, 23.
55. Dermot Quinn, "Distributism as Movement and Ideal," *Chesterton Review* 19 (May 1993): 165. For an entertaining account of life among the London members of the Distributist League, see Brocard Sewell, "Devereux Nights: A Distributist Memoir," in John Sullivan, ed., *G. K. Chesterton: A Centenary Appraisal* (London: Paul Elek, 1974), 141–55.

farmers as he might have seen the yeoman farmers of Gloucestershire or Herefordshire," and he heartily approved of their rough independence.[56] Another formative experience had been the Irish Land Act of 1903, by which Irish peasant farmers had been allowed, for the first time, to buy their own farmland, which they then did with alacrity. Hilaire Belloc had approved, noting that "the Irish people have deliberately chosen to become peasant proprietors . . . when they could have become permanent tenants under far easier terms."[57] The incident had contributed to Belloc's indictment of wage slavery in *The Servile State* (1913), the sacred text of distributism.[58] These examples demonstrated, said the distributists, that people would rather have landownership with poverty than wages and luxuries. Moreover, widespread farming would restrain the aggressive centralizing state.

Distributism made little practical headway, but as an anticapitalist *and* antisocialist vehicle it pottered along in the depressed English economy of the 1920s and 1930s. Across the Atlantic, Dorothy Day attempted to put it into practice on the Catholic Worker Movement's several rural communes, as did the Marycrest communards of rural New York in the late 1940s.[59] Both experiments were, in practical terms, pathetic failures; only Day, with her exceptional faith and endurance, could draw solace from an experience that most observers found purgatorial. It was certainly no advertisement for voluntary mass return to the land. The Catholic Rural Life Movement had a considerably more practical approach to the issue, though its members too were influenced by Chesterton, Belloc, and Gill. Among its own more outspoken theorists were the converts Willis Nutting (a Notre Dame history professor) and Allen Tate.[60]

The distributists knew that they were vulnerable to the charge of utopianism. When their antibanker rhetoric took on an anti-Jewish cast, as it usually did in the speeches and writings of Belloc, it provoked fears of fascism, but its assault on oligarchy capitalism laid it open to accusations of

56. Michael Ffinch, *G. K. Chesterton: A Biography* (London: Weidenfeld and Nicolson, 1986), 83.

57. Wilson, *Belloc*, 131.

58. Hilaire Belloc, *The Servile State* (1912; New York: Holt, 1946).

59. James Fisher, *The Catholic Counterculture in America, 1933–1962* (Chapel Hill: University of North Carolina Press, 1989), 119–25.

60. Edward S. Shapiro, "Catholic Agrarian Thought and the New Deal," in Edward Kanatowicz, ed., *Modern American Catholicism, 1900–1965: Selected Historical Essays* (New York: Garland, 1988), 202–18. See also (on Catholic rural life) Christopher Kauffman, *Mission to Rural America: The Story of Howard Bishop, Founder of Glenmary* (New York: Paulist Press, 1991). Allen Tate was co-author, with Herbert Agar, of an American Distributist manifesto, *Who Owns America? A New Declaration of Independence* (Boston: Houghton Mifflin, 1936). Tate became a Catholic in 1950.

communism from conservatives and businessmen. In short, distributism contained something to annoy everyone and never managed to make the turn from ideal to reality. Many of the distributists became ardent conservatives during the 1940s, especially when the outcome of the Second World War left "Godless communism" as the sole effective challenger to a U.S.-dominated "Christian West." The converts had been united from the start in their fear and hatred of Soviet communism, perceiving the atheist state as even more threatening to citizens' dignity and independence than monopoly capitalism. Under these circumstances it was a small step for Arnold Lunn to become an active contributor to William F. Buckley's conservative *National Review* or for Christopher Hollis to become a staunchly Conservative member of Parliament.[61]

Of all the convert distributists, none was so bitingly critical of capitalism as Eric Gill, and he leveled his accusations as much against the Catholic Church itself as against the rest of society. He held most English priests in low esteem, finding them far too willing to conform to conditions of decadent capitalism. "Like the rest of the world," he wrote in 1926, "they are only interested in getting and spending, keeping an eye meanwhile on their heavenly home and a sort of list of things no fellow should do. . . . The state of modern Europe—the mass of people totally engrossed in getting and spending—is apparently what they approve."[62] Despite his sweeping condemnations, however, Gill accepted lucrative commissions from the very corporations that, in theory, he held responsible for the destruction of society. His Ditchling community broke up over acrimonious money disputes in 1924 (he thought the others were not paying their fair share), and he moved first to Capel-y-ffin, a sublimely impractical hillside site in Wales, and thence, after four years of struggle and prolonged absences, to the more accessible High Wycombe in Berkshire. Always in demand and always well paid for his work, Gill and his commune-minded crowd of Dominican tertiaries were able to avoid the poverty and privation of their less fortunate American commune counterparts.[63]

Gill's brilliant creativity and outspoken opposition to both the commercial world and the everyday Catholicism around him made him a perpetual challenge to religious complacency. Gill discovered and translated into English Jacques Maritain's *Art et scholastique* in 1923. This French con-

61. See, for example, Arnold Lunn, "Spanish Ordeal," *National Review*, August 12, 1961, 91–92; Lunn, "Red Shadow on the Slopes," *National Review*, March 27, 1962, 212. On Hollis's parliamentary career, see *Along the Road*, 182–99.
62. Gill quoted in Speaight, *Life of Eric Gill*, 174.
63. Fiona MacCarthy, *Eric Gill* (London: Faber and Faber, 1989), 179–211, 225–28.

vert's work, says Gill's biographer Robert Speaight, "had the dramatic force of a revelation. For years to come it was to dominate all his thinking about the relation of Art to Prudence and of Art to Christianity. It clarified his own principles and at the same time enlarged them" and it gave him surer theoretical footing to stand his ground against Philistine critics.[64] In the face of sharp clerical opposition, Gill illustrated D. H. Lawrence's *Lady Chatterley's Lover* and defended Lawrence's philosophy of sex as consonant with Catholic teaching.[65] He hated the Catholic aesthetic of the 1920s and 1930s, the gimcrack statuary and gaudy painting of England's Catholic churches. In a succession of essays of breathtaking audacity (for their time and place) Gill declared: "It would be very pleasant if our churches were denuded of all their present sacred images and pictures—if all their carvings were carved off and all their windows filled with plain glass; but even then, though they would look better . . . it would only be whitewashing of the sepulchre unless that iconoclasm were really the expression of the mind of the congregations." "Cultured people," he added, "have got to take church-going as a penance . . . a well-deserved purgatory, a test of endurance."[66]

As alternatives to capitalism the Catholic revival and distributism made far less progress in the 1930s than communism, which generated more intellectual enthusiasm than at any other time in the two nations' history. In the United States, Malcolm Cowley, Edmund Wilson, and Theodore Dreiser, and in England Stephen Spender, W. H. Auden, C. Day Lewis, and George Orwell, looked to the far Left for salvation, and regarded the church, when they gave it so much as a glance, as reactionary and atavistic. The Catholic intellectuals' own view, of course, was that they alone had a program, based on the encyclicals, which blended sound economic and moral principles, but they could see which way the wind was blowing. Daniel Lord, a Jesuit, says Arnold Sparr, "always confessed to a sneaking admiration for the Communists" because of their success in inspiring youthful enthusiasm and idealism which his own church could not seem to match.[67]

Among the Catholics' misfortunes during the Great Depression was G. K. Chesterton's premature death in 1936 at the age of sixty-two. His disappearance from the scene was an irrecoverable loss to the English Catholics, who had no other larger-than-life champion to put in his place. His only rival as a profound, yet entertaining Christian apologist, C. S.

64. Robert Speaight, *The Life of Eric Gill*, (New York: P. J. Kenedey, 1966), 124.
65. MacCarthy, *Gill*, 256–59.
66. Eric Gill, *Beauty Looks after Herself* (London: Sheed and Ward, 1933), 47.
67. Sparr, *To Promote*, 45.

Lewis, said that "the contemporary book that has helped me the most is Chesterton's *The Everlasting Man*," but Lewis, despite a large Catholic following, never converted.[68] Distributism also received a mortal wound with Chesterton's death. His little magazines, the *New Witness* (1913–1923) and *G. K.'s Weekly* (1925–1936) had provided news and continuity for the movement. Nor could the United States fill the void created by his death. Its Catholic literary culture continued to lean heavily on British supports. As Sparr says, "The consequences of this Anglo-American Catholic cultural union were not always fortunate. . . . the example of English Catholic clannishness only reinforced already strong Catholic American tendencies in that direction."[69]

Cardinal Bourne, archbishop of Westminster, died the year before Chesterton but was not so sorely missed by the convert intellectuals. As distributists they had been shocked by Bourne's support for the British government during the General Strike of 1926, which seemed to fly in the face of the papal encyclicals' social teachings. Shane Leslie wrote of Bourne in 1934: "He has not shown imagination like Wiseman or originality like Manning. He has made his clergy a body of meek and unremarkable yes-men" and "given converts no promotion and little encouragement save as laymen."[70] Bourne's defensive narrowness had hampered the convert writers, and his chosen editor for the London Catholic weekly the *Tablet*, Ernest Oldmeadow, was an inflexibly humorless critic of the converts' imaginative work. Evelyn Waugh described him as "a man of meagre attainments and deplorable manners, under whom the paper became petty in its interests and low in tone."[71] When Oldmeadow reviewed Waugh's *Black Mischief* unfavorably Waugh replied in print: "Long employment by a prince of the Church has tempted him to ape his superiors, and, naturally enough, he gives an uncouth and impudent performance."[72]

Bourne's successor, Archbishop (later Cardinal) Arthur Hinsley was far more tractable and showed an eager interest in the converts' intellectual enterprises. Hinsley, who had been head of the English College in Rome and apostolic delegate to the Catholics of Africa, replaced Oldmeadow at the *Tablet* with Douglas Woodruff from the *Times*, a friend and admirer of the convert writers. Hinsley also appointed the convert historian Christopher Dawson to edit the monthly *Dublin Review* and encouraged Michael

68. C. S. Lewis, *God in the Dock: Essays on Theology and Ethics*, ed. Walter Hooper (Grand Rapids, Mich.: Eerdman's, 1970), 260.
69. Sparr, *To Promote*, 93.
70. Leslie, *Passing Chapter*, 205–6.
71. Waugh, *Knox*, 243.
72. Christopher Sykes, *Evelyn Waugh: A Biography* (1975; London: Penguin, 1977), 177.

de la Bedoyere's new newspaper, the *Catholic Herald*. De la Bedoyere was not himself a convert but his mother was, and she too was the daughter of an Anglican bishop.[73]

Hinsley, like all other clerics, collided with Eric Gill, but he was more flexible than Bourne and more willing to see that he was dealing with an eccentric genius rather than a mere troublemaker.[74] Hinsley appreciated the aesthetic dimensions of religious life and encouraged the nascent liturgical movement. In 1937 he commissioned Ronald Knox to rewrite the Catholic vernacular prayers, which had been composed originally in awkward and mannered English. Knox was delighted to help in this reform because "the prayers used by the Church of England are, by general admission, models of dignity and faultless prose rhythm," such that "no convert . . . has ever failed to experience a sense of loss over this difference."[75]

Since 1926 Knox had been chaplain to the Catholic students at Oxford University—a job he held until 1938. He never visited the United States but his books sold widely there and always gained enthusiastic reviews in the American Catholic press. One admirer wrote in the *Catholic World* that Knox knew how to temper his hard-hitting satire with "impish humor" and regretted that this ability was "unfortunately rare among Catholic writers."[76] Much of Knox's writing during his twelve Oxford years was indeed lightheartedly satirical, though always with an apologetic intention. A pair of more serious works from these years took aim at the influential public intellectuals of his day. In the first, *Caliban in Grub Street* (1930), Knox attacked Arnold Bennett, Arthur Conan Doyle, Israel Zangwill, Rebecca West, and other contributors to the English newspapers' "religion" supplements. Ridiculing their lack of theological knowledge, their dependence on feeling rather than reason in religious questions, their illogic, and their ill-concealed contempt for tradition, Knox declared that on no other subject would the press tolerate such ignorance. So secular had England become, he concluded, that the press now relied for religious enlightenment on people who had never studied it seriously but were famous for other accomplishments.[77]

73. Adrian Hastings, "Some Reflexions on the English Catholicism of the Late 1930s," in Garrett Sweeney, ed., *Bishops and Writers* (Wheathamstead, England: Anthony Clark, 1977), 107–26. On Hinsley, see Thomas Moloney, *Westminster, Whitehall, and the Vatican: The Role of Cardinal Hinsley* (Tunbridge Wells, Kent: Burns and Oates, 1985).

74. Moloney, *Westminister*, 65–71, 74.

75. Waugh, *Knox*, 254.

76. J. G. E. Hopkins, "Father Knox and a Great Victorian," *Catholic World* 146 (October 1937): 72–75.

77. Ronald Knox, *Caliban in Grub Street* (London: Sheed and Ward, 1930).

In the second of these more serious books, *Broadcast Minds* (1932), Knox aimed at a higher intellectual level, taking to task loose, illogical, and biased treatments of religion in the works of H. G. Wells, Bertrand Russell, Julian Huxley, and H. L. Mencken. He denied their contentions that there was a natural opposition between Christianity and science and that dogma was arbitrarily "imposed" on witless Catholics. Dogma, to the contrary, was a set of agreements on shared common beliefs. Here again he insisted that religious feeling was a less trustworthy guide than religious doctrine: "The whole traditional theology of Europe presupposes the Five Proofs [of the existence of God], or some modification of them, as the basis of belief in God, and does not appeal for a moment to any revelation, in Scripture or out of it, for the purpose." Even though his own conversion, movingly described in the *Spiritual Aeneid* (1918), had been a highly emotional event, Knox was almost as impatient with religious emotionalism as he was with agnosticism. Of Huxley's claim, in *Religion without Revelation* that moments of transcendent feeling were glimpses of the supernatural, Knox answered that "the sense of mystery and the sense of sacredness" were completely different, just as magic, the work of man, was completely different from miracle, the work of God.[78]

Knox maintained the British converts' tradition of criticizing evolutionary ideas applied beyond their proper biological limits. He noted that Freud in psychology and James G. Frazer in comparative religion had both assumed, rather than demonstrated, that societies progressed through stages analogous to those Darwin had outlined for species development. They claimed that monotheism was a relatively late development that had "evolved" from an earlier polytheism. Knox, to the contrary, echoed Orestes Brownson's theme from the previous century, that the fragmentary anthropological evidence we possess could as easily support the opposite claim, more harmonious with Scripture, that the "primitive" polytheistic tribes were degenerate descendants of formerly monotheistic peoples, rather than late starters up the evolutionary ladder. There was, Knox concluded, no hard evidence to show a gradual shift toward monotheism. He also contested the "assumption, half-consciously made, that each succeeding scientific hypothesis is more damaging to the credit of Christianity than the last."[79]

To read Knox today is to get the impression that he knew he was right but also that he knew he was failing to reach much of an audience. *Broadcast Minds* begins with the doleful recognition that the BBC (at that time a

78. Ronald Knox, *Broadcast Minds* (London: Sheed and Ward, 1932), 51–52, 82, 126.
79. Ibid., 72, 25.

government-controlled broadcasting monopoly) was in effect creating and authenticating a national orthodoxy of opinion made up of equal parts "science" and sentiment, in which dogmatic religion had no part. The popularizers of science, such as Julian Huxley and Bertrand Russell, had access to the airwaves. In Knox's view they did not want so much to enlighten the man in the street as to convince him of his ignorance. "They want to confuse him with the riddles of science, not to enlighten him with its lucidity; so confused, will he be able any longer to trust his own judgment, to hold, therefore, any beliefs at all?" Knox foresaw when broadcasting was in its infancy that it would have immense propaganda powers that could as easily be turned to mendacious uses as to good ones.[80]

A distinguished new recruit, meanwhile, was the poet, novelist, and historian Alfred Noyes, who had converted to Catholicism in 1927.[81] Noyes was already famous in Britain and the United States. Born in 1880, he had neglected to take his Oxford final exams in 1900 because a publisher, impressed by his poems, had summoned him to London and offered him a book contract. The offer had led the confident youth to believe that he could make his living as a professional writer. A succession of literary triumphs in the first decade of the century, including an epic, book-length poem on the life of Sir Francis Drake (full of stirringly Protestant declamation against Spanish Catholicism), justified this hope.[82] His verse, in the style of Tennyson, is easy and rhythmical: he could stand for the genteel poetic tradition against which Ezra Pound and T. S. Eliot rebelled. Like Chesterton, Noyes had a long sympathetic preparation for conversion and was the subject of laudatory articles in the British and American Catholic press for nearly twenty years before his formal reception. As an undergraduate he had read Bishop George Berkeley who "had delivered [him] for ever from the prison of nineteenth century materialism" and had set him on the road to the "perennial Philosophy."[83] In an article of 1911 he wrote that a modern materialist was "like a man who should explain a Beethoven symphony . . . by tracing to their source the wood and catgut of the instruments, and forget both the significance of

---

80. Ibid., 29–30.
81. Biographical information in the following passage is based on Alfred Noyes's autobiography *Two Worlds for Memory* (Philadelphia: Lippincott, 1953).
82. Like the young Arnold Lunn, Noyes equated Protestantism with freedom, Catholicism with tyranny. For example: "He fought for the soul's freedom, fought the fight, / Which, though it still rings in our wondering ears / Was won then and for ever— that great war / That last Crusade of Christ against His priests / Wherein Rome fell behind a thunderous roar / Of ocean triumph." Alfred Noyes, *Drake: An English Epic* (1906; New York: Frederick Stokes, 1909), 11.
83. Alfred Noyes, *The Unknown God* (1934; London: Sheed and Ward, 1949), 118.

the music and the mind of the composer, who, although He does not appear on the scene, speaks through physical instrumentalities to the minds of his listeners."[84]

He married an American in 1907, and the United States welcomed him on his first lecturing tour in 1911. By the age of thirty-three, in 1913, Noyes held an honorary doctorate from Yale and was taking up residence as the Murray Professor of English Literature at Princeton University, where he worked for half of every academic year until 1925. Two of his best students were F. Scott Fitzgerald (who told Noyes he planned to write for money, not fame) and Edmund Wilson, who had "unquestionable literary gifts and a critical flair quite unusual in a young student" and whose juvenile poems Noyes published in a 1916 Princeton anthology.[85] His own work, meanwhile, appeared in both countries and was equally well known on both sides of the ocean. Congressmen loved to quote him, and one enthusiast of his First World War poetry described him as "the poet laureate of the Allies."[86] He converted to Catholicism after his wife's premature death in 1927. His outspoken oppositon to publication of James Joyce's *Ulysses* on grounds that it was obscene made him popular among his new coreligionists, and his personal acquaintance with judges, press barons, members of Parliament, and nearly all the English and American literary lions of his age made him an instantly influential member of the Catholic community.[87]

His spiritual autobiography, *The Unknown God* (1934), described his early childhood religious experiences and his gradual realization of the existence of God. Noyes was excited by and respectful of the scientific achievements of the last century, and he paid tribute to the way in which good scientists pursued truth by patient experiment, contrasting their humility to the "arrogant effrontery" of agnostics philosophizing beyond the evidence of their discoveries. Darwin himself had known better than to overreach his evidence or use it to deny God, he said, and Noyes approved of his remark at the end of *The Origin of Species* that "this grand sequence of [evolutionary] events the mind refuses to accept as the result of blind chance." Noyes, like Bertram Windle, had no doubt that the theory of biological evolution was, in the main, true, but like recent developments in atomic physics, it had provoked as many fundamental questions as it had

84. Noyes, *Two Worlds*, 78.

85. Ibid., 100. The anthology was *A Book of Princeton Verse, 1916–1919*, ed. Alfred Noyes (Princeton: Princeton University Press, 1916).

86. Caroline Henderson Griffiths, Introduction to Noyes, *The Avenue of the Allies* (New York: Art War Relief Book Committee, 1918), v.

87. Noyes, *Two Worlds*, 223–28.

answered. "Science has not changed its austere determination, but quietly and unexpectedly it has met Religion at the cross-roads. Each was going its own way, and each is standing with new humility in the other's presence, before an unfathomable and eternal mystery."[88]

Noyes followed *The Unknown God* with a biography of Voltaire, having concluded after reading the complete works (seventy dense volumes) that he was far less the enemy of Christianity than Catholic writers usually assumed and that "he was probably as necessary to the well-being of Christianity as the Reformation."[89] In fact, said Noyes, Voltaire "had, beneath the polished surface of his Gallic wit, an *anima naturaliter Christiana*."[90] It was his dislike of lazy, corrupt, and dishonorable churchmen, of whom he encountered many, which provoked Voltaire's sharpest rebukes. Taken out of context, they might seem to indicate hatred of religion itself. In fact, Voltaire was intent on a new apologetics "which may one day transfigure the results of modern science as Aquinas attempted to transfigure the results of Greek philosophy." His efforts "to restore Reason to its proper throne, which it had always held in the *philosophia perennis* at its greatest periods" had won him "the full enmity of those who preferred to set Reason aside, and therefore fell into what Voltaire and Locke believed to be lazy, sensual and cowardly superstition."[91] Unfortunately the French Revolution had idolized Voltaire and depicted him as an enemy of the church. In later controversies atheists and skeptics had quoted him selectively, "quite unaware of the support which Voltaire himself, consciously or unconsciously, had given to the central principles and the central beliefs of the faith."[92] Sheed and Ward published *Voltaire* in 1936, the newly invigorated London *Tablet* serialized it, and secular and religious reviewers (with a few exceptions) praised it.[93]

But then a curt message came from the Vatican to Cardinal Hinsley that the book must be withdrawn and "corrected," or else it would be condemned. Author and cardinal alike were mystified, for the message did not specify which were the objectionable passages. The book was certainly designed as a tribute to the Catholic faith, not an attack on it. Nevertheless, the cardinal followed instructions from Rome to restrain its distribu-

88. Noyes, *Unknown God*, 54, 6.
89. Noyes, *Voltaire* (London: Sheed and Ward, 1936), 632.
90. Noyes, *Two Worlds*, 278.
91. Noyes, *Voltaire*, 528.
92. Noyes, *Two Worlds*, 278.
93. See the anonymous review in the *Times Literary Supplement*, October 10, 1936, 808; Paul Wilson review, *New York Times*, September 6, 1936; Paul Crowley review, *Commonweal*, November 13, 1936, 81. For a less laudatory view, see J.McS. [probably Joseph McSorley], *Catholic World* 144 (November 1936): 244.

tion. Frank Sheed, the publisher, describes in his autobiography how Noyes "did something without parallel in the history of [Catholic] censorship: he began a civil suit against the Cardinal for infringing his rights as a British citizen by sending on the Roman document to Sheed and Ward instructing them to withhold his book from continuing publication."[94] Correspondents to the London *Times* seized on the case to debate the extent to which English Catholics were hamstrung by censorship. Denis Gwynn, a popular Catholic writer, criticized Noyes in the *Dublin Review* for taking the controversy into the national press, instead of sympathizing with him as the victim of anonymous informers. Adrian Hastings says the incident shows how deferential most English Catholics still were to Rome: "With a few exceptions Catholics showed an almost complete inability to face up to the deeper issues of the case. At the time they simply had not the tools for mounting a challenge to Roman behaviour precisely on Catholic principles."[95]

Noyes's determination to avoid censorship finally led in 1939 to a conciliatory letter from Vatican Secretary of State Cardinal Eugenio Pacelli (who became Pope Pius XII later that year), after which Noyes abandoned his lawsuit, but he still had to face years of criticism. For example, an Irish author, Kathleen O'Flaherty, devoted a large part of her *Voltaire: Myth and Reality* (1945) to refuting Noyes's portrait. She asserted that Noyes was intellectually dishonest, misleading in his use of quotations, and unacquainted with the history of the Christian mystics. In high dudgeon she derided "the English critic" for his rhetorical tricks, his "great imaginative fertility and considerable ingeniousness," which she claimed had taken the place of sober research, and his implied rebuke that to object to his portrait of Voltaire "would be the sign of a prejudiced, petty mind."[96] But Noyes was adamant. Confident of his orthodoxy and not one to be overawed by authority, he had discovered that he could challenge the Vatican censors and make them bend, even if it cost him the sympathy of some coreligionists.

In the 1930s a group of French Catholics began to make their own mark on intellectual life in the United States, complementing the role of the British converts. Jacques Maritain and Etienne Gilson, Paul Claudel, Léon Bloy, Charles Peguy, and Gabriel Marcel were the principal figures in this new element of the Catholic revival. Sheed and Ward were the translators and publishers who brought their works before the English and Amer-

94. Sheed, *Church and I*, 188.
95. Hastings, "Some Reflexions," 117.
96. Kathleen O'Flaherty, *Voltaire: Myth and Reality* (Cork, Ireland: Cork University Press, 1945), 163.

ican audience. They were more indebted to scholasticism and less historical minded than their English counterparts, but these qualities gave them a
ready audience at the U.S. Catholic universities whose syllabi were often
organized around scholastic principles. As with the Britons, so with the
Frenchmen, some were strictly literary influences, and others showed up in
person, bringing their ideas to America and beginning to absorb American
influences. Gilson and Maritain both became Ivy League celebrities—
Gilson at Harvard, Maritain at Princeton. Frank Sheed confided to Maritain that he had long been hoping that T. S. Eliot would convert to
Catholicism, but Maritain joked, "Eliot exhausted his capacity for conversion when he became an Englishman."[97] Gilson became a professor at
Toronto, but two of his books, *Medieval Universalism and Its Present
Value* and *Reason and Revelation in the Middle Ages*, were based on his
Harvard lecture series. Between them they won among non-Catholics a
respect for neoscholasticism which no born Catholic in the United States
had been able to gain and which the British converts had not aimed to
foster.[98]

97. Sheed, *Church and I*, 89.
98. On these developments, see James Hitchcock, "Postmortem on a Rebirth: The Catholic Intellectual Renaissance," *American Scholar* (Spring 1980): 211–25.

# X

# FASCISTS, COMMUNISTS, CATHOLICS, AND TOTAL WAR

I TALY, THE CENTER of the Catholic faith, was a
magnet for English and American convert intellectuals
in the nineteenth and twentieth centuries. All who
could afford it visited Italy sooner or later, hoping to find
there a surrogate Catholic home to compensate them for
the Protestant home they had lost.[1] Anticipating an exem-
plary Catholic life in Italy, they found a more complex and
ambiguous reality. Encounters with cynical Curial officials,
anticlerical reformers, fraudulent innkeepers, and voracious
bedbugs offset their admiration for the beauties of Assisi,
Venice, Florence, and Rome. Ronald Knox was the exception in knowing beforehand that he would find Catholicism
at its worst in Rome, remarking "if you are a bad sailor, stay
away from the engine room."[2] With most converts, their
reactions to Italy—the landscape, the politics, the people,
and the Vatican—illuminate their ideas about the difference
between Catholicism in theory and in practice, about the
aesthetic and spiritual tensions in their new faith, and indirectly, about their hopes for the church in their home countries.[3]

1. The following passage is based on Patrick Allitt, "America, England, Italy: The Geography of Catholic Conversion, 1840–1960," *Notre Dame Cushwa Center Working Papers*, ser.
26, no. 3 (Fall 1994).

2. Knox, quoted in Frank Sheed, *The Church and I* (Garden City, N.Y.: Doubleday,
1974), 121.

3. For the Protestant view of Rome in the nineteenth century, see Jenny Franchot, *Roads
to Rome: The Antebellum Protestant Encounter with Catholicism* (Berkeley: University of
California Press, 1994), 16–34; C. P. Brand, *Italy and the English Romantics* (Cambridge:
Cambridge University Press, 1957). On Italy in American Catholic literature, see Paul Giles,

Italy represented not only the Catholic Church but also the Roman Empire. In Edward Gibbon's opinion, with which many of the converts were familiar, the rising church had destroyed the old Roman Empire and ushered in more than a millennium of Italian weakness. The heroes of Italian unification in the nineteenth century, Giuseppe Mazzini, Camillo Cavour, and Giuseppe Garibaldi, were all anticlerical, and the papacy's struggle to retain its temporal power cast it as a reactionary force. British and American Catholic converts would have liked to reassure potential converts that Catholicism was not synonymous with reactionary politics, but Italian affairs seemed to prove just the opposite. Unification, achieved by 1870, for the first time gave Italy an image of national strength rather than weakness.[4]

The clearest case of a conversion prompted by Italy's aesthetic spectacle is that of the Amerian art critic Bernard Berenson. A Lithuanian Jew by birth, he visited Italy after graduating from Harvard and was so enamored that he settled there permanently to build his career as an art historian and connoisseur. In February 1891 he was received into the church at the Benedictine monastery of Monte Oliveto Maggiore where he was studying the frescoes. To his English friend Mary Costelloe he wrote that at mass "I feel the bodily presence of God in such a way that prayer at the moment becomes the most naturally personal of things. . . . I had seen much before in Catholicism that attracted me irresistibly but not that. I wanted so much to thank God that he had led me to Him so much just by those beautiful pictures."[5] In London he was confirmed by the octogenarian Cardinal Manning, but outside Italy he found it hard to sustain his faith. "In Italy," he wrote in another letter, "it is easy to feel Catholic, just as in England it is so inevitable to feel antagonistic to it. Elsewhere it is repelling. Yet in Italy it is as much at home as the sun and the sky."[6] After reading Leopold von Ranke's history of the papacy he lost his reverence for the hierarchy and from then on attended church only when he was in Italy. There was, he came to believe, an intrinsically Catholic quality to Italy itself which faded as he traveled to England or America. His was the

---

*American Catholic Arts and Fictions: Culture, Ideology, and Aesthetics* (New York: Cambridge University Press, 1992), 76–108.

4. Thomas Bokenkotter, *A Concise History of the Catholic Church*, rev. ed. (Garden City, N.Y.: Doubleday, 1979), 327–39; Harry Hearder, *Italy: A Short History* (Cambridge: Cambridge University Press, 1990), 153–207.

5. Hanna Kiel, *The Bernard Berenson Treasury* (New York: Simon and Schuster, 1962), 57. Biographical summary is based on Ernest Samuels, *Bernard Berenson: The Making of a Connoisseur* (Cambridge: Belknap of Harvard University Press, 1979); and Ernest Samuels, *Bernard Berenson: The Making of a Legend* (Cambridge: Belknap of Harvard University Press, 1987).

6. Kiel, *Berenson Treasury*, 47–48.

quirkiest and most aesthetically driven Catholic conversion, unable to withstand the chilly Protestant wind of northern Europe or North America.[7]

Berenson stayed in Italy through the First World War and into the era of the Fascist dictator Benito Mussolini, who took power in 1922. Between 1870 and 1929, Popes Pius IX, Leo XIII, Pius X, Benedict XV, and Pius XI regarded themselves as "prisoners of the Vatican." They refused to acknowledge Italian unification, the nation's anticlerical constitution, and its appropriation of the Papal States. The Lateran Treaty of 1929 between Pope Pius XI and Mussolini was, therefore, a momentous event, ending this sixty-year standoff and restoring church-state relations. Mussolini recognized the special privileges of the church throughout Italy in return for Pius's acceptance of the fact that the Vatican's temporal empire had gone for ever.[8]

Nineteenth-century Italy had been, for American and British observers, a byword for political weakness and fragmentation. Under Mussolini, by contrast, it began to appear strong, especially by comparison with the United States in the grip of the Great Depression and Britain mired in the interminable "Slump." This appearance of vitality, along with the Lateran Treaty, made Italy seem a particularly attractive political-religious model to many American and British Catholics. Chesterton visited Rome in the year of the treaty and commemorated his visit in *The Resurrection of Rome* (1929), which depicted Rome as the literal and mystical center of Western civilization, a city of perpetual rebirth and self-renewal. He met the pope and "Il Duce" and praised them both. Believing that Britain and America were in the thrall of a godless plutocracy and that only an independent church and an independent regime, such as Mussolini's, could prevent Italy from being dragged down in the same way, he was lenient toward Fascist abuses and treated the regime as the scourge of the moneylenders and a bulwark against communism.[9]

Christopher Hollis was similarly enthusiastic. In one of his Notre Dame speeches, about 1936, Hollis described Mussolini as Italy's equivalent of a

7. Berenson's enthusiasm for Catholic teaching and art remained. In *The Venetian Painters of the Renaissance* (New York: Putnam, 1894), for example, he wrote: "From the earliest times it [the Church] employed mosaic and painting to enforce its dogmas and relate its legends . . . [and] as an indirect stimulus to moods of devotion and contrition. . . . No one can look at Bellini's picures of the Dead Christ upheld by the Virgin and angels without being put in a mood of deep contrition, nor at his earlier Madonnas without a thrill of awe and reverence" (2–3).

8. Bokenkotter, *Concise History*, 398–404.

9. G. K. Chesterton, *The Resurrection of Rome*, in *The Complete Works of G. K. Chesterton*, ed. Robert Royal, (San Francisco: Ignatius Press, 1990), 21:265–466.

distributist. He was "the peasant from the Lombard plains who could trace his ancestry back for six hundred years, a man of roots who knew how important roots were. He attacked capitalism because it was itself the revolution, destroying the traditions." He was "fighting to protect the ancient heritage of the Italian people."[10] Hollis told a South Bend reporter that Mussolini was justified in his attack on Abyssinia, that Italian rule would give the Ethiopian people access to "elementary medical knowledge and other aids of science," and that the League of Nations, which had imposed sanctions against Italy for its aggression, was "a body of weak kneed politicians" trying to defend an indefensible Versailles Treaty, which had deprived Italy of its rights in the first place.[11]

Another recent convert, the American historian of Europe Ross Hoffman (1902–1979), visited Italy in the summer of 1936, met the pope ("very thrilling"), and toured the ancient and Christian sites. He had read Chesterton's *Resurrection of Rome* and had himself recently published *The Will to Freedom*, which praised Mussolini as an effective barrier against "the pestilential heresy of Communism."[12] Fascism, he wrote there, "does not quarrel with traditional concepts of the nature of man. . . . Poor though it is in philosophy, it does insist that man is no mere economic animal," and to that extent it created "a spiritual environment favorable to the Christian religious tradition." But along with these attractions Hoffman could clearly see the dangerous side of the doctrine: "In places it tends toward a purely biological explanation of human behaviour, as is evident in the mad doctrines of racialism and eugenics which have gained such wide acceptance." If Italian Fascism could not purge itself of these accretions, he warned, it would midwife "one of the strangest and most malignant heresies that ever appeared in Christendom."[13]

Like nineteenth-century visitors to Rome, Hoffman was appalled at the general inefficiency of everyday life and the flood of counterfeit money circulating in Rome but consoled himself with the thought that conditions were improving. He wrote in his diary: "What a land this must have been before Mussolini began to crack heads! He knows his people well. They are either saints or devils."[14] While he was there the Spanish Civil War broke out, and he feared that at any moment the whole of Europe would explode into another world war, stranding him and his family in its midst.

10. Christopher Hollis, speech typescript, n.d. (about 1936), Hollis File, Notre Dame Archives, UDIS 106/074.
11. "Hollis Defends Stand of Italy," *South Bend News Times*, March 6, 1936, 2.
12. Ross Hoffman, Rome Diary, August 7, 1936, ms., courtesy of Mrs. M. E. Flinn, Professor Hoffman's daughter.
13. Ross Hoffman, *The Will to Freedom* (New York: Sheed and Ward, 1935), 52.
14. Hoffman, Rome Diary, July 28, 1936.

The immediate European war crisis passed, but news of Republican atrocities in Spain filled the Italian press. Hoffman compared the two Mediterranean nations:

What a contrast is shown between this country [Italy] and Spain. I wish some of my left-wing friends might have visited both these countries this summer. Here there is peace, there is order, there is a reasonable freedom, there is a fair measure of justice, there is public spirit, there is religion, there is hope, courage, faith in the future. Yet Italy might very well have gone through what rages today in Spain. Italy and Europe owe Benito Mussolini more perhaps than anyone yet realizes.[15]

Hoffman, like Chesterton, drew a radical distinction between Mussolini's pro-Catholic Fascism and Hitler's Nazism, which he opposed as a new form of militant paganism. He greeted with horror Mussolini's alliance with Hitler three years later, in 1939, which shattered Hoffman's hopes for an integral Catholic Italy. In dismay he abandoned his academic career in modern European politics (he taught at Fordham in New York) and retreated to eighteenth-century England, where he became a pioneer in the study of Edmund Burke, in whom he found an alternative source for a viable Anglo-American Catholic and natural law tradition.[16]

The Spanish Civil War had begun in 1936 when General Francisco Franco flew from Majorca to the Spanish mainland (in a plane chartered for him by an English Catholic right-winger, Douglas Jerrold) and led a rebellion against the unstable Republican government.[17] German and Italian forces aided Franco, while Soviet advisers and supplies flowed to the Republican side. The war, which dragged on until 1939 with horrifying brutality on both sides, became an ideological litmus test for intellectuals in Britain and America, whose governments remained officially neutral. Few had been well informed about Spanish affairs until then. Spain had been a political backwater for decades, even more so than Italy. Propaganda in the form of "news" coming from the two sides was wildly contradictory, and it was possible, depending on your sources, to believe either side saintly or demonic. To members of the English Labour Party, to

15. Ibid., August 22, 1936.
16. Ross Hoffman and Paul Levack, eds., *Burke's Politics: Selected Writings and Speeches of Edmund Burke on Reform, Revolution, and War* (New York: Knopf, 1949). On Hoffman and his search for non-Italian sources for a natural law tradition, see Patrick Allitt, *Catholic Intellectuals and Conservative Politics in America, 1950–1985* (Ithaca: Cornell University Press, 1993), 49–58.
17. This summary of the war is based on Hugh Thomas, *The Spanish Civil War* (New York: Harper, 1961).

the Communist-dominated Popular Front, and to most non-Catholic Americans, the Spanish Civil War was a clear-cut struggle between republican freedom and Fascist autocracy. Prominent writers, including George Orwell, Arthur Koestler, Stephen Spender, W. H. Auden, and Ernest Hemingway visited Spain (Orwell fought there with a group of Catalan anarchists on the Repubican side) and wrote openly as partisans of the Republic. They explained the Republicans' attacks on churches, priests, and nuns as a consequence of the church's long and close association with reactionary politicians.[18]

For most American and British Catholics, by contrast, the war represented a struggle between the church, championed by Franco, and militant, anticlerical communism. Arnold Lunn, who went to the war as a journalist and followed it from the Nationalist side, spoke for many Catholics when he wrote that "the only effective choice was between an authoritarian government which would protect and an authoritarian government which would persecute Christianity."[19] In *Spanish Rehearsal* (1937) he argued that the Nationalists were Spain's equivalent of the distributists. He supported them because "I accept the Christian tradition in favour of the economy of the farm, the village and the small town. . . [and] I dislike the tendency to transform small men working on their own land or in their own business into the employees of chain stores, and I regard Communism as the final form of the servile state." Franco's Nationalists, he said, were "more determined to redress the just grievances of the poor than their opponents."[20]

On a second visit to the war Lunn was the guest of a junior branch of the Spanish royal family (skiing friends from happier days) whose three sons were flying missions in the Nationalist air force (one died in action). Lunn witnessed what for the Nationalists were the exhilarating advances of 1938 and regarded each newly "liberated" town as a safe haven for the Catholic faith. The local people, he reported, were delighted to return to their churches. "In Spain," he wrote, "the burning of churches and the massacres of priests were, in the main, the work of small bands of itinerant gangsters. There, as in Communist Russia and in revolutionary France, the unorganized majority proved defenseless against an organized minority of terrorists."[21]

18. See, for example, George Orwell, *Homage to Catalonia* (1938; New York: Harcourt, Brace, Jovanovich, 1952); Ernest Hemingway, *For Whom the Bell Tolls* (New York: Scribner's, 1940).
19. Arnold Lunn, *Come What May* (London: Eyre and Spottiswoode, 1940), 129.
20. Arnold Lunn, *Spanish Rehearsal* (New York: Sheed and Ward, 1937), vii, i.
21. Lunn, *Come What May*, 344.

Lunn watched the combat through field glasses, usually from a reasonably safe distance. Closer to the fray was Roy Campbell (1901–1957), a hard-drinking poet and storyteller, who was beaten up by the Republican militia and had to escape from the besieged city of Toledo in the first months of the war.[22] Campbell, South African by birth but Oxford educated, had struggled as a writer in London from 1926 to 1929. An enthusiastic literary modernist at first, friend of T. S. Eliot, Aldous Huxley, and Wyndham Lewis, he had gradually turned against the modernist literary "establishment," especially when his wife, Mary, had a lesbian love affair with Vita Sackville-West. He published a bitingly satirical poem about the Bloomsbury group, the *Georgiad*, in 1931. Campbell had moved first to France and then (just ahead of debt collectors) to Barcelona, Spain, in 1933, where he wrote poems about the ancient sun-worshiping religion of Mithraism.[23]

Campbell, reunited with his wife when Virginia Woolf replaced her in Vita's affections, moved to a remote Andalusian village and asked the parish priest to receive them both into the Catholic Church. They were remarried as Catholics in 1935. Campbell's poem about his conversion, "The Fight," is an allegorical dogfight in modernist garb between a red plane (his earlier life of sin and radicalism) and a white plane of Christianity, which wins. The poem ends with a vision of the risen Christ oddly mixed with Mithraic solar imagery.[24] Uninterested at first in politics, Campbell witnessed the escalating Spanish conflict at first hand after moving to Toledo, where Cardinal Isidro Goma y Tomás confirmed him and Mary in a dramatic, secret nighttime ceremony. The persecution of the Spanish Catholic clergy in the March riots of 1936 horrified Campbell and he responded by sheltering a group of Carmelite friars in his house, for which he in turn was arrested and beaten by the militia. All seventeen of the Carmelite friars were later shot dead in the street by Republican soldiers, after bringing him a chest containing the papers of Saint John of the Cross for safe keeping. By judicious bribery Campbell, a marked man for his open Catholic sympathies, was finally able to escape from the city in a mortuary truck. These wrenching experiences, intensified by his farewell view of Toledo, with the Alcazar Palace under bombardment and partly aflame, gave him a crusader's view of the war as a struggle between Christendom and godless communism.

---

22. Biographical information in the following passage is based on Peter Alexander, *Roy Campbell: A Critical Biography* (Oxford: Oxford University Press, 1982).

23. Roy Campbell, *Mithraic Emblems: Poems* (London: Boriswood, 1936).

24. Alexander, *Roy Campbell*, 150–51. See also Katharine B. Hoskins, *Today the Struggle: Literature and Politics in England during the Spanish Civil War* (Austin: University of Texas Press, 1969), 40–55.

Campbell, according to his own account (in an autobiography full of tall tales), later returned, volunteered for the Nationalists, and fought through the war to victory. In fact he did return, but he spent the rest of the war as a correspondent for a Catholic newspaper, the London *Tablet*, rather than as a fighting soldier. He published an epic poem, *Flowering Rifle: A Poem from the Battlefield of Spain*, in 1939, which was so passionate in its admiration of Franco and the Nationalists and so vehement in its contempt for the left-wing English Republican sympathizers that it cost him nearly all his remaining English friends. Even his generally admiring biographer says that it is a poem of "stupefying monotony" and that it "provides some extraordinary examples of the shallowness and naiveté of Campbell's political judgment." In a section that glorifies the bloodshed of a Nationalist cavalry charge, Campbell compares the soldiers' exuberance to that of a crowd of soccer fans: "But of this match the wide earth is the ball, / And by its end shall Europe stand or fall."

Throughout the poem the enemy are "Bolshies" or "Communists" rather than Spaniards, and Campbell's eulogies to the Nationalists are replete with comparisons of the soldiers' virtues to those of Christ. Pro-Nationalist reviewers praised it and pro-Republicans condemned it; one of them, Stephen Spender, described it as the "ignoble sweepings of every kind of anti-Semitic and atrocity propaganda" and said that it made him feel physically sick.[25]

Despite Lunn's and Campbell's enthusiasm for Franco and the fiercely pro-Nationalist outlook of most other Catholic writers, a few English-speaking Catholics remained neutral or supported the Republicans. Once again, it was mainly converts who took the more independent line. Dorothy Day took a neutral and pacifist position but sympathized more with the Republicans than with the Nationalists. Jacques Maritain was horrified to learn that the Nationalists were executing prisoners and hostages in the name of defending religion. Writing in Day's *Catholic Worker*, he declared that Franco's troops revealed "a rare and singularly high level of cruelty and contempt for human existence." "It is as if the bones of Christ, which the executioners on Calvary did not touch, were being broken on the Cross by Christians." The Holy Cross Fathers' journal, *Ave Maria*, taking the more conventional Catholic line, professed amazement at Maritain's attitude and rebuked him for being "an incredibly ignorant and misinformed commentator" and probably a dupe of Communist propaganda.[26] Carlton Hayes, a convert and history professor at Columbia University in New York, also urged neutrality and resigned from the board of *Common-*

25. Alexander, *Roy Campbell*, 174, 175, 177 (quoting Spender).
26. Maritain and *Ave Maria*, quoted in J. David Valaik, "American Catholic Dissenters and the Spanish Civil War," *Catholic Historical Review* 53 (January 1968): 544, 545.

*weal* in 1937 when Michael Williams, one of the founding editors, yielded to the pressure of Catholic public opinion and supported Franco.[27] The war placed *Commonweal*'s entire future in jeopardy. The other founding editor, George Shuster, also resigned. A younger of group of editors, incensed by Williams, bought him out and forced him into retirement. Their neutralist editorials in turn enraged Charles Coughlin, the Detroit radio priest, who compared their refusal to take sides to Pontius Pilate's attitude toward Jesus.[28]

Among English Catholics, Eric Gill was almost alone in believing not merely that Franco was fallible but even that the Republicans deserved to win. He was also the most outspoken and would not back down even when a pair of Popular Front groups, Artists International and the Communist *Left Review*, used his name in their Spanish propaganda. Gill was so averse to commercial capitalism and the evils of industry, themes he had been spelling out in the Dominicans' *Blackfriars* magazine throughout the 1930s, that he was willing to be bracketed, on this issue, with the Communists and to criticize English Catholics for supporting Franco. His biographer Fiona MacCarthy shows how his outspokenness put the hierarchy in a quandary. "In his role of Catholic Artist the Church saw Gill as a good thing, someone to be nurtured. He was a point of contact between the Romish minority in Britain and more mainstream art and culture, and his influence on younger Catholics was profound. But as a Catholic Artist in the company of Marxists he was now becoming an increasing liability."[29] Cardinal Hinsley had a framed photograph of Franco on his desk (sent him by the "Caudillo" in person) and, while supporting the British government's policy of nonintervention, was quite clear about the desirability of a Nationalist victory. He reproached Gill in a private letter: "You have no right or justification for stating that the Catholic Church in Great Britain has identified itself with the Nationalists. But it is impossible to ignore the facts, and the comparison of the conditions prevailing in Government and Nationalist Spain is more than sufficient excuse for the present attitude of many Catholics in this country."[30]

Making a sharp distinction between Italian Fascism and German Naz-

27. Thomas E. Blantz, *George N. Shuster: On the Side of Truth* (Notre Dame, Ind.: University of Notre Dame Press, 1993), 84–88. George Shuster, coeditor of *Commonweal* with Williams, warned American Catholics not to support Franco. In the long run, he believed, fascism was as dangerous as communism to the welfare of the church. Shuster had made several visits to Nazi Germany and written perceptively about Hitler's regime, making him one of the first strongly antifascist American Catholics.

28. Valaik, "American Catholic Dissenters," 553.

29. Fiona MacCarthy, *Eric Gill* (London: Faber and Faber, 1989), 274.

30. Thomas Moloney, *Westminster, Whitehall, and the Vatican: The Role of Cardinal Hinsley* (Tunbridge Wells, Kent: Burns and Oates, 1985), 65.

ism, the English converts were among the earliest Catholic foes of Hitler. E. I. Watkin saw Nazism as a threat to the historical progress of civilization (a theory in which, unlike many of the other converts, he still had some faith): "I must confess that I could not have conceived that a civilized European people would have relapsed into the barbarous Jew-baiting of Nazi Germany," he wrote in 1936.[31] By the late 1930s a majority of British Catholics echoed this view. The Jesuit *Month*, for example, condemned Hitler's "insolent and wholly baseless claim" of Aryan superiority and declared that Germany was "following the example of Russia in turning its back upon Christian civilization"; yet the periodical continued to praise Mussolini for recognizing "the supremacy of the supernatural" and for giving "religion something of its due place in his system."[32] By the middle of 1937 the *Month* was making regular scathing attacks on Hitler and Stalin, "the Autocrat of all the Russias," but held off on fierce rebukes to Mussolini until his formal alliance with Hitler in 1939.[33]

Britain declared war on Germany in September 1939 in reaction to Hitler's invasion of Poland, but two and a quarter years were to pass before the Japanese attack on Pearl Harbor brought the United States into the conflict. Hitler's overwhelming successes in conquering Poland, Czechoslovakia, Belgium, Holland, Denmark, Norway, and France in the first year of the war tempted some Britons to consider making terms rather than carry on alone in a seemingly hopeless conflict. Catholics were among them, especially when Hitler's arrangement of a semiindependent Vichy regime in France seemed to mitigate the rigors of direct rule. German and Italian propaganda tried to foster the idea of a "Latin bloc" of nations, including Vichy France, Franco's Spain, and Mussolini's Italy, allied with Germany against the threat of Soviet Communism. The idea took on slightly more plausibility after July 1941, when Hitler broke his pact with Stalin and attacked the Soviet Union directly. In England the *Catholic Herald*, edited by Michael de la Bedoyere, favored this view of the international situation. De la Bedoyere had been an ardent supporter of Franco and, in 1940 as in 1936, regarded the threat of Stalin as much greater than that posed by Hitler.[34]

---

31. E. I. Watkin, Review of Jacques Maritain, *Freedom in the Modern World*, and Maritain, *The Freedom of the Intellect and Other Conversations with the Sage Theonas*, in *Dublin Review*, no. 396 (January 1936): 172–75.

32. Editorials, "The Olympic Games," *Month* 167 (February 1936): 108; and "Collectivism and the Absolute State," *Month* 167 (May 1936): 386–87.

33. See, for example, Editorials, "The Terror in Russia," *Month* 170 (July 1937): 4; and "False National Ideals," ibid., 7.

34. He subsequently recanted this view, saying, "We must now honestly admit that we underestimated the effective power for evil of the Nazi movement." But he continued to deplore the demand for unconditional surrender, foreseeing the possibility of a separate

The English convert writers offered a bracing contrast to this view and urged Britain to fight on. Arnold Lunn, for example, whose London home was damaged during a German air raid and who witnessed the conflagration of the East London docks at first hand, called de la Bedoyere a defeatist.[35] Christopher Hollis foresaw the inevitable and early collapse of the Vichy regime, and the historian Christopher Dawson described the "Latin bloc" idea as "treason to Christ the King." Hollis also urged British Catholics to enlist and fight, as the surest way of allaying their fellow citizens' suspicions, incurred during the Spanish war, that they were pro-Fascist.[36]

Several of the British and American converts also dedicated themselves to bringing the United States into the war as soon as possible. To do so, they had to overcome the anti-English views of the Irish-American population, many of whom shared Father Coughlin's strident isolationism. Arnold Lunn, on a lecture tour in the United States, emphasized the Irish element of his background and urged Irish Americans to reflect that Nazi victory in the war would be infinitely worse than British. "The English way of life . . . has many defects," but at least it honored "the Christian belief in man's high estate . . . conferred on him by his Creator." By contrast, "Christ the King is formally dethroned [and] the brutalities of the pagan world into which Christ was born have reappeared in the Germany of Hitler." Lunn met Father Coughlin, who harangued him for hours about Jewish and Masonic plots. Coughlin's deterioration—by 1940 he was an admirer of Hitler, who, he said, had morally purified Germany—was a great shame, wrote Lunn, because his earlier broadcasts had introduced the papal encyclical tradition to thousands of Protestants who would never otherwise have known about it and he had done as much as anyone to spread the idea that the Catholic Church was not just an apologist for wealthy capitalists. "The tragedy of Father Coughlin is that whereas he might have been one of the greatest of modern apostles, he has only succeeded in being one of the most futile of modern politicians."[37] Alfred Noyes also sailed to America in 1940 and spent the next two years criss-crossing the continent, lecturing in the United States and Canada until the

---

peace with Hitler to forestall Soviet dominance. See Michael de la Bedoyere, "The Catholic Press in Wartime," *Commonweal*, January 2, 1942, 263.

35. Arnold Lunn, *And the Floods Came: A Chapter in Wartime Autobiography* (London: Eyre and Spottiswoode, 1942), 63–64.

36. Thomas R. Greene, "Vichy France and the Catholic Press in England," *Recusant History* 21 (May 1992): 111–33.

37. Lunn, *And the Floods Came*, 19, 27–28, 143. On Coughlin in 1940, see Alan Brinkley, *Voices of Protest: Huey Long, Father Coughlin, and the Great Depression* (1982; New York: Vintage, 1983), 267.

nervous strain affected his eyesight.[38] Frank Sheed, the converts' publisher, went at the instigation of British military intelligence, in the hope that by lecturing to American Catholics in favor of intervention he could accelerate a U.S. commitment to the war. He ultimately crossed the Atlantic fifteen times during the war, without incident, though on one occasion military demands bumped his name from the passenger list of a ship that was then sunk by a German submarine.[39]

American converts—admirers of their English counterparts—were also hard at work speaking and writing in favor of early U.S. intervention. Ross Hoffman at Fordham and his Columbia University friend Carlton Hayes both urged early U.S. participation and had to withstand verbal brickbats from unsympathetic Irish Americans. Having lost his Italian illusions Hoffman now saw Britain and the United States as the best remaining guardians of Christian civilization. In a book titled *The Great Republic*, written in 1940 and 1941 but appearing just after Pearl Harbor, he described the Atlantic Ocean as the "inland sea" of Christendom and argued that, paradoxically, the Protestant nations were now guardians of the Christian flame, which was guttering out in Italy, France, and Germany. Against American historians who treated the United States as separate from, and spared the imperfections of, old Europe, Hoffman insisted that America was still part of European civilization, with the same convictions, faith, and spirit.[40] In a collaborative account of the origins of the war, written long before its successful outcome could be assured, Hoffman wrote that this Second World War was the greatest battle yet for the survival of Christendom.[41] President Roosevelt appointed Carlton Hayes U.S. ambassador to Spain, on the theory that a Catholic who had *not* been compromised by support for Franco during the Spanish Civil War was a suitable choice for the job of keeping Spain neutral. *Commonweal* praised the appointment of "a man who thoroughly understands the tradition of his hosts and shares the Faith that has inspired that tradition," especially since he was one of few prominent Catholics "who, from its inception, has been so forceful an opponent of modern totalitarianism."[42]

English converts also played a central role in a bold interreligious experiment in the early years of the war, the Sword of the Spirit Movement. The brainchild of Cardinal Hinsley, who supported a militant war policy, it

38. Alfred Noyes, *Two Worlds for Memory* (Philadelphia: Lippincott, 1953).
39. Sheed, *Church and I*, 245, 247; Wilfrid Sheed, *Frank and Maisie: A Memoir with Parents* (New York: Simon and Schuster, 1985), 121.
40. Ross Hoffman, *The Great Republic* (New York: Sheed and Ward, 1942).
41. Ross Hoffman and C. Grove Haines, *The Origins and Background of the Second World War* (New York: Oxford University Press, 1943).
42. Editorial, "Professor Hayes to Madrid," *Commonweal*, April 17, 1942, 637.

brought together Catholics, Anglicans, and nonconformists to clarify the moral and spiritual dimensions of the war.[43] Its origins, says Hinsley's biographer, "were rooted in the reverberating events of 1940: the fall of France, the shock to Catholic sentiment of Italy's entry into the war, the insidious allurements of a Latin Catholic bloc; and above all, the exuberant if fearful clarity of Britain's isolation."[44] Hinsley made Christopher Dawson, editor of the *Dublin Review*, its chief lay spokesman, and in essays and speeches to the group Dawson emphasized the preservation of the Christian spirit as a principal war aim. Never before had the moral issues in war been so pressing, for total war broke down the distinction between combatants and noncombatants, "requiring from the latter a standard of courage and endurance which is just as high as that of the professional soldier. Modern war is a struggle of mass wills and a test of moral strength for the whole population; and hence in the last resort it is a conflict which calls for the intervention of spiritual powers and demands a spiritual decision."[45] The Sword of the Spirit's moment of glory, a series of packed ecumenical meetings in the early months of 1941, soon passed. Other Catholic bishops and theologians feared it might encourage religious "indifferentism," and Britain's alliance with Stalinist Russia after Hitler's invasion in the summer of 1941 showed that realpolitik rather than moral purity would govern national war policy.[46]

Several members of this interwar generation of Catholic converts saw active service in the Second World War: Evelyn Waugh in Crete and Yugoslavia, Roy Campbell in East Africa, and Graham Greene in West Africa. Others were too old or sick. Eric Gill died in 1940 from lung cancer, and two years later Hilaire Belloc suffered a severe stroke that effectively ended his long writing career. Cardinal Hinsley, the convert writers' friend and patron, died in 1943. For the rest of this generation the war was a time of intensified literary effort, interrupted by such disasters as the obliteration of the London headquarters of Sheed and Ward in a German air raid. Born and converted Catholics alike hated communism and their wartime work blended condemnations of Hitler's Germany and Stalin's Russia. They were sure that being allied with Stalin to defeat Hitler should not lead Britons, least of all Catholics, to find the former in any way

43. Cardinal Hinsley, "The Sword of the Spirit," BBC radio address, reprinted in *Catholic Mind*, June 8, 1940, 201–8.

44. Moloney, *Westminster*, 186.

45. Christopher Dawson, "The Sword of the Spirit," *Dublin Review*, no. 416 (January 1941): 2. See also his "Democracy and Total War," *Catholic Mind*, August 22, 1940, 308–20; and "Spiritual Foundations of Order," ibid., May 8, 1941, 16–18.

46. For Hinsley's defense against the charge of indifferentism, see Hinsley, "The Sword of the Spirit Movement," *Catholic Mind*, November 22, 1941, 14–19.

preferable to the latter. Soon after the British-Russian alliance in the summer of 1941 the Soviet ambassador in London protested to the Foreign Office about anti-Soviet rhetoric in the Catholic press. The government sent cautionary notes to Catholic editors but declined to censor their work and told the Russians that Britain was proud of its free press. The Ministry of Information also reminded other government departments that "the Catholic press in England is watched with interest by Catholic circles in America" and that "a too sudden reversal of policy on Russia" would simply rob it of the leverage for U.S. intervention it was currently exerting. It remained untouched by government censors as the war progressed.[47]

Ronald Knox played no direct role in the war effort. Instead he dedicated himself to writing an elegant Catholic translation of the Bible, which he hoped the hierarchy would adopt in place of the stilted Douai Bible then in use. Knox had relinquished his Oxford chaplaincy in 1938 and gone to stay with Lady Acton, a recent convert who became his patroness, and he lived in spartan conditions on her estate, plodding along with the translation and assured of Cardinal Hinsley's support. A good translation of this kind had been proposed as far back as 1855, with the expectation that Newman would do it, but news that Archbishop Francis Kenrick of Baltimore was working on his own translation (never completed) had led to fears of an unseemly competition, and the idea had been dropped, to be picked up by one of his convert successors almost a century later. Catholics, said Knox, ought to read the Bible more. "Our first job is to make them love it. If they don't love it, they won't read it."[48] His translations first appeared in print only to subscibers: first the New Testament (1944), and then the Old (1949). The project caused Knox years of anguish and delay, especially after Hinsley died in 1943, and it was finished in the face of obstruction from bishops who lacked the old cardinal's open-mindedness. In September 1944, for example, they were on the verge of denying the imprimatur to his New Testament after many postponments of proper discussion. Knox wrote a revealing letter to Archbishop Bernard Griffin of Westminster, Hinsley's successor, comparing himself to other converts and pointing out how Protestants would interpret such a rejection:

Ever since I was received [into the Church] twenty seven years ago tomorrow, I have been incurably propaganda-minded, and the question "What will the Protestants think of this?" has never been absent from my thoughts. It is obvious that the Newman centenary will be written up by the [Anglican] *Church Times* and . . . they will say what they have always said—That

47. Moloney, *Westminster*, 231.
48. Penelope Fitzgerald, *The Knox Brothers* (London: Macmillan, 1977), 248.

the Church of Rome does not want converts, finds them an embarrassment and does not know what to do with them. That Newman, like all converts after him, found himself entirely wasted as a Roman Catholic, whenever he tried to do anything, authority always let him go a little way with it and then crushed him. . . . I can see the *Church Times* writing, "Father Knox should have known the Church of Rome better by now. He would have been wiser to stick to detective stories."[49]

Only after another year of delay and editing did the bishops finally relent and authorize the new Bible for sale with the imprimatur and for use in Britain's Catholic churches. Almost at once it became a best seller. Despite his vexations Knox donated all royalties to the church. The profits also guaranteed the prosperity of the publisher, Sheed and Ward, for over a decade, becoming, in Wilfrid Sheed's words, "our transatlantic meal ticket . . . Sheed and Ward's beefsteak mine" which "gave us illusions of vast prosperity."[50]

By the end of the war the British converts' role in American Catholic life was diminishing, though the last and most intellectually distinguished of them, Christopher Dawson, did not arrive in the New World until 1958, as we shall see. Having once seemed avant-garde the European Sheed and Ward writers were now duplicating a message that could be heard from many indigenous (convert) voices, notably those of Thomas Merton and Avery Dulles. Wilfrid Sheed recalled that by the 1950s "Sheed and Ward had begun to look awfully assimilated, somewhere on the edges of the Universal Church; it serviced the incurably brainy and kept them orthodox. In this its role was almost like the meliorism of the New Deal; Sheed and Ward led its public exactly as far out of the Dark Ages as the powers that be felt it safe to go."[51] The Catholic revival to which it was dedicated had never taken off among the Catholic population as a whole, in Britain or America. By comparison with the drama and upheaval to come in the 1960s, Catholic intellectual life from 1920 to 1960 looked quiescent and docile.

Christopher Hollis was a Conservative M.P. from 1945 to 1955 but never a minister. He resigned his seat after ten years to resume his career as a writer, and much of his work took on an elegiac quality. After the furies of the Second World War, he said, he had lost some of his old Bellocian illusions about Europe and the faith and now believed that Catholics were

49. Evelyn Waugh, *The Life of the Right Reverend Ronald Knox* (London: Chapman and Hall, 1959), 300–301.
50. Sheed, *Memoir with Parents*, 185.
51. Ibid., 102.

apt to be better people when they were a minority than when they became a nation's majority population. "Those Catholics who never come into [Protestants'] company remain in infancy," and "the Catholic machine, when it is unchallenged, becomes corrupt, just as much as does the machine of State or party."[52] But he was dismayed by what he regarded as the decline of religion in England and the United States. The ecumenical spirit had grown on Hollis, who had disliked religious polemics from the outset and now saw a pressing need for all Christians to join forces against a hostile secular world. In his biography of his Eton contemporary and lifelong friend George Orwell, Hollis overlooked Orwell's bitterly anti-Catholic remarks and found in him, at least latently, the spirit of Christianity. John Rodden, in a study of the politics of Orwell's reputation, is indignant that Hollis drew a portrait of an Orwell rather like himself—conservative at heart, antiurban, and alive to spiritual realities. From our point of view it is equally striking that Hollis made the attempt at all, that he was willing to extend a charitable hand to a man who had made starkly uncompromising anti-Catholic remarks throughout his literary life. Hollis's *Orwell* is a work that shows how the urbane, conciliatory side of the convert intellectuals laid the foundations for the ecumenical 1960s and the more adventurous Catholic generation that was to displace this one.[53]

The same conciliatory and elegiac note was struck in E. I. Watkin's *Roman Catholicism in England from the Reformation to 1950* (1957). Watkin noted many lost opportunities in England's Catholic history and many instances of uncharitableness and bad faith on both the Protestant and the Catholic sides. He ended each passage with a regretful summary. If only the Ultamontanes and Cisalpines had not dissipated their energies in squabbling against each other in the early nineteenth century. If only Newman and Manning had not been adversaries. That they were was "a major tragedy of the Church in England during the second half of last century." If only Tyrrell had been less pigheaded and Pius X's condemnation of modernism less harsh. If only parochial schoolchildren in England today were taught their faith in context, rather than being "crammed with doctrine imparted as isolated items of indigestible information, supplied with dry bones of text book theology, coated with devotional sugar." And like Hollis, Watkin was eager for a more ecumenical approach to the Protestants, in place of the "unreasonable, sectarian prejudice" that Catholics still often showed. "But a more truly Catholic vision is aware that,

52. Christopher Hollis, *Along the Road to Frome* (London: Harrap, 1958), 227.
53. Christopher Hollis, *A Study of George Orwell: The Man and His Works* (London: Hollis and Carter, 1956); John Rodden, *The Politics of Literary Reputation: The Making and Claiming of "St. George" Orwell* (New York: Oxford University Press, 1989), 362–74.

although Catholics cannot agree that Protestants are right *against* the Church in matters of faith, their practice may have lessons to teach Catholics and that, as Newman pointed out, heresies have often anticipated in an unbalanced and therefore unacceptable form, future Catholic developments."[54]

Among them, this group of British converts wrote a hundred good books and thousands of articles and lectures, and they drew interested and usually respectful press attention for more than half a century, in both Britain and the United States. They played a central role in the Catholic revival, and the novelists among them made Catholicism an important part of twentieth-century English literature. But they were no more successful than Newman and Brownson had been at stimulating a general turn to Rome. Many readers, particularly of Knox and Chesterton, admired the work without being moved to convert to Catholicism. This large audience was just as likely to respect T. S. Eliot, C. S. Lewis, or Dorothy Sayers, skilful Christian apologists for whom the denominational issue was insignificant. Lewis was closer to the popular view that the particular church was ceasing to matter; he was careful to avoid interdenominational squabbling.[55]

After the Second World War a religious revival began in the United States. Sociological studies suggested that the revival was as much a matter of community building in suburban settlements as passionate attachment to Christianity's more exacting demands. Few of its figures specified doctrinal rigor. From Billy Graham to Norman Vincent Peale it was more a matter of feeling and goodwill—"Peace of Soul."[56] England had no comparable postwar revival. Battered and weakened by German bombing and seven years of total war, its people seemed to the convert writers more than ever hardened to materialism and a grimly pragmatic this-worldliness. The converts' sense of dismay and failure was well captured by a disillusioned and nearly blind Alfred Noyes, who wrote in 1949:

The moral and spiritual catastrophe in which the whole of our civilization is involved is sometimes glibly described as a revolution, one of those changes

54. E. I. Watkin, *Roman Catholicism in England from the Reformation to 1950* (London: Oxford University Press, 1957), 150–70, 192, 215–20, 212, 230.
55. See, for example, C. S. Lewis, "Christianity and Culture" (1940), in his *Christian Reflections*, ed. Walter Hooper (Grand Rapids, Mich.: Eerdman's, 1967), 12–36.
56. On the revival and its characteristics, see Will Herberg, *Protestant, Catholic, Jew: An Essay in American Religious Sociology*, new ed. (1955; Garden City, N.Y.: Doubleday, 1960); Peter Berger, *The Noise of Solemn Assemblies: Christian Commitment and the Religious Establishment in America* (Garden City, N.Y.: Doubleday, 1961); Gibson Winter, *The Suburban Captivity of the Churches: An Analysis of Protestant Responsibility in the Expanding Metropolis* (Garden City, N.Y.: Doubleday, 1961).

to which we must surrender as a normal process of history. It is rather to be described as an insurrection of the lower faculties of man against the higher. In art and literature there has been a reversion to animalism, a triumph of brutality over the finer influences of the spirit. . . . There is only one remedy. Without it the human race is lost beyond recovery and the future holds nothing for mankind but evil heaped on evil. Either we must rediscover those absolute values of which the only source and foundation is the Supreme Being, or we go down in universal ruin.[57]

Noyes thus dramatically summarized a sense shared by the surviving members of his generation of converts, including Lunn, Knox, Hollis, Martindale, and Leslie, that they had been helpless to prevent the deterioration of religion and morality. It seemed to them that the hideous menace of Communism was now opposed only by a spiritually weakened West adrift from its moorings in Christian faith. "We Catholics may be unable to arrest the world's progress to self-destruction," wrote Arnold Lunn to Ronald Knox in 1949, "but at least we understand what is destroying us. We have at least the melancholy satisfaction of not being simultaneously bewildered and annihilated. . . . It is not only because the Russian Marxists destroyed the embryo of Kerensky democracy that the oppression in Russia is infinitely more evil than the worst tyrannies of the pagan world to which Christ was born. The key to Russia's troubles is not political but theological. They have substituted the worship of the proletariat for the worship of God."[58]

57. Alfred Noyes, Introduction to 1949 edition of *The Unknown God* (London: Sheed and Ward, 1949), 319–20, 321.
58. Arnold Lunn and Ronald Knox, *Difficulties: Being a Correspondence about the Catholic Religion* (1932; London: Eyre and Spottiswoode, 1958), 255. This edition of the two men's earlier debate contained a final exchange of letters, dated 1949.

# XI

# TRANSFORMING THE PAST
## *The Convert Historians*

T HE NOISIEST CATHOLIC historian of the early twentieth century was Hilaire Belloc, but despite his literary gifts, he often let polemics against Protestantism and industrial capitalism take precedence over historical accuracy. He was also given to an exaggerated veneration for the Catholic Middle Ages and the "organic" unity of Catholic Europe. Belloc's vision, amplified in much of Chesterton's historical work, supported a widespread Catholic enthusiasm for the Middle Ages in Britain and the United States in the first half of the century. Belloc's well-publicized historical controversies with H. G. Wells and G. G. Coulton in the 1920s and 1930s contained as much swagger as scholarship, and he was often downright wrong about facts. His high profile and his apparently inexhaustible productivity made him seem exhilarating to many converts, but to the more sober historians among them he was, in the long run, an embarrassment.[1]

Many of the convert intellectuals of the early and middle twentieth century were more reliable historians than Belloc, even when, like Noyes and Maynard, they saw history as secondary to their principal work as poets. They had learned historical method prior to conversion and, coming only later to scholasticism, found its deductive, ahistorical techniques unsatisfactory. They recognized that history, rigorously pursued, could be used to defend the Catholic Church in a way more likely than scholastic philosophy to win recognition from non-Catholic scholars.

1. A. N. Wilson, *Hilaire Belloc* (1984; London: Penguin, 1986), 297–317, 348–54. See also Philip Gleason, "American Catholics and the Mythic Middle Ages," in his *Keeping the Faith* (Notre Dame, Ind.: University of Notre Dame Press, 1987), 11–34.

Other converts were historians first and foremost. Among them were the American Carlton Hayes (1882–1964) and the Englishman Christopher Dawson (1889–1970). Together, they led a revival of Catholic historical study, making full use of nineteenth- and twentieth-century methodological refinements. They argued with a hitherto-unmatched display of learning that the disasters of the twentieth century could be traced to the demise of a united Christendom, first in the Reformation era, then in the era of the French Revolution, then ever more acutely in the materialistic nineteenth century. They perceived the contemporary political world as alien, icy, and disintegrating rather than brave and new. They tried to show, through meticulous historical research rather than by deduction or assertion, how this condition had developed.[2]

In some respects Dawson and Hayes make an odd couple, and each embodied something of his home country's stereotypes. Dawson, the Englishman, was born in a twelfth-century castle, grew up in wild, rural landscapes redolent of the ancient past, and lived the isolated life of a private gentleman-scholar. His first full-time academic appointment did not come until he was sixty-nine years old, and by then his students found him unapproachable and almost paralyzed by shyness. The American Hayes, by contrast, was a gregarious urbanite, a fraternity man, who had a rural background but spent nearly all his life at Columbia University in the noisy heart of Manhattan, apart from an equally bustling episode during the Second World War when he was the U.S. ambassador to Spain.[3]

Despite these contrasts the two men had much in common. Both received the best education their respective nations had to offer, and both then converted to Catholicism in their twenties. Each married a born Catholic but converted only after prolonged study and meditation on religious life and history. As Catholics they deplored the polemical war many of their coreligionists were waging against Protestants, and each played an active role in organizations for promoting interreligious harmony against the common enemies of religion. They also helped to found, and contributed regularly to, journals that aimed to raise intellectual standards within the Catholic Church, and they were on friendly terms with many of the apologists of Chesterton's generation. They built bridges to sympathizers in the non-Catholic world and deplored the insularity and

2. Biographical material in this chapter is based on Arthur J. Hughes, "Carlton J. H. Hayes: Teacher and Historian" (Ph.D. diss., Columbia University, 1970); and Christina Scott, *A Historian and His World: A Life of Christopher Dawson, 1889–1970* (London: Sheed and Ward, 1984).

3. On Hayes in Spain, see John P. Wilson, "Carlton Hayes in Spain" (Ph.D. diss., Syracuse University, 1969).

uncharitableness that sometimes marred Catholic writing and conduct. That outreach, in its turn, brought them under suspicion within their respective countries' Catholic communities.

Dawson and Hayes were wide-ranging historians, interested not merely in particular aspects of the past but in its entire sweep. They were theorists of civilization itself, working at the end of a hundred-year period in which "metahistorians" had flourished.[4] Hayes was one of the founders of the academic discipline of international relations, and Dawson was an inventive synthesizer of anthropological, archaeological, and sociological techniques in historical writing. Dawson in particular was one of the first scholars to incorporate the insights of cultural and social anthropology into historical interpretation and to see culture rather than nature as the basic building block of civilization. Unlike many of their distinguished predecessors and contemporaries, including Hegel, Marx, Comte, Spencer, Freud, Spengler, and Toynbee, they were skeptical about evolutionary paradigms in historical study. The idea of social and historical "evolution," adapted metaphorically from Darwinian biology, had made a deep impression on two generations of historical scholars but seemed to them fatally compromised by its materialist premises and deterministic implications.[5] They also rejected many of the commonplaces of late Victorian historiography, such as the Teutonic theory, which held that the Anglo-Saxons were a distinctive race singled out by biology for world dominance.[6] They were almost equally critical of the theory of progress as an innate force in history and criticized such advocates of rational, planned progress as H. G. Wells, though never in Belloc's intemperate style. Their shared choice of metaphors was revealing. They opposed mechanistic metaphors for society and favored organic ones. A society, they argued, is more like a living person than a machine. Its distinctive character comes from its spirit, not its structure. Like a person it can age, become sick, and die, and it is not destined to rise ever higher up a preestablished ladder. They both believed that Western society after the First World War was mortally wounded, an organism in danger of death. They prescribed spiritual rather than mechanical remedies.

No less than the liberals and Marxists of the 1930s they recognized the

4. On metahistory, see Hayden White, *Metahistory: The Historical Imagination in 19th-Century Europe* (Baltimore: Johns Hopkins University Press, 1973).

5. On the influence of evolutionary ideas on historical scholarship, see John Higham, *History: Professional Scholarship in America* (1965; Baltimore: Johns Hopkins University Press, 1983), 147–70.

6. On Anglo-Saxon and "Teutonic" history, see Peter Novick, *That Noble Dream: The Objectivity Question and the American Historical Profession* (New York: Cambridge University Press, 1988), 80–87.

Great Depression as a challenge to the political, economic, and moral orthodoxy of their era, and conducted a running debate with these antagonists over its meaning, significance, and potential resolution. In some respects they shared the liberals' concerns, praised liberalism for its scientific and technological achievements and for its dedication to liberty, equality, and abundance. Hayes's early support for welfare reforms, his sympathy for the New Deal, and his criticism of militant nationalism, won him liberal friends and admirers for a time. But in other respects they differed from contemporary liberalism. Since the late nineteenth century, they each believed, liberalism had separated from its Christian moorings and become increasingly materialistic and nationalistic. They both saw nationalism as a substitute religion, and they hated and feared the volatile combination of revolutionary communism with Russian nationalism embodied in the new Soviet Union. Like their fellow converts in the late 1920s and early 1930s they believed that, on balance, fascism represented a less dreadful threat to Europe than communism, and that certain theoretical elements of fascism—especially the idea of the organic state—were defensible. But both reacted in horror against Hitler's anti-Semitism and his European aggression.

The outbreak of the Second World War, confirming their gloomiest premonitions, lent a new urgency to their work. They reached their high point of intellectual influence in the Second World War and at the onset of the Cold War, when their theories of civilization's decline and the rise of political parody religions seemed to have been borne out by events. But their heyday was short. Hayes ended his career honored by half of his historian colleagues but suspected by the other half of harboring antidemocratic and profascist sympathies, especially when, in his seventies, he became an apologist for the Franco regime in Spain. Dawson's grand synthesizing technique, widely admired in the 1940s and just right for the postwar religious revival, seemed archaic by the early 1960s, and his life ended in an intellectual environment resistant to celebrations of Western Christendom.

Carlton Hayes, son of a Baptist doctor from Afton, New York, graduated from high school at the age of sixteen and did two years of intensive independent study alone before going as an undergraduate to Columbia University in 1900.[7] He was an outstanding undergraduate and stayed on for graduate study in history, gained the Ph.D. in 1910, and at once joined Columbia's dynamic history faculty. Among his teachers and colleagues

---

7. The biographical summary in this and subsequent paragraphs is based on Hughes, "Hayes."

the most influential were James Harvey Robinson and Charles Beard, both champions of the "New History," who tried to use historical studies in support of progressive reform projects.[8] Throughout his career, Hayes, too, linked his study of the past to contemporary political issues. Although he repudiated many of his teachers' explicit political and religious beliefs he learned from them to be a skeptical but wide-ranging reader of historical documents. His undergraduate thesis on the origins of Anglicanism and his master's thesis on the papal election of 1378 both showed the influence of Robinson's searching tutelage, and his 1909 doctoral dissertation on the Germanic invaders of the Roman Empire contributed to the attack on the Teutonic theory of Anglo-Saxon origins.[9]

On becoming an assistant professor at Columbia in 1910, Hayes shifted his focus to modern European history. Under Robinson and Beard's influence, he voted for the Socialist candidate, Eugene Debs, in the presidential election of 1912, and his critical attitude to industrial society is apparent in the anthology *British Social Politics* (1913), which he edited. It deplored the dislocations caused by the capitalist revolution and praised the nascent welfare state, begun by Asquith and Lloyd George.[10]

Hayes's conversion to Catholicism came in two stages. He was strongly attracted to Catholic ritual and romantic medievalism as a teenager and joined the church in 1904 when he was twenty-two. But it was not until his 1920 marriage to Evelyn Carroll, a graduate student at Columbia Teacher's College and herself a born Catholic, that Catholicism became a salient issue in his work. "Marriage to a born Catholic," says his biographer, "seems to have intensified his interest in his adopted religion and it certainly stepped up his public avowal of his faith." Hayes was disappointed by many elements of Catholic life in his native country. "As a Catholic, Hayes's ambition was to prod his fellow communicants out of their parochialism and into a meaningful role in American society, particularly in the intellectual life. . . . Following the same pattern he had adopted in propagating the ideas of the New History, he took part in a many-sided campaign to wean Catholics from the apologetical ghettos of the mind in which they lived."[11]

The outbreak of the First World War shocked Hayes and turned his thoughts to the problem of international politics, which was to preoccupy

---

8. On the New History, see Novick, *Noble Dream*, 90–106; and Richard Hofstadter, *The Progressive Historians: Turner, Parrington, Beard* (New York: Knopf, 1969), 180–85.

9. Hughes, "Hayes," 67–72.

10. Ibid., 125; Carlton Hayes, ed., *British Social Politics: Materials Illustrating Contemporary State Action for the Solution of Social Problems* (Boston: Ginn, 1913).

11. Hughes, "Hayes," 162, 165.

him for the rest of his life. Ironically, he developed his far-ranging critique of nationalism in just those decades when Catholic immigrants, eager for acceptance from their nativist neighbors, identified themselves passionately and sometimes uncritically with America. In this setting he wrote a textbook for schools and colleges, *A Political and Social History of Modern Europe* (1916), which first embodied his idea that the zealous nationalism of modern Europe could be traced to the breakdown of Catholic *inter*nationalism in the Reformation era. Extremely well written and far more engaging than most textbooks, it became a best seller over the next decade and sold more than a million copies by 1950, enriching Hayes and making his name synonymous with the study of European history for several generations of students. In line with the concerns of the New History it gave detailed attention to social, economic, and institutional affairs, upstaging an older generation of school and college histories which had been narrowly political.[12] He opposed American participation in the First World War but joined army intelligence after the United States became a belligerent, serving in Washington, D.C., from September 1918 to March 1919. He was among the contributors to *The League of Nations: The Principle and the Practice*, which urged the creation of an international group for the peaceful arbitration of national conflicts.[13]

Christopher Dawson, born in 1889, was raised first on the Welsh border, then on the south coast of England, and from 1896 onward, in a remote Yorkshire valley. His mother was the daughter of a Church of England clergyman and his father a landed gentleman and army officer. Dawson was tutored at home until the age of ten, then went to boarding school, first a preparatory school, Bilton Grange, and then Winchester, one of England's most prestigious private schools. By an odd coincidence he was a contemporary at Winchester of Arnold Toynbee, who, like Dawson, would become a leading theorist of the history of civilization. Being residents of different houses, however, they did not become friends until years later.[14]

Dawson converted to Catholicism at the age of twenty-five in 1914. Like many earlier English converts, he had enjoyed as a young Protestant a

12. Carlton Hayes, *A Political and Social History of Modern Europe*, 2 vols. (New York: Macmillan, 1916).

13. Hughes, "Hayes," 153–59; Carlton Hayes, "The Historical Background of the League of Nations," in Stephen Duggen, ed., *The League of Nations: The Principle and the Practice* (Boston: Portraits Press, 1919), 18–49.

14. Scott, *Historian*, 13–32. See also Christopher Dawson, "Tradition and Inheritance" (1949), *Dawson Newsletter* 8 (Summer 1989): 1–9.

rigorous education *outside* the church, which exposed him to contemporary currents in scientific and historical thought and made him familiar in early life with skepticism and atheism. A first premonition of his turn to Catholicism came with a visit to Rome in 1909 when he was an undergradute at Trinity College, Oxford. Unlike many predecessors this English visitor was delighted by the baroque atmosphere, recalling later that "the art of the Counter-Reformation was a pure joy, and I loved the churches of Bernini and Borromini no less than the ancient basilicas." This appreciation "led me to the literature of the Counter-Reformation, and I came to know St. Teresa and St. John of the Cross, compared to whom even the greatest of non-Catholic religious writers seem pale and unreal."[15] He visited the steps of the Ara Coeli church where Edward Gibbon, whom at that time he greatly admired, had vowed to write the history of Rome's decline and fall. There Dawson made a comparable plan, to write the history of culture, noting in his diary, "I believe it is God's will I should attempt it."[16] In the event he became a kind of anti-Gibbon, arguing in direct contradiction of the old master that Christianity, far from being the great destroyer of civilization, was the idea that vivified a moribund Europe and made possible its highest achievements.

In 1909 Dawson met his future wife, Valerie, who belonged to one of England's old Roman Catholic families. His conversion, however, was not simply an act of convenience to smooth the path of their marriage. He already felt doubtful about the Anglo-Catholicism of his childhood because it lacked a proper principle of authority. As a teenager he had learned about the rise of historical-critical biblical scholarship and its challenges to biblical literalism. "If it had been a frankly hostile attack from without it might have been successfully resisted, but the critics themselves were often men of high character and position in the church who could not lightly be dismissed as infidels." Initially, this approach to the Bible led Dawson to a period of agnosticism in his teens, but he found that he "could not acquiesce altogether in a view of life which left no place for religion." After graduating from Oxford, he resumed close study of the Bible and came to the conclusion that "the Incarnation, the Sacraments, the external order of the Church, and the internal working of sanctifying grace were all parts of one organic unity, a living tree, whose roots are in the Divine Nature and whose fruit is the perfection of the saints." Grasping the doctrine of sanctifying grace, he wrote a decade later, brought him to full acceptance of

15. Christopher Dawson, "Why I Am a Catholic," *Catholic Times*, May 21, 1926, reproduced in typescript by John Mulloy, courtesy of Mr. Mulloy.
16. Scott, *Historian*, 49.

Catholic claims, and he converted in 1914, despite his mother's opposition.[17]

Dawson was a lifelong sufferer from bronchitis, too ill to be drafted in the First World War. Having a small income, the rent of a manor given him by his father, he was able to devote nearly all his time to study and, after a brief, unsuccessful entry into politics at his father's request, worked almost entirely alone.[18]

His first articles appeared just after the First World War and then flowed steadily throughout his long life, impeded only by periods of acute depression. His ambition was to demonstrate how civilizations came into being, matured, and decayed, and to discover whether Western Christian civilization would be spared the fate of all the others. One admirer compares him aptly with Lord Acton, noting that both men "were isolated scholars with a background of British independence and German scholarship" and that both worked with "a high ethical fervour."[19] His system, as it developed, rivaled those of his near contemporaries Spengler and Toynbee, but he emphasized spiritual factors and the element of free will in the creation and preservation of a culture. In his opinion Spengler's fault was a counterfactual tendency to treat cultures as though they were isolated from one another, and Toynbee's error the tendency to treat the twenty-one civilizations of his *Study of History* as all morally equivalent. In Dawson's view, the *encounter* of two distinct groups, examples of which abounded throughout history, was the stimulus for new cultural creation. He also asserted, against Toynbee, that some civilizations, preeminently that of the Christian West, were superior to others.[20]

When Hayes returned to Columbia from the war he joined Peter Guilday in establishing the American Catholic Historical Association (ACHA) and became its first secretary. He had just been promoted to full professor. American Catholic historians at that time were marginal to the historical profession as a whole, partly because most of them worked at Catholic universities and colleges and partly because many of them blended apologetics with history, rather than pursue the austere "scientific" ideal of the

17. Dawson, "Why I Am a Catholic."

18. Scott, *Historian*, 57–58, 66–69.

19. James Oliver, "Christopher Dawson, An Appreciation," in Dawson, *The Gods of Revolution* (New York: New York University Press, 1972), xvii.

20. On Toynbee, see Christopher Dawson "Arnold Toynbee and the Study of History" (1955), in Dawson, *The Dynamics of World History*, ed. John J. Mulloy, (1956; New York: Mentor Omega, 1962), 381–94. On Spengler, see Dawson, "Oswald Spengler and the Life of Civilizations," ibid., 366–80. For this chapter the editor, Mulloy, combined two Dawson essays on Spengler, from 1922 and 1929.

secular professionals. Non-Catholic historians, meanwhile, treated Catholicism as an obstacle to freedom and truth. Reviewing the Catholic William Walsh's sympathetic biography *Philip II*, for example, Roger Merriam, wrote: "The standpoint from which it is written is violently Roman Catholic . . . and the author's ignorance and credulity are appalling. . . . his prejudices and ignorance are so obvious that no one with the slightest smattering of historical knowledge or training will be in any danger of taking it seriously." Walsh retaliated furiously that his book had annoyed Merriam because "it exposed the shabby and slipshod and bigoted methods by which he, and the whole anti-Catholic conspiracy to justify the wretched division of Christendom, have dealt with Catholic Spain and the Church."[21]

Hayes, one of very few Catholic professors of history at a prominent non-Catholic university, was well placed to arbitrate disputes of this kind. He hoped that the new ACHA could improve the quality of Catholic historical scholarship by encouraging more rigorous original research and less partisan writing, but also that it would expose the prejudices of the anti-Catholic historians. In the interwar decades it had something of a split personality, half of it being distinctly anti-Protestant. Its first president, Lawrence Flick, for example, wanted the organization to carry on the Counter-Reformation struggle by "correcting the false history which has evolved from the religious cataclysm of the sixteenth century."[22] The other half, by contrast, though also dedicated to advancing Catholic claims, exhibited a more irenic spirit and advocated impartial, "scientific" scholarship. Hayes led this group, along with several other distinguished historians who had also converted to Catholicism, including Parker T. Moon, Ross S. J. Hoffman, Robert Lord, Gaillard Hunt, Henry James Ford, Daniel Sargent, Herbert Bell, Marshall Baldwin, and Henry Lucas, all of whom became presidents of the organization.[23]

Growing up as Protestants Hayes and these other convert historians had learned to value the Reformation as one of the triumphs of history, which had brought truth out of the brutal, superstitious Dark Ages. But when they became Catholics, they turned this idea of the past on its head and

21. Novick, *Noble Dream*, 203n. It is worth noting as an example of the marginality of Catholic historians to the profession in the United States that in this generally superb 650-page book, Catholic historians as a group are mentioned only four times, all of them in footnotes.

22. Lawrence Flick, quoted in "The First Annual Meeting of the ACHA: Washington D.C.," *Catholic Historical Review* 6 (October 1920): 2–3.

23. On these historians, see Patrick Allitt, "Ross Hoffman and the Transformation of American Catholic Historiography" (unpublished paper delivered to the American Catholic Historical Association Conference, Oxford, Mississippi, April 1991).

learned to look on the Middle Ages as the great age of faith and the Reformation as a catastrophe. Hayes could see merit in both views and tried to conciliate them. Like other Catholic historians, he believed that "the Protestant Revolution of the 16th century and the consequent disruption of Chrstendom split and weakened the one force which might possibly have offered resistance to rampant nationalism, greedy imperialism, and immoral diplomacy. With the revolt of northern Europe against the Papacy and the Catholic church, the last bulwark of medieval internationalism went down in ruins, and there arose full-grown in its stead the state system of modern Europe with all its faults and vices."[24] But the Catholics were not blameless. Hayes admitted that in the Middle Ages "officials of the Catholic Church acquiesced in and then applauded and finally abetted the revival of intolerance throughout Christendom."[25] In his presidential address of 1931 he offered a nonpolemical survey of Reformation scholarship from both sides of the Protestant-Catholic divide. He noted that a consensus about the Reformation was emerging not entirely flattering to either side. But he was pleased to note "an almost revolutionary change in attitude on the part of non-Catholic historiography. No reputable historian of the Middle Ages now treats the period immediately antecedent to the Reformation as 'dark.' No non-Catholic historian now dreams of attributing all virtues, and no vices, of the present age, to Sixteenth Century Protestants."[26]

While trying to conciliate this old argument and still make a vigorously pro-Catholic case, Hayes also pointed to continuities across the great Reformation divide. In an early article for *Commonweal*, which he supported from the outset as a contributing editor, he maintained that the Declaration of Independence and the principles embodied in the Constitution had their antecedents in the Catholic natural law tradition, which arrived with the *Mayflower* at Plymouth as well as with the *Ark* and *Dove* in Maryland. "Although the bulk of the European emigrants . . . in the seventeenth century were Protestants they had been so briefly separated from Catholic ancestors and Catholic traditions that the best of what they brought with them, no matter how unwittingly, was Catholic."[27] The convert and ACHA president Gaillard Hunt (1862–1924), similarly, traced some of Thomas Jefferson's ideas on liberty to Catholic scholars such as

24. Carlton Hayes, "Medieval Diplomacy," in Edmund Walsh, ed., *The History and Nature of International Relations* (New York: Macmillan, 1922), 88.
25. Carlton Hayes, "The Significance of the Reformation in the Light of Contemporary Scholarship," *Catholic Historical Review* 16 (January 1932): 403.
26. Ibid., 395–420.
27. Carlton Hayes, "Obligations to America," *Commonweal*, December 31, 1924, 201.

Cardinal Robert Bellarmine and argued that the Constitution belonged to the Catholic tradition of natural law and limited government.

The American idea went far beyond Magna Carta, for that declared that certain rights and liberties could not be taken away save by the law of the land. America proclaimed that there were certain rights and liberties which could *never* be taken away, even by law. It set these rights above the law. Never before had a people voluntarily subscribed to certain definite principles of right which they bound themselves to regard.[28]

These claims stood in stark contrast to non-Catholic scholars' views of U.S. intellectual genealogy. If non-Catholic historians showed sympathy for any religion, it was for the radical Protestant churches. These were the years in which William W. Sweet, the Protestant church historian, declared: "All the great concepts for which American democracy stands today, individual rights, freedom of conscience, freedom of speech, self-government and complete religious liberty, are concepts coming out of the left-wing phase of the Reformation."[29] Sweet believed that Catholicism had always threatened liberty and did so still. The nonreligious sociologist Talcott Parsons agreed, noting "an authoritarian element in the basic structure of the Catholic Church itself which may weaken individual self-reliance and valuation of freedom."[30]

In other areas there was more scope for compromise. Hayes, Hunt, Hoffman, and their fellow convert historians had, after all, been educated outside the Catholic universities and had witnessed the intellectual achievements of Protestant and agnostic scholars at first hand, including their work in the developing field of comparative religion. In another series of *Commonweal* articles Hayes mentioned in passing that Christianity was syncretic, incorporating elements of paganism, Judaism, and Hellenism. An indignant subscriber wrote in to say that Catholic Christianity

28. Gaillard Hunt, "The Virginia Declaration of Rights and Cardinal Bellarmine," *Catholic Historical Review* 3 (October 1917): 276–89; Hunt, "The American Idea," *Catholic World* 109 (June 1919): 293. Hunt was a biographer of Madison and editor of the Continental Congress papers. He worked at the Library of Congress. For a discussion of this episode, see Philip Gleason, *Contending with Modernity: Catholic Higher Education in the Twentieth Century* (New York: Oxford University Press, 1995), 125–28; and William Halsey, *The Survival of American Innocence: Catholicism in an Era of Disillusionment, 1920–1940* (Notre Dame, Ind.: University of Notre Dame Press, 1980), 71.

29. Sweet, quoted in John McGreevy, "Thinking on One's Own: Catholicism in the American Intellectual Imagination, 1928–1954," 17–18, unpublished essay, courtesy of Professor McGreevy.

30. Ibid., 19. McGreevy points out that Parsons was the translator of Max Weber's *Protestant Ethic and the Spirit of Capitalism* (1930), which tended to treat Protestantism as the motor of progress against a more "backward" Catholicism.

had no debts to any earthly system; it came direct from Heaven. In his rebuttal Hayes made the crucial distinction; Catholicism alone is true and comes from God, he agreed, but in form its theology could not possibly be what it was without the prior existence of the pagan philosopher Aristotle. Similarly, Christmas would almost certainly not be celebrated on December 25 but for the existence of an ancient Mithraic festival at midwinter. Catholics need not shy away from these and other facts unearthed by biblical critics, historians, and archaeologists, even if they were Protestants, he said, since revelation could not clash with rigorous historical research.[31] Neither should Catholics grasp too eagerly at supernatural explanations of historical events. In an article for *Encyclopedia Britannica* he dismissed the Catholic legend of the Virgin giving the rosary to Saint Dominic, remarking instead that it too grew out of other religious practices: "Similar expedients to assist the memory in repetition of prayer occur among Buddhists and Mohammedans."[32]

Hayes was an active exponent of interfaith cooperation and a cofounder in 1927 of the National Conference of Jews and Christians (NCJC). The group included Protestant, Jewish, and Catholic members, who gave speeches and conducted goodwill debates throughout the United States. This work required Hayes to face the disapproval of many American Catholic bishops. A papal encyclical of 1928 "unequivocally spelled out doctrinal opposition to interfaith discussions with Protestants" from fear that "movements, conferences, meetings, and congresses with peoples of different religions might lead one to the totally erroneous conclusion that all religions are equal."[33] Hayes argued that he was working for the mutual understanding and cooperation of *social* groups and was thus beyond the scope of Pius XI's condemnation. He was always part of a small Catholic minority in this work; as late as the mid-1950s about one-fifth of U.S. Catholic bishops "absolutely forbade Catholic participation" in the NCJC.[34] And the former Baptist was hardly likely to mollify suspicious

31. Carlton Hayes, "Nationalism as a Religion," *Commonweal*, December 16, 1925, 149–50; December 22, 1925, 178–79; December 30, 1925, 212–13; January 3, 1926, 236–38; January 13, 1926, 262–63. Letter from C. E. Dougherty and Hayes reply, ibid., January 6, 1926, 242.

32. The incident is recounted in Arthur Hughes, "Carlton Hayes: The Historian as Man of Faith," unpublished paper, delivered to the Seventh Annual Conference of the Middle Atlantic Historical Association of Catholic Colleges and Universities at Saint John's University, Staten Island Campus, April 25, 1981, 12, courtesy of Professor Hughes.

33. Benny Kraut, "Jews, Catholics, and the Goodwill Movement," in William Hutchison, ed., *Between the Times: The Travail of the Protestant Establishment, 1900–1960* (New York: Cambridge University Press, 1989), 215.

34. Kraut, "Jews, Catholics," 219.

Catholics when he declared in *Commonweal* that Catholics should willingly embrace Prohibition![35]

But if Hayes was eager for good interfaith relations, he wanted to exact more sympathy for Catholics from Protestants and Jews in exchange for extending the hand of friendship. During the 1920s several of his attempts to advance Catholic principles and criticize Protestant and nationalist bias got him into trouble. In 1926, for example, he made a speech against veneration of the American flag and the Liberty Bell which, he believed, verged on nationalistic idolatry. "Superpatriot" organizations responded by urging Columbia Unversity to fire him, and one of them editorialized that as a Catholic convert he was particularly dangerous:

Could anyone but a renegade Protestant be guilty of such disrespect toward his flag, his country, and the Constitution? It simply goes to prove what traitorous ideas will enter the mind of a "convert" to Romanism. What would become of America under Romish rule and teaching? The observing ones see the danger of this papal element. Is the great American breast nourishing a Frankenstein monster, which will some day shamelessly devour its benefactor?[36]

Columbia resisted the appeal, and Hayes kept his job. Two years later, when Al Smith became the first Catholic presidential candidate in American history and encountered a hailstorm of anti-Catholic prejudice, Hayes helped to found the Anti-Bigotry Society and made speeches to refute allegations that Smith's religion disqualified him for the job.[37]

In 1930 his textbook came under attack. A Staten Island Episcopalian priest whose children had read it at high school, complained to the New York Board of School Superintendents in 1930 that "the book is objectionable on two grounds, civic and religious. It is written evidently in the interests of some visionary scheme of internationalism. By direct attack and persistent insinuation it breaks down respect for political democracy, patriotism, and everything that pertains to nationalism. It encourages radicalism by continual criticism of the economic basis of modern society under the name of capitalism, contrasting it unfavorably with conditions in the Middle Ages." As for its religious parts, the book was "out and out propaganda. The Roman Catholic Church is everywhere deliberately de-

35. Hughes, "Hayes," 170.
36. Ibid., 225. Unfortunately the name of the newspaper from which Hayes took this cutting was not kept.
37. See Thomas E. Blantz, *George N. Shuster: On the Side of Truth* (Notre Dame, Ind.: University of Notre Dame Press, 1993), 73.

fended and both the Church of England and all the branches of Protestantism are persistently criticized."[38] Hayes said the charges were "preposterous" but the school board dropped his text just the same. Under this provocation he and his friend and fellow convert Parker T. Moon wrote a more circumspect version of the book, taking advantage of advances in cultural anthropology in the last fifteen years. It was republished in 1932 as *A Political and Cultural History of Modern Europe* and drew another round of favorable reviews. For the *American Historical Review* a Princeton historian, J. E. Pomfret, wrote: "Hayes has been among the first in recognizing the importance of factors other than political in the treatment of general history. . . . He has adopted the term *cultural* with a broader anthropological connotation, to designate his interest in the whole range of the nonpolitical activities of mankind."[39]

Hayes, while involved in these community activities and controversies, was consolidating his reputation as a scholar within and beyond Catholic boundaries. His book *The Historical Evolution of Modern Nationalism* (1931) was his most distinctive and original contribution to historical research and writing. It argued that nationalism was a post-Reformation ideology which, from relatively benign origins, had gathered sinister impetus and ferocity by the early twentith century and taken on the character of a pseudoreligion. Before the Reformation, in this view, the empire and the church were transnational organizations that muted national sentiment. They were eclipsed first by dynastic absolutism, then later by the rise of humanitarian nationalism, apparent in the work of Henry Bolingbroke, Jean-Jacques Rousseau, and Johann Herder. Only with the French revolutionary wars, however, after 1792, did nationalism start to become a pernicious and intolerant doctrine. "Jacobin nationalism" had a secular missionary impulse and relied on Napoleon's armies for dissemination through Europe. Then, Hayes argued, the defeat of Napoleon led to the formation of a countervailing "traditional nationalism" among the Congress of Vienna powers, expressing the ideals of August Wilhelm von Schlegel, Edmund Burke, and Louis-Gabriel-Ambroise Bonald, but running into the stout opposition of antinationalist traditionalists such as Clemens Metternich. From Metternich's point of view, Hayes observed, "nationalism in every form [was] too closely associated with Jacobinism, as being essentially subversive of social order and security, as being inherently inimical to the traditional state and specifically to the historic Habsburg

38. "City Schools Bar Prof. Hayes's History," *New York Times*, May 2, 1930, 1.2.

39. Carlton Hayes, *A Political and Cultural History of Modern Europe*, 2 vols. (New York: Macmillan, 1932); J. E. Pomfret, review in *American Historical Review* 38 (July 1933): 839–40.

Empire." He foresaw that the triumph of nationalism augured "a series of great international wars." Hayes shared Metternich's view on the novelty and instability of nationalism.[40]

English "liberal nationalism," shaped by Jeremy Bentham and the utilitarians, though less bellicose than the Jacobin variant, was still an invitation to wars for national independence or national unity in the hands of Giuseppe Mazzini, Louis Kossuth, or Daniel O'Connell. Much worse was the "integral nationalism" of Charles Maurras and Action Française in the early twentieth century, with its anti-German, anti-Jewish flavor and belligerent xenophobia. The rise in the nineteenth century of mass education and mass literacy, along with European industrialization, had enabled governments to conduct mass propaganda and use early childhood training as a forcing ground for nationalist sentiments.[41] In another book, *France, a Nation of Patriots* (1930), which he researched with a grant from the Carnegie Endowment, Hayes showed how "Frenchmen of the present day are rendered supremely patriotic." He described "the agencies by which French national psychology is fashioned and fortified" and explained "a national psychology which has inspired Frenchmen to effect and maintain an extraordinary degree of national unity and national optimism not only during the awful military strain of 1914–1918 but also during the unparalleled economic stresses of the decade of reconstruction from 1919 to 1929." These achievements, and the bombastic national propaganda he found especially in French educational materials, provoked dread in Hayes. His fear of nationalism made him skeptical of its counterpart, mass democracy, and his work of the 1930s echoed the doubts of Dawson and their Spanish contemporary Jose Ortega y Gasset.[42]

Christopher Dawson's *Progress and Religion* (1929) was an achievement parallel to Hayes's *Historical Evolution of Modern Nationalism*. Its publisher, Maisie Ward, described it as "the immense sensation in our early career."[43] Dawson investigated the history of the concept of progress to show how it, like Hayes's nationalism, had developed after the Reformation and gained a central place in the Western intellectual tradition; how progress, like nationalism, had taken on religious connotations, making

40. Carlton Hayes, *The Historical Evolution of Modern Nationalism* (New York: Richard Smith, 1931), 117.

41. Ibid., chap. 5, "Liberal Nationalism," 120–63. On misuses of literacy, see 136–37.

42. Carlton Hayes, *France, a Nation of Patriots* (New York: Columbia University Press, 1930), v. The book is impartial in tone, but in interviews Hayes was more outspoken. See "Scores French Textbooks," *New York Times*, January 17, 1930, 14.4. See also José Ortega y Gasset, *The Revolt of the Masses* (1930; New York: Norton, 1957).

43. Maisie Ward, *Unfinished Business* (London: Sheed and Ward, 1964), 118.

men willing to sacrifice themselves to it. Dawson traced the destructive quality of the doctrine to Descartes, with his plans to place knowledge on a surer footing. "All the vast accumulation of knowledge and tradition which was the heritage of European culture, all the ideas and beliefs that men acquire from experience and literature and contact with other minds were to be set aside as an impure compound of truth and error, and to be replaced by a new knowledge of mathematical certitude which was derived from the infallible light of pure reason."[44] The Enlightenment confidently linked reason and progress and viewed tradition and religion as obstacles to truth.

The Cartesian epistemology and the theory of progress itself were both, in Dawson's view, fatally erroneous. He offered his own account of the rise of Western civilization to show that, although in certain respects and from certain vantage points it could be seen as a story of "progress," the dynamic force was Christianity. "At every step the religion of a society expresses its dominant attitude to life and its ultimate conception of reality." Far from being a retrogressive force, as the Enlightenment tradition alleged, religion alone had sustained it. "The secularization of a society involves the devitalization of that society. . . . the passing of a religion is not a sign of progress but a token of social decay." Liberalism and the idea of progress were, he continued, living on the borrowed energy of Christianity but could not do so for much longer:

The day of the Liberal Deist compromise is over, and we have come to the parting of the ways. Either Europe must abandon the Christian tradition and with it the faith in progress and humanity, or it must return consciously to the religious foundation on which these ideas were based. . . . The religious impulse must express itself openly through religious channels, instead of seeking a furtive, illegitimate expression in scientific and political theories to the detriment alike of religion and science. It must be recognized that our faith in progress and in the unique value of human experience rests on religious foundations, and that they cannot be severed from historical religion and used as a substitute for it, as men have attempted to do during the last two centuries.

Dawson was no foe of modern science and its achievements. Indeed, he argued forcefully that the great strength of Western civilization was that it had linked Christianity with the scientific heritage of Hellenism. Orthodox Christianity was strong by reason of its historical rather than merely meta-

44. Christopher Dawson, *Progress and Religion: An Historical Enquiry* (1929; New York: Sheed and Ward, 1938), 11.

physical claims. It did not take refuge in the Eastern religions' claim that the material world was ultimately unreal or unimportant, and so it paid serious attention to scientific discoveries about the material world. "The return to the historic Christian tradition would restore to our civilization the moral force that it requires in order to dominate external circumstances."[45]

Dawson was already an established author by the time he published *Progress and Religion*. Many articles through the 1920s and his first book, *The Age of the Gods* (1928), had demonstrated his encyclopedic learning in ancient history, anthropology, and archaeology and indicated that his summary interpretation of culture would begin right at the beginning. It also showed a radiant self-confidence in his ability to bring together and explain a vast array of diverse data through one general interpretive framework. Subtitled "A Study in the Origins of Culture in Prehistoric Europe and the Ancient East," it aimed to explain the development of the earliest civilizations, the religious forces that directed and gave them shape, and the material achievements and limitations that had flowed from their spiritual and psychological makeup.[46]

*The Making of Europe*, Dawson's next book, showed that his grasp of medieval history was equally sure. As in *Progress and Religion* he argued that the church was the thread that had preserved Latin culture through the Dark Ages and that the monasteries were the centers from which learning had revived.[47] The church, the barbarian societies, the remains of the Roman Empire, and the classical tradition had all played distinctive roles in this history. Like Hayes, Dawson was reacting against the Teutonists, who had overemphasized the barbarian element, and more distantly against Gibbon, who had treated the church as an element in the dissolution rather than preservation of civilization. As Dawson wrote at about this time: "[His] lack of sympathy and understanding for the religious forces which have exerted such an immense influence on Western culture is Gibbon's great defect as an historian: and it is a very serious one, since it invalidates his judgment on the very issues which are most vital to his subject."[48]

*The Making of Europe* was well received inside and beyond the Catholic

45. Ibid., 246, 256, 258–59.
46. Christopher Dawson, *The Age of the Gods: A Study in the Origins of Culture in Prehistoric Europe and the Ancient East* (Boston: Houghton Mifflin, 1928).
47. Christopher Dawson, *The Making of Europe: An Introduction to the History of European Unity* (1932; New York: Sheed and Ward, 1952). See in particular chap. 11, "The Western Church and the Conversion of the Barbarians," 189–213, emphasizing the role of the monasteries.
48. Dawson, *Dynamics*, 327.

community. Reviewers in England and America emphasized that Dawson was trying to break down the nationalist historiography of the recent past, which had retrospectively imposed modern national boundaries on the medieval era. A reviewer for the *Nation*, an habitually anti-Catholic journal at that time, commented that "this is probably the best short history of the Dark Ages that has appeared in England. Dr. Dawson writes with an impartiality very unusual in a Catholic historian."[49] An enthusiastic Catholic reviewer meanwhile noted that *The Making of Europe* "marks a complete break with many historical conventions and traditions. [Dawson] has striven to write history from the Catholic standpoint and to depict events and forces which have contributed to the welfare of mankind at large rather than to the pride and glory of any race or nation." The book is "singularly free from insularity and prejudice."[50] That the book could seem both "impartial" and yet come from "the Catholic standpoint" was a tribute to Dawson's moderation and scholarly care. In this respect it differed vastly from Hilaire Belloc's idea that "Europe is the Faith," frequently delivered with the rhetorical hammer. "From this provincial view of the Faith and Europe," wrote Maisie Ward, "Christopher Dawson saved us."[51]

In these books from the late 1920s and early 1930s Dawson balanced praise for the intellectual system builders of the nineteenth century with criticism of their reductionism. He tried to avoid oversimplification even while analyzing history on a scale as broad as theirs. It seemed clear to him that there was a much more complex interplay of material, psychological, and spiritual forces in any culture than Hegel, Marx, Comte, or Spencer had admitted. He did not deny, for example, that material forces vitally influence the shape of a culture, but far more insistently than Marx he declared that to understand the material setting alone was only the beginning. The Eskimo, for example, appeared to live under the most exacting material conditions, he wrote in 1928. "At every point—in his use of skin for boats and tents and clothing, of bone for weapons and tools, of blubber for warmth and light—he is bound down to an absolute dependence on the little that nature has given him. Yet his culture is not a necessary result of climatic and economic determinism, it is a work of art, a triumph of

49. Anonymous review of *The Making of Europe*, in *Nation*, September 7, 1932, 575. See also the anonymous review in the *Times Literary Supplement*, June 23, 1932, 457.

50. Patrick Healy, review of *The Making of Europe*, *Commonweal*, January 4, 1933, 274–75.

51. Ward, *Unfinished Business*, 119.

human inventiveness and endurance, and it is the fruit of an age-long cultural tradition."[52]

At the center of every culture was religion, but metahistorians and sociologists from the Enlightenment to the early twentieth century had treated cultures as, *in essence*, responses to economic, geographic, or environmental forces. The fallacy either sprang from their ignorance of religion or else was part of a polemic against it. They had forgotten or suppressed the knowledge that until the most recent times all peoples had lived in a world full of magic and of gods needing to be propitiated at every turn.

The apostles of the eighteenth century Enlightenment were, above all, intent on deducing the laws of social life and progress from a small number of simple rational principles. They hacked through the luxuriant and deep-rooted growth of traditional belief with the ruthlessness of pioneers in a tropical jungle. They felt no need to understand the development of the historic religions and their influence on the course of human history; for, to them, historic religion was essentially negative, it was the clogging and obscurantist power ever dragging back the human spirit in its path towards progress and enlightenment.[53]

For Dawson, by contrast, "the essential unity of a civilization consists in a common consciousness," and "behind the cultural unity of every great civilization there lies a spiritual unity." These psychological and spiritual issues transcended, without contradicting, all material issues.[54]

Dawson's sensitivity to psychological issues did not make him receptive to the ideas of Sigmund Freud, another of his rivals in the interpretation of civilization. Freud's general works on religion, *Totem and Taboo* (1913), *The Future of an Illusion* (1927), and *Civilization and Its Discontents* (1930) were almost contemporaneous with Dawson's early cultural explorations, but they seemed to him fallacious. Freud, he noted, treated religion as a "sublimation of the irrational" and "an illusory substitute for reality." But if this were true, Dawson argued, "it would be useless to look to religion as a source of spiritual power; on the contrary it would be a source of weakness, a kind of collective neurosis which perverts and saps

52. Dawson, "The Sources of Culture Change," in *Dynamics*, 18. Dawson's contemporary Antonio Gramsci, aware of these deficiencies, was working toward a refinement of Marxist cultural theory in the same period.
53. Dawson, "Religion and the Life of Civilization," in his *Enquiries into Religion and Culture* (1933; Freeport, N.Y.: Books for Libraries Press, 1968), 95.
54. Dawson, "Cycles of Civilization," in ibid., 70.

social energy." Dawson claimed to have shown, by detailed historical investigation of a sort Freud never attempted, that "religion has undoubtedly been one of the greatest motive powers in human history" and that it had "increased collective energy rather than diminishing it." Dawson found it "impossible to believe that the power of the spirit is nothing but a perversion and consequently a degradaton of physical energy. . . . It is as though one were to say that reason itself arises from the perversion of the irrational. It is a line of thought that leads to the blank wall of nihilism and nonsense."[55]

Dawson's more popular contemporaries echoed this harsh judgment of Freud, often without the self-restraint. Arnold Lunn, for example, said that "there is not a page in Freudian literature which betrays any knowledge of Christian philosophy, history, or apologetics" and that Freudianism was really a contemporary form of laziness.[56] Other, more temperate convert intellectuals realized the need to distinguish between sense and nonsense in contemporary psychology. For example Reginald Dingle (born 1889, converted 1919), author of *The Faith and Modern Science* (1935), acknowledged the fertility of Freud's ideas and the acuteness of perception he often showed, even if he organized his findings according to a wrongheaded materialist and "pan-sexualist" scheme. Let us not ask whether Freudianism can prove Catholicism, cautioned Dingle. "It is more useful to say: 'What can Catholics learn from these discoveries which Freud cannot, because there are things which they know and he doesn't?'" Dingle added that "there is a work calling out to be done in the development of a Christian psychology of the sense of sin."[57]

Dawson was indebted to anthropology and throughout his career used the term "culture" in its anthropological sense and not to mean "high culture." He lamented the tendency of nineteenth-century sociologists, starting with Comte, to mix pseudotheological utopias into their "scientific" study of society, judging that of all the social scientists only the anthropologists had escaped this pitfall, keeping their eyes fixed on particular realities and generalizing guardedly, on the basis of observation. Like his secular contemporaries, he aimed to write "scientific" history, informed by painstaking observation and excluding wish fulfillment and special pleading. Among the pernicious quasi-religious "scientific" theo-

55. Dawson, *The Judgment of the Nations* (London: Sheed and Ward, 1942), 127–28.
56. Arnold Lunn, *A Saint in the Slave Trade: Peter Claver (1581–1654)* (London: Sheed and Ward, 1935), 17.
57. Reginald Dingle, "Psychology and Original Sin," *Dublin Review*, no. 400 (January 1937): 137; Dingle, *The Faith and Modern Science* (London: Burns, Oakes, and Washbourne, 1935).

ries were those based on race. But races, said Dawson, were in fact the *creations* of cultures rather than the biological raw materials out of which cultures were made. He theorized that a cultural group, living in fixed material conditions over many centuries and remote from other such groups, gradually developed certain physical characteristics that differentiated it from other cultural groups. In other words he took race to be a consequence of the more fundamental phenomenon, human culture, and not the biological basis on which a culture was later built. This view, similar to that of Franz Boas, Alfred Kroeber, Ruth Benedict, and other leading anthropologists of the interwar years, grounded his opposition to Nazi racial theory, which was inspiring a pseudo-religious zeal in the Germany of the 1930s and would eventuate in the Holocaust.[58]

Marxism was vulnerable to the same criticism, and Dawson understood it as another substitute religion. "Communism," he wrote in 1933, "supplies its own refutation, for while its philosophy is materialistic, the driving force in its historical development has been essentially religious. It owes its success not to the impersonal evolution of capitalist society but to the religious fervor of its disciples, their spiritual revolt against the practical materialism of modern culture and their apocalyptic hopes in the realization of a Messianic reign of social justice on earth."[59] He also anticipated, presciently, that once Communism had become "an established order," this revolutionary religion was destined to pass away, leaving a demoralized and cynical state dependent on manipulation of fear and naked power.[60]

Dawson's reaction to European Fascism was more complicated than his sharp condemnation of Nazism and Communism. Unlike analysts on the Left he did not think of Fascism and Nazism as similar. In one of his earliest essays, written during the First World War and published in 1920, he had said that only a drastic transformation of society, restoring "organic" principles of social organization, could save England from "the hideous edifice of Victorian industrial society." Among the necessary changes were production-oriented guilds and a new role for the rural classes, since the wealth and welfare of a community spring from the soil. This essay also contained a criticism of "cosmopolitanism" and maintained that the inclusion of radically different groups such as Polish Jews and Armenians in the

58. Dawson, "Sources of Culture Change," 17–18. On the development of cultural anthropology, see Carl Degler, *In Search of Human Nature: The Decline and Revival of Darwinism in American Social Thought* (New York: Oxford University Press, 1991), 61–83.

59. Dawson, *Enquiries*, vii.

60. Dawson, "The Conflict between Christianity and Communism," in his *Religion and the Modern State* (New York: Sheed and Ward, 1935), 59–72.

polyglot United States was likely to bring about "a loss of social personality" from which "only the worst elements are apt to survive."[61] These
remarks, written before Mussolini's rise to power in Italy, now look like
auguries of Fascism. In the early 1930s Dawson added that "the Fascist
State as such is not consciously or intentionally hostile to religion" and
that in Italy, since Mussolini's concordat with the pope, "it has given a
much fuller recognition to the place of religion in national life than did the
democratic regime that it replaced."[62]

In the early 1930s Dawson believed that the growth of technology,
harnessed by the state, threatened to turn even the Western democracies
into totalitarian powers. In places he implied that the West was left with
only a grim choice between competing forms of tyranny. He feared that
economic planning of the sort tried by the national government in England and the New Deal in the United States was likely to stifle individual
freedom. Under these grim circumstances Fascism at least catered to the
sense of national community and embraced the church, whose authority
marked a limit to state pretensions.[63] One of the first scholars to write at
length about Dawson's work, Bruno Schlesinger, faulted him for implying
a latent moral equality between democracy and Fascism in the early 1930s.
Schlesinger, writing after the Second World War, was indignant.

How could Dawson mistake the iron cage of Hitler's Volksgemeinschaft,
where spontaneity and freedom of action were altogether missing, for a true
community? A community cannot be organized from above, least of all by
unmitigated terror. It is a tragic coincidence that a writer as high-minded as
Christopher Dawson unwittingly pleaded in behalf of people who were
utterly unprincipled in the choice of their political means, and thereby
contributed to the confusion of already confused minds.

In fact Dawson never did applaud Hitler's idealized German community
and always condemned the view that the state was its own end, not subject
to any higher law.[64]

It would even be misleading to call him a Fascist sympathizer, because
he was inflexibly opposed both to racism and to militant nationalism. In
1932 he was invited to speak at what he thought was an academic conference in Italy. On arrival he learned that it was, at least in part, a Fascist
rally. At one of the conference dinners his wife was seated beside the

61. Dawson, "The Passing of Industrialism," in *Enquiries*, 48, 60.
62. Dawson, *Religion and the Modern State*, 52.
63. Ibid., 46–51.
64. Bruno Schlesinger, "Christopher Dawson and the Modern Political Crisis" (Ph.D.
diss., Notre Dame University, 1949), 45.

German representative at the conference, Hermann Goering! Undeterred by this setting or the guests, Dawson unequivocally condemned scientific racism and its political effects:

The relatively benign Nationalism of the early Romantics paved the way for the fanaticism of the modern pan-racial theorists who subordinate civilization to skull measurements and who infuse an element of racial hatred into the political and economic rivalries of European peoples. . . . If we were to subtract from German culture, for example, all the contributions made by men who were not of pure Nordic type German culture woud be incalculably impoverished.[65]

It was a source of special regret to see these ideas taking root in Italy, which Dawson had long admired.

In the 1930s Dawson met T. S. Eliot, who invited him to contribute to *Criterion*: Algar Thorold, editor of the *Dublin Review* (himself a convert), who offered the pages of his journal; and Seward Collins, editor of the *American Review*, who coaxed an article from Dawsom for his first issue.[66] He also started to publish with Frank Sheed and Maisie Ward. Dissatisfied with the censorious atmosphere of English Catholicism, Dawson joined Maritain, Eric Gill, and other intellectuals, nearly all of them converts, to found a Catholic literary and political journal, *Order*. It took a less triumphalist tone than many Catholic publications of the era and continued Dawson's efforts to distance himself from the Chesterton-Belloc outlook. "Catholicism was not always a jolly tavern, nor were Catholics necessarily medievalists and Europe was not necessarily always the faith."[67] When the journal collapsed for lack of funds in less than a year, Sheed and Ward took up its mission and published a series "Essays in Order," using Dawson as series editor and his book *The Modern Dilemma* (1932) as an early title.[68]

For Sheed and Ward, he wrote a more accessible prose than hitherto. His style was mild, meticulous, and generally nonpolemical. He continued to win high praise from Catholic reviewers in the 1930s for his services to the faith, giving intellectual ballast and learning to Catholic claims and showing, with weighty erudition, that Christianity was the foundation,

65. Scott, *Historian*, 106.

66. See, for example, Christopher Dawson, "The End of the Age," *Criterion* 9 (April 1930): 386–401; "Religion and the Totalitarian State," *Criterion* 14 (October 1934): 1–16; "The Significance of Bolshevism," *American Review* 1 (April 1933): 36–49.

67. Scott, *Historian*, 96.

68. Ibid., 95–98. Christopher Dawson, *The Modern Dilemma: The Problem of European Unity* (London: Sheed and Ward, 1933).

rather than a dispensable buttress, of Western Civilization. Arnold Sparr has traced the extensive use of Dawson's work—along with that of Maritain and Virgil Michel—among professors and promoters of the American Catholic revival curriculum, and the rise of "Dawsonian" as an adjective to indicate Catholic intellectual gravity.[69] Dawson made a dramatic contrast with Belloc, whose fulminating pro-Catholic polemics made tendentious use of history. Their contrasting styles can be seen side by side in the articles each contributed to the first issue of the *American Review*.[70] Unlike Belloc, Dawson never appealed to the anti-Protestant prejudices of his readers; he reasoned every point, appealing to the judgment of a wider literate audience.

Dawson stood in equally sharp contrast, on the other side, to H. G. Wells, whose *Outline of History* (1924) was a kind of secularist rendering of Western history, in which Christianity was a force of obscurantism and obstruction from which the world had struggled to escape. Belloc had criticized it so venomously that Wells's friends said it contributed to his nervous breakdown. "In many accounts of the controversy," notes his biographer, "Belloc has been represented as a callous sadist, bullying and kicking poor little Wells when he was down."[71] With characteristic generosity, Dawson admitted that no other historian had been willing to undertake a history of the whole world in the early 1920s and that "no one could have done it better than Wells." In its way it had been an astonishing achievement. Wells, like Dawson himself, had a "religious faith" that enabled him to see history as "a creative process out of which a new world and a new humanity must ultimately emerge." What is more, Wells, "despite his notorious hostility to Catholicism," had paid "remarkable tribute to the idea of Christendom as the world-city of God, and especially to the papacy as the first clearly conscious attempt to provide a spiritual government for mankind." Yet, "at the same time," Dawson went on, *The Outline of History* "shows the typical defects of Wells' mind, his Philistinism, his intolerance, the superficiality of his judgment, and the serious gaps in his knowledge and his intellectual sympathies."[72]

Carlton Hayes was dismayed by the rising tide of war in the 1930s. A member of the Catholic Association for International Peace, he criticized

69. Arnold Sparr, *To Promote, Defend, and Redeem: The Catholic Literary Revival and the Cultural Transformation of American Catholicism, 1920–1960* (Westport, Conn.: Greenwood, 1990), 104–13.

70. Hilaire Belloc, "The Restoration of Property," *American Review* 1 (April 1933): 1–16; Dawson, "Significance of Bolshevism," ibid., 36–49.

71. Wilson, *Belloc*, 300.

72. Dawson, "H. G. Wells and *The Outline of History*," in *Dynamics*, 362.

the Italian attack on Abyssinia (Ethiopia) in 1935. He was also more willing than most American Catholics to believe that Franco's troops in the Spanish Civil War, which began in 1936, were committing atrocities as horrible as those of the Republicans. As we have seen, he requested that his name be removed from *Commonweal*'s masthead when Michael Williams organized a pro-Franco rally in 1937. Declining to support Franco in the mood of the late 1930s was an unusual step for an American Catholic, another measure of Hayes's resistance to intra-Catholic conformity and of his awareness of non-Catholic opinion. Dorothy Day, who was on good terms with Hayes, joined him in declaring neutrality in the Spanish war and so becoming "an outcast from the broad mainstream of articulate opinion in the American Church."[73]

Hayes, a familiar figure in New York public life, was much in demand as a speaker and writer in the late 1930s. He made a series of speeches about the rising danger of Nazism and wrote a sharp condemnation of Nazi racial theory for the *New York Times Magazine* in 1937. "Biologically," he declared, in a passage reminiscent of Dawson, "there is no German race or Slavic race, no Irish or Jewish race. . . . The very word 'Aryan' denotes a type of language—only sheer imagination can make it connote race." At the heart of German aggression Hayes beheld the most militant form of nationalism exacerbated by the quest for economic autonomy. Germany as a whole seemed to him to be reverting to a form of primitive barbarism, rejecting nearly all the most humane elements of its Christian heritage.[74] In 1938 he exhorted a convention of Brooklyn's Catholic teachers that they must be as implacable in their opposition to Nazism as they were to Communism (giving an implicit rebuke to the anti-Jewish Catholic demagogue Father Charles Coughlin, who regarded Communism as the more serious threat).[75] And in a speech at the bicentennial of the University of Pennsylvania he betrayed a growing dislike of popular participation in mass politics: "The immemorial age of patricians has closed with Bismarck, Cavour, Nicholas II, perhaps Winston Churchill, and the age of the plebe-

---

73. Blantz, *George Shuster*, 88. On Dorothy Day, see Mel Piehl, *Breaking Bread: The Catholic Worker and the Origin of Catholic Radicalism in America* (Philadelphia: Temple University Press, 1982), 123. Hayes had been one of the first speakers at the New York House of Hospitality (ibid., 74). When shabby Peter Maurin of the Catholic Worker Movement came early on a visit one day, Mrs. Hayes mistook him for a plumber and escorted Maurin to the basement, where he sat uncomplaining among the leaky pipes until Hayes himself showed up to set matters straight. See James Fisher, *The Catholic Counterculture in America, 1933–1962* (Chapel Hill: University of North Carolina Press, 1989), 37.

74. Carlton Hayes, "Patriotism Swings back to Pagan Tribalism," *New York Times Magazine*, January 24, 1937, 3, 20.

75. "Catholic Beliefs Held Anti-Fascist," *New York Times*, December 4, 1938, 44.1.

ians is definitely ushered in by the porter's son Hitler, the blacksmith's son Mussolini, the cobbler's son Stalin, and who will it be in England?"[76]

Hayes realized that the United States was likely to be drawn into the Second World War following the Hitler-Stalin pact and the German invasion of Poland in September 1939. In his view, the sooner the Americans committed themselves, the less difficult it would be to prevail in the long run, and between then and Pearl Harbor he was an active interventionist. He fretted at the folly of Americans who simply did not understand the gravity of the issue. "It is well-nigh incredible," he declared in one speech about Hitler's recent actions, "how, in the face of all these shocking developments, most democratic peoples behaved. They continued to sit apart, in self-righteous isolation, and to chatter about the rapidly extending war as a 'phony war.'"[77] In one of his most impassioned speeches, delivered to the American Philosophical Association in November 1939, Hayes drew an extended parallel between Communism and Nazism as enemies of the Judeo-Christian tradition, and called on all religious and civilized Americans to arm themselves for the fight. The idiom was strongly reminiscent of Dawson.

[Nazism] is a revolt against the moderation and proportion of classical Greece, against the righteousness and justice of the Jewish prophets, against the charity and mercy and peace of Christ, against the whole vast cultural heritage of the Christian church in the Middle Ages and modern times, against the Enlightenment, the reason and the humanitarianism of the eighteenth century and against the Liberal Democracy of the nineteenth. . . . In Russia Christians and in Germany Jews are first gotten rid of. Presently it will be the turn of Christians in Germany and Jews in Russia for if you are to erase the most constant memory in the Western mind you have to destroy Judaeo-Christianity both in its roots and in its flowers.[78]

The Japanese attack on Pearl Harbor in December 1941 annihilated isolationism, but by then the Soviet Union had become an enemy of Germany and a presumptive ally of the United States, blurring the ideological clarity of the war Hayes had hoped to fight.

Hayes published *A Generation of Materialism, 1871–1900* in 1941. Commissioned for William Langer's series on European history, "The Rise of Modern Europe," it was hardly a testament to the principle suggested in

76. Pennsylvania speech quoted in Novick, *Noble Dream*, 244.
77. Carlton Hayes, *This Inevitable Conflict* (New York: Columbia University Press, 1942), a prointerventionist pamphlet, based on a pre–Pearl Harbor speech.
78. "Despots Pictured against the Ages," *New York Times*, November 18, 1939, 18.5.

the series title. Instead, Hayes depicted the last three decades of the nineteenth century as a time in which Europe had grown materially more wealthy but spiritually more impoverished, materialist in the philosophical and the crass, acquisitive sense, and coarsening all its sensibilities as it wrestled for colonies, grabbed at wealth, and armed for total war. Hayes's tone of haughty irony occasionally broadened out into sharp condemnation of the era's self-serving politicians and the ruthless "sectarian liberals," whose "horror of possible ecclesiastical dictation was prodigious. Religion [secular liberalism] would concede to be a tolerable and probably temporary peccadillo of the individual's conscience, provided, of course, one's conscience was not too imperative."[79]

His eloquent prointerventionism had drawn the notice of President Franklin Roosevelt, and in 1942, with the United States at war against Japan and Germany, Roosevelt asked Hayes to be his ambassador to Spain. In some respects it was a shrewd choice. Hayes was a Catholic but also, as a Columbia professor and a prominent public figure in New York life, very much a part of the Eastern Democratic "establishment." He was not tainted by the pro-Fascist views to which many Catholic intellectuals had succumbed in the 1930s, but neither was his name associated with Popular Front anti-Franco groups. It was a drawback that Hayes did not speak Spanish and had no expertise in Spanish history. Neither did he have any practical political or diplomatic experience to prepare him for a senior posting. Even so, the *New York Times* applauded the president's choice, describing Hayes as "a Catholic who has done yeoman's work to break down [religious] intolerance."[80] Hayes's mission was to prevent Franco from joining the war on Hitler's side and to make Spain a benevolent neutral.

Hayes succeeded in his mission but in a way that cost him much of the esteem he had won from American liberals. When he arrived in Madrid, he found many of Franco's advisers assuming that Hitler would win the war and advocating a timely Spanish intervention on the German side. The gradual turning of the tide, however, enabled him to impress Franco with the idea that the postwar world would be far easier for him if he did not bear the stigma of having supported the Axis. Spain was chronically short of gasoline, and Hayes promised petroleum imports as a reward for Franco's neutrality. He criticized the continued use of Fascist paraphernalia and Nazi-style salutes by Spanish Falangists and pointed out that American onlookers who remembered the role of Hitler's bombers in bringing Fran-

79. Carlton Hayes, *A Generation of Materialism, 1871–1900* (New York: Harper and Bros., 1941), 50.
80. Editoral, "Ambassador to Spain," *New York Times*, April 4, 1942, 28.

co to power received the impression that Spain was a Fascist country. An admiring article about Hayes in *Harper's* declared, "There are few examples in the annals of diplomacy of such frank criticism of the domestic policies of a country by a foreign ambassador accredited to it."[81]

But there was another side to the picture. Hayes did little to help refugees, including many European Jews, seeking sanctuary in Spain, and he paid little attention to the opinions of ordinary Spaniards, with whom, in any case, he had no common language. He appears to have succumbed to one of the occupational hazards of diplomatic life: identifying too much with the outlook of the government to which he was accredited and coming to share its concerns. He enjoyed rubbing shoulders with the Spanish aristocracy and took pleasure in the ostentatiously Catholic atmosphere of the restored church in Madrid. He could also foresee that Franco, for all his sins, would be a staunch ally in the coming confrontation with Communism. Paul Preston, in his biography of Franco, suggests that a diplomatically inept Hayes (whom he treats as a schoolmasterish amateur, out of his depth) gave "indiscreet assurances . . . that Roosevelt would never under any circumstances contemplate intervention in Spain." Franco certainly seemed satisfied with the ambassador; he commissioned a portrait of Hayes from a fashionable Spanish artist of the day, and gave it to him as a farewell gift when he left in January 1945.[82]

At the war's end Hayes received Notre Dame's Laetare Medal and congratulations from Catholic groups throughout the country. But many American liberals believed that Hayes had been too friendly with Franco and had done nothing to help persecuted opponents of the Spanish regime. They saw a continuum between Franco and Hitler where he saw a sharp distinction. One critic wrote that in diplomatic wrangling over Spanish tungsten exports to Germany Hayes "went out of his way to yield to rather than try to diminish Franco's blackmail."[83] He angered liberals further by advocating Spanish admission to the new United Nations as a reward for its neutrality—a recommendation which the State Department and the UN itself rejected until 1951. His memoir *Wartime Mission in Spain* won the ACHA John Gilmary Shea prize, but it also drew harsh reviews in liberal journals such as the *Christian Century*, the *Nation*, and the *New Republic*.[84] One reviewer noted as an example of Hayes's bias

81. Ernest K. Lindley and Edward Weintal, "How We Dealt with Spain," *Harper's Magazine* 190 (December 1944): 23–33.

82. Paul Preston, *Franco: A Biography* (New York: Harper Collins, 1993), 524.

83. Percy Winner, "Special Pleader," *New Republic*, November 26, 1945, 718.

84. Carlton Hayes, *Wartime Mission in Spain, 1942–1945* (New York: Macmillan, 1945); W. E. Garrison, "Two Views of Spain," *Christian Century*, June 19, 1946, 780–81; Winner,

that he "goes into considerable detail about the looting of churches, the murder of priests and nuns and the desecration of holy places by the godless leftists" in the Civil War but entirely omits "the virtual extermination of all known liberals, including Protestants," by Franco's men.[85] Another critic, who had seen Hayes in Spain, noted his scorn for American public opinion, accused him of "vanity and ambassadorial despotism," and said his book was really an apologia for Franco's regime.[86] And a third wrote that the book would "lay to rest the curious supposition that Hayes had any affection for liberalism or democracy."[87] More conservative reviewers, by contrast, such as the historian Crane Brinton, praised the book as accurate and evenhanded.[88]

Despite the controversy, Hayes was honored for his scholarly achievements by being elected president of the American Historical Association— the first Catholic to hold the post. A "Popular Front" faction of the AHA, however, led by Frank Friedel and Kenneth Stampp and supported by Richard Hofstadter, opposed Hayes's election on the grounds that he was too friendly to Franco, the last remaining Fascist ruler in Europe, that his earlier writings showed him to be antidemocratic, and that he had been too willing to surrender the refugees to the needs of realpolitik.[89] At an uncharacteristically dramatic business meeting of the AHA Arthur Schlesinger Sr. made a speech on his behalf and Hayes won the contested election by 110 votes to 66.[90] Such elections had traditionally been unanimous, however, and the opposition marred his enjoyment of the honor. His presidential address to the association criticized the insular tendency of American historians, their neglect of the U.S. role in the wider Atlantic world, and their provincialism. While technology had been making the

---

"Special Pleader"; Thomas J. Hamilton, "Hayes Tells All," *Nation*, December 22, 1945, 692–94. On the press controversy, see John LaFarge, S.J., "Carlton Hayes and Friendship for Spain," *America*, December 1, 1945, 232–35. LaFarge and Hayes had worked together before the war to promote interracial Catholicism. Here LaFarge seeks to exonerate Hayes from the charge of profascism and to remind readers that he is a true liberal and a Catholic antifascist.

85. Garrison, "Two Views," 781.

86. Winner, "Special Pleader," 719.

87. Hamilton, "Hayes Tells All," 692.

88. Crane Brinton, review of Hayes, *Wartime Mission*, in *Weekly Review* (of the *New York Herald-Tribune*), December 2, 1945, 3.

89. On the AHA presidency incident, see Novick, *Noble Dream*, 321–22. On Hofstadter's equivocal role in the affair, see Susan Stout Baker, *Radical Beginnings: Richard Hofstadter and the 1930s* (Westport, Conn.: Greenwood, 1985), 180–81.

90. The rebels proposed to vote for Sidney Fay, an association vice-president, but Fay was indignant and declared that he would not accept the presidency if elected over Hayes. See Guy Stanton Ford, "Minutes of the Business Meeting . . . ," *American Historical Review* 50 (April 1945): 663–65.

world smaller, American historians had retreated into an intellectual isolationism that made it seem larger and had exaggerated American exceptionalism. They had, for example, fixed on Frederick Jackson Turner's "frontier thesis" without asking themselves, "Frontier of what?" Of Western Civilization, he answered, and now more than ever American historians must recognize their intimate links to a jeopardized Western Europe, the legatee of Christendom. The address can be read today as a historically illuminated manifesto for the creation of a strong North Atlantic treaty (such as was realized a few years later in NATO) and a continued American presence in Europe against the Soviet threat. It sustained his earlier criticism of exclusive nationalism and argued for the moral superiority of a Greater Europe, of which both the United States and Spain were members.[91]

Hayes retired from his Columbia professorship in 1950, aged sixty-eight, but remained active in lecturing and writing, always aware of his role as a prominent Catholic spokesman and of the attitudes of non-Catholic listeners. In that decade he joined the lament about low educational achievements among Catholics, declaring in one speech that "the restrictions and rigidities of 'ghetto Catholicism' are quite impossible to anyone who aspires to a position of influence in contemporary society and thought."[92] Yet he was losing his own "position of influence in contemporary society and thought" by repeating and elaborating his unpopular views of Spain. *The United States and Spain* (1951) showed that by the early 1950s Hayes had become a fairly orthodox cold warrior, viewing the history of the previous decades through the lens of current preoccupations. He again criticized Americans' ignorance about Spain and the fickleness of public opinion and reminded readers that "there cannot be a [solidified Atlantic Community] without the inclusion of Spain along with her eighteen daughter nations in America." Besides, such an alliance made strategic sense in terms of the apocalyptic confrontation with Soviet Communism.[93] The book provoked another round of unfriendly reviews, with one critic, Herbert Matthews, noting that his account of the Spanish Civil War was "intensely partisan" in Franco's favor and that "Hayes the adherent writes in a way that Hayes the historian would have flunked any

91. Carlton Hayes, "The American Frontier—Frontier of What?" *American Historical Review* 51 (January 1946): 199–216.

92. Hayes, quoted in Hughes, "Hayes," 333. The debate, sparked by John Tracy Ellis in 1955, is well summarized by Gleason in *Contending with Modernity*, 287–93.

93. Carlton Hayes, *The United States and Spain: An Interpretation* (New York: Sheed and Ward, 1951), 175. Publishing with the Catholic house of Sheed and Ward rather than Macmillan, whose favored client he had been for thirty years, marked a step back into the Catholic subculture for Hayes which, in earlier times, he had tended to keep at arm's length.

student of his at Columbia for doing." The book's great weakness, Matthews added, was "its premise that those who disagree with the author are innocent dupes of Moscow or Communists, or fellow travelers," making it a kind of literary McCarthyism.[94]

In 1940, as the Second World War raged, Christopher Dawson was working as editor of the *Dublin Review* and, as we have seen, he was a founding member of Sword of the Spirit, an organization to advance Britain's spiritual welfare. He worked with Barbara Ward, a gifted journalist and Labour Party enthusiast who had become foreign affairs editor of the *Economist* at the age of just twenty-four and was herself beginning a distinguished career in the study of international development.[95] Cardinal Hinsley, the archbishop of Westminster, supported their work, though other members of the English Catholic hierarchy continued to frown on them for making conciliatory gestures to the Anglicans. *The Judgment of the Nations*, which Dawson published in 1942, was the most anguished work he ever wrote, complementary in theme and message to Hayes's *Generation of Materialism*. Dawson, like Hayes, traced this new war to the rise of secular, materialist liberalism in the late nineteenth century and the failure of the older liberal tradition. "It is no accident that the period that has seen the culmination of the modern development of scientific and economic power should have brought Western civilization to the brink of ruin." Again like Hayes, Dawson was particularly frightened by the ability of mass literacy and propaganda to arouse entire nations in the struggle. "The most characteristic feature of the totalitarian system against which we are fighting is its claim to control men's minds as well as their bodies, and in order to enforce this claim it mobilizes all the resources of the new black arts of mass suggestion and propaganda." He warned that achieving victory could corrupt Britain and the United States by tempting them to use the same corrosive spiritual weapons.[96]

In the 1930s he had scanted the difference between the totalitarian dictatorships and the Western democracies, maintaining that the growing reach of the state in all things was rendering the democracies totalitarian too. He now decisively abandoned that line of reasoning and began to assert that democracy and totalitarianism were polar opposites. He continued to blame secularization for the disasters that had befallen Europe, to see Soviet Communism as a perverted descendant of the Orthodox form

94. Herbert Matthews, "No Middle Ground," *New York Times Book Review*, October 28, 1951, 14.

95. "Barbara Ward," *Current Biography, 1977* (New York: H. W. Wilson, 1977), 424–27.

96. Dawson, *Judgment of the Nations*, 5, 16.

of Christianity, and to understand the war itself in eschatological terms.[97] In an early editorial for the *Dublin Review* he wrote that "the present conflict is not just a material struggle for markets and territory, it is a battle for the possession of the human soul. Western civilization is threatened not by the blind violence of the barbarian, but by a far more sinister power which strikes directly at the foundations of our civilization and releases the forces of destruction which have been held in check by a thousand years of Christian culture."[98] Like Hayes he was dismayed to be fighting alongside one totalitarian power in order to defeat the other after the bracing ideological clarity of the early war years when Britain was fighting against a Hitler-Stalin alliance.[99]

Dawson's reputation continued to grow in the war years and he was given one of the highest honors to which a religious scholar could aspire, an invitation to deliver the Gifford Lectures at Edinburgh University. The series had traditionally shown a strongly Protestant bent. Among his illustrious predecessors were William James, Josiah Royce, Karl Barth, and Reinhold Niebuhr. The two series of lectures were then published as *Religion and Culture* (1948) and *Religion and the Rise of Western Culture* (1950), which codified and elaborated his work from the foregoing decades.[100] Catholic reviewers were delighted. Waldemar Gurian, himself a convert and a refugee from Nazism working at Notre Dame, wrote that Dawson had blended the highest achievements of historical scholarship with defense of Christian principles: "Dawson's book shows that the Catholic scholar must master all modern methods of analysis and investigation but that he cannot be satisfied with naive use of them—that is, without intellectual-spiritual interpretation and general ideas."[101] Other reviewers were not so sure. Hugh Trevor-Roper, a rising star among English historians, later to be Regius Professor at Oxford, agreed that Dawson was a brilliant synthesizer and stylist but found his concentration on Christianity as the chief source of European recovery from the Dark Ages excessive: "What are we to deduce? . . . That Christianity alone is a formative religion, alone can change the world? . . . This is Mr. Dawson's conclusion. . . . It seems inconceivable that he should draw it, that so learned a scholar should appear, in this one respect, so parochial."[102]

97. Dawson, "Democracy and Total War," ibid., 15–32. See also Schlesinger, "Dawson and Crisis," 60–70.

98. Dawson, "editorial note," *Dublin Review* 104 (1940): 1.

99. Dawson, *Judgment*, 21.

100. Christopher Dawson, *Religion and Culture* (New York: Sheed and Ward, 1949); Dawson, *Religion and the Rise of Western Culture* (New York: Sheed and Ward, 1950).

101. Waldemar Gurian, "Dawson's Leitmotif," *Commonweal*, June 3, 1949, 202–4.

102. Hugh Trevor-Roper, review of Dawson, *Religion and the Rise of Western Culture,* in *New Statesman*, March 11, 1950, 276–77.

Dawson was a central part of the Catholic college curriculum by the late 1940s. In 1949 Bruno Schlesinger wrote a laudatory political science dissertation about him, faulting Dawson's early sympathy for Fascism but enthusiastically praising his maturation, after 1939, into an uncompromising foe of the dictators. His unswerving emphasis on spiritual affairs, wrote Schlesinger, differentiated Dawson from "other critics of culture who have tried to ascertain the causes of the modern crisis, such as Spengler, Mannheim, and Lewis Mumford. Dawson looks at history in the light of Christian principles, *sub specie aeternitatis*, like St. Augustine whose spiritual descendant he is." Dawson's outlook was reminiscent, said Schlesinger, of those of two social theorists who were enjoying a Catholic revival in the early postwar years, Edmund Burke and Alexis de Tocqueville, men who had loved the accumulation and preservation of tradition and feared mass democracy.[103] Schlesinger, himself a convert from Judaism and a Viennese refugee, tried to put Dawson's "Christian Culture" program into practice at Saint Mary's College, Indiana, in the early 1950s.[104]

In the early 1950s Dawson began a long correspondence with a Philadelphia schoolteacher, John Mulloy, who was captivated by Dawson's intellectual power. It ultimately ran to more than two hundred letters on each side. Dawson wrote dozens of articles for the American Catholic press in the 1940s and 1950s though he had never been to the United States. Mulloy, who made a pilgrimage to visit Dawson in Oxford, urged him to consider the possibility and tried to arrange for him to visit Notre Dame University in Indiana. He also became the aging historian's leading exponent in America. Mulloy then edited a selection of Dawson's works on the nature and history of civilization titled *Dynamics of World History* (1956), which drew wide and generally admiring press notices.[105]

The following year another American convert, Chauncey Stillman, gave money to Harvard Divinity School to found a chair of Catholic studies. This entry into one of the old temples of Protestant learning was a symbolically important step in the "coming of age" of American Catholicism in the 1950s. Douglas Horton, the Divinity School Dean, invited Dawson to be the first to hold the chair, and Dawson, under the influence of Mulloy's long campaign of persuasion, accepted for a five-year term. Stillman, the donor, was pleased by the choice and wrote to Dawson, explaining how dramatic an innovation it was to have a Catholic scholar at Harvard. "Harvard has always considered Catholicism intellectually contemptible,

103. Schlesinger, "Dawson and Crisis," 84.
104. Personal communication from Philip Gleason, May 21, 1996.
105. Scott, *Historian*, 167–178. Author's telephone conversation with Mr. Mulloy, March 17, 1992.

socially negligible, and dangerous politically." Dawson's visa was almost blocked when American doctors alleged that he was suffering not merely from the bronchitis that had afflicted him through much of his life but from tuberculosis. Appeals to Massachusetts Senators Leverett Saltonstall and John Kennedy and finally to the surgeon general removed this obstacle, and Dawson took up his duties in the fall of 1958. Stillman befriended Dawson and his wife, Valerie, and helped ease their cultural transition to a full-time job and life in America.[106]

Dawson was a shy man and found it difficult to adapt to the easy, gregarious manner of his students. Maisie Ward said, "Christopher can talk of anything though you can also find him plunged in an almost unbreakable silence and impervious to things around."[107] Despite some early difficulties, Dawson soon came to admire the energy of American Catholicism, and on his seventieth birthday, in 1959, he declared: "When I began writing it was the days of Charles Peguy and Belloc and Chesterton and my eyes were fixed on Europe and the European tradition. But today I have come to feel that it is in this country that the fate of Christendom will be decided."[108] With Mulloy's help Dawson had developed a proposed curriculum for the thoroughgoing study of Christian culture, which would make religion central to every element of the course, along with a sharply critical account of American progressive education.[109]

But the days of "integral" Catholic education in America were numbered. In 1955 John Tracy Ellis, S.J., had published an epoch-making article in *Thought* deploring the intellectual defensiveness and apologetical tone of most Catholic higher education.[110] A chorus of other Catholic intellectuals joined Ellis in urging a shift to a model closer to that of the secular universities rather than an elaboration of the "Christian culture" theme advocated by Dawson. American conservatives, including Russell Kirk (who converted to Catholicism a few years later), praised Dawson's approach, but liberal Catholics, such as Justus George Lawler, were critical. Lawler pointed out that Dawson had made a series of undocumented accusations about U.S. society as godless and conformist; a series of false analogies, comparing ordinary students' ideas, based on polling data, against Christian classics like Augustine's *City of God*; and many errors of fact. What's more, said Lawler, Dawson was always implying that earlier

106. Scott, *Historian*, 183, 185.
107. Maisie Ward, *Unfinished Business*, 117.
108. Scott, *Historian*, 197–98.
109. Christopher Dawson, *The Crisis of Western Education* (New York: Sheed and Ward, 1961).
110. John Tracy Ellis, "American Catholics and the Intellectual Life," *Thought* 30 (Autumn 1955): 351–88.

ages possessed a humaneness and integrity that our own lacked. But was that true, or was it mere romantic projection? "I see no reason to believe that there is any difference, save in implementation, between the kind of acquisitive urge that led, say, to the Hundred Years' War and World War II; and who is to say that Raymond of Toulouse or Philip II had greater control of their subrational drives than contemporary power-mad hegemonists? . . . Nor do I feel that such vents for the subrational as an *auto da fe* had more 'spirituality' about them than the Moscow purge trials." The whole conception of "Christian culture," Dawson's watchword, had an antiquated sound to Lawler. "It is a usage which may have had some proselytizing value a few decades ago, when Chesterton and Belloc or the patriots of the Action Française were lobbying for a militant *renouveau Catholique*. In the present moment it is precisely the identification of Christianity with any specific temporal achievements that seems most likely to inhibit its mission."[111]

In other respects, too, Dawson's work was out of tune with the scholarly direction of his times. The era of great syntheses of civilization was closing, and in one of the most curious intellectual fads of the century, historians and critics of the early 1960s began to argue that the whole world was accelerating, leaving no time for grand generalizations on the nature of things, but only a flux in which to make pragmatic gestures. This was the intellectual climate not only of Vatican II but also of the "death of God" movement. "Christopher Dawson, T. S. Eliot and other defenders of 'Christian culture' have been urging us to try to maintain the core values of the past in the name of our civilization itself," wrote "new breed" theologian Michael Novak in 1965, but "what I am suggesting is that we are on the threshold of a *new* civilization, and that we are witnessing the birth of a *new* form of life [which will not be] serenely continuous with the past."[112]

The optimistic excesses of the "death of God" moment soon passed in the supercharged political environment of the late 1960s, but the trend away from grand synthesizing persisted. In the ensuing decades professional historians became more intent on explaining the details of cultures—the conflicts, the variety of ideas at work in a society—and they became ever-more-suspicious of the kind of vast generalization about civilization which was Dawson's forte. No matter how immense his learning, Dawson could not enter with equal assurance into the microhistory of all

111. Justus George Lawler, review of *The Crisis of Western Education*, with rejoinder by John Mulloy and discussion, *Harvard Educational Review* 32 (Spring 1962): 214–27.
112. Michael Novak, "Christianity, Renewed or Slowly Abandoned?" (1965), in *A Time to Build* (New York: Macmillan, 1967), 30.

the cultures and civilizations he studied, with the result that each of his glittering apothegms was vulnerable to attack from younger historical generations. His scholarship and his religious attitudes were both being superannuated by the 1960s, when a generation of Catholic scholars was inspired by Vatican II and the mood of the "Secular City." He suffered a stroke in 1962, the year of his retirement from Harvard, and spent the remaining eight years of his life back in England, in Budleigh Salterton, Devonshire. John Mulloy continued to publish anthologies of his writings and later founded the *Dawson Newsletter*, but by the late 1960s Dawson's ideas imparted a flavor of ultraconservatism, such as they had never done in his heyday.

The end of Carlton Hayes's career was embittered by conflicts over Spain. Perhaps the surprise is that a man of his views and convictions should have been so central and influential among American historians and political theorists in the first place. One commentator on his life, Carter Jefferson, remarked that although for a while he was "a leading member of what might be called the historical establishment, he ended his career an embattled figure, alienated from many of the colleagues whose praise had brought him recognition. His later estrangement is not surprising for, basically, he did not share their views."[113] The history and theory of nationalism were his most lasting work and subsequent students paid tribute to him as a "pioneer," who "did much to dispel the fog surrounding the nature of nationalism." At the same time his largely European view of the issue was expanded by later interpreters, who investigated new forms of nationalism in other parts of the world.[114] Hayes's last book, *Nationalism, a Religion* (1960), published when he was seventy-eight, restated this central issue in his work and extended it to the nationalism of postcolonial Africa and Asia. Paying tribute to Christopher Dawson and his analysis of the development of civilizations, Hayes admitted that nationalism had emerged first in the Christian lands and borrowed fervency and ritual from the church.

Nationalism, like any religion, calls into play not simply the will, but the intellect, the imagination, and the emotions. The intellect constructs a spec-

---

113. Carter Jefferson, "Carlton Hayes," in Hans A. Schmitt, ed., *Historians of Modern Europe* (Baton Rouge: Louisiana State University Press, 1971), 15.
114. See, for example, Louis L. Snyder, *The New Nationalism* (Ithaca: Cornell University Press, 1968), 48.

ulative theology or mythology of nationalism. The imagination builds an unseen world around the eternal past and the everlasting future of one's nationality. The emotions arouse a joy and ecstasy in the contemplation of the national god who is all-good and all-protecting, a longing for his favors, a thankfulness for his benefits, a fear of offending him, and feelings of awe and reverence at the immensity of his power and wisdom; they express themselves naturally in worship, both private and public.[115]

Nevertheless, he believed that only Christianity had the potential to save the world from the scourge of nationalism, and he was pleased to discover "an ecumenical trend among leaders of its major divisions toward greater mutual charity and understanding." It was all the more necessary by 1960 because of the scourge of communism. "As a Christian," wrote Hayes on the last page of his last book, "I earnestly believe that in measure as lands of Africa and Asia tolerate Christian missions (that are themselves without taint of imperialism) and come under the influence of Christian faith and morals, the rising obsessive nationalism on those continents will be rendered less exclusive and belligerent and more in keeping with international cooperation and peace."[116]

He had contributed to the "secularization" of Catholic scholarship, detaching it from apologetics and elevating its credibility in the eyes of non-Catholic judges. He had also contributed to the theoretical defense of Catholic Americanism against the old anti-Catholic tradition. In the last decade of his life John Courtney Murray, S.J., refined arguments that Hayes and his fellow convert historians had outlined thirty years before: that the American Constitution owed its origins not to quirks of Protestant separatism but to the Catholic natural law tradition. Murray, elaborating on Hayes's ecumenical work from the interwar years, also developed a theory of religious freedom on strictly Catholic premises and got it embodied in one of the declarations of Vatican II.[117] But Hayes did not live long enough to see his work vindicated in this way. He died in 1964, eclipsed within the historical profession and within the church. By then the "new breed" of Catholic scholars were making much greater concessions to their secular counterparts' views than Hayes ever did but, in the process, losing much of the distinctively Catholic vision of America's role in Western civilization that his work had promoted.

115. Carlton Hayes, *Nationalism: A Religion* (New York: Macmillan, 1960), 164.
116. Ibid., 182.
117. Patrick Allitt, "The Significance of John Courtney Murray, S.J.," in Mary Segers, ed., *Church Polity and American Politics: Issues in Contemporary Catholicism* (New York: Garland, 1990), 51–65.

Hayes and Dawson both gained widespread favorable notice for their historical works of the 1930s and 1940s but neither escaped censure. Both had to face the accusation that their Catholicism had led them to distort aspects of historical interpretation. They were powerless to alter the fact that most practicing historians were not fellow Catholics and that the standards and canons of the historical profession were strictly this-worldly, based on secular scientific ideals. In this situation they disagreed with their contemporaries on the nature of human life itself and the meaning of existence. For them the tension between the mundane and the supernatural worlds, though always kept under close control in their interpretation, never disappeared, and it lent their work an air of apologetics to unconvinced readers.

Hayes and Dawson were at the height of their powers just when "scientific history" was becoming the universal norm in the historical profession. They aimed, like their contemporaries, for the highest degree of technical accuracy and competence, even though they directed it to different ends. But they also lived and worked at a time when there were scattered signs of a reaction against reductionistic scientific metaphors in historical study. The 1920s, when they were in their thirties and forties, was the decade in which the most influential American intellectuals wrote off Protestant "fundamentalism" as an atavistic remnant. But it was also the decade in which J. Gresham Machen made a rigorous and telling criticism of secularism and liberal Protestantism from fundamentalist premises.[118] Similarly in the 1920s and 1930s most American and British historians were in revolt against "puritanism" as a repressive and destructive force. Yet it was in the early thirties that Perry Miller conceived and wrote *The New England Mind*, a scholarly masterpiece that revived the Puritans' reputation for intellectual brilliance and transformed conceptions of early American history.[119]

Each man has had some lasting influence. Aspects of historical study which Dawson helped pioneer are now commonplace among British and American historians. The concept of culture, in the anthropological sense, was a novelty among historians when Dawson began to use it in the 1920s but has been indispensable to the social historians of the last three decades, though they have used it to very different ends. The study of international relations remains indebted to Hayes's pioneering work, and more recent

118. On Machen, see D. G. Hart, *Defending the Faith: J. Gresham Machen and the Crisis of Conservative Protestantism in Modern America* (Baltimore: Johns Hopkins University Press, 1994), esp. 78–102.

119. Perry Miller, *The New England Mind: The Seventeenth Century* (Cambridge: Harvard University Press, 1939).

studies of international politics and of nationalism itself often include respectful references to Hayes in their long first footnote, though few scholars now pause to debate him in detail. To the degree that their influence persists, however, it is despite, rather than because of, the Catholic faith that animated them.

# XII

## NOVELS FROM *HADRIAN*
## TO *BRIDESHEAD*

EVELYN WAUGH (1903–1966) and Graham
Greene (1904–1991) have enjoyed critical acclaim
and commercial success on both sides of the Atlantic. Many critics place them in the first rank of twentieth-century novelists. In the generation before theirs, Compton
Mackenzie (1883–1972) held a place of almost equal esteem. All three were converts to Catholicism—Mackenzie
at the age of thirty, Waugh and Greene in their mid-twenties—and all three made this religious experience central to
some of their most effective fiction. All three, in addition,
were prolific critics and commentators on the literature and
politics of their age, which they approached from the vantage point of their new faith. Their success gave Roman
Catholics a place in English literature which they had not
previously enjoyed and introduced Catholicism itself and
conversion to Catholicism as subjects for sympathetic treatment in fiction. But like many converts in the nineteenth
and early twentieth centuries, they found that conversion
led to personal, artistic, and intellectual tensions, involving
them in complex relationships with both the community
they had embraced and the one they had left.

By blending the techniques of literary modernism with the advocacy of
orthodox religion Mackenzie, Waugh, and Greene were able to show that
their Catholicism was neither a throwback to old superstitions nor a mental surrender in the face of contemporary pressures. They were, each in his
own way, philosophical antimaterialists and opponents of the idea of progress. They were strongly influenced by the major modernists, Ezra

Pound, T. S. Eliot, and James Joyce, whose view of "progress" was also equivocal. In the first and second decades of the twentieth century, Mackenzie experimented with stream-of-consciousness writing and showed a psychological insight that anticipated Freud. Henry James admired Mackenzie's early work and expected him to carry on the development of English fiction where he himself had left off. Mackenzie, though he later drew back from the daring style of his early works, acknowledged Joyce's *Ulysses* as "the major piece of literature this time has witnessed." It was, he said, "the second part of *Faust* written at last, and the most convincing proof ever penned of the possibility of human damnation, the profoundest revelation of evil ever set down upon paper."[1] Greene also grappled with the unconscious mind, was psychoanalyzed as an unhappy teenager, and in his fiction used dreams as signs of conflict in the unconscious mind.[2] Waugh's debt to modernism can be seen particularly in his novel *A Handful of Dust* (1934). Like Eliot's poem "The Waste Land," from which its title is taken, this novel is a bleak indictment of life in a decadent and godless world.[3] As David Lodge notes, "The disorderliness, the contingency, the collapse of value and meaning in contemporary life" all link Waugh with the modernist movement.[4] As a critic Waugh praised Ernest Hemingway and emulated his terse style, economical dialogue, and dramatic understatement.[5]

Mackenzie, Greene, and Waugh were at odds with modernism in other respects, but they deplored the antimodernist cheap shots of lesser Catholic controversialists. They worked from a deeply convinced Catholicism but caused as much distress as reassurance to many Catholic contemporaries by shunning traditional apologetics and avoiding didacticism. The Catholic characters they drew were not morally better than the Protestants or atheists, were no more successful in living their lives in the mid-twentieth century (and often less so), and rarely had much luck in converting others to their faith. The antithesis of older Catholic propaganda fiction,

1. Compton Mackenzie, *Literature in My Time* (1934; Freeport, N.Y.: Books for Libraries Press, 1967), 203. He also believed that "such a revelation could only have been made by an Irishman and a Catholic," 103.
2. Biographical information on Greene in this chapter is based on Michael Shelden, *Graham Greene: The Man Within* (London: Heinemann, 1994); and Norman Sherry, *The Life of Graham Greene*, vol. 1 (1989; London: Penguin, 1990). On Greene's psychoanalysis, see Sherry, *Greene*, 95–103.
3. Evelyn Waugh, *A Handful of Dust* (1934; London: Chapman and Hall, 1964).
4. David Lodge, *Evelyn Waugh* (New York: Columbia University Press, 1971), 5.
5. Martin Stannard, *Evelyn Waugh: The Early Years* (London: Dent, 1986), 209–10. See also Waugh's later review of Hemingway, "Winner Take Nothing," in *The Essays, Articles, and Reviews of Evelyn Waugh*, ed. Donat Gallagher (London: Methuen, 1983), 391–93.

which treated conversion to Catholicism as the solution to earthly suffer-
ings, these authors' novels portrayed Catholicism as more often a harrowing burden than a rest for weary souls. Their avoidance of happy
resolutions by a spiritual deus ex machina, in addition to their superb
technical skills, explains both their appeal to skeptical critics and the
doubts of orthodox churchmen. Each of them would have endorsed this
remark by Greene: "I belong to a group, the Catholic Church, which
would present me with grave problems as a writer were I not saved by my
disloyalty. . . . There are leaders of the Church who regard literature as a
means to an end, edification." Greene could not endorse such a view. He
found himself unable to emulate the French novelist François Mauriac's
scrupulous adherence to orthodox claims. As a novelist, he declared, "I
must be able to write from the point of view of the black square [on a
chessboard] as well as of the white: doubt and even denial must be given
their chance of self-expression." Otherwise, said Greene, his Catholic fiction would be as lame and one-sided as the "socialist realism" enjoined on
novelists by the Communist Party.[6] Of Greene's novel *The Heart of the
Matter* (1948) Waugh wrote: "There are loyal Catholics here [Britain] and
in America who think it the function of the Catholic writer to produce
only advertising brochures setting out in attractive terms the advantages of
Church membership. To them this profoundly reverent book will seem a
scandal. For it not only portrays Catholics as unlikeable human beings but
shows them as tortured by their Faith."[7]

Mackenzie, Waugh, and Greene were raised in the solid center of the
English middle class and all three attended elite Church of England "public" (i.e., private) schools and then Oxford University, following the educational regimen that prepared generations of British politicians,
administrators, Anglican clergy, and a great many of their fellow converts.
The political and social stigma attached to conversion was slighter by their
day than it had been for Newman's generation and none of these three
suffered material or social hardships through becoming a Catholic. Each
undertook special overseas military duties in time of war, Mackenzie and
Greene as secret agents, the former as Britain's spymaster in the Eastern
Mediterranean during the First World War, the latter in West Africa during
the Second War. During the Second War Waugh was sent as a special
military envoy to the provisional government of Yugoslavia, in the company of the prime minister's son, Randolph Churchill, where he tried to

6. Greene, quoted in A. A. DeVitis, *Graham Greene* (Boston: Twayne, 1986), 15.
7. Evelyn Waugh, "Felix Culpa," in *Essays, Articles, and Reviews*, 361. The review originally appeared in *Commonweal* in July 1948.

influence British policy against Tito's Communist partisans and in favor of the Catholic Croatians.[8] In peacetime all three were influential pundits, appearing frequently on British radio and television. Greene's brother Hugh was head of the British Broadcasting Corporation and Graham worked for him on many commissioned radio and film projects; Mackenzie was heard regularly on British radio through the 1930s and 1940s before becoming an early British television celebrity, and even Waugh, appearing less often, was prized by broadcasters for his unashamed snobbery and his ingenious presentation of unpopular ideas.[9]

These three novelists were exceptional individuals, quite distinct from one another, and their similarities need not be exaggerated. From the political point of view Greene and Waugh might seem a particularly incongruous couple, for Waugh is remembered as a crusty, irritable reactionary who once justified his refusal to vote on the grounds that he thought it presumptuous to advise his queen on her choice of ministers, whereas Greene was a luminary of the political Left, one of the first to denounce ideological anticommunism and to support third-world revolutionaries. Their view of civilization also differed in a critical way. Waugh, in the tradition of Hilaire Belloc, regarded the Reformation and the breakup of "Christendom" as a catastrophe and often lamented the passing of a nobler age, whereas Greene wrote in a mood of estrangement from a civilization that, as he drew it, had always been inimical to Christian truth and in which the man or woman of genuine faith had always been an alien. Their ideas of Catholicism itself differed too. One critic writes: "The world of Waugh's faith is spacious, open, logical: Greene's is claustrophobic, decaying, full of violence, giving an occasional glimpse of goodness that is far more inexplicable and mysterious than the evil that surrounds it."[10] But along with these differences their work exhibited many common themes and shared ideas on questions of religion and morality which illuminate some of their shared outlook as Catholic converts. No one has yet written about them as figures in British or Atlantic Catholic history or linked them more broadly to the history of conversion, in which light certain of these similarities become clear.

Other Catholic converts before them had tried to use fiction to advance Catholic claims; the two most notable were Frederick Rolfe (1860–1913)

8. Christopher Sykes, *Evelyn Waugh: A Biography* (1975; London: Penguin, 1977), 367–68; Martin Stannard, *Evelyn Waugh: No Abiding City* (London: Dent, 1992), 136–43.

9. Stannard, *No Abiding City*, 333–38.

10. Robert Murray Davis, "The Rhetoric of Mexican Travel: Greene and Waugh," *Renascence* 38 (Spring 1986), 161.

and Robert Hugh Benson (1871–1914).[11] None of Benson's novels rose much above the level of propaganda, however, and he makes a poor showing beside his more accomplished successors. His father, Edward White Benson, was the Anglican archbishop of Canterbury, a Victorian eccentric in the grand manner who chose his future wife when she was a child of eleven and trained her for the role over the next six years before marrying her with her family's full connivance.[12] None of their children ever married, but all wrote prodigiously: E. F. Benson as a popular society novelist and memoirist, Arthur Benson as a don and master of Magdalene College, Cambridge, and Hugh himself as a religious polemicist. Ordained by his father to the Anglican priesthood in 1894, he converted to Catholicism in 1903 after concluding that the Church of England was a geographically isolated anomaly on the fringe of Christendom and that, on dogmatic questions, it made a point of not knowing its own mind. Yearning for religious certainty he reached out to Rome, but as his brother Arthur later remarked, it was not any spirit of submissiveness but rather Hugh's "isolation, his independence, his lack of any real deference to personal authority, which carried him into the Church of Rome," where he could "repose on something august, age-long, overpowering."[13]

Benson was reordained as a Catholic priest after nine months' study in Rome. He spent most of his time from then on writing novels but also for a time worked as chaplain to the Catholic undergraduates at Cambridge University, among them the young Shane Leslie, who left a vivid record of his preaching style. "He mastered his stammer in the pulpit by convulsions and gestures. It was difficult to say if he were wrestling with his stammer or with Satan. He would begin slowly, anxiously, as though he had a secret, and from the moment he possessed his audience he ceased to keep his possession of himself. He gave the feeling that he was preaching his last sermon on the eve of the Day of Judgment. He began to mop his brow; he waved his arms and his eyes stared out of his face in agony. He seemed to fall back into convulsions, and to collapse out of the pulpit, whence he was led into a hot bath."[14]

Always histrionic, Benson made three successful preaching tours of America (1910, 1912, 1914), admired the vigor of American Catholicism,

11. Biographical information in the following passage is based on C. C. Martindale, *The Life of Monsignor Robert Hugh Benson*, 2 vols. (London: Longmans, Green, 1916).

12. E. F. Benson, *As We Were: A Victorian Peepshow* (1930; London: Hogarth Press, 1985), 56–66.

13. Arthur C. Benson, *Hugh: Memoirs of a Brother* (New York: Longmans, Green, 1915), 140–41.

14. Shane Leslie, *Long Shadows* (London: John Murray, 1966), 106.

and said he hoped to see an increase in the Anglo-Saxon element of the church (shades of Isaac Hecker). In an appreciative article on conditions he had found there Benson wrote that American Catholicism

inspires the visitor from Europe with an extraordinary sense of life; the churches are not exquisite sanctuaries for dreaming—they are the business offices of the supernatural; the clergy are not picturesque advocates of a beautiful medievalism—they are keen and devoted to the service of God; the people are not pathetic survivals from the Ages of Faith—they are communities of immortal souls bent upon salvation. There is a ring of assurance about Catholic voices; an air of confidence about Catholic movements . . . a swing and energy about Catholic life, that promise well indeed for the future of the Church in this land.[15]

Back in England he lived a life of splendid isolation in a Hertfordshire country house, one room of which he decorated with paintings of "highly disquieting robed skeletons, stepping the Dance of Death. He merrily consecrated this room to the use of heretic Anglicans who stayed with him, in the pious hope that waking in the night and finding themselves encompassed with these gruesome reminders of mortality they might be moved to fly to the only true fountain of salvation."[16]

Like many other British converts from privileged backgrounds, Benson found the Catholics of England a poor crowd, given to backbiting and jealousies, showing all the weaknesses that flesh is heir to. Aloof from parish life after his brief stint in Cambridge, he was a poor judge of character and formed only one close attachment, which proved disastrous. This was with Frederick Rolfe, another convert.[17] Rolfe, a dandy and a dilettante without money (his father was a London piano tuner) sought ordination but was twice ejected from seminaries, first in England, then in Rome, for idleness and debt. Rolfe, always protesting his innocence, had an unrivaled talent for feeling aggrieved and persecuted, and turned against many generous patrons when they displeased him (as all did sooner or later) with a vengeful, paranoiac bitterness. Among many other oddities he was convinced that the Jesuits were trying to assassinate him. He would show new acquaintances a barbed ring he wore on his finger, claiming that

15. Quoted in Martindale, *Life of Benson* 2:177.
16. E. F. Benson, *Final Edition* (1940; London: Hogarth Press, 1988), 89.
17. Biographical information in the following passage is based on Miriam Benkovitz, *Frederick Rolfe, Baron Corvo: A Biography* (London: Hamish Hamilton, 1977); and A. J. Symons, *The Quest for Corvo* (1934; London, Penguin, 1963).

he had once thwarted a Jesuit assassination attempt by slashing at his assailant's forehead with the ring and blinding him with his own blood.[18]

Rolfe's weird qualities and experiences are apparent in his novel *Hadrian VII* (1904), which is a tour de force of vanity and wish fulfillment but brilliant nonetheless.[19] Its main character, George Arthur Rose, a Catholic convert wrongfully denied ordination in Rome twenty years before, is suddenly elevated to the priesthood and then to the papacy when there is a deadlock in conclave. He adopts the title Pope Hadrian VII, recalling that the only other English pope in history, nearly a thousand years before, was Hadrian IV. At once he sets about cleansing the church of its abuses. He sells the Vatican's treasures, gives the proceeds to the poor of Italy, and reforms corrupt seminaries (including the one from which he had been ejected). His bull *Regnum Meum*, based on Christ's declaration "My Kingdom is not of this world," renounces the temporal power and, in doing so, implicitly criticizes the real popes, Pius IX, Leo XIII, and Pius X, for refusing to take the same step. He heads off an incipient world war (whose character Rolfe foresaw presciently) and, by his concern for the poor and his radiant faith, nullifies the appeal of revolutionary socialism. At the end, bowed under the weight of his responsibilities but successful in restoring harmony to the world, Hadrian is shot and martyred by an embittered cynical socialist.

Rolfe, like many British and American converts, had a love-hate relationship with Italy. He claimed at one point to have been granted an Italian title of nobility, and he posed in England as Baron Corvo, using the raven (Italian: *corvo*) on his signet ring and as an emblem on all his property.[20] But more often he shared Isaac Hecker's sense that what Catholicism really needed was less of Italy and more of the Anglo-Saxon spirit. In *Hadrian VII* he depicted the Vatican as stifling under "the mysterious gloom of the stage, its smallness, its air of cavernous confinement; the sour, oppressive, septic odour of architectural and waxen and human antiquity." The curial officials are reluctant to obey Hadrian, and Rolfe portrays the briskly businesslike English pope as a new broom sweeping away old Roman cobwebs. "Dear, deliberate Rome simply gasped at a Pontiff who said 'Tomorrow' and meant it. The Sacred College found it had no option. Naturally it looked as black as night." "Cardinals and their familiars cackled and cooed and squeaked and growled in corners; or arranged for return to their distant sees." Many of the Catholic

18. Symons, *Quest for Corvo*, 169.
19. Frederick Rolfe, *Hadrian VII* (1904; London: Wordsworth, 1993).
20. Symons, *Quest for Corvo*, 70.

officials are sinister obstructionists, above all the Jesuit superior, whom Hadrian harangues about his order's corrupt ways.[21]

As for the English Catholics, whose church he had joined, Rolfe felt only contempt. In his "Epistle to the English" Hadrian/Rolfe makes it quite clear that the only Catholics he considers worthy of respect are the converts:

He pointed out that the Penal laws, which from 1534 to 1829 had deprived them of "that culture which contact with a wider world alone can give" had rendered the Catholic aborigines corporeally effete and intellectually inferior to the rest of the nation. He did not blame involuntary defects; but facts were facts, and only fools would refuse to face them. These defects would find their remedy in the influx of new and vigorous blood and unexhausted brains. . . . He bade them to welcome and to comfort accessions to their number not (as was the present custom) with slavering sentimentality giving place to slights, snubs, slanders, and sneers; but with brotherly love, putting in practice the Faith which they professed and letting their light shine.

Like Hecker in America, Rolfe's plan was to encourage more English conversions to Catholicism, to minimize the influence of the Old Catholics, and to affirm "that the English Race naturally was fitted to give an example to humanity."[22]

Robert Hugh Benson thought *Hadrian VII* was a masterpiece: he wrote Rolfe an enthusiastic letter of praise, and the two became friends. Together they went on a walking tour of England and planned to write a biography of Thomas à Becket. But while the project was still in its planning stages, the church authorities warned Benson of Rolfe's disreputable past and his promiscuous homosexuality. Then Benson's publishers told him that the book would sell better if just his own name was on the cover. After a period of wrangling the two authors broke their connection and from then on Rolfe poured vitriolic abuse on Benson for the remainder of his life.[23] Rolfe pilloried Benson in his novel, *The Weird of the Wanderer*, portraying him as Father Bobugo Bonsen, "a stuttering little Chrysostom of a priest with the Cambridge manners of Vaughan's Dove, the face of the Mad Hatter out of *Alice in Wonderland*, and the figure of an Etonian who insanely neglects to take any pains at all with his temple of the Holy Ghost, but wears paper collars and a black straw alpine hat."[24] Rolfe spent his last

21. Rolfe, *Hadrian VII*, 72, 83, 97, 247.
22. Ibid., 167, 166.
23. E. F. Benson, *Final Edition*, 34–42.
24. Rolfe, quoted in Benkovitz, *Frederick Rolfe*, 185. See also E. F. Benson, *Final Edition*, 38.

years in Venice, enjoying sexual affairs with teenage gondoliers and still writing furiously, with the help of long-suffering patrons. But at last, after alienating every possible benefactor, he died penniless and alone on the Venice dockyards in 1913.

Benson was a loner, more than ever after this fiasco, and although he talked periodically of creating a religious community, "his later life was," said his shrewd brother Arthur, "a complete contrast to anything resembling community life: his constant restlessness of motion, his travels, his succession of engagements both in all parts of England as well as in Rome and America, were really, I do not doubt, more congenial to him."[25]

Among Hugh Benson's dozens of novels, all written with the aim of promoting Catholic claims, several used incidents in pre-Reformation English history to make a didactic point about current religious life. In *The History of Richard Raynal, Solitary* (1905), for example, his own favorite, he described a hermit sent by God to warn King Henry VI of his impending martyrdom. Raynal the "solitary" is despised by the regular clergy, persecuted at court, and condemned to torture by a cardinal who suspects him of being an assassin. When king and cardinal realize their mistake, it is too late, and the saintly man dies. Perhaps Benson, himself a "solitary," was projecting himself backward in time. His harsh portrayal of English Catholic officialdom suggests that he thought the institutional Catholic Church of his own day remained insensitive. "I think," says the narrator in this novel, "that [Raynal] was hardly treated and flouted, for the professed monks like not solitaries except those that be established in reputation; they call them self-willed and lawless and pretending to a sanctity that is none of theirs. Such as be under obedience think that virtue the highest of all and essential to the way of perfection."[26]

Other Benson novels depict a Catholic Church in which the dross is ten times as plentiful as the gold and give the impression that, much as he admired its intellectual system and its grip on truth, he deplored many of its human manifestations. In *Confessions of a Convert* (1913), a book modeled on Newman's *Apologia* and first serialized in the American journal *Ave Maria*, he remarked that born Catholics were often insensitive to the plight of converts. "It does not seem to me that Catholic controversialists as a body in the least realize what Anglicans have to go through before they can make their submission. . . . I mean the purely internal conflict. One is drawn every way at once; the soul aches as in intolerable pain; the only relief is found in a kind of passionless Quietism. To submit

25. A. C. Benson, *Hugh*, 139.
26. Robert Hugh Benson, *The History of Richard Raynal, Solitary* (London: Hutchinson, 1905), 59.

to the Church seems, in prospect, to be going out from the familiar and the beloved and the understood into a huge, heartless wilderness, where one will be eyed and doubted and snubbed." Of the Catholic Church he said: "I had no kind of emotional attraction towards it. I knew perfectly well that it was human as well as divine, that crimes had been committed within its walls . . . that I should find hardness there, unfamiliar manners, even suspicion and blame. But for all that it was divine; it was built upon the Rock of rocks." These remarks he set side by side with an evocative tribute to the Church of England, her "hundred virtues" and her "gracious ways." Benson made it seem almost a stroke of hard luck that he had been driven into the unlovely Catholic Church with its "truth as aloof as an ice-peak."[27]

Whatever his emotional misgivings, however, Benson became a blazing champion of the church militant and delighted a vast Catholic readership by smiting the Reformation churches hip and thigh. In *The Holy Blissful Martyr Saint Thomas of Canterbury* (1908), the book he had originally planned with Rolfe but ultimately wrote alone, Benson explored the perpetual conflict of church and state. He condemned royal usurpations while making frequent analogies with earlier and later conditions. "King Henry II [represented] earthly dominion, seeking, as Herod against Jesus Christ, and Nero against Peter, and the French Republic against Pius X, to bring the kingdom of God into subjection to his own." Benson added that the Reformation and a long tradition of English Protestant jingoism had clouded the issue and obscured Thomas's true greatness as an opponent of erastianism. "It is perfectly easy for a clever and bigoted historian to make [Henry II's depredations on the church] out as trifles about which no 'loyal Englishman' need trouble his head; yet to those who understand, as Thomas understood, that Christ's Church must bow her head to none save Divine Authority in matters that concern her life, years of exile, tears, disappointments, and sorrows, even life itself, are a small price to pay in such a cause."[28]

Benson, as son of the Anglican primate, was a great catch for the Catholic Church, whatever his quirks. One enthusiast, writing in an English Catholic monthly, exulted that he "has won for himself a unique position amongst contemporary writers, in the eyes of Catholics and non-Catholics alike. The former regard him with pride and satisfaction as a living example of the compatibility of great intellectual keenness with a sincere and hum-

27. Robert Hugh Benson, *Confessions of a Convert* (New York: Longmans, Green, 1913), 89, 126, 111, 129.
28. Robert Hugh Benson, *The Holy Blissful Martyr Saint Thomas of Canterbury* (London: Macdonald and Evans, 1908), 72, 106–7.

ble acceptance of all the claims of faith; the latter are astonished to find themselves, under his attractive guidance, taking an interest in things quite outside their usual concern, and becoming curious to study the inner workings of a religion which they had hitherto despised too much ever to think about seriously."[29] Benson himself, always an exotic bloom, served the church to the point of exhaustion and died prematurely in 1914 at the age of forty-three, bequeathing his country home with all its furnishings to the cardinal archbishop of Westminster. As his brother Fred later wrote, "Cardinal Bourne much enjoyed being a small English Squire and often used the place as a holiday home and . . . thus it happened that a Cardinal of the Church of Rome ate his dinner under a portrait of the Archbishop of Canterbury."[30]

Compton Mackenzie was the first of the Catholic convert novelists who worked from more than propaganda motives.[31] Born in 1883, the son of successful actors and theatrical entrepreneurs, he was a precocious child, learned to read before the age of three, and began early to devour the classics of English literature at high speed. He recalled that one summer, while vacationing as a teenager in France, he read 150 English, French, Italian, and Russian novels. He studied at Saint Paul's School in London, an Anglican establishment famed for its scholarly successes, where he befriended Leonard Woolf. Singled out as a likely scholarship winner, he disappointed his teachers by devoting too much of his time to Church of England controversies and then to the homosexual demimonde of London in the decadent 1890s. He even flirted with the half-extinct cause of legitimism, arguing that the Catholic Stuart claim to the British throne, last asserted by Bonnie Prince Charlie in 1745, outweighed that of the Hanoverians. At Magdalen College, Oxford, he launched a literary magazine, drew the attention of influential dons, and with their encouragement, prepared himself for the life of a poet after turning down lucrative offers for a theatrical career.

Reversals checked Mackenzie's rapid ascent after Oxford and obliged him to live on an allowance from his father. His first book of poems was rejected by several publishers; he could attract no company to perform early plays; and his first novel suffered many rejections before appearing from a new press in 1910 as *The Passionate Elopement*. It enjoyed mixed reviews but then its successors, *Carnival*, *Guy and Pauline*, and above all

29. J. Keating, "Monsignor Benson, 'De Civitate Dei,'" *Month* 118 (October 1911): 389.

30. E. F. Benson, *Final Edition*, 121–22.

31. Biographical information in this passage is based on Arno Linklater, *Compton Mackenzie: A Life* (London: Chatto and Windus, 1987).

*Sinister Street*, won critical acclaim for him on the eve of the First World War, just as he was converting to Catholicism.

The first part of *Sinister Street* was written while he was still a member of the Church of England, the second after he had converted. It is a fictionalized version of Mackenzie's childhood, whose young protagonist is beset by terrifying dreams and ruled in the daytime by a sadistic nurse.[32] Early on, Mackenzie had become ardently religious and at the age of fourteen, while on holiday in Dorset, had had a profound religious experience:

As I sat there looking out to sea I suddenly seemed to become more alive than I had ever been, and in this awareness of life in myself to feel what might be described as a new and tremendous responsibility towards life. . . . I was equally aware that this life of myself had been bestowed upon me by a force immeasurably greater than any force in me. I knew that God must be and that therefore God must have a purpose for my being.[33]

This and other childhood episodes were artfully incorporated into *Sinister Street*, which experimented with stream-of-consciousness narrative. Becoming a Roman Catholic was not a vivid emotional experience for Mackenzie, who was living on the Italian island of Capri at the time. Rather, he said, it was "not to be regarded as a conversion but as a submission, a logical surrender to an inevitable recognition of the fact that Jesus Christ had founded his Church upon the rock of Peter."[34] He was hardly the ideal convert. Already flagrantly disloyal to his wife, Faith, he had a long series of love affairs with chorus girls, one of whom was the inspiration for *Carnival*. He and Faith made periodic, unsuccessful attempts at reconciliation, but although they remained married until the end came with her death in 1962, they rarely lived together.

As a British military spymaster in Athens during the First World War, Mackenzie enjoyed a swashbuckling notoriety among the authorities, who ultimately dismissed him. Secrecy seems to have been at a discount, and he often drew attention to himself with dandyish clothes: later he sported a black sombrero and velvet-lined cape. The war as a whole, not only its carnage (which he witnessed at Gallipoli) but its bureaucratic monotony, horrified him, and he made his disillusionment plain in postwar novels. "What he had witnessed," writes his biographer Arno Linklater, "was the end of the old England he knew and the beginnings of the modern, or . . .

32. Compton Mackenzie, *Sinister Street*, 2 vols. (London: M. Secker, 1913, 1914).
33. Mackenzie, quoted in Linklater, *Mackenzie*, 44.
34. Ibid., 136.

'Hunnish' state, in which individuality was subsumed within the laws and regulations of officialdom."[35]

Mackenzie's thousand-page novel *The Parson's Progress*, written in the early 1920s and published in three installments as *The Altar Steps*, *The Parson's Progress*, and *The Heavenly Ladder*, is his longest religious work. It carries his protagonist, Mark Lidderdale, through forty years of life and every phase of High Anglicanism before coming to a climax with his conversion to Roman Catholicism. Written a decade after his own conversion, it builds up an indictment of the Church of England but in an affable and intimate way, drawing heavily on his own experiences and those of other Anglo-Catholics Mackenzie had known. As a young graduate he had lived for a time in a Cornish village and preached lay sermons while leading a children's Sunday school. Lidderdale becomes vicar in a comparable Cornish village in *The Heavenly Ladder* and suffers persecution at the hands of his insular Methodist neighbors when he introduces what to them seem like unfamiliar "popish" idols in his church. Accused unjustly of having an affair with an unattached lady parishoner whom he despises and of corrupting innocent children, Lidderdale is ultimately ejected from his living, after which he enlists as a private soldier and suffers horrific wounds in the First World War. The villagers are hardly more to blame than the church itself, however. Mackenzie depicts Anglican bishops as time-serving trimmers corrupted by their deference to the civil power, made arbitrary and capricious by the lack of a universally agreed-upon liturgy or ritual system to unite them. Like Benson and like Cardinal Manning a generation earlier, he hated the servility of church to state.[36]

Lidderdale talks of himself as a "Catholic" throughout his travails but is brought up short by a cynical stranger who, hearing his tale, remarks: "You will admit that I am, religiously speaking, a disinterested observer? Very well, I assure you that the claim of the High Church Anglicans to be Catholics strikes a disinterested observer as merely funny. I hate Catholicism, which I regard as nothing but an elaborate trap to ensnare the individual, but at least it is a well-made trap. The mechanism is perfect of its kind."[37] On the brink of his conversion to Rome at the war's end, Lidderdale talks with a kindly Benedictine, who tells him that the new League of Nations is unlikely to succeed because it lacks even the organic unity of the Catholic Church, which has itself failed to bring peace to the world. The remark prompts Lidderdale to realize that the Church of

---

35. Ibid., 181.

36. Compton Mackenzie, *The Altar Steps* (London: Cassell, 1922); *Parson's Progress* (London: Cassell, 1923); *The Heavenly Ladder* (London: Cassell, 1924).

37. Mackenzie, *Heavenly Ladder*, 288.

England is analogous to the League of Nations, created by the victors in an earlier struggle but essentially an unstable hybrid.[38] By contrast the Church of Rome, for all its imperfections, offers unity and the possibility of coherent truth, outwardly symbolized by the monastery of Monte Cassino, which he visits while under instruction:

He had rejected the idea of driving up by the modern carriage road, preferring to ascend on foot by the ancient mule track so that he might follow as it were the natural curve of the progress of European civilization, for Monte Cassino is the very abstract of history in the external evidence it offers of what man was and is and may be, and the very essence of humanity in the way it shows the activity of evil transformed to produce the activity of good, turned back sometimes toward evil, but always by the grace and mercy of Almighty God rescued finally for good.[39]

The trilogy ends with Lidderdale on the doorstep of the Catholic church. Along the way he gives a glimpse of one of the long-simmering disputes in English Catholicism since Newman's time, the question of adaptation to, or resistance against, English conditions. An English Roman Catholic priest, Monsignor Cripps, tells Lidderdale: "the English people will not have Irish priests to rule them. They don't like it and I don't blame them." Later the monsignor adds: "So long as they think at Westminister that we're going to convert England with a tag rag and bobtail mob of Irish priests we never shall make the right men. . . . You cannot expect a decent English family to confess to an Irish peasant."[40] Although Mackenzie could be sentimental about Scotland (in the interwar years he became a demonstrative Scottish nationalist) he resisted the allure of Ireland and shared the monsignor's view.

Much of Mackenzie's fiction from the interwar years was inferior to his earlier works. His extravagant way of life, which extended to the purchase of several islands in the English Channel and in western Scotland, left Mackenzie permanently in debt. He tried to pay off his debts by writing more books (he ultimately produced more than a hundred), dictating many of them at high speed to a secretary, along with hundreds of letters and short articles for the press. His friend D. H. Lawrence wrote a merciless short story, "The Two Bluebirds," about a once-great novelist now dictating trivial works to his secretary under the compulsion of debt.[41]

38. Ibid., 319–20.
39. Ibid., 327.
40. Mackenzie, *Altar Steps*, 235–37.
41. Linklater, *Mackenzie*, 194, 206, 209.

Out of this great outpouring of work the central ideas of Mackenzie's maturity stand out clearly. He was a fierce opponent of Protestantism and its intellectual heritage. Plainest in books such as *Catholicism and Scotland* and his biography of Bonnie Prince Charlie, both from the early 1930s, his anti-Protestantism also shone through all his literary criticism.[42] He theorized that puritanism, the characteristic religious expression of northern Europe, was the source of modern science, industrial civilization, and the odious cant and moralism that accompanied them. Ironically, this view coincided with the voguish American antipuritanism of H. L. Mencken and Clarence Darrow in the 1920s, though Mackenzie's Catholic solution to the problem was the antithesis of their atheism. But this polemic against the Protestant heritage was tempered by his acknowledgment of the brilliance to which it had also given rise. For example, at a time when H. G. Wells was a scapegoat for many Catholic writers, Mackenzie, like his contemporary Christopher Dawson, admitted that Wells's *Outline of History* was an "astonishing feat." He admired Wells for "his magnificent refusal to compromise with his ideas and his profound indifference to opinion. He is the only personality thrown up by modern English democracy who suggests the grand style."[43]

Mackenzie was slightly too old to be drafted into the trenches; Waugh and Greene were slightly too young. They spent their schooldays watching boys four or five years their senior go straight from school to basic training and from there to the murderous front lines. The war influenced every aspect of British life, literature included, and although Mackenzie was one of the "grand old men" of Catholic literature by the time they published their first novels at the end of the 1920s, he represented the literary generation against which they were in rebellion. The contrast was less complete than they might have supposed, however. Like Mackenzie they spent several years coming to terms with conversion. Just as nearly a decade passed between Mackenzie's conversion and its literary rendering in *The Parson's Progress*, similarly it was not until the end of the 1930s that Catholicism became the central issue in a Greene novel (*Brighton Rock*) and the early 1940s for Waugh (*Brideshead Revisited*).

Again like Mackenzie, they did not experience conversion as euphoric. Greene was received into the church in February 1926, after writing laconically to his mother: "I expect you have guessed that I am embracing the Scarlet Woman." He wrote later, "I rememeber very clearly the nature

---

42. Compton Mackenzie, *Catholicism and Scotland* (1931; Port Washington, N.Y.: Kennikat Press, 1971); Mackenzie, *Prince Charlie (De Jure Charles III, King of Scotland, England, France, and Ireland)* (London: P. Davies, 1932).

43. Mackenzie, *Literature in My Time*, 165.

of my emotion as I walked away from the Cathedral [in Nottingham]; there was no joy at all, only a somber apprehension."[44] Waugh told Father Martin D'Arcy, who instructed him in 1930, "On firm intellectual conviction but with little emotion I was admitted to the Church." D'Arcy added, "Evelyn . . . never spoke of experience or feelings. He had come to learn and understand what he believed to be God's revelation, and this made talking with him an interesting discussion based primarily on reason."[45] Intellectually convinced, the two novelists gradually developed powerful emotional attachments to the Catholic Church, which they expressed in their fiction after the late 1930s.

Both suprised secular critics by asserting the continuing importance of the Catholic faith. As Waugh's biographer Christopher Sykes wrote of *Brideshead Revisited* (1945) "not since the time of Robert Hugh Benson . . . over thirty years before had novelists of high ambition taken Christian religion as the main subject of a fiction to be treated without skepticism. . . . Evelyn was doing something which seemed in England to have gone out of fashion for ever; he was making religion the central point of a story about contemporary English life, and approaching his theme with respect and awe."[46] Waugh followed the success of *Brideshead* with his *Sword of Honor* trilogy which viewed the disillusioning experiences of the Second World War through the eyes of a devout but struggling Catholic. Much of its literary power comes from the narrator's awareness that religion, especially so demanding a religion as Catholicism, means nothing to most of his contemporaries, to whom he seems merely quixotic. Greene in *Brighton Rock* (1938) and *The Heart of the Matter* (1948) achieved the same effect, showing the special difficulties and temptations faced by Catholics in a world utterly indifferent to religion and running according to quite different principles.

In their own lives Greene and Waugh experienced the conflict between the Catholic ideal and the contemporary reality as it affected marriage. Waugh's early marriage, before his conversion, soon failed, and after his wife's adultery it ended in separation and then divorce.[47] In becoming a Catholic soon afterward Waugh recognized the possibility that he was denying himself the chance of ever marrying again. In the event, however, after protracted negotiations, he got an annulment from the Vatican in 1936, after which he married Laura Herbert and subsequently fathered six

44. Graham Greene, *A Sort of Life* (New York: Simon and Schuster, 1971), 168–69.
45. D'Arcy quoted in Stannard, *Early Years*, 228.
46. Sykes, *Waugh*, 338.
47. Stannard, *Early Years*, 181–85.

children.[48] Divorce haunted his writings, notably in *A Handful of Dust*, where he portrayed the dilemma of rootless, irreligious people whose marriage broke down, and *Sword of Honor*, where the divorced Catholic protagonist, Guy Crouchback, struggles with the religious prohibition against remarriage. Greene's marriage also foundered and he had a succession of mistresses in the years after the Second World War.[49] Ironically it had been his infatuated love for Vivien Dayrell-Browning which led him to the Catholic Church in the first place, before his learning about the faith took on a life of its own. He knew that Waugh, whom he liked and admired, frowned on extramarital affairs and could be vengefully rude to people who pursued them. He therefore introduced Waugh to his lover Catherine Walston only with great trepidation and was relieved to find Waugh merciful.[50]

Both men recognized that they were influential figures in English-language Catholicism and both wrote extensively for the Catholic press in England and America for far smaller sums of money than they earned from the commercial press. Like so many converts since Newman's day, they received much encouragement and praise from the British and American Catholic communities but also plenty of animosity. Waugh's early novels, in particular, infuriated Ernest Oldmeadow, editor of the *Tablet*, who saw them as degenerate, cynical, and more likely to undermine than fortify the faith of readers. Waugh had not undertaken *Vile Bodies* or *Black Mischief* in a missionary spirit, however, and greatly resented Oldmeadow's attacks, which he reciprocated wth interest.[51]

Greene's fiction also suffered official attacks; *The Power and the Glory* was condemned by the Holy Office at Rome, whose head, Cardinal Giuseppe Pizzardo, requested that he change certain passages. Greene stoutly refused. Later, he recalled, "when Pope Paul VI told me that among the novels of mine he had read was *The Power and the Glory* I answered that the book he had read had been condemned by the Holy Office. His attitude was more liberal than that of Cardinal Pizzardo. 'Some parts of all your books will always,' he said, 'offend some Catholics. You should not worry about that,' a counsel which I find it easy to take."[52] Neither author saw himself as simply a "Catholic novelist." While taking their religion seriously, they would not let it compromise their craft.

48. Sykes, *Waugh*, 153–56, 178, 216; Stannard, *Early Years*, 351–53.
49. Shelden, *Greene*, 368–75.
50. Stannard, *No Abiding City*, 219–20, 293–94.
51. Sykes, *Waugh*, 176–78.
52. Greene, *A Sort of Life*, 79.

Waugh, son of a London publisher, had been raised in a mild Anglican environment and had rebelled against conventional Anglicanism at Lancing School. Charles Ryder's description of his religious education in *Brideshead Revisited* seems to correspond closely with Waugh's own experience.

The view implicit in my education was that the basic narrative of Christianity had long been exposed as a myth, and that opinion was now divided as to whether its ethical teaching was of present value, a division in which the main weight went against it: religion was a hobby which some people professed and others did not; at the best it was slightly ornamental, at the worst it was the province of "complexes" and "inhibitions"—catchwords of the decade—and of the intolerance, hypocrisy, and sheer stupidity attributed to it for centuries. No-one had ever suggested to me that these quaint observances expressed a coherent philosophic system and intransigent historical claims; nor, had they done so, would I have been much interested.[53]

Waugh espoused a kind of joyous atheism in his iconoclastic debut, *Decline and Fall* (1928). The only even nominally religious figure there is a defrocked Anglican priest, Mr. Prendergast, who teaches at a boys' boarding school and is hopelessly bad at it. He confides to Paul Pennyfeather, the protagonist, that he had been forced from his parish by fundamental doubts. Later Prendergast learns of the existence of "modern churchmen" who permit no theological scruple to stand in the way of their careers and decides he can be one too. Back in the clergy once more and working as a prison chaplain (in the prison where Pennyfeather is serving time after inadvertently working in the white slave trade) Prendergast is hacked to pieces by a demented prisoner who is religiously or demonically possessed.[54] Waugh here makes the same ruthless fun of the modern Church of England as of all other institutions and offers no counterweight of sanity.

His next novel, *Vile Bodies*, also written before his conversion, has no ostensible religious content, though its stock Catholic figure, the sinister Jesuit, of whom he later felt rather ashamed, is, as his biographer Martin Stannard says, "the most nearly admirable figure" in the book. It was written only a few months before Waugh's conversion, and Stannard speculates that the comparatively sympathetic treatment of Father Rothschild,

53. Evelyn Waugh, *Brideshead Revisited: The Sacred and Profane Memories of Captain Charles Ryder* (Boston: Little, Brown, 1945), 85.
54. Evelyn Waugh, *Decline and Fall* (1928; Boston: Little, Brown, 1949).

S.J., is a subconscious augury of later developments.[55] Waugh's early postconversion novels and travel books, however, also have little ostensible religious content. They show, rather, the development of his political conservatism and the sense (shared by many Catholics of his age) that the modern world was in a state of moral decay and practical dissolution.[56]

Greene published no novels before his conversion. His youth had been troubled. Son of the headmaster of Berkhamstead School in the northern suburbs of London, he also attended it, suffering both from the bullying of other boys who goaded him as a teachers' favorite and from his family's meticulous care to show him no favors. When he had a nervous breakdown, his parents sent him for psychoanalysis, then still in its infancy (especially in Britain). He enjoyed it.[57] As an undergraduate at Oxford he was visited by periodic bouts of acute melancholy, and on several occasions he played Russian roulette with a revolver he had found at home, discovering that the possibility of immediate death made his spirits soar when the hammer fell and life went on.[58] An early book of poems was published, but he first made a living as a newspaper editor in the midlands city of Nottingham, and there he converted. At first he was drawn to Catholicism only as a way of persuading a young Catholic woman, Vivien Dayrell-Browning, whom he had met at Oxford, to marry him. He met a certain Father Trollope for instruction.

At the first sight he was all I detested most in my private image of the Church. A very tall and very fat man with big smooth jowls which looked as though they had never needed a razor, he resembled closely a character in one of those nineteenth century paintings to be seen in art shops on the wrong side of Picadilly—monks and cardinals enjoying their Friday abstinence by dismembering enormous lobsters and pouring great goblets of wine.[59]

Later he came to like and admire Trollope for his moral goodness and his persuasive account of Catholicism, but conversion was never by syllogistic reasoning. Rather, "I can only remember that in January 1926 I became convinced of the probable existence of something we call God . . . and my belief never came by way of those unconvincing philosophical arguments

55. Stannard, *Early Years*, 201; Evelyn Waugh, *Vile Bodies* (Boston: Little, Brown, 1930).
56. See, for example, his satire on the British press and the political Left in *Scoop: A Novel about Journalists* (London: Chapman and Hall, 1938).
57. Sherry, *Greene*, 65–99.
58. Ibid., 154–60.
59. Greene, *A Sort of Life*, 165.

which I derided in a short story called 'A Visit to Morin.'"[60] Reception into the church and marriage to Vivien were followed by publication of his early novels, *The Man Within* (1929), *Stamboul Train* (1932), and *It's a Battlefield* (1934), adventure stories that, like Waugh's novels of the early 1930s, had little religious content.

Greene's first major religious novel was *Brighton Rock* (1938) which began as another adventure story but changed into a profound study of the idea of evil. Outwardly it describes the efforts of a seventeen-year-old gangster, Pinkie, to outwit a rival gang and to cover up a murder. Pinkie is a Catholic, surely one of the most vicious and depraved ever to appear in literature. He is convinced of the reality of hell and damnation, and seems determined to fly in the face of God's goodness. "Of course there's Hell," he declares to his girlfriend, Rose: "'Flames and damnation,' he said. . . . 'And Heaven too?' Rose said with anxiety. . . . 'Oh Maybe,' the boy said, 'maybe.'"[61] Inexperienced, Pinkie longs for worldliness and glamour, but has a horror of sex, drinking, and smoking. The ignorant and credulous Rose is Catholic too, and she marries Pinkie believing he loves her, whereas his only motive is to put her in a position where she cannot testify against him in court, as might otherwise happen. After the marriage he reflects: "She was good but he'd got her like you got God in the eucharist—in the guts. God couldn't escape the evil mouth which chose to eat its own damnation" (221).

As Catholics, Pinkie and Rose see a significance in every event and every act which others might miss. This is a frequent theme in Greene's work and in Waugh's, where the surface meaning of events and scenes is penetrated by the Catholic gaze. When he sees a disgusting tramp woman in the street Pinkie thinks first, "It was like a sight of damnation," but then he sees the woman's fingers moving and hears her praying the rosary. He realizes: "This was not one of the damned; he watched with horrified fascination. This was one of the saved" (234). And when Rose gets up from her nuptial bed, she realizes that she might be pregnant and that as a mother she could "raise an army of friends for Pinkie. . . . There was no end to what the two of them had done last night upon the bed: it was an eternal act" (249). At the end of the novel, after Pinkie's gruesome death, Rose confesses that she wants to be damned with him, but the priest tells her not to despair or to be too sure that Pinkie has been damned. "You cannot conceive, my child, nor can I or anyone, the appalling strangeness of the mercy of God" (308). This was a theme Greene was to develop

60. Ibid., 168.
61. Graham Greene, *Brighton Rock* (1938; London: Heinemann and Bodley Head, 1970), 61–62, herafter cited in the text.

further in *The Heart of the Matter* (1948), and this idea of God's strangeness sets the tone for *Brighton Rock*. Of these religious novels an admiring
Evelyn Waugh wrote that they "have been baptized, held deep in under
the waters of life. The author has said: 'These characters are not my
creation but God's. They have an eternal destiny. They are not merely
playing a part for the reader's amusement. They are souls whom Christ
died to save.'"[62] Greene wrote later that, with the publication of *Brighton
Rock*, "I was discovered to be—detestable term!—a Catholic writer. Catholics began to treat my faults too kindly, as though I were a member of a
clan and could not be disowned, while some non-Catholic critics seemed
to consider that my faith gave me an unfair advantage in some way over my
contemporaries."[63]

Catholicism signifies no definite political views, but during the 1930s, a
decade of acute political polarization, most British and American Catholics
became vigorous anticommunists. In a few cases anticommunism led to
flirtation with fascism but more often to a denunciation of both "isms."
Waugh was certainly no enemy of Mussolini when he accepted Italian
government aid to visit the Italian-Abyssinian War in 1936, and he was
pro-Franco in the Spanish Civil War.[64] But while a generation of writers
struggled to get into Spain to fight or report, Waugh and Greene instead
visited Mexico, where an anticlerical revolution had led to persecution of
the Catholic Church. Although Waugh was much more politically conservative than Greene, both of them wrote critical commentaries on the
Mexican Revolution, Greene's *The Lawless Roads* and Waugh's *Robbery
under Law*.[65] Waugh went there at the expense of an oil company which
faced expropriation by the revolutionary government and doubtless satisfied his patrons in this most openly political of his books. It included a
summary statement of his mature Catholic view of politics and human
nature.

Let me warn the reader that I was a Conservative when I went to Mexico
and that everything I saw there strengthened my opinion. I believe that man
is, by nature, an exile and will never be self-sufficient or complete on this
earth; that his chances of happiness and virtue, here, remain more or less
constant through the centuries and, generally speaking, are not much affected by the political and economic conditions in which he lives; that the

---

62. Waugh, quoted in DeVitis, *Graham Greene*, 27.
63. Greene, Introduction to *Brighton Rock*, vii.
64. Stannard, *Early Years*, 425–26.
65. Graham Greene, *The Lawless Roads: A Mexican Journey* (London: Longmans, Green,
1939); Evelyn Waugh, *Robbery under Law: The Mexican Object Lesson* (London: Chapman
and Hall, 1939).

balance of good and ill tends to revert to a norm; that sudden changes of physical condition are usually ill, and are advocated by the wrong people for the wrong reasons; that the intellectual communists of today have personal, irrelevant grounds for their antagonism to society, which they are trying to exploit.[66]

*Robbery under Law* was published in the summer of 1939, by which time anxiety about the imminent outbreak of European war doomed it to obscurity. Waugh later felt ashamed of the compromised circumstances under which it was produced and declined to revive it in an anthology of his travel writings.[67]

Greene's novel on the Mexican Revolution, *The Power and the Glory*, written after a long visit and extensive travels in 1938, was much more successful than Waugh's book and, Greene said, "gave me more satisfaction than any other I had written."[68] It followed publication of *The Lawless Roads*, a documentary account of the revolution which showed the positive achievements of the Plutarco Calles and Lázaro Cárdenas regimes as well as their drawbacks.[69] The visit to Mexico was also important to Greene's religious life. "It was in Mexico," he recalled "that I discovered some emotional belief in myself, among the empty and ruined churches from which the priests had been excluded, at the secret masses of Las Casas celebrated without the sanctus bell, among the swaggering pistoleros."[70]

Revolutionary persecution of the Catholic Church made a tempting subject for any apologist. Greene avoided the easy route of depicting the situation in Tabasco province as a simple conflict between good and evil. Instead, he was at pains to show that the priest protagonist of the novel had been slack and slothful before the revolution, a chronic drunkard (he is known as "the whisky priest" and the reader never learns his name), that he had fathered an illegitimate child, performed religious services for money, and taken advantage of pampering parishioners. Another cowardly priest in the novel, Father José, has completely sold out to the revolution by marrying his bullying housekeeper and renouncing the church. By contrast the revolutionary lieutenant of police is a man of stern principle, dedicated to improving the lives of the downtrodden peasantry. The events of the novel show how power corrupts the lieutenant and pow-

66. Waugh, quoted in Sykes, *Waugh*, 256.
67. Stannard, *Early Years*, 487.
68. Graham Greene, *Ways of Escape* (London: Bodley Head, 1980), 89.
69. Greene, *Lawless Roads*.
70. Greene, Introduction to *Brighton Rock*, x.

erlessness brings out the heroic piety of the bad priest. Its exploration of sin, forgiveness, and duty is riddled with paradox, and Greene shows how the most heroic and most despicable characteristics jostle together in the same individual. The priest's final willingness to risk his life by following a Judas figure back into danger after his escape across the mountains illuminates the power of faith in adversity. His final conversations with the lieutenant before being shot by firing squad suggest the durability of the church, its ability to outlive the revolution. In this sense Greene's conclusion was similar to Waugh's: human nature and the propensity to sin made the revolution more dangerous than beneficial and prevented any chance of permanent improvement. The church, made up of men with feet of clay, would certainly never be perfect but neither would it perish.

As in *Brighton Rock*, Greene's characters in *The Power and the Glory* muse on the power of evil, the ability and desire of individuals knowingly to defy God. When he listens to the confession of the half-caste man who will later betray him, the whisky priest reflects on the greatness of Christ's sacrifice: "How often the priest had heard the same confession—Man was so limited he hadn't even the ingenuity to invent a new vice: the animals knew as much. It was for this world that Christ died; the more evil you saw and heard about you, the greater glory lay in the death. It was too easy to die for what was good or beautiful, for home, or children or a civilization—it needed a God to die for the half-hearted and the corrupt."[71]

This was the novel the Holy Office condemned on the grounds that it was morally paradoxical. Greene refused to make changes, alleging that copyright now lay with the publisher and was out of his hands. "The price of liberty, even within a church, is eternal vigilance," wrote Greene in the introduction to a later edition of the novel, "but I wonder whether any of the totalitarian states, whether of the right or of the left, with which the Church of Rome is often compared, would have treated me as gently when I refused to revise the book. . . . There was no public condemnation, and the affair was allowed to drop into that peaceful oblivion which the Church wisely reserves for unimportant issues."[72]

Waugh and Greene both wrote superb novels based on their experiences during the Second World War, and both used the war as a dramatic backdrop to further religious explorations. In Waugh's *Brideshead Revisited* (1945) and Greene's *Heart of the Matter* (1948) it is the boredom rather than the danger of war which provides the stimulus for the narratives. Waugh found the experience of wartime highly uncongenial. Eager to

71. Graham Greene, *The Power and the Glory* (1940; London: Heinemann and Bodley Head, 1971), 114.
72. Greene, Introduction, ibid., xi.

serve his country, he found it reluctant to accept his services, and much of his wartime experience consisted of being passed around from one unit to another, partly because he was pulling strings and partly because his commanding officers could not abide his prickly personality and pulled strings of their own to dislodge him.[73] Finally Waugh was granted an extended leave, which he spent living in a hotel and working on a new novel. The result of this odd leave, *Brideshead Revisited*, takes the form of an extended reverie by Charles Ryder, a low-ranking officer in Waugh's situation, bogged down in the irksome duty of moving sullen troops from one camp to another, still in Britain, with no sign of the real war to break the monotony. Arriving at one more station Ryder suddenly realizes that he is at Brideshead, home of a Catholic family to which he has been intimately bound for twenty years, and the place prompts his reminiscences.

The patriarch of the family, Lord Marchmain, is separated from his wife and lives in exile at Venice. Lady Marchmain comes from an old English Catholic family (his lordship converted at the time of their marriage) and now runs the house, surrounded by a coterie of admirers. Ryder befriends her son Sebastian Flyte when they are carefree undergraduates at Oxford in the 1920s. Through Sebastian he meets the other Flyte children, Julia, Cordelia, and "Bridey," and at crucial moments in later years finds his fortunes interwoven with theirs. Bit by bit he discovers that the Catholic faith, of which he has no experience and for which he has no patience, is central to all their lives and makes them judge all things according to criteria quite different from his own. When Charles tells Sebastian early on that Catholics seem to be just like everyone else, Sebastian answers: "My dear Charles, that's exactly what they are not—particularly in this country, where they're so few. It's not just that they are a clique—as a matter of fact they are four cliques all blackguarding each other half the time—but they've got an entirely different outlook on life; everything they think important is different from other people. They try to hide it as much as they can but it comes out all the time."[74] The novel tells of Charles's gradual education in the truth of that remark. As in Greene's *Brighton Rock*, Catholicism changes everything, but usually in the subtlest ways, which superficial observers cannot grasp.

One of the great achievements of Waugh's earlier fiction had been his creation of modern, rootless, metropolitan individuals, who see themselves as worldly, clear-sighted, and realistic but who, under Waugh's piercing and satirical gaze, seem pitifully inadequate, representatives of a

73. Sykes, *Waugh*, 270–320.
74. Waugh, *Brideshead*, 89, hereafter cited in the text.

world in decline. With Rex Mottram, the character who marries Julia Flyte, Waugh perfected the type. Mottram is a member of Parliament, well connected in business and government, Canadian by birth but super-ficially at home everywhere. He agrees to convert to Catholicism to marry Julia but regards it as no more significant than learning the ins and outs of any other business. The priest instructing Mottram reports to Lady Marchmain:

The first day I wanted to find out what sort of religious life he had had till now, so I asked him what he meant by prayer. He said: "I don't mean anything. You tell me." I tried to, in a few words, and he said, "Right, so much for prayer. What's the next thing?" I gave him the catechism to take away. Yesterday I asked him whether our Lord had more than one nature. He said: "Just as many as you say, Father." . . . Lady Marchmain, he doesn't correspond to any degree of paganism known to the missionaries. (192)

Julia, besotted, marries Mottram anyway, and only years later does she tell Charles, when she has become his lover after the marriage has failed: "You know Father Mowbray hit on the truth about Rex at once that it took me a year of marriage to see. He simply wasn't all there. He wasn't a complete human being at all. He was a tiny bit of one, unnaturally developed, something in a bottle, an organ kept alive in a laboratory. . . . he was something absolutely modern and up to date that only this ghastly age could produce" (200). Ryder, the narrator, feels himself to be symbolic of a decadent age too. An architectural artist, he finds that he is often em-ployed to paint dignified old houses just before they are destroyed, so that his own success is "a symptom of the decline" (227).

The climax of the novel is the return of the ailing Lord Marchmain from Venice to Brideshead where, it becomes clear, he has come to die. At first he resists the urging of family and friends that he should see a priest and resume his lapsed Catholic faith, but as the crisis approaches he makes his peace with the church and dies making the sign of the cross. Ryder is horrified, first that the church should pursue the dying man against what seemed to be his wishes, then that the man should succumb, but in the midst of the crisis he realizes that his beloved Julia has also been trans-formed by witnessing her father's recovery of the faith. She too is re-claimed by the church, and although both she and Ryder are now divorced, her return to the faith prevents them from marrying. At the very end of the novel we see Captain Ryder himself worshiping in Brideshead chapel and suddenly realize that he too has converted and that we have been listening, in effect, to the retrospective confession of a new Catholic.

Earthly bliss is denied, the lovers are torn apart, and only the gruesome boredom of the war comes along to take its place. Like Greene, Waugh gave his characters no supernatural sanctity and insisted that, in worldly terms, adherence to Catholicism was more likely to entail painful privation. David Lodge comments, "As so often in modern Catholic literature . . . the descent of God's grace, because of the human sacrifice it demands, has an aspect of the catastrophe—here conveyed through the iterative image of an avalanche."[75]

Greene's *Heart of the Matter* is in some respects a parallel work, stressing the boredom of war, the seeming irrelevance of faith, along with its ultimate power to transform men's destinies. Like *The Power and the Glory*, it is set in "Greeneland," an area infested with mosquitoes, vultures, and derelict Europeans much the worse for drink, but where sudden glimpses of virtue and faith transform the sordid scene. Its central character, Scobie, is a Catholic convert who, like Greene himself, had converted initially because of his intended marriage but had then become convinced of Catholic truth. Greene spent several of the war years as an intelligence agent in West Africa and the novel is set there amid the tropical heat and decay. "Why do I love this place so much?" Scobie asks himself. "Is it because here human nature hasn't had time to disguise itself? Nobody here could ever talk about a heaven on earth. Heaven remained rigidly in its proper place on the other side of death, and on this side flourished the injustices, the cruelties, the meannesses, that elsewhere people so cleverly hushed up. Here you could love human beings nearly as God loved them, knowing them at their worst."[76]

In this setting Scobie, an assistant commissioner of the colonial police, is ruined by his pity for others, which, the novel shows, can be a powerful temptation to sin. Pitying his wife, Louise, who hates life in the colony, he borrows money from a Syrian merchant so that he can send her to the greater luxury and safety of South Africa. In doing so, he compromises his police work, for colleagues believe the Syrian to be a smuggler. While his wife is away he falls in love with a nineteen-year-old girl, Helen, a shipwreck survivor who has already been widowed. He soon feels the same pity for her as he does for his wife and promises her that he will never abandon her, even when he learns that Louise is returning. To test his fidelity to her, Louise, back in the colony, asks Scobie to take communion with her, and to protect the secret of the affair he does so, without first going to confession or repenting, which puts him in a condition of mortal

75. Lodge, *Evelyn Waugh*, 33.
76. Greene, *Heart of the Matter* (New York: Viking, 1948), 32, hereafter cited in the text.

sin. He cannot confess without the intention of reforming, but having promised not to desert Helen, he cannot make that intention. Scobie rebukes God for his situation and says that these women are more in need of his sympathy and pity than God himself: " 'God can wait,' he thought; how can one love God at the expense of one of his creatures? Would a woman accept a love for which a child had to be sacrificed?" (203).

Scobie comes to realize that by committing suicide he can save both women from despair, Louise from knowing about his adultery and Helen from her dread of abandonment. He is willing to do it even though suicide means eternal damnation. "The priests told you it was the unforgivable sin, the final expression of an unrepentant despair, and of course one accepted the Church's teaching. But they also taught that God had sometimes broken his own laws, and was it more impossible for him to put out a hand of forgiveness into the suicidal darkness and chaos than to have woken himself in the tomb, behind the stone? Christ had not been murdered: you couldn't murder God: Christ had killed himself; he had hanged himself on the Cross" (206). Thus Scobie internally argues the issue back and forth with God and determines to go ahead with his suicide plan, but unlike Pinkie in *Brighton Rock*, he does it with a feeling of shame rather than defiance: "He had no love of evil or hate of God: how was he to hate this God who of His own accord was surrendering Himself into his power?" (247). Greene builds up a vivid sense of God's powerlessness in the face of the human will to sin and shows that each sin perpetuates the pain of Christ's scourging and crucifixion. "He had a sudden picture before his eyes of a bleeding face, of eyes closed by the continuous shower of blows; the punch-drunk head of God reeling sideways" (264). Even so he persists in his plan. He feigns attacks of angina to make it seem he is dying of natural causes, so that Louise will benefit from his life insurance policies. But after Scobie has taken his own life another police agent, Wilson, realizes that it is a suicide, Louise reveals that she has known about his adultery all along, and Helen falls listlessly into a sexual affair with an air force officer. Scobie's self-sacrifice, honorable in one light but mortally sinful by Catholic standards, has been in vain.

Some secular readers understood Greene to be arguing against Catholic teaching and to be presenting Scobie as a moral hero superior to the inflexible church. Catholic journals, by contrast, debated whether or not Scobie was damned eternally. Evelyn Waugh, writing in *Commonweal*, said that "the reader is haunted by the question: is Scobie damned?" Waugh was impressed by Greene's storytelling skill but puzzled by the reasons for Scobie's suicide. "To me," he wrote, "the idea of willing my own damnation for the love of God is either a very loose poetical expression or a mad blasphemy, for the God who accepted that sacrifice could be neither just nor lovable."[77] Greene, writing later in an autobiography, reminded readers that Scobie and Greene were two very different men and added that "the character of Scobie was intended to show that pity can be the expression of an almost monstrous pride," so that "the motive of his suicide, to save even God from himself, was the final twist of the screw of his inordinate pride."[78]

By the end of the Second World War, Greene and Waugh were critical successes on both sides of the Atlantic, despite a shared broad streak of anti-Americanism. But their success was certainly not beyond challenge. Mary McCarthy, a rising star in the *Partisan Review* circle and an angry lapsed Catholic, made a slashing attack on Greene, whom she described as "an ersatz serious novelist." She found his characters, particularly Scobie, unrealistic and suspected Greene of highbrow evangelizing: "One cannot imagine a character whose behavior is wholly governed by pity, and one feels that Greene, in pretending that it is possible, is being pious and insincere."[79]

In the 1950s Waugh and Greene diverged more emphatically in their work and ideas. Despite the experiences in Mexico which had given rise to *The Power and the Glory* and the onset of the Cold War, Greene showed more sympathy for communism than virtually any Catholic contemporary. Impressed by the radical implications of the papal encyclical tradition and annoyed by the social quiescence of English Catholics, he wrote, "In this country Catholicism which should produce revolutionaries produces only eccentrics (eccentricity thrives on an unequal social system)." In his view, "Conservatism and Catholicism should be as impossible bedfellows as Catholicism and National Socialism."[80] But even as he said it, he had to face the increasingly crotchety conservatism of his friend Waugh, who was coming to believe by 1950 that Parliament itself was an impertinent affront to monarchical rule. After spending four winters in French Indochina (1950–1953) Greene became convinced that the French (and then the American) interventions there were doomed to failure and that if any cause there was just, it was the position of the Vietnamese Communists.[81] His novel *The Quiet American* (1955) prophesied victory for the Viet Minh, much to the indignation of American Catholic reviewers, for whom

77. Waugh, *Essays, Articles, and Reviews,* 365.
78. Greene, *Ways of Escape,* 125–26.
79. Mary McCarthy, "Graham Greene and the Intelligentsia," *Partisan Review* 11 (Spring 1944): 229.
80. Graham Greene, *Collected Essays* (London: Bodley Head, 1969), 349–50.
81. Norman Sherry, *The Life of Graham Greene,* vol. 2: *1939–1955* (London: Jonathan Cape, 1994), 364–93.

anticommunism at that time was the sine qua non of their faith.[82] He opposed the American mission in Vietnam on the grounds that it embodied a liberal utopianism based more on wishful thinking than real assessment of the political situation.

In the same years he also put his life at risk on visits to Malaya and Kenya during anticolonial uprisings, and his increasing doubts about the sureness of his faith were reflected in *A Burnt-Out Case* and "A Visit to Morin."[83] The sympathetic characters in *A Burnt-Out Case* are Colin, the atheist doctor, and the Father Superior, who thinks far more about the brick-and-mortar problems of his African leper hospital than about faith and salvation. The narrator, Querry, is an egotistical cynic who has won renown as a Catholic architect; the zealous Father Thomas masks religious doubts with dogmatism; and the "good Catholic" layman, Ryckert, is a bigot and a bully. Casual readers could almost take the novel as an anti-Catholic tract, and Greene seemed to sympathize with Doctor Colin when he justified his faith in secular evolution and progress:

Evolution today can produce Hitlers as well as St. John of the Cross. I have a small hope, that's all, a very small hope, that someone they call Christ was the fertile element, looking for a crack in the wall to plant its seed. I think of Christ as an amoeba who took the right turning. I want to be on the side of the progress which survives. I'm no friend of pterodactyls.[84]

His secular love of his fellow men, the leprosy victims, is Colin's substitute for the divine love of Christ.

*A Burnt-Out Case* occasioned an anxious correspondence between Waugh and Greene. Waugh, after reading it, refused to review it for the *Daily Mail* and wrote that he hoped the novel did not signal a loss of faith by Greene. Greene, without confirming or denying that he had reached a stage of religious crisis, answered that the book sought merely to "give expression to various states or moods of belief and unbelief." Waugh was unconvinced and replied: "I don't think you can blame people who read the book as a recantation of faith." Greene renewed his usual defense: "What I have disliked in some Catholic criticism of my work . . . is the confusion between the functions of a novelist and the functions of a moral teacher or theologian. I prefer the statement of Newman. 'I say . . . if Literature is to be made a study of human nature, you cannot have a

82. See, for example, William Clancy's review in *Commonweal*, March 16, 1956, 622.
83. Graham Greene, *A Burnt-Out Case* (New York: Viking, 1961); Greene, "A Visit to Morin" (1963), in Greene, *Collected Stories* (London: Bodley Head and Heinemann, 1972), 238–56.
84. Greene, *Burnt-Out Case*, 160.

Christian literature. It is a contradiction in terms to attempt the sinless Literature of sinful man.'"[85]

While Greene's faith seemed to waver in the 1950s, a triumphal era for many British and American Catholics, Waugh's remained unruffled. Only the possibility of liturgical novelties and the gathering auguries of Vatican II provoked his wrath. Ever since his conflict with Ernest Oldmeadow in the 1930s he had been eager to mollify English Catholic opinion. One gesture in this direction had been his biography of Edmund Campion (1935), the first study of the Elizabethan martyr since that written by another convert, Richard Simpson, sixty years before. Deeply sympathetic to the Catholic tradition without falling into hagiography it showed the English Catholics in Elizabeth I's reign as true followers of the ancient faith and the Anglicans as opportunist "hedge priests."[86] In Waugh's telling the Tudors opened the way to industrialization, commercial corruption, and the woes of the modern world, against which Campion's dwindling Catholic band had opposed themselves in the name of religious truth. It was the first of Waugh's books to make his religious and political views explicit. The royalties from *Edmund Campion* went to the Jesuits' Campion Hall in Oxford, designed by Edward Lutyens and built in 1934 by the man who had instructed Waugh in the faith, Father Martin D'Arcy.

In *Helena* (1950) Waugh returned to the apologetic formula with a historical novel about Saint Helena, Emperor Constantine's mother. He even claimed in the last years of his life that it was his best book, but no one else ever thought so. It is embarrassingly bad, embodying all the weaknesses of hagiographical fiction against which he, Mackenzie, and Greene had earlier struggled. Apart from its sly anachronisms it could almost have been written by Hugh Benson.[87] Far more successful was his biography of Ronald Knox, whom Waugh nursed as he died of cancer in 1957. Elegiac in mood, it suggests that Knox, who had begun life as a brilliantly promising Anglican, paid a high price for his conversion, becoming marginal in English life, fated to spend his time among Catholic dullards. Cardinal Bourne had received Knox into the church, and Waugh's description of Bourne, whom he also knew, is a miniature masterpiece of denigration:

He was not a man with whom Ronald had any natural sympathies. Devout, industrious, well-instructed, the Cardinal was quite devoid of anything which would have passed for scholarship, taste, or humor in Ronald's Angli-

85. Greene, quoted in Stannard, *No Abiding City*, 444–45.
86. Evelyn Waugh, *Edmund Campion* (1935; Boston: Little, Brown, 1946), 2.
87. Evelyn Waugh, *Helena* (Boston: Little, Brown, 1950).

can circle. He had no felicity of expression in speech or writing. . . . He knew no life except that of religious institutions; he had no acquaintance that was not professional and official. Moreover he combined a genuine personal humility with an exceedingly lofty conception of the dignity of his position and with an absolute confidence in all his opinions (which he believed to have been revealed to him in prayer). He was thus singularly disqualified from normal social intercourse.[88]

Waugh described Knox's life as a Catholic schoolteacher and emphasized the theme of the convert's sense of being out of place among his new fellow religionists, a feeling Waugh and Knox appear to have shared: "He became a Catholic in violation of all his tastes and human sympathies, in obedience to his reason and in submission to what he recognized as the will of God. . . . He had grown up to believe . . . that, except for a few illustrious converts, the Roman clergy were a rough and rather tricky lot. He now sought to identify himself with them completely, eschewing all religious dandyism."[89] The book carries a sorrowful air, through which Waugh shows that Knox's life was greatly impoverished by his conversion, whatever the eternal rewards might be.

More important than these churchly works were Waugh's three novels about the Second World War, which collectively made the *Sword of Honor* trilogy. Picking up many of the themes of *Brideshead Revisited*, it tells a story of the betrayals and disappointments of Britain's role in the war, seen through the eyes of Guy Crouchback, another divorced Catholic. The trilogy is packed with comic episodes but has a deeply serious core. At the outset of the war Guy returns from a long personal and spiritual exile in Italy to Britain, exultant to learn that the Hitler-Stalin pact makes Britain the enemy of both. Now, he believes, he can take up the sword of honor which an ancestor, the Blessed Gervase Crouchback, had wielded centuries before in the age of the crusades. But just as Gervase, "il santo Inglese," never reached the Holy Land but died a pointless death en route in a parochial Italian squabble, so Guy Crouchback never gets his chance to fight the great dictators. His only moments in action are against Vichy Frenchmen at Dakar, as part of the headlong British retreat at Crete, and in the company of cynical Yugoslavian Communist partisans at the war's end. All are backwaters of the war; all are morally compromised. Waugh himself had been in Yugoslavia in 1944–1945 and had been horrified to see the British government backing the Communist leader Tito despite his

88. Evelyn Waugh, *The Life of the Right Reverend Ronald Knox* (London: Chapman and Hall, 1959), 166–67.
89. Ibid., 176–77.

contempt for the Catholics of Croatia. He had written a long memorandum arguing the case for the Croatians and against Tito, which concluded: "Great Britain has given great assistance to the establishment of a regime which threatens to destroy the Catholic faith in a region where there are now some five million Catholics." He had even visited the pope to press the Croatians' claims but had been powerless to change the course of British policy.[90]

The war itself loses its sharply etched moral dimensions for Guy Crouchback when the Soviet Union becomes an ally instead of an enemy. Guy's old uncle Peregrine, a memorable Catholic bore, declares in mid-1944: "Shocking news from the Eastern Front. The Bolshevists are advancing again. Germans don't seem able to stop them. . . . If one can believe the papers we are actually helping the Bolshevists." In place of Gervase's crusader sword, only a pseudoheraldic sword plays any role in the war effort, a goodwill gift from the British government to the Soviets in 1944. Visited in Westminster Abbey and admired by a credulous British public, it plays an ironic role in Guy's disillusionment.[91]

In 1964, publishing a recension of the trilogy, Waugh noted that the rapid changes in Catholic life of the last decade had led him to do "something quite outside my original intention. I had written an obituary of the Roman Catholic Church in England as it had existed for many centuries." He had never considered, he said, "that the church was susceptible to change. I was wrong and I have seen a superficial revolution in what then seemed permanent."[92] His writings in these last years before his death (in 1966) left no doubt in a reader's mind that so far as Waugh was concerned these changes were strictly for the worse.

Waugh was outlived by the inexhaustible Compton Mackenzie, who, now in his eighties, was working steadily on his ten-volume autobiography. Graham Greene lived on through the 1970s and 1980s, taking the transformations of the church with equanimity. His work lost much of the intense religious preoccupation of his middle years, and he noted wryly that he had not long to wait before learning one way or another the truth of the faith in which he had placed his hopes. He died in 1991.

90. Sykes, *Waugh*, 372.
91. Evelyn Waugh, *Unconditional Surrender* (London: Chapman and Hall, 1961), 159, 18–22.
92. Evelyn Waugh, *Sword of Honor: Final Version* (London: Chapman and Hall, 1964), 9.

# XIII

## THE PRECONCILIAR
## GENERATION
### *1935–1962*

THE SECOND VATICAN COUNCIL (1962–1965) transformed British and American Catholicism. The conciliar decrees and the much-vaunted "spirit" of the council together diminished the idea of an exclusive Catholic claim to religious truth, and under their influence, the Catholic quest for converts slackened. By then, moreover, a generation of talented and well-trained intellectuals had grown up within Catholic ranks, and they were less dependent on recruits from outside. Catholic intellectuals in both countries were less committed to the idea that their church should oppose the spirit of the age. Even so, the council and its aftershocks took many Catholics by surprise. The two decades preceding it had witnessed, at least officially, no letup in the stern opposition to "indifferentism" and to intellectual modernism that the church had mounted earlier in the century. Many Catholics believed in the 1940s and 1950s that their rearguard action against the world was succeeding, and a few even entertained the illusion that the age of mass conversions was about to begin.[1]

In the United States particularly, old interfaith tensions persisted after the Second World War. Catholics still had to face the hostility of such anti-Catholic intellectuals as Paul Blanshard, who made sinister comparisons between the Kremlin and the Vatican as dual foreign conspiracies against

1. See, for example, Frederick Wilhelmsen, "Catholicism Is Right, So Why Change It?" *Saturday Evening Post*, July 15, 1967, 10, 12.

Amerian freedom.[2] The editors of the *Nation* and the *Christian Century* gave Blanshard the royal treatment. They saw Catholicism as the antithesis of American freedom, faulting it for foreign loyalties, domestic intransigence, censoriousness, and opposition to a free and vigorous intellectual life.[3] Eleanor Roosevelt, the darling of the liberal New Dealers, got into a well-publicized squabble with Cardinal Spellman of New York in the late 1940s over government aid to parochial schools and birth control prohibition, both of which he favored and she opposed.[4] Many other liberal intellectuals linked Catholicism to narrow-mindedness and McCarthyism as the nation's public culture became increasingly secular and scientific.[5] Edmund Wilson, for example, whose novel *Memoirs of Hecate County* (1946) had been banned as obscene in some states under Catholic pressure, was openly scornful of Allen Tate's conversion in 1950 and linked it to what Wilson saw as Tate's reactionary "southern agrarian" politics. "I hope that becoming a Catholic will give you peace of mind," wrote Wilson, "though swallowing the New Testament as factual and moral truth seems to me an awful price to pay for it. . . . Christianity seems to me the worst imposture of any of the religions I know of. Even aside from the question of faith, the morality of the Gospel seems to me absurd."[6]

At the same time, however, the broad religious revival of the late 1940s and 1950s marked something of a high point for Catholics, a few of whom became famous among the general population. Thomas Merton, the convert and Trappist monk, was one, and few men did more than Merton to improve Catholicism's public image. In 1950, moreover, he was selling a thousand books for each one of Edmund Wilson's, and his inspirational autobiography found a readier audience than Wilson's skeptical fiction.[7]

The events of Merton's life have been told often, in his autobiography

2. Paul Blanshard, *American Freedom and Catholic Power* (Boston: Beacon, 1949); Blanshard, *Communism, Democracy, and Catholic Power* (Boston: Beacon, 1951).

3. John McGreevy, "Thinking on One's Own: Catholicism in the American Intellectual Imagination, 1928–1954," unpublished essay, courtesy of Prof. McGreevy, 5–9.

4. John Cooney, *The American Pope: The Life and Times of Francis Cardinal Spellman* (New York: Times Books, 1984), 176–79.

5. On the secularization of public culture, see David Hollinger, *Science, Jews, and Secular Culture: Studies in Mid-Twentieth-Century American Intellectual History* (Princeton: Princeton University Press, 1996).

6. Wilson, quoted in Jeffrey Meyers, *Edmund Wilson: A Biography* (Boston: Houghton Mifflin, 1995), 139. On Tate's conversion, see Peter Huff, "Allen Tate and the Catholic Revival," *Humanitas* 8 (1995): 26–43.

7. Meyers emphasizes how poor Wilson's sales were throughout the 1940s. See Meyers, *Wilson*, 238. On the commercial success of *The Seven Storey Mountain*, see Michael Mott, *The Seven Mountains of Thomas Merton* (Boston: Houghton Mifflin, 1984), 243. Mott's is the best biography of Merton, though massive. Shorter and also very good is Monica Furlong, *Merton: A Biography* (San Francisco: Harper and Row, 1980).

*The Seven Storey Mountain* (1948) and in a string of later biographies. Born in France in 1915 and raised partly in the United States, partly in France and England (he held a British passport until he became a U.S. citizen at the age of thirty-five), he led a dissolute life as an undergraduate, first at Cambridge in England, then at Columbia University in New York. Only on a visit to Rome at the age of eighteen did he feel moved to pray, being inspired by the Christian architecture and repelled by the colossal Roman imperial remains.[8] An aspiring poet, novelist, and critic, Merton made a favorable impression on Mark Van Doren and stayed on at Columbia to write a master's thesis on William Blake. He recalled that when he saw the Catholic imprimatur in Etienne Gilson's *Spirit of Medieval Philosophy*, which he had bought in 1937, it inspired a "feeling of disgust and deception . . . like a knife in the pit of the stomach." His first thought was to throw the book contemptuously from the train on which he was traveling. "They should have warned me that it was a Catholic book!"[9] In the event, he restrained himself and found it affected him profoundly. Gilson, a French layman writing philosophy and theology in the vernacular rather than addressing himself in Latin to priests, was, along with the convert Jacques Maritain, an exceptional figure in the Catholicism of the era. He was just the man to make an impression on the restless Merton, who, after a period of developing conviction and a series of supernatural experiences, converted to Catholicism in November 1938.[10]

For a while Merton was content in the practice of his new faith and began teaching at a Catholic college, Saint Bonaventure's, in upstate New York. He was impressed by the self-sacrificing work of Dorothy Day and Catherine de Hueck, at whose Fellowship House in the slums of Harlem he worked one summer. He felt energized and cleansed by Catholicism, but the possibility of a more arduous vocation nagged at him and eventually he joined the Trappists at Gethsemani, Kentucky, in 1940, accepting thereby a life of austere mortification and the penance of perpetual silence. Ironically this dramatic withdrawal from the world was the gateway to a literary fame that had eluded him before. His religious autobiography, approved for publication by his superiors, became a surprise best seller in 1948. Written in a dogmatic and "triumphalist" tone that made him wince in later years, it deprecated the world and the flesh and praised the contemplative, peaceful life he had found in the monastery. It was so success-

8. Thomas Merton, *The Seven Storey Mountain* (New York: Harcourt, Brace, 1948), 107–8.
9. Ibid., 171.
10. On Gilson, see Laurence K. Shook, *Etienne Gilson* (Toronto: Pontifical Institute of Medieval Studies, 1984). On Merton's conversion, see Mott, *Seven Mountains*, 120–21.

ful and Merton hit such a responsive chord in thousands of readers that the Trappists found themselves overrun with aspiring members eager to follow Merton's lead, and soon had to open extra monasteries to deal with the rush.[11]

Despite some bombastic passages, *The Seven Storey Mountain* is a superb book. It speaks with the personal intensity of Augustine's *Confessions* and shares its sense of the delicious allurements of sin. On the other hand, it lacks the intricate historical and doctrinal to-and-fro of Newman's *Apologia*. Merton, like Augustine but unlike Newman, regarded himself as choosing Catholicism not as an alternative to another branch of Christianity but as a shelter from a world that was becoming a godless secular wilderness.

From then on and throughout the 1950s and 1960s Merton, writing from Gethsemani, was one of the most prolific and influential Catholic writers in America, addressing himself not only to spiritual and contemplative questions but also to the Cold War, communism, nuclear weapons, and the Civil Rights Movement.[12] But like so many of his convert predecessors, he did not find it at all easy to fit into the daily life of his Catholic community and was constantly negotiating with his superiors for further isolation, first in a fire lookout tower, later in a "hermitage" bungalow on the Gethsemani estate. Friction with his abbot over the commercialization of the monastery, the attention of fans, the eagerness of agents and publishers to get more books from him, even a dalliance with a local nurse, showed that Merton, after his ardent Catholic "honeymoon," found the life ceaselessly demanding and difficult.[13] Success hard on the heels of self-surrender was not the only paradox of Merton's life. He also could not make up his mind whether he wanted his Catholicism to represent the antithesis of the America beyond the monastery or to be engaged in the gritty details of the Civil Rights and the antiwar movements, with which he became increasingly involved in the early and mid-1960s. Some scholars speculate that he was on the verge of a complete change in his way of life when he died in a freak accident in 1968.[14]

11. Mott, *Seven Mountains*, 226–28; James Fisher, *The Catholic Counterculture in America, 1933–1962* (Chapel Hill: University of North Carolina Press, 1989), 230.
12. On the Cold War see, for example, Thomas Merton, "Christianity and Totalitarianism," in his *Disputed Questions* (1960; New York: Harcourt, Brace, Jovanovich, 1985), 127–48. On the Civil Rights Movement, see "Black Revolution," in his *Seeds of Destruction* (1964; New York: Farrar, Straus, and Giroux, 1980), 3–90.
13. On his conflict with the abbot, see Mott, *Seven Mountains*, 278–83; on his relations with the nurse, "S," ibid., 435–62.
14. See, for example, Eugene McCarraher, "The Land of Unlikeness: A Cultural History of the Social Gospel in the United States, 1920–1965" (Ph.D. diss., Rutgers University,

A near contemporary of Merton who made a similar conversion journey at the same time was Marshall McLuhan. Born in western Canada in 1911 and raised by strict Baptists, he flourished at the University of Manitoba and won a two-year fellowship to Cambridge. Despite his Protestant background, McLuhan had discovered G. K. Chesterton while still an undergraduate and relished his paradoxical style, his veneration for the Middle Ages, and his dislike of the Reformation. When he got to England he joined the Distributists—sometimes going to London by train for their meetings—and met the great man in 1935. From Chesterton he moved on to the study of Maritain, and in November 1936 he converted to Catholicism. As with many predecessors his conversion shocked his parents. His ambitious mother "felt Marshall, a bright, potentially outstanding scholar, was going to lose every opportunity he might otherwise have had in the academic world. She saw Harvard going down the drain."[15] At Cambridge he received an intensive education in literary modernism from the critics I. A. Richards and F. R. Leavis, which laid the foundations for much of his life's work. Under their guidance he learned the principles of the New Criticism: the scrutiny of texts, the methods of rhetoric, and the deliquescence of language. He would later apply New Critical principles to the study of advertising and media rather than the literary canon, but his Cambridge teachers' influence endured.

Again like many convert predecessors, McLuhan was disappointed to find the fires of the Catholic faith smoldering rather than burning bright. U.S. and Canadian Catholics seemed to him self-satisfied conformists rather than zealous challengers of a decadent society. As his biographer says, "Individual Catholics around him, he was always disappointed to note, were no different from other people. He complained that as far as his own work was concerned his fellow Catholics were, if anything, more hostile and uncomprehending than non-Catholics."[16] In a letter to his fiancée, Corinne Lewis, in 1939 he wrote of his discovery that "most Catholics are too lazy or feeble to use what they possess. And particularly in America where the main currents of life are profoundly anti-Catholic, the average Catholic is too timid, too over-awed by the surrounding material 'splendor' to feel able to be anything but an 'interior' Catholic." And

---

1995). "By the time the order granted him special permission to attend a conference of Eastern and Western monks," writes McCarraher, "Merton had clearly decided not to return to Gethsemani. His old friend Ed Rice recalled that on several occasions Merton had told him emphatically that he intended to remain permanently in Asia, and that he hoped to earn enough money as a writer to support himself."

15. Philip Marchand, *Marshall McLuhan: The Medium and the Messenger* (New York: Ticknor and Fields, 1989), 45.

16. Ibid., 46.

yet, in his early exhilaration as a new Catholic, McLuhan made the common error of believing that the English-speaking nations as a whole were now showing signs of returning to the old faith.[17]

It seemed essential to McLuhan that Catholic intellectuals should go beyond neoscholasticism, the philosophical foundation of the interwar Catholic revival, and take up new intellectual challenges. "Increasingly I feel that Catholics must master C. G. Jung," he wrote in 1944. "The little self-conscious . . . area in which we live today has nothing to do with the problems of our faith. Modern anthropology and psychology are more important for the Church than St. Thomas today."[18] Two years later he wrote a Jesuit friend: "It seems obvious that we must confront the secular in its most confident manifestations and, with its own terms and postulates, to shock it into awareness of its confusion, its illiteracy, and the terrifying drift of its logic." But he noted sadly, "this cannot be done by any Catholic group, nor by Catholic individuals trained in the vocabularies and attitudes which make our education the feeble simulacrum of the world which it is."[19]

Whatever their limitations, the Catholics were glad to make use of this gifted new convert, and almost at once he was offered a job at the Jesuits' Saint Louis University, which he held from 1938 until 1944 (apart from another year in Cambridge to research his doctoral dissertation). Like the historian Ross Hoffman, whose conversion had preceded his own by four years and who moved straight after conversion from a secular to a Catholic university (New York University to Fordham), McLuhan became an influential teacher whose Catholic graduate students went on to lead distinguished academic careers beyond the "Catholic ghetto."[20] Among his more talented students at Saint Louis was Walter Ong, S.J. In another expression of dismay at the state of Catholic education McLuhan told Ong in 1946 that most American Thomists had not yet mastered the developmental insights of Newman, from whom they could learn so much:

They are painfully in the position of lacking that general culture, vitalized by a genuine community, which alone confers relevance. Gilson and Maritain do belong to a community in which a general awareness of our age at all its points is cultivated. Yet both these men have evaded (or for lack of time and

17. Marshall McLuhan, *Letters of Marshall McLuhan*, ed. Matie Molinaro, Corinne McLuhan, and William Toye (Toronto: Oxford University Press, 1987), 102.
18. Ibid., 166.
19. Ibid., 180.
20. Patrick Allitt, "Ross Hoffman and the Transformation of American Catholic Historiography" (unpublished paper, delivered to American Catholic Historical Association Conference, Oxford, Mississippi, April 1991).

faculty they have done nothing) the application of Thomistic principles to the area of Freud, Fraser, and Malinowski—psychology and anthropology. These are the areas of most intense contemporary awareness and they have not found their Newman. . . . The question of training in sensibility, the education of the passions, the fluid interplay of thought and feeling in the development of value judgments apropos of particular works of art. . . . This question no Thomist has ever faced. I mention this to you Walter because you can do something about it.[21]

Ong did his best to live up to McLuhan's hopes. He wrote a master's thesis on the recently "canonized" (in the literary sense) Gerard Manley Hopkins. McLuhan urged Ong to enter a secular rather than Catholic graduate school (Harvard), where he wrote a doctoral dissertation on the Reformation rhetorician Peter Ramus. Later he became the first Catholic president of the Modern Language Association.

In the mid-1940s McLuhan moved to Saint Michael's College, Toronto, where he spent the rest of his career. Once again he was able to supervise the early career of a subsequently famous critic, Hugh Kenner, whom he guided out of the Catholic educational ghetto and into the secular mainstream. His introduction to Kenner's book *Paradox in Chesterton* (1948) shows the two of them in close accord, arguing that Chesterton had addressed the vital moral and psychological issues of his era while the formal Thomists had failed. He used a tribute to Chesterton as a way of reproaching Catholic scholars:

The Catholic teaching of philosophy and the arts tends to be catechetical. It seeks precisely that Cartesian pseudo-certitude which it officially deplores, and divorces itself from the complex life of philosophy and the arts. This is only to say that the Catholic colleges are just like non-Catholic colleges; reflections of a mechanized world. The genuine critical discoveries, on the other hand, made by T. S. Eliot and F. R. Leavis, about how to train, simultaneously, esthetic and moral perceptions in acts of unified awareness and judgment: these major discoveries are ignored by Catholic educators. . . . That is where Chesterton comes in. His unfailing sense of relevance and of the location of the heart of the contemporary chaos carried him at all times to attack the problem of morals and psychology.[22]

---

21. McLuhan, *Letters*, 187.
22. Marshall McLuhan, Introduction to Hugh Kenner, *Paradox in Chesterton* (London: Sheed and Ward, 1948), xviii.

McLuhan was a nonstop talker, full of unconventional notions, and a negligent classroom teacher. His abrasive personality would have made him a problem on any college faculty, and most of his Catholic colleagues were baffled by the directions his work was taking.[23]

McLuhan always shied away from the label "Catholic scholar" and made no attempt to incorporate apologetics into his mature work. Nevertheless, it is easy to see the influence of midcentury Catholic attitudes in his media analysis in *The Mechanical Bride* (1951), *The Gutenberg Galaxy* (1962), and *Understanding Media* (1964). The Reformation, in McLuhan's telling, coincided with the invention and dissemination of print technology, a "hot" medium, which worked in a concentrated way on just one of the senses—sight. In doing so it displaced the "cooler" sensibility of the Catholic Middle Ages, which had worked on all the senses and which the invention of television was bringing back in a degraded form.[24] Some critics mistook his analysis of cartoons, advertisements, and television for celebrations of the new media, but most of his analysis was bitingly critical. These were, he believed, the decadent manifestations of a culture adrift from its religious moorings. McLuhan's biographer Philip Marchand points to the tension in his work between pre- and postconversion influences. "McLuhan maintained to the end that his theories of communication were 'Thomistic'; certainly he would have felt uncomfortable severing connections entirely with the official philosophy of his Church. Nonetheless, he always remained rooted in the tradition he admired, that of the Sophists and rhetoricians, rather than in the more logical and dialectical tradition of Aquinas."[25]

A third figure who moved from the heart of the secular modern world into the embrace of Catholicism at the same time as Merton and McLuhan was Avery Dulles (born 1918). Comparing his experience with theirs, Dulles later wrote:

The pattern in Merton's generation was relatively constant. You find a student, full of youthful energy and passion, still unable to find any meaning in life. The diluted Protestantism of his youth seems to offer no answers. He dabbles with modern literature, becomes intrigued for a while with the psychology of Freud and flirts briefly with ideologies such as Fascism and

23. See Jonathan Miller, *Marshall McLuhan* (New York: Viking, 1971). This acerbic book is a valuable part of the literature on McLuhan because Miller finds McLuhan wholly unconvincing, almost a charlatan, and knows exactly how to deflate the media prophet's pretensions.

24. Marshall McLuhan, *Understanding Media: The Extensions of Man* (New York: New American Library, 1964), chap. 2, "Media Hot and Cold," 36–45.

25. Marchand, *McLuhan*, 82.

Marxism, which present themselves as superior alternatives to a failing liberal capitalist system. But these ideologies prove to be blind alleys. . . . Then, almost by chance, . . . our young student comes across the work of living Catholic philosophers such as Etienne Gilson and Jacques Maritain. They convince him that European civilization took a false turn with Luther and Descartes and that the human community cannot be regenerated except by recovering the principles of Christian philosophy.[26]

He and his contemporaries, wrote Dulles, had "made a spiritual emigration to the Middle Ages."[27] As with so many others, his conversion came as a shock to his parents, especially his father, John Foster Dulles, who was an elder in the Presbyterian Church and was later to become President Dwight Eisenhower's secretary of state.[28]

Maritain (1882–1973), as we have seen, influenced the conversions of Merton, McLuhan, Dulles, and many others. He had become a Catholic in 1906, along with his wife, Raissa, an artist, after agreeing with her to commit suicide if they could find no spiritual purpose in life. He became a leading exponent of neo-Thomism, getting back to Aquinas himself, rather than the later schoolmen, and applying the old principles to modern existentialism and to contemporary political, social, and aesthetic issues. Outspokenly opposed to the totalitarian dictatorships, Maritain spent the Second World War years in Canada and the United States, teaching in both Catholic and secular universities (Notre Dame, Toronto, Chicago, and Columbia). After a spell as French ambassador to the Vatican in the late 1940s, he was invited to teach at Princeton, where he presided until 1961, the living embodiment of urbane, worldly-wise scholasticism at the headquarters of American Presbyterianism.[29] His work had been affecting American and British converts since Eric Gill discovered and first translated it in the early 1920s, but the 1950s marked the zenith of his prestige and helped along the cause of Catholic intellectual respectability. The major books he wrote there, *Man and the State* (1951), *Creative Intuition in Art and Poetry* (1953), and *On the Philosophy of History* (1957) were in English, not translations, and they placed him among the foremost

26. Avery Dulles, "The Lure of Catholicism: Merton's Generation and Our Own," Thomas Merton Lecture, Columbia University, November 16, 1994 (typescript), 3–4.
27. Ibid., 21.
28. On Dulles and his relationship with Harvard Catholics, especially Leonard Feeney, see Mark Silk, *Spiritual Politics: Religion and America since World War II* (New York: Simon and Schuster, 1988), 72–75.
29. Biographical information in this passage is based on John Dunaway, *Jacques Maritain* (Boston: Twayne, 1978); and Deal Hudson and Matthew J. Mancini, eds., *Understanding Maritain: Philosopher and Friend* (Macon, Ga.: Mercer University Press, 1987).

contributors to English-language Catholic work in philosophy and theology.[30]

Converts continued to play a prominent role in Catholic journalism as well as theology in the postwar era. Already important contributors to *Commonweal*, they also helped launch new journals. Among them was *Integrity*, founded in 1946 by the convert Carol Jackson and the born Catholic Ed Willock. As James Fisher has shown in his engrossing study of the *Integrity* group, their way of criticizing the official church was to take its teachings *more* seriously and *more* literally than most of their fellow Catholics, struggling at all hazards to avoid becoming middle class. In this striving they owed an obvious debt to Dorothy Day. Their heroic poverty in the rural Marycrest commune, harking back to Eric Gill's Ditchling community, their daunting fecundity (twelve couples with seventy-nine children), and their refusal to give a thought to the morrow, made them a headache to more conventional bishops and priests, while their nutty methods doomed their enterprises to a short, if spectacular, life. Carol Jackson had converted in 1941, and like Merton, she saw the church as a refuge from a corrupt world: "I started considerably below scratch, misshapen, and neurotic [but] gradually my neurosis unwound itself (courtesy of grace, and without benefit of psychoanalysis) and my ideas straightened out and I started writing."[31] She published under the pen name Peter Michaels and indulged in fantasies of a mass turning-away from consumerism:

It might conceivably happen that presently, under the terror of atomic bombing, and urged by holy and fiery preachers, possibly over the radio, several million Americans would take to the traditional sackcloth and ashes. It would be an edifying sight. Imagine an army of Franciscan-like penitents filling the highways from coast to coast and refusing to eat anything more tasty than the scraps of old hot dogs left by the Sunday picknickers. Converted psychiatrists might form a special elite of flagellants, scourging themselves constantly for their sins.[32]

In its early years (1946–1951) *Integrity* treated prudence and self-restraint with contempt until the calmer editorial influence of Dorothy Dohen laid a restraining hand on Jackson and Willock's wilder schemes.

*Jubilee* was a more level-headed contribution to Catholic journalism. Founded by two of Thomas Merton's close college friends, Robert Lax,

30. Jacques Maritain, *Man and the State* (Chicago: University of Chicago Press, 1951); *Creative Intuition in Art and Poetry* (New York: Pantheon, 1953); *On the Philosophy of History*, ed. Joseph Evans (New York: Scribner, 1957).

31. Fisher, *Catholic Counterculture*, 104.

32. Ibid., 106.

who had converted from Judaism to Catholicism under the inspiration of his friend's example, and Edward Rice, a born Catholic, its first issue appeared in May 1953. *Jubilee* was a Catholic version of *Life* or *Look*, just as *Commonweal* was a Catholic *New Republic*. It ran stories and pictures about the more colorful and daring aspects of Catholic life and emphasized its variations throughout the world. Outwardly orthodox, it nevertheless offered an implicit challenge to what its editors saw as the philistine everyday life of most American Catholics. They wrote extensively about the convert intellectuals who provided a more bracing alternative. Photo essays of converts Christopher Dawson at Harvard and Thomas Merton at Gethsemani, articles by and about Dorothy Day, Catherine de Hueck, and the convert novelist Sigrid Undset were sprinkled liberally through its pages right from the beginning.[33] *Jubilee* invariably used Ronald Knox's translations when it carried passages from the Bible and often decorated articles with Eric Gill's woodcuts.[34] Theodore Maynard, the dean of Catholic historians in those days, commemorated the 150th anniversary of Orestes Brownson's birth in *Jubilee* in December 1953.[35] Writing after the Second Vatican Council, Garry Wills noted that in the 1950s (in his days as a Jesuit novice) the Cathoic liberalism symbolized by *Jubilee* had seemed to him an oasis of civilization in a Catholic intellectual wasteland.[36]

One staff writer at *Jubilee* was Richard Gilman, another convert from Judaism, whose autobiography, *Faith, Sex, Mystery* (1986), forms a dramatic successor to the confessional literature that is so central to the lives of British and American Catholic converts, and to this history. Written thirty years after Gilman's faith had dissipated it inevitably sees the events that led to his conversion through the filter of subsequent disillusionment, but it is also full of the power that conversion exercised over him at the time. And it is notably free of the kind of self-justification and self-righteousness that impairs many conversion narratives.[37]

Gilman, brought up in a mildly observant family for which Jewishness

33. Thomas Merton, "Bernard of Clairvaux," *Jubilee* 1 (August 1953): 33–37; Harold C. Gardiner, S.J., "Sigrid Undset," *Jubilee* 1 (October 1953): 34–39; editorial, "Friendship House Crisis," *Jubilee* 1 (November 1953): 60; Dorothy Day, "I Remember Peter Maurin," *Jubilee* 1 (March 1954): 34–39. On Dawson, see editorial, "Undisturbed Philosopher," *Jubilee* 8 (April 1961): 24–27, including an interview with Dawson by Michael Novak.

34. See, for example, "The Creation of the World" (June 1953): 6–15; "The Christmas Story" (December 1953): 5–11; Graham Carey, "Eric Gill" (January 1954): 16–21, all in the first volume of *Jubilee*.

35. Theodore Maynard, "Orestes Brownson," *Jubilee* 1 (December 1953): 47–51.

36. Garry Wills, *Bare Ruined Choirs: Doubt, Prophecy, and Radical Religion* (Garden City, N.Y.: Doubleday, 1972), 43–45.

37. Richard Gilman, *Faith, Sex, Mystery* (New York: Penguin, 1986).

was more a form of social identity than a religion, was struggling in an unsuccessful marriage in the early 1950s, living off his wife's income, and dreaming of a literary career. He found the sight of Catholics entering local churches thoroughly unsavory and remarked, "Everything I thought I knew about contemporary Catholicism tended to fill me with contempt; its intellectual narrowness, its hostility to new ideas, and especially its enmity to all that I valued in present-day art and literature." But visiting a branch library one day, he felt irresistibly drawn to a shelf of religious books and to one volume in particular, Etienne Gilson's *Spirit of Medieval Philosophy*. Checking it out almost against his will, he had to fight down the temptation to throw it from the bus as he rode home, but then he sat down to read it, all day and all night, in a rapture of intellectual excitement. Only years later did he learn of the uncannily similar experience Thomas Merton had had with the same book fifteen years before. He began to attend church, read Greene, Mauriac, Newman, and Merton, and entered into a passionately cerebral relationship with "Ruth," an ascetic Catholic woman he had met in another library.[38]

Gilman does not try to excuse conduct that often strikes the reader as cowardly and unkind. He arbitrarily cut off this relationship with "Ruth," left his wife, and drove out to Colorado so that he could be received into the Catholic Church in a place where he was unknown. And after converting in a church full of Hispanic Americans, whom he saw as exotic, instead of among the irksomely familiar Catholics of New York, he continued to keep this great change in his life secret from his close friends and all his family. Even when he went to work for *Jubilee*, he reassured his parents that it was a "liberal" Catholic journal and did not require all its contributors to be Catholic. Despite these deceptions, Gilman describes his early life as a Catholic as exhilarating. The faith enabled him to discipline his aberrant sexual fantasies (he longed to be dominated by oversized athletic women and squeezed between their thighs). But gradually he learned that the moral demands of Catholic life were taking a toll on nearly all his new Catholic friends. One of them, a woman involved in a doomed love affair, fell from a high building, having apparently committed suicide, and a chilling passage describes the *Jubilee* group's common reluctance to admit what had happened. Gilman was visited by this suicide's ghost but even this supernatural experience was not enough to prevent his reversion to old habits, and he felt God's presence ebbing away.[39]

Ironically the waning of his faith coincided with the takeoff of his career.

38. Ibid., 61, 49–52, 57, 86–94.
39. Ibid., 97–98, 140–56, 156–57.

He had begun at the bottom, selling subscriptions to *Jubilee*. He wrote reviews for the journal from early 1954, full of conventionally pious remarks ("Catherine of Siena is surely one of the most astounding women who ever lived. . . . what we learn from Catherine is how love of God turns all pain to joy, and how residence in His house grants one the power to open doors for others").[40] He moved on to work with *Commonweal* and became its drama critic in the early 1960s. In 1964 he became theater critic at *Newsweek* and graduated from there to a professorship of drama at Yale University.[41] Gilman, in *Faith, Sex, Mystery*, manages to combine a sense of the impossibility of Catholicism for a modern urbanite with the paradoxical sense that his Catholicism was, nevertheless, much richer and more compelling than any other part of his life.

Gilman, considered in the light of other midcentury converts, demonstrates some of the special characteristics of conversion in that era. The first is that sex had become a more prominent issue than in the nineteenth or early twentieth centuries. Many of the nineteenth-century converts, Newman included, had taken vows of celibacy *before* becoming Catholics. Married Catholics usually had no access to contraceptives, but neither did most Protestants, and birth control was not yet the public issue it would become in the twentieth century. Big families in Britain and America were just as likely to be Protestant as Catholic. This situation changed after about 1920. In the United States the Comstock Laws, prohibiting dissemination of information about contraception, began to be flouted. Margaret Sanger led an aggressive campaign on behalf of contraception as benign and necessary. Then, in 1930 the Anglican Church made a declaration in favor of family planning for married couples, and other Protestant churches followed suit. Pius XI responded with a sharp condemnation of contraceptives, *Casti Conubii* (1930), with the result that sexual theory and practice now became an area of marked difference between Catholics and everyone else and therefore a badge of identity.[42]

To some Catholics this new point of difference indicated the decadence of the Protestants and agnostics. Denis Gwynn, writing in England in the late 1920s, observed that "when once the national birth-rate begins to fall suddenly through the adoption of birth control, a general weakening of

---

40. Richard Gilman, "Sigrid Undset's Last Book," *Jubilee* 2 (June 1954): 61. See also Gilman, "St. Thomas More," *Jubilee* 2 (July 1954): 27–31. "The manner of Thomas More's dying won him the crown of a saint, but martyrdom is not the work of one day only. More's entire life had prepared him to accept joyfully the burning imprint" (27).

41. Gilman, *Faith, Sex*, 233–37.

42. John T. Noonan Jr., *Contraception: A History of Its Treatment by the Catholic Theologians and Canonists*, enlarged ed. (Cambridge: Belknap of Harvard University Press, 1986), 407–9, 424–34.

the nation's moral fibre sets in, and only the more hardy and hopeful elements retain their former rate of natural increase." But there was a pleasant aspect to this situation from the Catholic point of view. Gwynn predicted that "while the more sophisticated and pleasure-loving drift inevitably towards race-suicide," a high birthrate would give Catholics a larger role in British life because "in an age of universal suffrage . . . the argument of numbers is unanswerable."[43] It was left to another English convert, C. C. Martindale, to remind his coreligionists that sex was not a bad thing in itself, so long as it was well regulated. In *The Difficult Commandment* (1925) he was one of the first Catholic priests to write about sex in an upbeat way, noting that "if sexual actions were not pleasurable, no one would want to do them." "Never confuse yourself," he told young men, "by thinking that somehow, if you were all you should be, you would be as it were body-less; or that your sex-instinct is a wicked thing; or that you are expected to trample it out, or that sex actions ought necessarily to disgust you, or that women are a regrettable necessity, or inferior to man, or that you ought not to be attracted by them." On the contrary, sex was wonderful but it must be carefully disciplined and directed toward procreation.[44]

As the life of Eric Gill plainly shows, the forsaking of contraceptives did not necessarily mean that profound Catholicism and active sexual lives never collided. But it is clear that for some converts, becoming a Catholic was a way of symbolically repudiating a life of sexual profligacy. Dorothy Day had been sexually active, had had an abortion and then later had a child by her common law husband, and for her conversion was, among other things, an escape from sexuality. The same is true of Thomas Merton. He had had a series of sexual affairs at Cambridge and Columbia to which he refers obliquely in *The Seven Storey Mountain* (Michael Mott addresses them more matter-of-factly), and he had been involved in a paternity suit. At the age of fifty he told an interviewer: "One thing on my mind is sex, as something I did not use maturely and well, something I gave up without having come to terms with it. That is hardly worth thinking about now—twenty-five years nearly since my last adultery."[45] Gilman too describes the period following his conversion, when the nagging and perverse sexual fantasies were, at least for a time, laid to rest. But the world and the flesh began to creep up on him once more, and as he

43. Denis Gwynn, *A Hundred Years of Catholic Emancipation, 1829–1929* (London: Longmans, Green, 1929), xxvii–xxviii.
44. C. C. Martindale, *The Difficult Commandment: Notes on Self-Control Especially for Young Men* (London: Manresa Press, 1925), esp. 15–17.
45. Mott, *Seven Mountains*, 83–84.

describes it, he resumed his old habit of masturbation and then went off to New Orleans in search of a prostitute.[46]

Gilman's experience, like Merton's, also shows that by the middle of the twentieth century Catholicism was attracting some converts in the same way that communism attracted others. Both offered a complete philosophical system and a rich intellectual tradition. Each claimed to have an answer for every human dilemma and each stood in judgment over a world in crisis. Each possessed a set of venerated texts that, taken in the right spirit at the right time, had a transforming effect on readers, so that Gilson's *Spirit of Medieval Philosophy* could act on Merton and Gilman in the way that the works of Marx and Lenin had acted on a generation of young Communists. The Great Depression showed capitalism at its worst and drove many Western intellectuals to seek radical solutions. No wonder Catholic conversion narratives from these middle years of the twentieth century are sometimes reminiscent of Communist conversion narratives. Whittaker Chambers, for example, became a Communist in 1925 after his brother's death by suicide led him to the brink of despair. He described his turn to communism as a way of reviving his sense of purpose in life, by surrendering his bourgeois identity to the great forces of history which the party represented.

The ultimate choice I made was not for a theory or a party. It was—and I submit that this is true for almost every man and woman who has made it—a choice against death and for life. I asked only the privilege of serving humbly and selflessly that force which from death could evoke life, that might save, as I then supposed, what was savable in a society that had lost the will to save itself. . . . For it offered me what nothing else in the dying world had power to offer at the same intensity—faith and a vision, something for which to live and something for which to die.[47]

Another famous ex-Communist of the 1940s and 1950s, Louis Budenz, made a similar case, that in joining the party he was struggling for the

46. Gilman, *Faith, Sex,* 127–31. See also Gilman's meditation on the nature of lust (193), which he categorizes as different from the other "deadly sins" because "largely unconscious" in psychological origin.

47. Whittaker Chambers, *Witness* (New York: Random House, 1952), 196. Chambers's role in the Alger Hiss espionage and perjury cases made him a controversial figure in the 1950s, and he remains one for historians. Nevertheless *Witness* seems to me an ideal source because it is written with great self-knowledge. Even though Chambers had abandoned and denounced communism the early sections of the book made a vivid case *for* communism and for the state of his mind on joining the party. Incidentally, *Witness* was a best seller just four years after Merton's *Seven Storey Mountain* and both books are stirring "conversion" accounts from the ideological crisis of the mid-twentieth century.

safety and future of the world while sacrificing himself. His autobiography, *This Is My Story* (1947) describes his conversion to communism (1935) and then his reconversion (1945) to the Catholicism he had abandoned as a young man.[48]

It would certainly be easy to exaggerate the similarities between Catholic and Communist converts, and I do not mean to be psychologically reductionist. Still the converts did share a dramatically restored sense of well-being and an awareness of working for an unpopular minority cause, opposed by a hostile world and supported by an outwardly humble but inwardly privileged community. And just as Catholic converts often faced a rude awakening when they discovered that most of their new coreligionists had feet of clay, so many Communists, including Chambers and Budenz, had their new faith tested by the far harsher discovery of the party line's icy Machiavellianism.

College-educated young American Catholics, embarrassed by the low level of Catholic intellectual life, which was becoming an open scandal in the mid-1950s, were delighted by the work of American converts such as McLuhan, Merton, Dulles, and Gilman. This generation of aspiring liberal intellectuals was, wrote Garry Wills in "Fifties Catholicism," becoming dissatisfied with "those breezy debaters spawned in England by Chesterton and Belloc—e.g. Theodore Maynard, Arnold Lunn, C. C. Martindale, Christopher Hollis." And they looked at their church as "a mass of Irish pastors truckling to Italian cardinals. . . . Ireland subject to Rome, with England providing diversionary camouflage."[49] McLuhan's friendship with Wyndham Lewis and Ezra Pound and his articles about T. S. Eliot and James Joyce indicated a willingness to get to the heart of modern literature of the most demanding kind, without any special pleading for the church. Merton's poetry and far-ranging essays, and Dulles's proximity to national power gave Catholic liberals a vicarious sense of power and urbanity. "The liberals' most acutely experienced urge," Wills adds, "was to prove that something recognizably Catholic need not be as cramped, ugly, and anti-intellectual as they found at the corner church."[50] And in a revealing passage, reflecting on his own youth, Wills continues:

The Catholic liberal was . . . a kind of honorary convert. He tried . . . to cast himself out of the ghetto of his upbringing and come back at the church from some entirely new direction, sacred or secular. He would even be a Thomist, so long as he could be a Bergsonian "neo-Thomist" with Maritain;

48. Louis Budenz, *This Is My Story* (New York: McGraw-Hill, 1947).
49. Wills, *Bare Ruined Choirs*, 41.
50. Ibid., 45.

a medievalist if it meant interesting experiences as a weekend monk with Tom Merton; a menial laborer, if it meant spending time at a *Catholic Worker* house with Dorothy Day, a "Christian humanist in the marketplace" if it meant escaping the coercive pulpit politics of Cardinal Spellman.[51]

Wills was a Jesuit seminarian in the 1950s before switching to a career as a secular academic and journalist.[52]

The Catholic converts of the 1950s nevertheless enjoyed the intellectual presence of more born-Catholic colleagues than their predecessors. Merton and Dulles, the religious writers, for example, were matched in intellectual rigor by John Courtney Murray, S.J., whose theological arguments in favor of religious toleration were controversial in the 1950s but fully vindicated in the 1960s by being incorporated into Vatican II's declaration on religious liberty.[53] By most measures the quality of Catholic intellectual life was improving. But in 1955 John Tracy Ellis, a born-Catholic historian, published "American Catholics and the Intellectual Life," which sparked a heated controversy about low standards in Catholic universities. Ellis showed that nowhere in the world had Catholics devoted as much money and energy to education as in America and yet had so little to show for it: few geniuses and only a cramped and narrow mental horizon. It was particularly galling that nearly all the prominent American Catholic intellectuals were *converts*, men and women who had escaped the process of Catholic education in childhood. Declining to blame outsiders' prejudice, Ellis placed responsibility firmly on the Catholics' own doorstep and blamed the defensive and apologetic outlook that had hamstrung too many Catholic educators.[54]

Ellis's lament can be taken in various ways. On the one hand, Ellis was certainly right that Catholic universities had produced few or no distinguished American intellectuals. On the other hand, he was basing his whole argument on the premises of his secular adversaries, who understood intellectual life as the pursuit of an unattainable, infinitely receding truth through the trial of tentative hypotheses. He was no longer content with the Thomist consensus on which the Catholic curriculum of the early twentieth century had been based, which assumed that all the really important truths were already known. In this sense Ellis might be faulted for

51. Ibid., 48.
52. On his early life and his move from seminary to *National Review*, see Garry Wills, *Confessions of a Conservative* (Garden City, N.Y.: Doubleday, 1979), 3–16.
53. Peter McDonough, *Men Astutely Trained: A History of the Jesuits in the American Century* (New York: Free Press, 1992), 230–33, 320.
54. John Tracy Ellis, "American Catholics and the Intellectual Life," *Thought* 30 (Autumn 1955): 351–88.

being too ready to yield to his secular contemporaries and to take "intellectual life" according to their definition rather than on the terms of his own tradition.[55]

In the following decade dozens of books, articles, and speeches addressed the issue, most admitting the justice of Ellis's analysis and urging a radical reform of Catholic higher education toward a more adventurous approach. Only a handful of participants in the debate wanted the Catholics' educational approach to remain as distinct as it was, warning against the excessive "assimilation" implicit in Ellis's plans.[56] This debate too can be understood in different ways. That it drew in so many Catholic commentators and that the self-criticism was so widespread might be taken to confirm that the state of affairs was indeed very bad, or might suggest that an improving situation was not improving quickly enough to satisfy a community that now placed more emphasis on education than ever before—a revolution of rising expectations. In these postwar years the U.S. Catholic middle class was expanding rapidly, and its members placed a high value on education because it offered them potential access to the learned professions and the managerial elite, the "new class." The "military-industrial complex" relied on highly trained technicians and citizens capable of abstract thought and rational planning. Catholics who wanted to be part of it had to get the training, so they clamored for their universities to deliver, even if that meant surrendering the old Thomist approach. Paul Giles and Eugene McCarraher, writing in the 1990s, have interpreted the Catholic education debate in this light and faulted Ellis's generation for its eagerness to join the "warfare state."[57]

The debate did not involve English Catholics, who had never had an educational system of their own. Young Catholics, born or convert, were free throughout the twentieth century to attend the secular universities and had less opportunity to build a parallel Catholic subculture. David Lodge (born 1935), a born Catholic studying at London University in the 1950s, wrote his first novel, *The Picturegoers* (1960), as a study of Catholic conversion and deconversion. He set the scene in a seedy, undistinguished part of south London just like the one in which he had grown up and organized the drama around two competing institutions, the cinema and

55. See McGreevy, "Thinking on One's Own," 14–17.

56. On the debate, see Philip Gleason, *Contending with Modernity: Catholic Higher Education in the Twentieth Cetury* (New York: Oxford University Press, 1995), 287–96. On warnings against assimilation, see Patrick Allitt, *Catholic Intellectuals and Conservative Politics in America, 1950–1985* (Ithaca: Cornell University Press, 1993), 41–48.

57. Paul Giles, *American Catholic Arts and Fictions: Culture, Ideology, and Aesthetics* (New York: Cambridge University Press, 1992), 440–43. McCarraher, *Land of Unlikeness*, 273–82.

the Catholic Church. Each has its guardian—the cinema manager and the priest; each has its heroes and heroines; and each offers visions of a brighter and more thrilling world—Hollywood and heaven. Many of the same people attend them both and try to organize their moral lives around the contradictory messages they teach. As in several of his later novels Lodge used the device of parallel characters moving in opposite directions. The first, Mark Underwood, is a skeptical student preparing to take his final examinations. He boards with a Catholic family whose daughter, Clare Mallory, the other principal character, has failed in her vocation to be a teaching sister. At first she is shocked by his irreverence. He sits meditating in the cinema on one of their first dates, shifting his thoughts from the "walking nightmare" of the audience members' daily lives to the vision offered them on screen. "It was in a way a substitute for religion—and indeed a fabulously furnished penthouse, and the favours of awesomely shaped women, offered a more satisfactory conception of paradise than the sexless and colourless Christian promise—the questionable rapture of being one among billions of court-flatterers." As he becomes more involved with the family and the church, Mark drops his scornful tone and develops the paradoxical idea that Catholicism's imperfections are signs of its truth. "If it was true that at the Consecration God was really present on the altar, whole and entire, under the appearance of bread and wine, as Clare's dog-eared Catechism stated—then it was quite simply the most important thing in life." And one Sunday in church he experiences a moment of conversion. "The priest stretched up, lifting the Host on high. Mark stared at it, and belief leapt in his mind like a child in the womb. . . . It was as if for an instant the scales had been lifted from his eyes, and he had seen how simple it was really, how it all fitted together."[58] Lodge was already too shrewd a novelist to offer this conversion as pure gain. Mark becomes priggish, a quality he had hated in other Catholics, disdains Clare's love, and instead declares his intention to become a priest.

Lodge was not alone in seeing the cinema as a source of liturgical, moral, and quasi-religious significance. Walker Percy's first novel *The Moviegoer* (1962) addressed the same themes in an American setting. Percy (born 1916), scion of a distinguished old southern planter family, had trained at Columbia University as a doctor but chronic tuberculosis (contracted while working in a TB ward) had forced him to abandon medicine.

58. David Lodge, *The Picturegoers* (1960; London: Penguin, 1993), 58, 109, 111. The last passage is strongly reminiscent of C. S. Lewis's spiritual autobiography, *Surprised by Joy*, which describes instantaneous moments of religious illumination followed by "dry" periods spent in a vain effort to recapture the sense of spiritual exaltation. C. S. Lewis, *Surprised by Joy* (New York: Harcourt, Brace, Jovanovich, 1955).

During a long recuperation he had read the whole of Thomas Aquinas's *Summa Theologia* and converted to Catholicism in 1947. He had also read Thomas Merton's *Seven Storey Mountain* enthusiastically, and begun contributing to Catholic journals.[59]

Percy wrote for *Commonweal* and *America* in the 1950s on the developing Civil Rights Movement, taking what now seems a deplorably cautious approach to desegregation and arguing on behalf of southern traditionalism.[60] *The Moviegoer* is the story of a well-connected young southerner, Binx Bolling, who is squandering his talents by working as a broker and flirting with his secretaries in the undistinguished New Orleans suburb of Gentilly. Traumatized by a wound he suffered in the Korean War, he treasures the memory of the moment because it made a breakthrough into clarity from a life lived mainly in a mental fog of malaise and unreality. His cousin Kate lives even more insecurely, permanently on the brink of nervous dissolution and the two of them appear like odd intruders into an unreliable world. Like Lodge's characters in the *Picturegoers*, Binx finds a brighter, more gratifying existence in the films he watches avidly than in his own prosaic life. And again like Lodge's characters, he knows that God provides no easy solutions to his life's dilemmas. The only "sacred" person in the novel is the movie star William Holden whom he sees by chance in the street one day, around whom looms "an aura of heightened reality."[61]

Lodge and Percy both included scenes of Catholic families going to church, again with oddly parallel effects. Lodge emphasized the sorry appearance of the congregation in the London church:

The church was stuffy. . . . The congregation did not seem to mind. But they were stuffy too, in ugly felt hats and buttoned raincoats, behinds tilted ungracefully on the edges of the benches. . . . Here and there a child fretted, bored and uncomfortable, penned in by dull, sabbatical childhood. Rows of grey, cross faces. Why were churchgoers so unlovable? There was no getting away from it, all the beautiful, witty, intelligent people were sufficient unto themselves. It was only the failures and defectives who slunk into the temples and listened greedily to their promised revenge.[62]

59. Biographical summary based on Jay Tolson, *Pilgrim in the Ruins: A Life of Walker Percy* (New York: Simon and Schuster, 1992).
60. Walker Percy, "The Southern Moderate," *Commonweal*, December 13, 1957, 279–82. "Even a liberal southerner cannot fail to regret the passing of an era of true intimacy between Negro and white and cannot help contrasting it with what he sees as somewhat shallow friendships between educated whites and Negroes" (282).
61. Walker Percy, *The Moviegoer* (1961; New York: Avon, 1980), 21.
62. Lodge, *Picturegoers*, 103–4.

Percy emphasized the harsh, businesslike aspect of the service: "The church, an old one in the rear of Biloxi, looks like a post office. It is an official looking place. . . . By the time Mass begins we are packed in like sardines. A woman comes up the aisle, leans over and looks down our pew. She gives me an especially hard look. I do not budge. It is like the subway."[63]

For Percy's characters, indeed, as for Graham Greene's, Catholicism is a challenge and source of grief as often as comfort. They are as lost and bewildered as any modern atheist, and Percy holds out none of the reassurance that Catholic novelists had provided a century before. He was strongly influenced by French existentialists, and he himself usually cited Dostoevsky, Kierkegaard, and Camus, but he put a distinctly Catholic turn to their idea of the isolated, alienated being in the world. After all, "alienation is nothing more or less than a very ancient, orthodox Christian doctrine. Man is alienated by the nature of his being here. He is here as a stranger and as a pilgrim, which is the way alienation is conceived in my books."[64] He told an interviewer that although "the deeper themes of my novels are religious" he found it difficult to use "the standard words like 'God' and 'salvation' and 'baptism,' 'faith,'" because they were "pretty well used up. They're old words, but the trick of the novelist, as the Psalmist said, is to sing a new song, to use new words." And Percy did not want to be considered an apologist, knowing that it would condemn him in the eyes of most critics. "The so-called Catholic or Christian novelist nowadays has to be very indirect, if not downright deceitful, because all he has to do is say one word about salvation or redemption and the jig is up, you know."[65]

Lodge, Percy, and McLuhan were all established authors by the eve of the Second Vatican Council. For all of them modern visual media, film and television, stood squarely in the center of contemporary consciousness, seeming to personify the challenge and threat of the modern world to traditional religious life. Pius X had aimed, at the beginning of the century, to protect his flock by shutting out entire realms of contemporary intellectual life. The last preconciliar generation of Catholic converts saw this kind of denial as an inadequate response and added their voices to proposals for change. As Arnold Sparr notes: "If the focus of Catholic self-criticism in the 1930s and 1940s was that Catholics were not Catholic enough, that of

---

63. Percy, *Moviegoer*, 129.
64. Walker Percy, interview with Carlton Cremeens, in Lewis A. Lawson and Victor A. Kramer, eds., *Conversations with Walker Percy* (Jackson: University Press of Mississippi, 1985), 28–29.
65. Percy, interview with Charles Bunting, in Lawson and Kramer, *Conversations*, 41.

the 1950s implied that Catholics, at least as intellectuals, could be *too* Catholic."[66] Members of this generation took pleasure in Harvey Cox's *Secular City* (1965), which urged religious thinkers to involve themselves fully in secular life. Cox argued that secularization was not the antagonist of Christianity, as theologians had traditionally assumed. Rather, it was the *product* of Christianity, the mature condition to which it led, away from a magical, supernaturalized world view.[67] Although Cox was a Baptist, his message seemed particularly apt for Catholics, who wanted to become involved in the great issues of their day, the Civil Rights Movement and the Vietnam controversy, instead of hunkering behind defensive church barricades.[68]

Historians of the last three decades have usually treated the Second Vatican Council as a "liberalizing" moment in Catholic history. In light of subsequent events that interpretation is understandable. It is, perhaps, too easy to forget that Pope John XXIII's intention, and certainly the intention of the Curia, was to *strengthen* the church in its relations with the secular world by taking advantage of an already strong position. Certainly church leaders had no thought of abandoning the Catholic claim to religious truth or the principle of Catholic unity, and none could have anticipated with equanimity the Catholic history of the ensuing decades.[69] In paving the road to Vatican II convert intellectuals played an ambiguous role. On the one hand, they showed by their own example that the Catholic Church was alluring to intellectuals. On the other hand, it was in part converts' criticisms that goaded Catholic universities into undertaking more rigorous studies, accepting the learning of the wider intellectual world, and facing its secular temptations. They led the church toward a step that most of them approved in itself even while being horrified by its consequences. Evelyn Waugh detested the liturgical and theological

66. Arnold Sparr, *To Promote, Defend, and Redeem: The Catholic Literary Revival and the Cultural Transformation of American Catholicism, 1920–1960* (Westport, Conn.: Greenwood, 1990), 165.

67. Harvey Cox, *The Secular City: Secularization and Urbanization in Theological Perspective* (New York: Macmillan, 1965), 17–37.

68. On the impact of *The Secular City* for restless Catholic intellectuals, see Wills, *Bare Ruined Choirs*, 89–96. For Catholic reactions to the "death of God," see Michael Novak, "The Christian and the Atheist," in Bernard Murchland, ed., *The Meaning of the Death of God* (New York: Vintage, 1967), 70–80; and John S. Dunne, C.S.C., "The Myth of God's Death," ibid., 165–69; Daniel Callahan, "Radical Theology or Radical Titillation?" in J. L. Ice and J. J. Carey, *The Death of God Debate* (Philadelphia: Westminster Press, 1967), 107–17.

69. The sense of dismayed realization that the church got weaker rather than stronger is embodied in George Kelly, *The Battle for the American Church* (Garden City, N.Y.: Doubleday, 1979), in particular 4–20.

330

THE PRECONCILIAR GENERATION

changes of Vatican II.[70] Jacques Maritain recoiled too. His memoir, *The Peasant of the Garonne* (1966), rejected many of the dramatic changes in the conciliar church, much to the disappointment of the "new breed" theologians, his former champions. Walker Percy struck a similar note in 1977, justifying his faith by a paradox. In an "auto-interview" he asked: "But isn't the Catholic Church in a mess these days, badly split, its liturgy barbarized, vocations declining?" and answered, "Sure. That's a sign of its divine origins, that it survives these periodic disasters."[71]

In the years after Vatican II the Catholic Church continued to win converts in Britain and America, but it no longer sought them as actively as it had in the foregoing century. Among postconciliar American converts such as the conservative theorist Russell Kirk, the editor of *New Oxford Review* Dale Vree, and the editor of *First Things* Richard Neuhaus, or English converts such as Malcolm Muggeridge, however, it is still possible to trace a concern with doctrinal clarity and a deep strain of antiutopianism. Converts still play a prominent role in British and American Catholic life, but the story of these postconciliar converts, who moved into a vastly changed world, is so different from the experience of their forebears that it would require a book of its own.

70. Martin Stannard, *Evelyn Waugh: No Abiding City* (London: Dent, 1992), 461–65.
71. Lawson and Kramer, *Conversations*, 177.

# INDEX

Acton, Charles, 38
Acton, John, 2, 27, 78; career as historian, 37–42; and *Rambler*, 92–97, 100
Adams, Henry, 40, 185
Addams, Jane, 147
Adrian (Hadrian) VI, pope, 82
*Aeterni Patris*, 8–9, 121
Alcott, Bronson, 68
Alexander, Calvert, 195–96, 198
Allen, George, 132
Allies, T. W., 6
*America*, 137, 150, 192, 199, 328
American Catholic Historical Association, 244–45, 264
American Catholic Sociological Association, 155, 157
American College, Rome, 73
American Historical Association, 265–66
*American Review*, 259–60
"Americanism," 107, 112, 115–16, 126
Andrews, William E., 26–27
Anglican bishops, as fathers of converts, 161–62
Anglicanism (Church of England), 3, 5, 6, 35, 43–45, 51–60, 231, 241, 286, 289, 321; doctrinal vagueness of, 63, 162–63, 205, 289–90
Anglo-Catholicism, 5, 119, 174, 186–87, 243
Anglo-Saxons, 69, 112–13, 181–82, 241, 253, 283
Anti-Catholicism, 17–25, 30, 36, 46, 165, 289

*Apostolicae Curae*, 5
Aquinas, Thomas, 10, 84, 119–20, 137, 171, 316–17, 328
Arbues, Pedro de, 39
Armada, Spanish, 19, 23, 65
Arnold, Thomas, 5, 8
Asquith, Herbert, 176, 183, 241
*Ave Maria*, 191–92, 226, 285
Aveling, Eleanor, 145
Avery, Martha Moore, 144–47

Baines, Peter, 34, 48
Baker, Alfred, 71
Baker, Francis, 71–73
Barberi, Dominic, 23
Baring, Maurice, 177
Barnes, Arthur, 203
Barry, Edward, 47
Batterham, Foster, 149
Beard, Charles, 241
Beaumarchais, Pierre-August Caron de, 136
Bebel, August, 145
Bedoyere, Michael de la, 210–11, 228–29
Bellarmine, Robert, 246–47
Belloc, Hilaire, 160, 187, 198, 231; and Chesterton, 175–76, 188–89; and distributism, 206–7; early career, 173; as historian, 237, 254, 260; and parliament, 176–77
Benson, Edward White, 281
Benson, Robert Hugh, 11, 162, 184, 281–87; *Confessions of a Convert*, 285–86; *Richard Raynal, Solitary*,

Benson, Robert Hugh (*cont.*)
285; *Saint Thomas of Canterbury*,
286
Bentham, Jeremy, 95, 251
Berenson, Bernard, 220–21
Bergson, Henri, 121
Biblical criticism, 80, 111, 116–17,
120, 134, 243
Biblical translation, 232–33
Bilio, Luigi, 102
Binet, Alfred, 138
Blanshard, Paul, 309–10
Block, Maurice, 100
Blondel, Maurice, 120
Bloomsbury Group, 97, 225
Boas, Franz, 155
Boer War, 173, 206–7
Bourne, Francis, 166, 180, 210, 287,
306–7
Bregy, Katherine, 141–42
Britain, cultural influence of in Ameri-
ca, 159–60
Brook Farm, 68
Bronte, Charlotte, 23, 36–37
Brownson, Orestes, 1–4, 41; compari-
son with Newman, 74–85; *Convert*,
64–65, 67, 77; conversion of, 67;
correspondence with Ward, 77;
criticism of Hecker's *Aspirations*,
92; and Hecker, 68, 99–100; on
Hewit, 99–100; on history, 82; on
science and evolution, 82–84;
youth, 65–67
*Brownson's Quarterly Review*, 65–66,
71, 75, 77, 92, 99
Buckley, William F., Jr., 208
Budenz, Louis, 323–24
Bull, George, 196
Bunyan, John, 142
Burke, John, 142
Burton, Katherine, 127, 130, 152–54
Bushnell, Horace, 95

Calvert, Caecelius, 19
Cambridge Movement, 43–45, 53–54
Campbell, Roy, 225–26, 231

Campion, Edmund, S.J., 19, 30, 100–
101, 306
Capes, John Moore, 92–93
Carey, Arthur, 62–63
Carroll, Charles, 21, 23–24
*Casti Conubii*, 321
Catholic Church: in Britain, 17, 25–
27, 35, 162, 282, 284–85, 290,
304, 308; and sexuality, 321–23; in
United States, 26, 64, 197, 232,
241, 266, 282, 309–10, 313, 320,
324
Catholic Evidence Guild, 197
*Catholic Herald*, 211, 228
*Catholic Magazine*, 31–32
Catholic Relief Acts and Emancipa-
tion, 21–23, 27–28, 52
Catholic revival, 189, 191–96, 202,
206, 233, 260
Catholic Rural Life Movement, 207
Catholic Truth Guild, 146
Catholic University, Dublin, 78–79
Catholic University of America, 114,
167, 196
Catholic Women's League, 131
*Catholic Worker*, 148, 150–52, 226
Catholic Worker Movement, 148,
207
*Catholic World*, 71, 99–100, 118,
179, 192, 199, 211
Chambers, Whittaker, 323
Channing, William Ellery, 65, 74, 90
Charles I, king of England, 19
Charles II, king of England, 20
Charles III, king of Spain, 26
Chesterton, Cecil, 176–77
Chesterton, Gilbert Keith, 1, 3, 11,
160–61, 198, 237; and America,
192, 196, 199; conversion, 188;
death, 209; distributism, 206; on
eugenics, 180–81; *Eye Witness*,
176–77; Father Brown, 177; *Heretics*, 174; and Lunn, 200; and
Maynard, 178–79; and McLuhan,
313–15; *Orthodoxy*, 3, 173–75,
177–78, 188; pleasures of Catholi-

cism, 163, 165; on Rome, 221; on
Teutonic fallacy, 181–82; and
World War I, 183; youth, 172–74
Cisalpines, 26–27, 30–32, 234
Civil War, English, 20
Clark, Richard, 111, 117, 124
Claver, Peter, 202
Clement XIV, pope, 26
Collins, Seward, 259
Collinson, James, 5–6
Commonweal, 142, 150, 169, 171,
192–94, 199, 226–27, 230, 246,
318, 321, 328
Communism, 149–50, 152, 208–9,
224–28, 232, 236; conversions to,
323–24; pseudo-religious character,
163, 236, 240, 257, 262, 267–68
Connelly, Cornelia, 143
Constant, Benjamin, 65–67
Contraception, 154, 310
Cooper, James Fenimore, 41
Corriere della Sera, 122–23
Corvo, Baron. See Rolfe, Frederick
Coughlin, Charles, 205–6, 227, 229,
261
Coulton, G. G., 200, 237
Cousin, Victor, 66–67
Cox, Harvey, 330
Craigie, Pearl, 129
Cranmer, Thomas, 18
Crashaw, Richard, 25
Creighton, Mandell, 40
Croatia, 308
Croce, Paul, 104
Curtis, George William, 24

Daly, Mary, 130
Darwin, Charles, 14, 33, 159, 164;
and Brownson, 83–84; and Chesterton, 174; and Mivart, 108–10;
and Newman, 80; and Noyes, 214–
15; and Simpson, 100; and Windle
168, 170
Davidson, Randall, 205
Dawson, Christopher, 12, 160, 198,
210, 237–75; on Communism,

267–68; conversion, 242–43; and
Dublin Review, 267–68; on fascism,
257–59; on Freud, 255–56; Gifford Lectures, 268; at Harvard,
233, 269–71, 319; as historian,
251–60, 274–75; Judgment of the
Nations, 267; and Mulloy, 269–70;
on nationalism, 258–59; Progress
and Religion, 251–52; on race,
256–57; and Schlesinger, 258, 269;
style, 259–60; on Wells, 260; and
World War II, 229, 231, 267–68;
youth, 242
Day, Dorothy, 205, 311, 318; and
Catholic Worker Movement, 148–
52, 207; conversion, 149–50; early
career, 148–49; and Maurin, 151–
52; pacifism, 151, 226, 261; radicalism, 130; reputation, 1, 12, 319;
and sex, 322
Death of God theology, 271
Debs, Eugene, 146, 241
Delany, Selden, 153
Dell, Robert Edward, 118
Dengel, Anna, 154
Descartes, Rene, 252
Deshon, George, 92
Dickens, Charles, 18, 96
Digby, Kenelm, 44, 48, 54
Dingle, Reginald, 256
Distributism, 167, 176, 206–10, 224
Dohen, Dorothy, 318
Dolling, Robert, 119
Dollinger, Ignatz, 38–40, 93, 98,
100, 103
Dorsey, Anna, 131–32
Draper, John, 171
Dreyfus case, 116, 184
Dryden, John, 25
Dublin Review, 34–35, 54, 60, 110,
161, 175, 210, 216, 231, 259,
268
Dulles, Avery, 233, 316–17, 324
Dupanloup, Felix, 99
Duportail, Louis, 136
Dwight, Thomas, 109

Education, 78–80, 166–67, 203, 325–26

Edward VI, king of England, 17

Eliot, T. S., 189, 217, 225, 235, 259, 278, 324

Elizabeth I, queen of England, 18–19, 30

Elliott, Walter, 114–15

Ellis, John Tracy, 156, 167, 270, 325

Emerson, Ralph Waldo, 70, 74, 90

English College, Rome, 23, 29, 31, 210

Episcopalians, 5, 61–64

Erastianism, 52–60, 61

Errington, George, 97, 101

Eugenics, 14, 137–40, 180–81, 186n, 222

Evolution, 14, 33–34, 80, 83, 108–12, 122, 156, 164; and history, 239; and Knox, 212; and Noyes, 214–15; and Windle, 168, 170

*Eye Witness*, 176–77, 179

Faber, Frederick, 56, 97

Fascism, 221–24, 229, 240, 257–59

Fawkes, Guy, 19,

Fay, Sigourney, 185

Feeney, Leonard, 154

Fitzgerald, F. Scott, 185, 194, 214

Fitzpatrick, John, 41, 67, 76–77

Flick, Lawrence, 245

Forbes, John Murray, 73–74

Fox, James J., 118

Foxe, John, 18

Franco, Francisco, 151, 223–28, 240, 261, 263–65

French Revolution, 22, 28, 39n, 215, 250

Freud, Sigmund, 155, 212, 255–56, 278

Froude, Hurrell, 51, 53–54, 63

Galileo, 9, 110–11, 172

Garibaldi, Giuseppe, 98, 220

Gaskell, Elizabeth, 37

General Strike of 1926, 210

General Theological Seminary (New York), 62–64, 74

George III, king of England, 22

George IV, king of England, 46

George V, king of England, 169

Gethsemani, 311–12, 319

Gibbon, Edward, 28, 74, 81, 220, 243, 253

Gibbons, James, 114, 116, 185

Gill, Eric, 192, 231, 319; anti-capitalist, 179, 206, 208, 227; and communal life, 179, 208; as craftsman, 160, 179–80; and English Catholicism, 209, 211; and Maritain, 208–9; and sex 164, 180, 209, 322

Gilman, Richard, 319–23

Gilson, Etienne, 203, 216–17, 311, 320, 323

Gladstone, William, 36, 40, 58, 100, 105

Gmeiner, John, 110

Goddard, Henry, 137–40

Goering, Hermann, 259

Goldstein, David, 145–47

Gompers, Samuel, 146

Gordon Riots, 22

Gorham, George: "Gorham Case," 10, 57, 59, 204

Gothic revival, 45–51

Greene, Graham, 1, 12, 277–308, 329; *Brighton Rock*, 291–92, 296–97; *Burnt-Out Case*, 305; conversion, 291–92, 295–96; *Heart of the Matter*, 279, 292, 297, 299, 302–4; political views, 280, 304; *Power and the Glory*, 293, 298–99; *Quiet American*, 304–5; World War II, 231; youth, 295

Griffin, Bernard, 232

Guilday, Peter, 167, 244–45

Guiney, Louise Imogen, 141

Gurian, Waldemar, 268

Gwynn, Denis, 216, 321–22

Haeckel, Ernst, 108, 171

Hagerty, Thomas, 144
Halifax, Lord, 5
Hardy, Thomas, 169
Harnack, Adolf von, 116, 120–21, 159
Harvard, 12, 41
Hawthorne, Nathaniel, 143
Hayes, Carlton, 12, 137, 237–75; Ambassador to Spain, 230, 238, 263–65; at Columbia, 240–41, 266; and *Commonweal*, 192, 226–27, 246–47, 261; conversion, 241; as historian, 241, 244–48, 262–63, 265–66, 273; interfaith relations, 248–49, 273; interventionist, 262; last years, 272–73; on nationalism, 242, 246, 249–51, 272–73; on Nazism, 261; political views, 240, 265–66; and Spanish Civil War, 226–27, 261; textbook controversy, 249–50; and World War II, 230; youth, 240–41
Hecker, Isaac, 1, 5, 7, 10, 64; and "Americanism," 107, 112, 114–15; and Anglo-Saxons, 112–14, 181–82; *Aspirations of Nature*, 7, 70, 90–92; *Church and the Age*, 112–13; conversion and seminary, 68–69; criticized by Brownson, 92; and Mivart, 112; *Questions of the Soul*, 69–70; and Simpson, 89–91, 103; and *Testem Benevolentiae*, 115–16; and Vatican I, 102–3; youth, 67–68
Hell, 111
Henry VIII, king of England, 17, 170
Herron, George, 144–45
Hewit, Augustine, 10, 71–73, 99, 109
Hinsley, Arthur, 210–11, 215–16, 227, 230–32, 267
Hiroshima, 164
Historiography: and 1960s, 271–72; and Acton, 38–42; American, 230, 265–66; and Anglo-Saxon theory, 181–82, 239, 241; Catholic, 2–3, 193n, 201–2, 238, 244–45, 273–74; of Catholic converts, 97–98; and evolutionary metaphors, 239; and Kite, 136–37, 139; and Lingard, 28–30; and metahistory, 239, 244; "New History," 241; and Newman, 81–82; "scientific," 274; and Simpson, 93–94. *See also* Acton, John; Belloc, Hilaire; Brownson, Orestes; Dawson, Christopher; Hayes, Carlton; Hoffman, Ross; Hunt, Gaillard; Kite, Elizabeth; Lingard, John; Lunn, Arnold; Newman, John Henry; Noyes, Alfred; Simpson, Richard
Hitler, Adolf, 14, 228, 231, 240, 258, 262–63
Hobart, John Henry, 61–62
Hobbes, John Oliver [Pearl Craigie], 129
Hoffman, Ross, 12, 137, 222–23, 230, 245, 247, 314
Hollis, Christopher, 12, 160–62; and America, 165–66, 203–4; interfaith relations, 165, 234; on Mussolini, 221–22; on Orwell, 234; in parliament, 161, 208, 233; and World War II, 229
*Home and Foreign Review*, 100. *See also Rambler*
Honorius, pope, 102
Hopkins, Gerard Manley, 142
Huber, Alice, 143
Hudson, Daniel, 192
Hueck, Catherine de, 151, 311, 319
Hugel, Baron von, 120–22
Hughes, John, 73–74, 92
Hull House, Chicago, 147–48
Hume, David, 28–30
Hunt, Gaillard, 137, 245–47
Huxley, Aldous, 225
Huxley, Julian, 212–13
Huxley, Thomas, 107–9, 159, 165, 171
Huysmans, Joris, 150

*Integrity*, 318

Ireland, John, 114–15, 185
Irish, 42, 60; in America, 78, 184–86, 229; Easter Rising, 186; in England, 161, 290; Home Rule, 169, 182–86; and World War I, 183–86
Irving, Washington, 41
Italy, 55, 102–3, 114, 219–23, 283

Jackson, Carol, 318
James, Henry, 278
James, William, 121, 201, 268
James I, king of England, 19
James II, king of England, 20
Januarius, Saint, 32
Jefferson, Thomas, 246–47
Jerrold, Douglas, 223
Jesuits (Society of Jesus), 40, 55, 196, 228, 314; in disguise, 64, 282–83; in Elizabethan England, 26–27, 101; and Tyrrell, 119–24
Jesus, 66, 123, 145–46
Jews, 173, 248–49, 264
John XXIII, pope, 330
Joyce, James, 214, 278, 324
Jubilee, 318–21

Kallikak Family, The (Goddard and Kite), 138–40
Keane, John, 114
Keble, John, 4, 51–52, 57
Kenner, Hugh, 315
Kenrick, Francis, 131, 232
Kirk, Russell, 331
Kite, Elizabeth, 12, 127, 134–41
Klein, Abbe Felix, 115
Knox, Ronald, 11, 160–65, 198; Bible translation, 232–33, 319; conversion, 187; on Italy, 219; and Lunn, 200–201; as Oxford chaplain, 211–12; and prayers, 211; on science and religion, 212–13; Spiritual Aeneid, 187–88, 212; and Waugh, 306–7; youth, 186
Know-Nothing Party, 24, 78, 132, 134
Kroeber, Alfred, 155
Kuhn, Thomas, 172

Laberthonniere, Lucien, 120
Lafayette, Marquis de, 136
Lamarckian theory, 33–34
Lamentabili Sane Exitu, 9, 123
Lateran Treaty, 221
Lathrop, Rose Hawthorne, 143
"Latin Bloc," 228–29
Lawler, Justus G., 270–71
Lawrence, D. H., 209, 290
Lax, Robert, 318–19
Leo XIII, pope, 5, 8–9, 115–16, 144, 147, 221
Lepanto, Battle of, 81–82
Leroux, Pierre, 66
Leslie, Shane, 12, 160, 198; in America, 184–86, 204–6; on Benson, 281; on Bourne, 210; and eugenics, 186n; and Fitzgerald, 185; Irish Question, 186; on Manning, 101; and Notre Dame, 204; and World War I, 184–86; youth, 184
Lewis, C. S., 189, 209–10, 235, 327n
Liberalism, 93–97, 100, 240, 252, 264
Lilley, A. L., 123
Lingard, John, 27–31, 37, 59, 100
Litany of Loreto, 32
Lloyd George, David, 169, 176, 241
Locke, John, 137
Lodge, David, 326–29
Loisy, Alfred, 120–21, 126
Lord, Daniel, 195, 209
Lord, Robert, 167, 245
Louis XIV, king of France, 20
Louis XVI, king of France, 136
Loyola, Ignatius, 120
Luce, Clare Boothe, 130
Lunn, Arnold, 12, 160–61; in America, 199, 201–3, 229; as anticommunist, 208, 236; on celibacy, 164; conversion, 201; on distributism, 206; on Freud, 256; as historian, 202; at Notre Dame, 202; Roman Converts, 200; Spanish war, 224–25; and tourism, 166; on Wesley, 165; and World War II, 229; youth, 198–99

Luther, Martin, 82
Lyell, Charles, 80, 83, 159

Macaulay, Thomas, 36, 81
Mackenzie, Compton, 12, 185, 277–
  80, 287–91, 308; *Parson's Progress*
  trilogy, 289–90; *Sinister Street*,
  288
Macmillan, Harold, 187
Maignen, Charles, 115
Manning, Henry Edward, 7, 9–10,
  220; archbishop, 101–2; compari-
  sons with Newman, 97–98; early
  career, 57–60, and Wiseman, 97;
  and Vatican I, 101–2
Mannix, Edward J., 194
Marconi affair, 176–77
Maritain, Jacques, 203, 208–9, 216–
  17, 226, 259–60, 313, 317–18,
  331
Martindale, C. C., 160, 162, 198,
  322
Marx, Karl; Marxism, 14, 144, 197,
  227, 254, 323
Mary, Queen of Scots, 19
Mary, Virgin, 129, 187–88, 248
Mary I, queen of England, 17, 20, 30
Mary II, queen of England, 20
Marycrest, 318
Maturin, Basil, 125, 160, 162, 184
Mauriac, Francois, 279
Maurin, Peter, 151–52, 261n
Maurras, Charles, 251
Maynard, Theodore: as Catholic his-
  torian, 160, 196–97, 237, 319; and
  Chesterton, 178, 188; and *Com-
  monweal*, 192–93; conversion 178–
  79; youth, 177–78
McCarthy, Mary, 304
McGlynn, Edward, 144
McGrady, Thomas, 144
McIlvaine, Charles, 62
McLaren, Agnes, 154
McLuhan, Marshall, 313–16, 324,
  329
McMaster, James, 63, 68–69

McNabb, Vincent, 180, 206
Media, 316, 329–30
Medieval Europe, Medievalism, 43–
  51, 75, 82, 124–25, 147, 175,
  179, 237, 246, 253, 316
Mendel, Gregor, 168
Mercier, Joseph, 124–25, 184
Merriam, Roger, 245
Merton, Thomas, 1, 12, 151n, 233,
  310–13, 319, 322, 324
Metternich, Clemens, 250–51
Mexico, 297–99
Michel, Virgil, 260
Military-industrial complex, 326
Mill, John Stuart, 4
Milner, John, 26, 30–31
Mithraism, 225, 248
Mivart, St. George, 8, 107–12, 116–
  18, 126
Modernism, 87, 106, 123, 125–26,
  205, 313
Moise, Lionel, 149
Monk, Maria, 24, 132
*Month, The*, 105, 120, 228
Moody, Dwight, 178
Moon, Thomas, 245, 250
Morris, William, 45, 147, 160
Muggeridge, Malcolm, 331
Mulloy, John, 269–70, 272
Mundelein, George, 166,
Murray, John Courtney, S.J., 13, 273,
  325
Mussolini, Benito, 221–23, 228, 258

Nashotah, Wisconsin, 63–64
National Catholic Welfare Conference,
  147–48
National Conference of Jews and
  Christians, 248–49
Nationalism, 164, 240, 242, 246,
  250–51, 257–59, 261
Nazism, 163, 223, 227–31, 257,
  261–62
Neuhaus, Richard, 331
*New Witness*, 193, 210
*New York Review*, 126

Newman, John Henry, 1, 3, 5, 7, 12, 63, 166; *Apologia Pro Vita Sua*, 54, 97–98, 168, 174, 188; centenary, 232–33; compared to Brownson, 74–85; *Essay in Aid of a Grammar of Assent*, 104–5, 196; *Essay on Development of Christian Doctrine*, 54, 76, 94, 122, 196; on history, 81–82; *Idea of a University*, 79; influence of Wiseman on, 35–36; influence on Baker and Hewit, 71–72; and Leslie, 205; *Loss and Gain*, 55–56; and McLuhan, 314–15; and Merton, 312; and Mivart, 117; and Oxford Movement, 52–55; on Pugin, 75; and *Rambler*, 95–96; on science, 80–81; "Second Spring," 87–88; and Simpson, 88–89, 101; and Tyrrell, 120; and Vatican I, 103–4

Nightingale, Florence, 59

North Atlantic Treaty Organization, 266

Notre Dame, University of, 75, 126, 127, 160, 199, 202–4, 221–22, 264

Novak, Michael, 271

Noyes, Alfred, 160–61, 164–65; in America, 214, 229–30; on decline of civilization, 235–36; on evolution, 214–15; on history, 237; *Unknown God*, 214–15; *Voltaire*, 215–16; youth, 213

Nutting, Willis, 207

O'Connell, William, 166

O'Connor, John, 177, 180, 183

O'Flaherty, Kathleen, 216

O'Hara, John, 203

Oldmeadow, Ernest, 210, 293

O'Neill, Eugene, 149

Ong, Walter, 13, 314–15

*Order*, 259

*Orthodox Journal*, 26–27

Orwell, George, 224, 234

Oscott College, 36, 38

Oxford Movement, 4, 6n, 31, 43, 51–60, 72, 186, 204–5

Pacifism, 149, 151

Papal infallibility, 7–8, 39–40, 59, 102, 121

Papal temporal power, 40, 98, 100

Paris, Treaty of, 21

Parker, Theodore, 131

Parliament, 175–77,

Parliament, Houses of, 47

Parsons, Talcott, 247

*Pascendi Dominici Gregis*, 9, 11, 107, 123–24, 126, 161, 164, 187, 195

Paul VI, pope, 293

Paulist fathers (Congregation of Saint Paul), 5, 68, 71–72, 90, 92, 114

Percy, Walker, 327–29, 331

Petre, Maud, 122

Philip II, king of Spain, 17

Phillipps de Lisle, Ambrose, 44–45, 47, 60

Pius V, pope, 18, 81–82

Pius VII, pope, 26

Pius IX, pope, 48, 55, 87; appoints Manning, 101; and Italian unification, 98, 221; and Mivart, 110; Munich Brief and *Syllabus of Errors*, 98–99; restores English hierarchy, 36; and Vatican I, 8, 39–40, 102–3

Pius X, pope, 9, 87, 122–23, 169, 221, 329

Pius XI, pope, 169, 221, 248, 321

Pius XII, pope, 216

Pizzardo, Giuseppe, 293

Poe, Edgar Allan, 41

Pope, Alexander, 25

Popular Front, 224, 227

Pretenders, Old and Young, 21

Progress, theory of, 11

Prohibition, 165–66, 249

Protestantism, 17–18, 23, 70, 82, 112, 120, 124, 165, 230, 232–33, 291. *See also* Anglicanism; Luther, Martin; Reformation

*Providentissimus Deus*, 9, 116

Pugin, Augustus Welby, 36, 38, 45–51, 75, 89, 133
Pusey, Nathan, 4, 57

*Quadragesimo Anno*, 206
Quakers, 134–35
Quebec Act, 21
Queen's College, Cork, 168–69

Racism, scientific, 113–14, 222
Radio, 212–13
*Rambler*, 7, 38, 92–97, 100, 105. *See also Home and Foreign Review*
Rand, Carrie, 144–45
Rand, Elizabeth, 144
Ranke, Leopold von, 94, 220
Redemptorists, 68–71, 91–92
Redmond, John, 169, 183
Reed, Rebecca, 132
Reformation, 17–20, 29–30, 42, 49, 316; and Brownson, 82; and Froude, 53; and historians, 242, 245–46; historical continuities across, 165. *See also* Anglicanism; Protestantism
*Regnans in Excelsis*, 18
Reich, Emil, 135–36
Renouf, Peter de Page, 38, 102
Repplier, Agnes, 141
*Rerum Novarum*, 144, 146, 173, 178, 206
Revival of religion, 235. *See also* Catholic revival,
Rice, Edward, 319
Ridolfi Plot, 19
Ripley, George, 68
Ripley, William Z., 113
Ritschl, Albrecht, 116
Robinson, James Harvey, 241
Rolfe, Frederick ("Baron Corvo"), 280–85; *Hadrian VII*, 283–84
Roosevelt, Eleanor, 310
Roosevelt, Franklin, 205, 230, 263–64
Roosevelt, Theodore, 146, 185
Ross, Eva, 12, 127, 130, 154–57

Rossetti, Christina, 5–6
Ruether, Rosemary, 130
Ruland, George, 91
Ruskin, John, 45–46, 50–51, 147
Russell, Bertrand, 212–13
Russell, Charles, 54
Russell, John, 36
Russell, Odo, 192
Russian Revolution, 146

*Sacrorum Antistitum*, 123
Sanger, Margaret, 321
Schlesinger, Bruno, 258, 269
Scholasticism, 10, 67, 121, 171, 196, 204, 314, 317, 325–26
Schweitzer, Albert, 120
Science, 32–34, 107–12, 117, 167–72. *See also* Brownson, Orestes; Darwin, Charles; Evolution; Huxley, Thomas; Mivart, St. George; Newman, John Henry; Windle, Bertram
Scott, Gilbert, 50
Scott, Walter, 45, 170
Scripture. *See* Biblical criticism
Searle, George, 71, 109–10, 118
Secularization, 16
*Servile State* (Belloc and Chesterton), 176, 207
Shakespeare, William, 105–6, 169, 204
Shaw, George Bernard, 159, 174–75, 177
Sheed, Frank, 166, 197–98, 202–3, 216, 230
Sheed and Ward, 197–98, 215–17, 231, 233, 259
Sheen, Fulton, 130
Shuster, George, 192–94, 202, 227
Sibthorpe, Richard Waldo, 54
*Sign*, 153, 192, 199
Simpson, Richard, 7, 38, 56; on Campion, 100; on Darwin, 100; early life, 88–90; friend of Hecker, 89–92, 103; on philosophy, 94–95; and *Rambler*, 92–97, 100; on Shake-

Simpson, Richard (*cont.*)
  speare, 105–6, 142; and Vatican I,
  105; and Ward, 97
Sinclair, Upton, 192
Sinn Fein, 169, 184–86
Smith, Al, 249
Socialism, 65, 144–48, 206
*Sociological Analysis*, 157
Spain, 114–15, 225, 230, 263–65
Spanish Civil War, 151, 222–27
Spellman, Francis, 151, 166, 310
Spencer, George (Ignatius), 44, 53
Spencer, Herbert, 110, 159, 165
Spender, Stephen, 209, 226
Spengler, Oswald, 244, 269
Stalin, Joseph, 14, 228, 231
Starr, Eliza Allen, 127, 131–33
Starr, Ellen Gates, 128, 147–48
Stillman, Chauncey, 269–70
Stokes, Scott Nasmyth, 96
Stonyhurst, 119, 203
Strachey, Lytton, 56, 57n, 97–98
Strong, Josiah, 114, 181
Suarez, Francisco, 119–20
Suffrage, women's, 147, 154
Sullivan, William, 126
Sweet, William, 247
Sword of the Spirit Movement, 230–
  31, 267
*Syllabus of Errors*, 8, 98–100
Synthetic Society, 120

*Tablet*, 105, 117, 210, 215, 226, 293
Talbot, Msgr. George, 98
Tate, Allen, 207, 310
*Testem Benevolentiae*, 115–16
Teutons. *See* Anglo-Saxons
Theology, converts avoid, 130, 161
Thirty-Nine Articles, 18, 43, 53, 56,
  62–63
Thomas, Norman, 145
Thomism. *See* Scholasticism
Thompson, Francis, 149
Thorold, Algar, 161, 259
Throckmorton, Sir John, 100
Tiernan, Frances, 129, 131–32

Tierney, Mark, 34
Tillotson, Robert, 71
Tincker, Mary Agnes, 129, 133–34
Tobey, Barkeley, 149
Tolstoy, Leo, 184
Toynbee, Arnold, 242, 244
Tractarians. *See* Oxford Movement
Tracts, Oxford, 35, 52–60, 62, 67
Transcendentalism, 67–69, 74
Trappists, 44, 310–12
Trevor-Roper, Hugh, 268
Trollope, Anthony, 24–25, 55–56
Tyrrell, George, 6, 9, 107, 161; *Chris-
  tianity at the Crossroads*, 125;
  *Church and the Future*, 122; con-
  troversies, 120–26; and Leslie, 205;
  "Letter to a Professor of Anthropol-
  ogy," 122–23; *Medievalism*, 125;
  and Mercier, 124–25, 184; youth,
  118–20

Ullathorne, William, 103
Ultramontanism, 7, 10, 26, 32, 59,
  96–97, 101, 234
Universities, American Catholic, 166–
  67, 217, 269, 325. *See also* Educa-
  tion; Catholic University of
  America; Notre Dame
Urquhart, Francis "Sligger," 162n,
  187
Ushaw, 28, 31

Van Doren, Mark, 311
Vatican, 2, 25, 31, 39, 49, 221; and
  "Americanism," 115–16; architec-
  ture of, 48; Hecker at, 71; and
  Tyrrell, 125; and *Voltaire*, 215–16
Vatican Council, First, 7–8, 39–40,
  59, 101–4, 126
Vatican Council, Second, 13–14, 272,
  309, 325, 330
Vaughan, Herbert, 118, 179–80
Vichy France, 228–29
Victoria, queen of England, 36
Vietnam, 304–5, 330
Vikings, 182

Vineland, N. J. Training School, 137–39

Virey, Julien-Joseph, 32–33

Voltaire, 165, 215–16

Vree, Dale, 331

Wadhams, Edgar, 64

Walsh, William, 245

Walworth, Clarence, 63–64, 68

War of Independence (American Revolution), 21, 23–24, 136–37, 139, 246

Ward, Barbara, 267

Ward, Maisie, 166, 197–98

Ward, Wilfrid, 120, 175

Ward, William George, 4, 7, 9, 56, 63, 77, 97–99, 105

Watkin, E. I., 18, 204, 228, 234–35

Watson, John B., 195

Waugh, Evelyn, 1, 12, 162, 166, 277–308, 330–31; *Brideshead Revisited*, 291–92, 294, 299–302; conversion, 292; *Decline and Fall*, 294; *Edmund Campion*, 306; on Greene, 279, 297, 303–5; *Handful of Dust*, 293; and Knox, 162, 306–7; and Oldmeadow, 210, 293; on politics, 280, 295, 297–98; *Sword of Honor* trilogy, 292–93, 307; *Vile Bodies*, 294–95; and World War II, 231, 279–80, 299–300, 307–8

Weiss, Johannes, 120

Wells, H. G., 174, 212, 260, 291

Wesley, John, 165

Westminster Cathedral, 179–80

White, Andrew Dickson, 9, 171

Whittingham, William, 72

Wilberforce, Henry, 104

William III, king of England, 20

Williams, Michael, 192–94, 227

Willock, Ed, 318

Wills, Garry, 319, 324–25

Wilson, Edmund, 209, 214, 310

Wilson, Woodrow, 113, 183, 185, 191

Windle, Bertram, 108, 160–61, 164–65; on Britain's Roman legacy, 182; on Catholics and science, 171–72; and *Commonweal*, 192; conversion, 168; in Cork, 168–69; early career, 167–68; on eugenics, 180; on evolution, 168, 170; on Protestant psychology, 178; in Toronto, 169–70, 193; on Vitalism, 171

Wiseman, Nicholas, 27–28, 31–37, 58–60, 101; ordains Hecker and Walworth, 69; relations with *Rambler*, 95–96, 100

Wolff, George Dering, 71

Woodruff, Douglas, 210

Woolf, Virginia, 225

World War I, 12, 181–86, 191, 214, 239, 242, 279, 288

World War II, 151, 208, 228–33, 240, 262–68, 279–80

Young, Alfred, 71

Yugoslavia, 307–8

Zahm, John, 126

Patrick Allitt is Associate Professor of History at Emory University.